Elke Zobl, Ricarda Drüeke (eds.)
Feminist Media

D1798612

Critical Media Studies
Band 9

ELKE ZOBL, RICARDA DRÜEKE (EDS.)
Feminist Media
Participatory Spaces, Networks and Cultural Citizenship

[transcript]

This book was funded by the Austrian Science Fund (FWF) within the research project P21187-G20 (»Feminist Media Production in Europe«) which has been conducted at the University of Salzburg, Department of Communication and the Program Area Contemporary Arts & Cultural Production within the Focus Area Art & Science, a cooperation between the University of Salzburg and Mozarteum University.

Bibliographic information published by the Deutsche Nationalbibliothek
The Deutsche Nationalbibliothek lists this publication in the Deutsche Nationalbibliografie; detailed bibliographic data are available in the Internet at http://dnb.d-nb.de

Cover layout: Kordula Röckenhaus, Bielefeld
Cover illustration: Elke Zobl, Salzburg
Layout & typeset by Brigitte Geiger, Wien
Proofread by Jason Heilman, New York
Printed by Majuskel Medienproduktion GmbH, Wetzlar
Printed on FSC certified paper
ISBN 978-3-8376-2157-0

Table of Contents

Chapter 2:
Participatory Spaces, Networks and Technology

Chapter 3:
Cultural Citizenship and Social Change

Appendix

Foreword

This anthology grew out of a research project and has gone through many different visions, stages, and forms of collaborations. The idea of this book was developed within the research project "Feminist Media Production in Europe," which was started at the Academy of Fine Arts in Vienna and then moved to the Department of Communication at the University of Salzburg, Austria. A warm thank you goes out to Elisabeth Klaus, the department head in Salzburg, who has been very enthusiastic about the project. The project was funded by the Austrian Science Fund (P21187) from December 2008 until November 2012. The study was conducted by a team: Elke Zobl, as the project leader, post-doctoral researchers Rosa Reitsamer (2009–2011) and Jenny Gunnarsson Payne (2008–2009) and doctoral student Red Chidgey (2008–2010), with research support from Stefanie Grünangerl (2010–2012). In the context of this project, we have been interested in such questions as: What are the content, forms, processes, and functions of feminist media production in Europe today? How far are these media used as sites of feminist news, activism and engagement? How can media produced by women at the grassroots level be a means to foster participation and civic engagement? What are the implications of women as active media producers for civic society? What is the potential of feminist grassroots media in Europe for cultural, social and political changes? Discussions of these and other questions can be found in this book (esp. see the research report by Elke Zobl and Rosa Reitsamer).

At first, an open call to contribute to this anthology with academic essays and case studies, as well as activist reports, practitioner interviews and visual commentaries, was issued in 2008 by Red Chidgey, Jenny Gunnarsson Payne and Elke Zobl. We received many contributions from various countries for which we have been very grateful, and we would particularly like to thank everyone who contributed at this stage. However, due to the difficulty in finding a publisher willing to publish a mix of theory and practice, as well as project personnel changes, we had to make the decision to focus the current volume on academic essays. At that stage Rosa Reitsamer and Elke Zobl were able to secure transcript Verlag as the publisher. We thank the editors of the Critical Media Studies series for their immediate enthusiasm for the book and their productive collaboration. As Rosa Reitsamer left the project for another job posting, Elke Zobl teamed with Ricarda Drüeke at the Department of Communication in Salzburg to edit the present anthology. As the project leader, Elke Zobl would like to thank all team members warmly and deeply!

The information that has been collected during the project has been continuously documented at the digital archive *Grassroots Feminism: Transnational archives, resources and communities* (www.grassrootsfeminism.net), which was set up in December 2008. By providing an interactive network portal and research platform for researchers, activists and media producers, this Web 2.0 archive makes contemporary feminist, queer and antiracist media and cultural practices more broadly accessible. The site is organized and maintained by Elke Zobl in collaboration with Rosa Reitsamer, Stefanie Grünangerl and Red Chidgey. Above all, we would like to thank everyone who continues to contribute to a diverse, engaging and critical feminist media landscape – and consequently to this website. At the end of this book you will find a selected list of feminist media projects in Europe for further consultation.

Another important impetus for this book were the annual Civil Media Conferences organized by Radiofabrik in Salzburg, where from 2008 to 2011 we invited feminist media producers from various countries to present their work and engage in discussions around media, social change, participatory culture, networks and cultural citizenship. We are deeply indebted to everyone who accepted our invitation and came to Salzburg, as well as to Radiofabrik!

Such an anthology is dependent on the help and enthusiasm of many: It would have not been possible without the patience of the contributors who revised their articles according to our input. For the detailed proofreading, we thank Jason Heilman (USA), and for the layout, we are greatly indebted to Brigitte Geiger (Austria). At transcript Verlag we would like to thank Anke Poppen for being our competent contact person.

In short: the development of this book has involved many people in various countries. We cannot name them all, but we would like to thank them from our deepest hearts!

We are looking forward to feedback and further discussions!

Elke Zobl & Ricarda Drüeke

Introduction
Feminist Media: Participatory Spaces, Networks and Cultural Citizenship

Ricarda Drüeke and Elke Zobl

Feminist Media

Women have always played an important role in movements for social justice. Using media to transport their messages, to disrupt social orders and to spin novel social processes, feminists have long recognized the importance of self-managed, alternative media. In the past two decades an increasing number of women have taken the tools of media production into their own hands. With the rise of new media and communication technologies, women have started to use these technologies for the production and distribution of feminist media. These demographics are often described as part of 'third wave feminism', 'pop feminism' or 'do-it-yourself-feminism'. We understand feminist media as any self-identified feminist and/or women's media project engaged in processes of social change. Feminist media – in this broader understanding – encompasses text production, e. g. zines, magazines and flyers, as well as practices of performance, graffiti and art. For this reason, we are interested in how feminist media producers create and engage in participatory spaces, networks and cultural practices, and how they assume a cultural citizenship and initiate processes of social change. Questions arise such as: What kinds of processes, strategies and mechanisms of inclusion and exclusion are at work in feminist media production? How does one assume a cultural citizenship within feminist media? How do feminist media producers engage with feminism, anti-racism and social change? Can we identify a 'new feminism' in feminist media – one that creates a new participatory culture?

The present volume offers several components for the analysis of feminist media in relation to participatory spaces, networks and the theoretical concept of cultural citizenship. The articles in this volume clearly illustrate the complexity and diversity of the issues that arise in this constellation concerning the character of the involvement and participation by feminist public spheres as well as reinterpretations of the hegemonic gender relations. In doing so, the articles incorporate approaches and findings from various humanities and social science disciplines, thus showing at the same time the productiveness of interdisciplinary openness. By problematizing the existing power-political configurations, changes in hegemonic practices as well as alternative paths for appropriating media and culture become evident. At the same time the articles have a theoretical as well as an empirical orientation. The common objective of all of the contributions is to analyze the broad topic of media and gender from a social-theoretical – but above all, feminist – perspective. In different ways, the articles pose questions concerning the specific production conditions of feminist media, the interplay between art and gender, the options for opening up new participatory spaces as well as for the creation of feminist public spheres. From a theoretical viewpoint, the articles are based for the most part on feminist theories of the public sphere and on the concept of cultural citizenship. Starting from different perspectives, the empirical analyses in the individual chapters place the focus on feminist activism. The book is organized in three main sections: *Feminist media production and alternative economies*, *Participatory spaces and networks* and *Cultural citizenship and social change*.

Feminist media production and alternative economies

Feminist movements make use of their own media for information and as a means of mobilization. In addition, the media form a platform for criticizing the dominant structures and the contents of the mainstream media. The feminist media landscape is at the same time extremely diverse. Small-scale alternative media share a low level of professionalization, which is marked by a do-it-yourself culture. Thus, an alternative (and sometimes gift-based) economy is developed by media producers and consumers that distinguishes itself from the global media conglomerates. Their primary aim is not to commodify media; rather, alternative economies focus on the exchange of knowledge and information, the spread of emancipatory concepts and activism, and they envision social change.

The six articles in the book's first section dealing with feminist media production and alternative economies examine the effects, potentials, and limitations of grassroots women's and feminist media production from different perspectives and disciplinary viewpoints. The reflections focus on such questions as: What kind of mechanisms are at work in the production and distribution of feminist media? How do feminist media producers develop and engage in alternative economies? In which ways do these alternative economies make low-threshold feminist media possible?

The diversity of feminist media production in Europe becomes clear in the article by **Elke Zobl** and **Rosa Reitsamer** (with Stefanie Grünangerl). Based on the findings of a research project, the authors show what common and distinguishable features are evident in feminist media production in Europe, making visible the varied modes according to which feminists produce and use media. This feminist media production forms the basis for the emergence of a new social movement in the context of third wave feminism, one which appropriates the discursive and participatory spaces of the public sphere. Underlying these production processes is the negotiation of feminist discourses in relation to a do-it-yourself (DIY) feminism, intersectional perspectives of feminism, and pop feminism in the context of the German-speaking debate on "new feminisms", leading to the development of alternative feminist media practices. Alternative media are also the focus of the contribution by **Jenny Gunnarsson Payne**, who discusses the fundamental issue of the extent to which feminist media can be considered alternative media at all. Based on this, the author develops a concept linking poststructuralist approaches to alternative media together with conceptualizations of political subjectivity in order to carry out empirical analyses of the users and producers of feminist media.

The subsequent three articles are devoted to distinct areas of feminist media production. On the basis of a history of the archiving of feminist grassroots media, **Brigitte Geiger** and **Margit Hauser** show how from the very beginning these activities played a significant role within the women's movement in order to make visible its history and politics. In particular, magazines resulting from feminist media production form a significant part of such archives. Nevertheless – as the authors' analysis shows – the history of this archiving is not linear: individual feminist magazines were discontinued and new media are increasingly being used. Thus it remains to be seen how the print media landscape will evolve in the future. Continuing the theme of do-it-yourself culture in feminist media, **Red Chidgey's** article deals with the practices and forms of collective memory in DIY feminist networks. On the basis of two examples from the Riot Grrrl movement, the author elaborates the concept of feminist cultural memory. Other feminist practices become evident in the contribution by **Verena Kuni**, who introduces the concept of 'gender jamming'. Gender jamming is in the tradition of 'culture jamming' and looks mainly at the relationship between gender, queer and 'post-gender' in order to make clear that one's chosen identity does not depend on such externals as a beard, one's sexual preferences or biological sex.

The concluding article in this chapter features a discussion involving feminist media activists Sonja Eismann from *Missy Magazine* (Germany), Jenni from *Emancypunx* (Poland/international), Jessica Hoffmann and Daria Yudacufski from *make/shift* (USA), and Jeanna Krömer from *AMPHI magazine* (Belarus), conducted by **Stefanie Grünangerl**, which again illustrates that the common objective of many media producers is the creation of networks and participatory spaces. It becomes clear from this discussion that feminist media producers have to confront numerous challenges in their work – challenges that have just as much to do with involving young feminists in media production as they do with the lack of financial resources.

Participatory spaces and networks

The contributions in the book's second section are concerned with the creation of the participatory spaces and networks that were already thematized in the previous chapter. A participatory culture has been described as offering low-threshold access, support to each other, informal mentorship to pass on knowledge, meaningful exchange and an acknowledgement of one's own creation (Jenkins et al. 2006). Hence, the focus lies on participatory processes in community involvement and civic engagement. How do feminist media create, engage in and negotiate spaces that are characterized by such participatory practices? In which ways are feminist media producers involved in such spaces that envision social change? Can we identify a 'new feminism' in feminist media that creates a participatory culture? How do feminist media producers engage in and create local, transnational and virtual networks? Which kinds of networks are developed in relation to the production, distribution, geographic spread, content and aims of their media?

The six contributions in this section deal with the topic of feminist activism and the role of media users from different theoretical perspectives. With this, the focus of the empirical studies is just as much on political actions as it is on theoretical reflections on the possibilities and limits of feminist participation.

The article by **Tea Hvala** thematizes the ways in which feminist and lesbian activism can occupy public spaces in concrete terms. Through the streetwise politics of feminist activists, the possibilities and the limits of alternative norms of public speech and of political expression in the public space are tested. Referring to the theoretical conception of counter-public spheres, the author shows how these spheres in Ljubljana, Slovenia, prove themselves to be sporadic, fleeting and mostly anonymous interventions in the public sphere. In historical terms, feminist public spheres mostly constituted counter-public spheres which sought to reach the hegemonic public by articulating alternative positions (Fraser 1990). The women's movement which created these public spheres was not, however, homogeneous. Black feminists in particular pointed out the differences within the women's movement, because they did not see themselves as adequately represented within a white feminism that remained captive of the middle class (hooks 1990). Feminist postcolonial theory opened up additional perspectives on the relation between gender and race (Rodríquez 2008). At the same time the categories of gender and race are understood as social constructs and discursive productions constructed through processes that go hand in hand with structural and identitary effects. Postcolonial theorists thematized especially the ambivalent role of marginalized women, who in feminist discourse often remain invisible and voiceless (Spivak 1988). In the context of these theoretical debates, **Jessalynn Keller's** article examines the identity constructs of non-Western feminists. The negotiations concerning different identity positions are shown in India especially on the website the 'fbomb'. Feminist blogs of this type play a decisive role in the participation of girls as well as in feminist activism and in the end are responsible for the emergence of a feminist blogosphere.

Sandra Chatterjee and **Cynthia Ling Lee** also raise the issue of the networking of feminists through the internet. On the basis of the Post Natyam Collective, these two authors investigate how transnational collaboration is made possible. Through a joint critical examination of South Asian dance by activists scattered across different countries, specific networks and participatory spaces come into being. Alongside the neglect of the category of race, queer theory points out another blank space in the early women's movement. Particularly by not thematizing the topic of sexuality this category ended up becoming a category of difference. At the center of the women's movement was for the most part an inexplicit heteronormative matrix. Mustached female youth on the platform flickr.com call into question this heteronormativity, as the article by **Marcus Recht** and **Birgit Richard** makes clear. These individual cases of self-depiction admittedly remain initially at the level of self-presentation but they have considerable political potential. Without the advent of new technologies – including the so-called Web 2.0 – such participatory spaces and networks would be hardly conceivable. In a study on the role of users in the production of Web 2.0 media, **Tanja Carstensen** highlights the fact that their role still remains ambivalent. Thus, on the one hand, one struggles with a feminist design of the internet while, on the other, numerous anti-feminist tendencies manifest themselves on the internet. One example of this can be seen in the German Wikipedia website, where suggestions were regularly made calling for the deletion of the entries for such topics as Ladyfest or Riot Grrrl. In the context of second wave feminism, **Linda Steiner** discusses the use dimensions of old and new media by the feminist collective *New Directions for Woman* to show how users make use of different technologies in order to make their goals and agendas visible.

Cultural citizenship and social change

The political potential of feminist media and the emerging public spheres are in the focus of the book's third section. One concept that theoretically captures the ongoing processes of social and cultural transformation is 'cultural citizenship'. T. H. Marshall described three main categories of citizenship rights: civil rights, political rights and social rights. Subsequently, the concepts of cultural citizenship (Hermes 2006; Lünenburg and Klaus 2004) and DIY citizenship (Hartley 1999) have been added and discussed. Alternative feminist media offer and constantly negotiate productive spaces to express opinions, experiences and political views – to actively construct meaning and make sense of the world – in which a critical and self-reflexive political education and a cultural citizenship could take place. Which expressions of citizenship can we observe in feminist media? How is cultural citizenship articulated in feminist media? How and under which circumstances and in which contexts does cultural citizenship take place? And what kind of processes of social change are intended and initiated?

This is the focus of the articles gathered here, which deal with social change as well as with theoretical reflections on the shaping of cultural citizenship. The article by **Elisabeth Klaus** and **Margreth Lünenborg** provides a fundamental introduction to the concept of cultural citizenship; here, the authors explain how cultural citizenship can serve as a key concept in examining cultural production. As Fiske (1986) argues, cultural studies are both an intellectual and a political project. Culture is the site of political critique and intervention. Therefore the concept of cultural citizenship is part of the circle of meaning production, which is located between fact and fiction, information and entertainment, privacy and public or political discourse, rationale and emotional debate. The authors clarify the complexity of the concept using the example of reality television – especially talent shows – and its portrayal of migrants and queers. Furthermore, participatory spaces for social change are increasingly being created online, as the article by **Anita Harris** shows. Through the use of online DIY culture and social networking sites, new participatory communities are being established for young women, which in turn open up new forums for negotiating citizenship identities in the confrontation with the increasingly neoliberal tendencies of society. These new forms of activism do not, however, lead automatically to a strengthening of political activism, which is also continued offline. The article by **Ricarda Drüeke** is based on the assumption that the underlying theoretical concept is the determining factor for analyzing political communication via the internet. Based on a theoretical approach combining the insights of gender studies and cultural studies, this article explores how questions of participation and the public sphere are linked to online political communication. Participation and, above all, the empowerment of women can take place in a variety of ways, as the article by **Sigrid Kannengießer** makes clear. The method of digital storytelling illustrated in her article serves as a tool for narrating the life stories of sex workers in South Africa in short films, and for thus opening up the opportunity for contributing to the visibility of different individual life plans. The focus of the article is on the meanings of such films for the producers with respect to possible empowerment.

Feminist zines, as it becomes clear in the article by **Alison Piepmeier**, can perfectly well develop into alternative strategies of political intervention. Based on the example of the zine *Doris*, the author works out the cultural and political aspects of zines in general. In doing so, forms of political intervention become evident which can transform the subject position of the female reader and thus open up a moment of resistance. A pedagogy of imagination then becomes a pedagogy of hope, which has an inherent political character. Finally, **Elke Zobl** deals with the concept of participatory spaces in a visual contribution. The collection, which ranges from DIY to collaborative fields of experimentation, shows on the one hand the changes of feminist media, while demonstrating on the other hand the diverse production of feminist blogs, print zines and e-zines. The subsequent appendix encompasses a selected list of feminist and women-led media projects from all over Europe including links to print media, blogs, e-zines, radio and TV shows as well as to networks, databases and visual material. It aims to provide a first insight into the variety of feminist media production in Europe without claiming to be exhaustive and thus also shall function as a reference list or starting point for the reader's own encounter with feminist media.

The present volume covers a broad spectrum of topics. In the variety of the problems that are discussed here and the distinctiveness of the approaches and perspectives, essential dimensions of feminist media and of the resulting participatory spaces and networks emerge. At the same time, however, the articles also reveal the increasingly pressing issue of the social and societal conditions which are necessary to share in the public sphere and its cultural resources. The diversity of feminist activism as well as the variety of feminist forms of involvement and theoretical reflections nonetheless provide hope that contributing to social and societal change will continue to be the main objective of feminist media production.

References

Fiske, J. 1992. *Understanding Popular Culture*. 2nd Edition, London: Routledge.

Fraser, N., 1990. Rethinking the Public Sphere: A Contribution to the Critique of Actually Existing Democracy. *Social Text* 25–26, pp. 56–80.

Hartley, J., 1999. *Uses of Television*. London: Routledge.

Hermes, J., 2006. Citizenship in the Age of the Internet. *European Journal of Communication* 21(3), pp. 295–309.

hooks, b., 1990. *Yearning: race, gender, and cultural politics*. Boston, MA: South End Press.

Jenkins, H., Puroshotma, R., Clinton, K., Weigel, M. and Robison, A. J. 2006. Confronting the Challenges of Participatory Culture: Media Education for the 21st Century [online]. Available at: http://www.newmedialiteracies.org/files/working/NMLWhitePaper.pdf

Klaus, E. and Lünenborg, M., 2004. Cultural Citizenship. Ein kommunikationswissenschaftliches Konzept zur Bestimmung kultureller Teilhabe in der Mediengesellschaft. *Medien und Kommunikationswissenschaft* 52(2), pp. 193–213.

Rodríquez, E. 2008. Postkolonialismus: Subjektivität, Rassismus und Geschlecht. In: R. Becker and B. Kortendiek, eds. *Handbuch Frauen- und Geschlechterforschung. Theorie, Methoden, Empirie*. 2nd edition. Wiesbaden: VS-Verlag, pp. 239–247

Spivak, G. C., 1988. Can the Subaltern Speak? In: C. Nelson and L. Grossberg, ed. *Marxism and the Interpretation of Culture*. Basingstoke: Macmillan Education, pp. 271–313.

Chapter 1:
Feminist Media Production
and Alternative Economies

"Zines can function as a participatory alternative medium to give alternative views on the society that can't be found in the mainstream media."
Nina Njisten (Belgium)

"I hope to be able to show people how anyone can share ideas and feelings without needing much money or without having to use the traditional ways of communication, which in most of the cases are ruled by influences and power."
Editor of *Dos Chicas* zine (Perú)

Drawing by Nina Nijsten (originally published in *Missy Magazine*, Germany, no. 7, 2010)

"Every girl out there should take some photos or write some poems or rants or essays or short stories and start her own true, passionate, heartfelt zine."
Editor of *Persephone is Pissed* (USA)

Feminist Media Production in Europe: A Research Report

Elke Zobl and Rosa Reitsamer (with Stefanie Grünangerl)

Introduction: Feminist media in the context of new social movements

Throughout history, feminists have used media individually and collectively to inform, motivate, and mobilise political action on behalf of women, as well as to critique the structures and content of dominant media. As Linda Steiner aptly puts it, alternative feminist media suggest "a model for oppositional media" (Steiner 2000: 1331) as they document women's attempts to improve themselves and remake the world. Chris Atton champions alternative media in general as "counter hegemonic" because they challenge hegemonic structures in society "whether on an explicit political platform, or employing the kinds of indirect challenges through experimentation and the transformation of existing roles, routines, emblems and signs" (2002: 27). What makes media "alternative" to the mainstream of corporate media conglomerates are the processes of production, the content and the interpretive strategies of its audiences (Atkinson 2010: 22). Grassroots media projects "are fundamental in breaking the fear of speaking and in challenging the myth of women's silence" (Riaño 2000: 1335), the dominant metaphor used to refer to the marginal position of women in the communications industry. While challenging the absence of women's voices in public space, women media producers develop creative, analytical and literary skills within this cycle of analysis, reflection, and action. James Hamilton (2000) argues that three general principles underpin alternative media production, namely de-professionalisation, de-capitalisation, and de-institutionalisation. These three principles speak of how alternative women-led and feminist media are usually accessible to women without the necessity of professional training and expensive capital outlay, and how they take place outside of institutional or formalised settings. Alternative women-led and feminist media offer participatory forums for debate and the exchange of politically, socially and culturally engaged ideas by those who are marginalised within mainstream political debates. In her book *Changing the Wor(l)d: Discourse, Politics and the Feminist Movement* (1997), Stacey Young conceptualises feminist publishing as discursive politics and activism. Starting from a thesis that enduring social change is possible according to changes in people's awareness of their situations and their prospects for change, she argues that "progressive changes in consciousness come about through discourses that challenge oppressive constructions of social phenomena" and that language acts, such as publishing, "can play a crucial part in bringing about individual and collective social change" (ibid. 25).

Taking this theoretical framework and research findings as a starting point for our empirical study, we will explore the following questions: So how does a younger generation of feminist media producers in Europe participate in society by producing print magazines, weblogs ("blogs") and electronic magazines ("e-zines") in grassroots, alternative contexts relating to "new social movements"? How do they engage in discourses on feminism(s), challenge the status quo and effect social change? In this article we will suggest a few answers to these questions. We will refer to the empirical data collected throughout the "Feminist Media Production in Europe" research project, which was affiliated with the Department of Communication at the University of Salzburg from 2008 to 2012[1]. Drawing upon theories of alternative and activist media as well theories on new social movements (NSMs), we understand alternative feminist media projects as part of and contributions to "new social movements".

"New social movements" emerged in the late 1960s and marked "an important cultural shift away from the hierarchical social relations and bureaucratic control structure of industrialism, and toward a new 'postindustrial' or 'programmed' society built on the foundations of networked information technologies, media culture, and an emerging class of highly educated, creative 'knowledge workers'" (Lievrouw 2011: 46). Suzanne Staggenborg (1995) has identified three main outcomes of social movements, namely political and policy outcomes, mobilization outcomes and cultural outcomes. Whereas changes in policies and practices, and the creation and sustaining of organizations are the more visible successes of social movements, cultural change is perhaps the longest-lasting form of social change. In the context of feminist media production, the cultural outcomes are of special interest because they "include changes in social norms, behaviours, and ways of thinking among a public that extends beyond movement constituents or beneficiaries, as well as the creation of a collective consciousness among groups such as women" (Staggenborg 1995: 341). In her book *Alternative and Activist New Media* (2011), Leah Lievrouw identified several characteristics that distinguish new social movements in the postmodern era from previous social movements of the industrial age such as the labour and the anti-war/peace movements: NSMs are seen to be of smaller scale, tackling a wide range of issues or focused on group identities,

1   The study was conducted by a team, encompassing project leader Elke Zobl; post-doctoral researchers Rosa Reitsamer (2009–2011) and Jenny Gunnarsson Payne (2008–2009); doctoral student Red Chidgey (2008–2010); with research support from Stefanie Grünangerl (2010–2012). This article has benefited from contributions by Red Chidgey and Jenny Gunnarsson Payne in the beginning of the project as well as from comments on this report, for which we kindly thank them. For documentation of the project see *Grassroots Feminism*: www.grassrootsfeminism.net. Contact: elke.zobl@sbg.ac.at.

often supporting cultural or symbolic (rather than for example economic) values and causes. NSMs are focused more on "the shared identities, professions, interests, values, and experiences of individual actors" (ibid. 47) who are mostly well-educated, articulated, creative knowledge workers, and their participants are primarily concerned with forming their own identities while avoiding the domination of formal institutions (ibid. 49). As a result, they "are more likely to identify with and organise around their youth, gender, sexual orientation, ethnicity, language, or professional background than with abstract categories like class", and NSMs are profoundly cultural rather than economic in nature, focusing instead on their symbolic capital (ibid. 50–51). Feminism – both as a movement and a plurality of feminist discourses in general – and contemporary feminist media in particular are profoundly cultural and represent these characteristics of new social movements.

In the first part of this article, we apply Lievrouw's genre framework for alternative, activist new media (2011) to the feminist media projects in Europe which we have identified in our empirical research. We present the scope (1.1) and the stance (1.2) of the feminist media projects as well as the action and agency of the feminist media producers (1.3). In the second part of the article we discuss how feminist media producers in Europe relate to and adopt feminist theories and activism and develop their own agenda and standpoints. Drawing upon theories on third wave feminism and our own empirical findings, we introduce three interrelated discourses: do-it-yourself feminism (2.1), intersectional perspectives on feminism (2.2) and pop feminism in the context of the German-speaking debate on new feminisms (2.3). In the conclusion we take up the central questions of this article and situate feminist media production within a larger social context.

Methodological approach

Grounded Theory (Glaser and Strauss 1967) served as the basis for the methodological approach for our study, as it allows for a combination of qualitative and quantitative research methods. In particular, the archival documentation of women-led and feminist media projects, a quantitative online survey of consumer habits and in-depth interviews with feminist media producers provided us with the empirical data to contextualise and analyse feminist alternative media production in Europe. In a first step, we conducted virtual ethnographic fieldwork (Hine 2000) to identify as many feminist media projects in Europe as possible, whereby the self-identification of the media producer as "feminist", their relation to the women's movement, feminist theory and (media) activism as well as the chosen media format (print and/or online) were essential selection criteria. In total, our sample includes 425 women-led and feminist media projects which are produced in grassroots and alternative on- and offline contexts in Europe, and which were analysed in reference to country, founding year, publishers, publication language, frequency of publication, main content and use of social media. On the basis of this descriptive statistic of feminist media projects, we identified feminist media producers for in-depth interviews and selected case studies to explore the meaning, vulnerabilities and significance of feminist grassroots media products (step 2). We conducted 47 in-depth interviews with feminist media producers from 19 European countries as well as five in-depth case studies on *Plotki Femzine*, a post-Soviet Central and Eastern European feminist print and online zine project (Chidgey, Gunnarsson Payne and Zobl 2009), several German-speaking comic producers (Reitsamer and Zobl 2011), feminist zines (Chidgey 2009a; Zobl 2009, 2011a, 2011b), the feminist music network *Female Pressure* (Reitsamer 2012) and feminist blogs (Reitsamer and Zobl 2012). The in-depth interviews lasted between 30 and 60 minutes and were conducted face-to-face in different European cities as well as online via Skype or email between 2009 and 2011. The interviewees, who included producers of weblogs, fanzines and other print media, were mainly white and middle class, and the majority studied at universities or already had a university degree. They were able to give detailed information on the access to alternative media production, their media projects and their feminist education.

In a third step, a quantitative online survey was conducted to explore the habits of feminist media consumers in Europe. In total 230 persons participated in this survey from January 2009 until April 2012. Additionally, all collected data was continuously documented on the digital archive *Grassroots Feminism: Transnational archives, resources and communities* (www.grassrootsfeminism.net), which was set up in December 2008. The website hosts three digital archives – "Grassroots Media in Europe", "Festivals: Ladyfest & Queer-Feminist" and "Zines" – and offers a chronological and geographical map of grassroots feminist media across Europe from the 1960s onwards, embracing digital and analogue media forms. By providing an interactive network portal and research platform for researchers, activists and media producers, this *Grassroots Feminism* Web 2.0 archive makes contemporary feminist, queer and antiracist cultural practices more accessible to researchers and the general public.

Image 1: A screenshot of Grassroots Feminism: Transnational archives, resources and communities

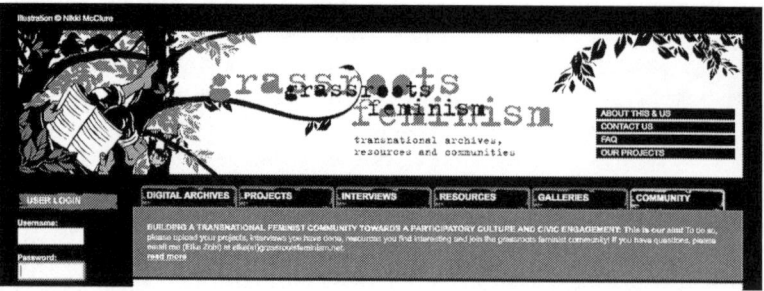

1   Scope and stance of feminist media projects

In *Alternative and Activist Media* (2011), Lievrouw describes the artistic and political practices of Dada and the Situationist International and other new social movements as central influences for today's alternative and activist uses in particular of new media. As such, activist art movements, new social movements and online activism, which emerged with the development of and access to the internet, are linked by three major themes: first, the scope or size of alternative and activist new media projects; second, the stance of movements and projects relative to the mainstream society and culture; and third, the nature of projects as action and activists as agents of social change (Lievrouw 2011: 59).[2] Lievrouw explores these three themes – scope, stance, and action and agency – as a "genre framework for alternative and activist new media." We have taken this distinction in scope, stance, and action and agency as a flexible toolbox and applied it to our empirical research. The analysis of the empirical data was oriented on the coding paradigm of Grounded Theory whereby Lievrouw's genre framework guided the identification of codes and concepts in the empirical material. In the following we will apply this framework to feminist media projects in Europe, beginning with their scope.

1.1   The scope of feminist media projects in Europe

According to Lievrouw's genre framework, scope includes two related features: the small-scale and the collaborative nature of alternative and activist new media projects. As "micro media" (Peretti 2001) or "tactical media" (Garcia and Lovink 1997), new media projects tend to be relatively small, low-cost projects with a do-it-yourself aesthetic as access to resources (e. g. in terms of funding and staff) is limited and a critical attitude towards dominant mass and consumer culture is taken. Moreover, compared to "mainstream" media, the outreach of alternative and activist media projects is relatively small, but as such they can provide their audience with a sense of familiarity and intimacy as they address their readers as insiders (Lievrouw 2011: 62). We have identified the following features to illustrate the small-scale nature of feminist media projects in Europe: media types, the number of media by European country, publisher, publishing frequency, and the use of language and social media platforms.

Media types: The 425 women-led and feminist grassroots media projects, which we have recorded in our survey, encompass 150 print media, including zines, magazines and journals, 140 blogs, 70 e-zines, 35 radio shows, five community TV shows, 17 archives, networks and databases, as well as eight artistic or visual interventions (posters, stickers, adbusting, subvertising). During the course of this survey, we found that some media projects distrib-

---

2   For an application and analysis of Lievrouw's genre framework in relation to participatory feminist interventions into cultural production, see Zobl forthcoming.

ute their content through multiple different media channels, such as by operating a blog or an e-zine in addition to publishing a print zine or magazine.
For example, the British feminist art journal *n.paradoxa* has been published
as a print magazine since 1998; its website has since 2010 provided an online
archive of previously published magazines and articles and an extensive
bibliography on feminist art and feminist art theory. The Czech riot grrrl
zine *Bloody Mary*, combining punk and riot grrrl feminism, was founded in
2000 by a collective, and in 2005 added a *Bloody Mary* blog. While each zine
edition is dedicated to a specific theme, the collective blog is used for the an-
nouncement of feminist-queer events and the publication of feminist-queer
news and articles about LGTBQ issues. The publishers of the Belgian blog
De Tweede Sekse decided in 2010 to publish selected articles in a zine format
with the aim of reaching a wider audience for their feminist-queer and anti-
racist content. One of the editors explains the extension of the blog to a zine
as follows: "We made the zine because we didn't want to limit ourselves just
to people who have a broadband internet connection. A zine is easy to distribute and people can read it anywhere – on the train or at your home, even
if you don't have internet."[3] Another example of the publication of content
in both blog and zine formats is the Ukrainian anarcha-feminist *Svobodna*
blog, edited since 2007 by a collective. In 2010 they published a zine on the
issue of domination and violence in activism and the anarchist movement,
and distributed it also as a download via their blog.

In addition to the use of varying media channels, we also observed
changes of media format. In 2010 the Swiss magazine *l'émiliE* stopped publication as a print magazine and now appears as an e-zine, expanded to
include a digital archive in which all the back issues since 1912 can be accessed. The Slovak print magazine *ASPEKT* (1993–2004) was discontinued
in 2004 due to a reduction in funding; a smaller version of the magazine has
been published on the internet since then.

Media by country: Of the total of 360 print media, blogs and e-zines, 56 are
located in Germany and 51 in the UK, followed by 25 feminist media projects
in Spain, 19 in Poland and 18 in Italy. In Austria, Belgium, France and Sweden
we could identify 17 media projects per country. The reasons for the varying
geographic distribution of feminist media projects in Europe were not investigated more specifically; in the interviews, however, the media producers
point out that the relative lack of feminist media in their country is based on
the country's size, the political orientation of the government, the state funding situation for feminist (media) projects and the influence of feminist theory
and activism on a younger generation of women. (Table 1)

Publishing frequency: Of the total of 150 print media, 39 were issued quarterly, 33 semi-annually and 34 were published at irregular intervals; in addition, 17 print media were published yearly, 12 published three issues per

---

3 All quotations in this article (unless otherwise indicated) stem from face-to-face or
online interviews with feminist media producers conducted throughout our research.
All quotations from other sources are marked as such. Quotes in the original German
language of the interviews and other sources have been translated by the authors.

Table 1: Media by country

Country	Print	Blogs	E-Zines	Total
Germany	21	25	10	56
UK	16	30	5	51
Spain	8	10	7	25
Poland	6	5	8	19
Italy	3	11	4	18
Austria	11	2	4	17
Belgium	11	6	–	17
France	7	9	1	17
Sweden	10	4	3	17
Switzerland	8	1	3	12
Croatia	3	1	5	9
Russia	3	4	2	9
Czech Republic	5	1	2	8
Netherlands	4	2	2	8
Slovenia	2	5	1	8
Portugal	3	3	1	7
Romania	3	4	–	7
Denmark	2	2	2	6
Hungary	1	4	1	6
Ireland	3	2	1	6
Serbia	4	1	1	6
Ukraine	2	3	1	6
Norway	3	1	1	5
Finland	4	–	–	4
Belarus	–	1	1	2
Bulgaria	2	–	–	2
Georgia	–	1	1	2
Macedonia	1	1	–	2
Slovakia	1	–	1	2
Turkey	–	–	2	2
Albania	1	–	–	1
Estonia	1	–	–	1
Greece	1	–	–	1
Iceland	–	1	–	1
	150	140	70	360

year, eight were monthly and seven bimonthly. Sixteen print media were founded before the year 1980, 20 between 1980 and 1989, 47 in the 1990s, and from 2000 to 2010, an average of six new print media were founded per year. In 2006 a high point was reached with 13 start-ups. Unlike print media, which have longer lead times for their publications, the publishers of blogs and e-zines are frequently able to make new content available to their readers. 44 blogs and 27 e-zines provide new content daily, 28 blogs and 12 e-zines offer weekly updates, and 21 blogs and seven e-zines update their content monthly. The first e-zine recorded in our survey was founded in 1995; the first blog was launched in 2001. 32 of the 70 e-zines were founded between 2006 and 2009, with a peak in 2006 with 11 new e-zines; 2008 was a high point in the creation of blogs with 33.

Language: The vast majority of the content of a total of 360 print media, blogs and e-zines is published in the native language of the editors; 30 media products are offered in two languages, whereby the second language is usually English. The collective that publishes the Romanian zine *Love Kills (Dragostia Ucide)*, for example, publishes both a Romanian and an English edition. While the Romanian zine edition is dedicated to local events and gives insight into international anarchist texts, the aim of the English zine edition, partially with other content, is to raise money for the activities of the collective. Other examples of a multilingual orientation are the Spanish technology blog *Dones i noves* (since 2006), with content in Spanish, English and Catalan; the Belgian *Scumgrrrls* magazine (since 2002), with content in English, French and Dutch; and the Georgian e-zine *CaucAsia* (2005–2009), which has published its issues in Russian, Georgian and English (becoming a Russian-speaking blog in 2009, however). A few media projects make use of four or even more languages to disseminate their content, such as *Trikster – Nordic Queer Journal* (Denmark, since 2008), with content in English and three other Nordic languages (Swedish, Norwegian and Danish), or *Migrazine* (Austria, since 2006), with content in a variety of languages, such as German, English, French, Portuguese, Spanish and Turkish. In their use of various languages they aim to transcend language barriers by addressing readers with differing language skills and knowledge as well as an international community.

Table 2: Language

Language	Print	Blogs	E-Zines	Total
Monolingual	131	125	57	313
Bilingual	9	12	9	30
Trilingual	6	2	1	9
Multilingual (≥ 4)	4	1	3	8
	150	140	70	360

Use of social media platforms: Contrary to our assumption that feminist media producers would use social media platforms to a large extent, only 110 producers of online and print media used one or more social media platforms to a great extent. In other words, two-thirds of feminist media projects went without the use of social media platforms. The most frequently used social media platform is Facebook, followed by Twitter and MySpace, and feminist online media (blogs and e-zines) use these services more frequently than feminist print media.

Table 3: Social Media

Social Media*	Print**	Blogs**	E-Zines**	Total**
no social media	121	82	47	250
social media	29	58	23	110
Facebook	21	37	19	77
Twitter	9	27	9	45
MySpace	10	6	7	23
flickr	0	12	3	15
YouTube	2	7	4	13

* multiple matches possible
** Print: n = 150; Blogs: n = 140; E-Zines: n = 70; Total: n = 360

The range of feminist media projects in relation to media type, publishing frequency, the use of social media platforms and publication language illustrate to the heterogeneity of small-scale, low-cost "micro-media."

The second aspect of scope that Lievrouw identifies for alternative and activist new media is their specific form of organization. The majority of these projects are not produced individually but in collaboration. They are the product of cooperation by individuals and groups and as such they are group efforts. This "new collectivism" (Lievrouw 2011: 62) is based on community building, interactivity and participation in the design of the media as well as the organization of the working and operation processes, and is associated with postmodern artistic practices and activism. The "new collectivism" of feminist media producers becomes clear when we researched the publishers of the media in the sense that they are mostly collaboratively produced.

Publisher: The majority of feminist media is published by independent collectives and groups (129), followed by independent women's organizations and NGOs (102), individuals (74), independent editors in the academic context (37) and small independent, self-founded corporate-structured publishers and editors as part of larger corporate publishers (13); in addition, five feminist media projects are published by public institutions, labour unions and political parties. While print media (53) and e-zines (30) are edited mainly by NGOs or independent women's organizations, blogs are overwhelmingly produced by groups (61) and by individuals (56) rather than by NGOs or women's organizations (19).

The collaborative, shared and volunteer efforts of feminist media producers are illustrated by the co-editor of the queer print magazine *Hugs and Kisses. Tender All Your Gender,* which has been published in German twice a year since 2007:

Hugs and Kisses has many supporters. There are people for the distribution; we have several proofreaders and graphic designers. That's a good thing, as not everyone can allow themselves at any time to be part of a non-profit project, even if they want to. We have a webmaster who only attends to the homepage.

The co-editor of *Hugs and Kisses* points to the decisive group effort of feminist media projects as well as to the constraints these projects face due to access to resources in terms of time, funding and staff.

Another example for a collaborative effort is *Plotki Femzine*, a post-Soviet Central and Eastern European (CEE) feminist print and online zine project that is part of a larger youth generated media project called "Plotki". *Plotki Femzine* was launched by a group of young women as a response to what they saw as increasing hierarchical and patriarchal attitudes within the network. Through collaborative acts of discussion, experimental art, autobiographical essays, and critical fiction, the *Plotki Femzine* project brings together women living and working in CEE countries to create an emerging, collaborative space for feminist discussions and an articulation of feminist identities and connections (for a further discussion of *Plotki Femzine* see Chidgey, Gunnarsson Payne and Zobl 2009).

The scope of the feminist media projects, as well as their small-scale and collaborative nature, says little about their relationship to the "mainstream" media and hegemonic culture, however. In what follows, therefore, the stance of feminist media projects is described in more detail, as well as what they share with alternative and activist new media projects, namely their heterotopic nature, their subcultural quality and their use of irony and humour (Lievrouw 2011).

1.2 The stance of feminist media projects in Europe

Feminist media producers describe their projects often as countersites to "mainstream" media because they offer a space where people can experiment with ideas, express themselves and describe their experiences. The Belgian editor of such zines as *Flapper Gathering* and *(Different Worlds) Same Heartbeats* and organizer of *The Feminist Poster Project* articulates such an approach: "Zines can function as a participatory alternative medium to give alternative views on the society that can't be found in the mainstream media."

In this respect feminist media projects reflect what Lievrouw identifies as characteristics in relation to the stance of alternative and activist new media projects. Firstly, these projects are heterotopic because they "act as 'other spaces' or 'countersites' for expression, affiliation, and creativity apart from the dominant culture" (Lievrouw 2011: 63). We see this heterotopic stance especially in feminist zines which often function as a heterogeneous, "culturally productive, politicized counterpublic space" (Nguyen 2000) for feminist networking and reflection by a younger generation of women in different parts of the world (Zobl 2010). Zine makers discuss topics – often taboo issues – that are left out, marginalized or underrepresented in dominant media, culture and politics, such as abuse, incest and complex interactions of sexism, homophobia, transphobia and racism. In addressing and critically discussing such issues, they not only point to the challenges and conflicts of their societies but they also bring "new, alternative, 'other' values and practices for the rest of society" (Lievrouw 2011: 64) to the table.

Second, the heterotopic nature of feminist media projects is associated with their "subcultural quality" (Lievrouw 2001: 65), which is rooted in shared insider knowledge and a "hyper self-reflexivity about the nature of pop culture" (Collins 1995: 2; quoted in Lievrouw 2011: 66). Accordingly, feminist media producers require a certain access to and knowledge of (sub) cultural codes, language and symbols. The co-editor of *Hugs and Kisses* emphasizes the strong connections to queer-feminist scenes and their shared "subcultural capital" (Thornton 1995):

> *Hugs and Kisses* shows the plurality of the queer movement by reporting about this movement. That's the reason why the contacts to subcultural initiatives and organisations that follow a political claim are very important. We know many of these organisations and we try to extend our networks further.

Similarly, the Love Kills Collective from Romania, which publishes the *Love Kills* zine and translates anarchist literature into Romanian, notes:

> Since four years we are also organizing an anarcha-feminist festival in Romania with international participation. The aim [. . .] is to establish and strengthen the bounds and links between activists involved and interested in anarcha-feminism and to develop a network. [. . .] But we know that our work is visible mostly in our own small scene and not on a large social scale. But as we are aiming towards anarchism, and as we see anarchism as an ongoing emerging occurrence, we strongly believe that even the slightest effort has its own meaningful importance and contribution.

The collective is aware of the specific local embeddedness of their activities in the feminist-queer scenes in Romania, but they assume that their work feeds into broader translocal cultures of social change.

Zine makers like the Love Kills Collective often speak about the advantages of networking with alternative media producers and media activists who share the same or similar (sub)cultural, social and political interests. A common feature of the analysed media projects is that they refer to networking discourses through which the affiliation of feminist groups and positions as well as collectivity is established. Networking occurs on a local, transnational and virtual level. In fact, this aspect of networking across national borders using the internet proves to be a major difference compared to the more restricted (in terms of geography, time, etc.) communication exchanges that took place during the era of second wave feminism. Networking among contemporary feminist media occurs over a wide range: from linking to other media projects (where further interactions between media producers do not occur) through editorial references to other feminist media projects with similar orientations in content and perspectives (with cluster-building in regards to content), to a pooling of online and offline activities of feminist media projects which often share the same spoken language (with cluster-building in regards to geography).

Zines, for example, circulate within a transnational peer-to-peer network that can be characterised as a system of online and offline exchange, dissemination and distribution outside of the mainstream (Zobl 2009). This network includes not only print and e-zines but also mail-order catalogues, so-called distros, online resources, mailing lists, message boards as well as zine meetings and conferences, exhibitions, workshops, libraries and archives. In this decentralized network, zine producers not only trade their zines via the mail – and virtually via email and social networking sites – but sooner or later they frequently become acquainted personally through zine picnics, festivals or workshops. Many of the zine editors we interviewed stress that they got to know similar-thinking people in other countries via the internet and got to know new and different perspectives by exchanging zines with them. Embedded in local and transnational contexts, zines can function as "a kind of backbone to subcultural feminist activism, allowing zine makers to link personal experiences to larger political activist work" (Schilt and Zobl 2008: 187).

However, the often subcultural quality of feminist media projects also has its drawbacks and has been criticized by media producers for its structural and individual mechanisms of exclusion. Misster Raju Rage (formerly known as Misster Scratch), producer of the English-speaking zine *Masculine Femininities* (UK), points to the underrepresentation of people of colour and of certain topics as well as to the limitations of access and demographics:

> I enjoy the variety and creativity of what there is out there but [. . .] I would like to see more people of colour, more about issues of race and sexuality, more about gender and surviving violence and things that don't get discussed much in our communities or from certain perspectives. The limiting thing about zines is getting access to them. Often they are distributed at events that are mainly white and middle class dominated, in specific scenes, which is problematic.

As such, by employing certain cultural codes, symbols, language, style and aesthetics, an orientation and associated affiliation toward a specific – subcultural – community occurs that involves overwhelmingly a white, middle-class and well-educated demographic. Whilst constant failure is inscribed in processes of media production and in building networks and coalitions, the distribution of subcultural capital (Thornton 1995) is essential. Feminist media producers such as Misster Raju Rage point to the fact that these challenges need to be further negotiated and interrogated within feminist media networks and subcultural scenes.

The third characteristic Lievrouw (2011: 66) describes in relation to the stance of alternative and activist new media projects is the use of irony and humour. In feminist media projects, especially zines, humour and irony manifests itself in cut-and-paste collages to subvert and deconstruct the hegemonic representations of femininity as beautiful, successful and young and to challenge the commodification and sexualisation of women's bodies as a dominant advertising and marketing strategy. Janice Radway (2002) describes such playful experimentations with subject positions as "narrative gleaning" and "insubordinate creativity" in the lives and cultural practices of girls and young women. Producing zines and using the format of a collage, Radway argues, becomes a means for young women to express intertextuality and multiplicity as well as their resistance to dominant modes of femininity.

The collectively produced zine *Riot Grrrl London*, for example, overwrites in a black-and-white collage an image of a face of a young, beautiful woman – as often used in advertising – with a cut-and-paste typeface declaring "boring meaningless crap", and juxtaposes it below in small letters with the question: "How many skinny airbrushed models can you stand?"

Image 2: Collage in the Riot Grrrl London zine (issue 3, 2003)

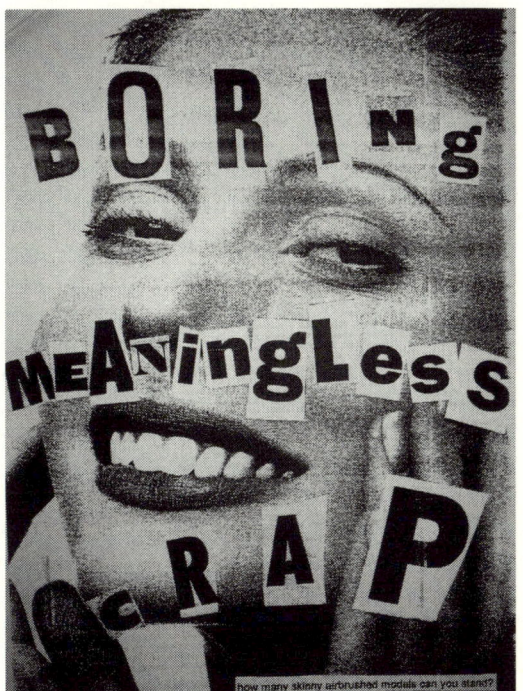

The culture jamming actions by street artist Princess Hijab (Paris) are a further example of the appropriation of advertising images to create new meanings in unexpected ways.[4]

---

4 For a discussion of the culture jamming activities of Princess Hijab, see the article by Jenny Gunnarsson Payne in this volume.

1.3 Action and agency of feminist media projects

The third theme of Lievrouw's genre framework connecting activist art movements, new social movements and online activism is action and agency – "that is, the extent to which projects are conceived and executed as *action*, by participants who see themselves and their projects as *agents* of social change" (Lievrouw 2011: 68). Activist art, social movement theory, and alternative/activist new media projects are characterized by being interventionist – as their creators aim to interrupt or alter existing conditions, often by direct action – and by being perishable – that is short-lived, nomadic, ephemeral, temporary, with rapid response (ibid. 60, 68–69). In our study, the interventionist and perishable features of action and agency are clearly exemplified by media producers who situate themselves in a do-it-yourself context of queer-feminist scenes. In the following we will describe the social practices of the two German comic producers The Artist of *Trouble X Comics*[5] and Ka Schmitz to give a more precise picture of their self-organized participation in the media landscape and their activist and interventionist practices (for a detailed discussion see Reitsamer and Zobl 2011).

The Artist of *Trouble X Comics* and Ka Schmitz consider their drawings as an activist practice, intended to break heteronormative notions of gender and sexuality in their interplay with other categories of social differentiation, and situate their comics generally outside the mainstream in a queer-feminist do-it-yourself culture. The two illustrators use varying publishing formats (such as comics, zines, blogs, games) and distribution channels and address heterogeneous topics. With their critique of social power relations, they share the interventionist aim of breaking open and changing hierarchical gender relations. The distribution of their comics takes place primarily through decentralized networks of queer-feminist scenes such as alternative bookstores, Ladyfest music and art festivals, exhibitions, workshops, online distros, mailing lists or message boards. Within the "network turn" in New Social Movement theory, such a dissemination of information and the building of temporary communities has been termed "networked activism" (Atkinson 2010: 10). Ka Schmitz and The Artist of *Trouble X Comics* are part of this "networked activism" and they contribute to "new social movement networks" (Atkinson 2010: 10) by circulating their comics at copy/print cost or completely free. Access to the comics is ensured primarily by the internet, where they can be found on blogs, MySpace, Flickr and Facebook and can be downloaded. As a result, Ka Schmitz and The Artist of *Trouble X Comics* describe the free distribution of their comics as "a kind of queer action" which aims at minimizing social inequalities. Consequently, they attempt to break through the boundaries between consumers and producers by actively involving comic readers, supporting individual initiatives with "how-to" instructions and passing along knowledge away from traditional educational institutions

---

5 At her/his express wish, The Artist of *Trouble X Comics* will not be mentioned by name, but will be represented in the text anonymously and ambiguously.

in self-organized workshops. In the "how to DIY a comic" zine,[6] The Artist of *Trouble X Comics* describes her/his approach to drawing, which she/he does not wish to have understood as formal guidance, but rather as an encouragement to begin on one's own through this "DIY practice". In the context of DIY culture, drawing queer-feminist comics becomes, through the interconnection of feminist self-empowerment strategies with a leftist critique of capitalism, an interventionist practice in social power relations. The focus is on emancipatory bottom-up processes through "learning by doing" and "skill-sharing"; the established standards and guidelines for "perfect" drawings are nullified, deconstructed and ignored. For example, Ka Schmitz holds comics workshops for girls, women and trans youth. In these workshops, a low-threshold opportunity to enter into comic drawing and a platform for informal learning is accelerated by Ka Schmitz into a collective self-empowerment process. The execution of instructions by the workshop participants and an orientation to results takes back seat. An artistic practice is mediated that rejects individual authorship and the established topos of the "artistic genius" through collective ways of working. Drawing comics is, in the workshops, dialogically and collectively conceived; it serves a tool for individual and collective agency and action. Therefore, comics, comic zines and comic workshops can be understood as an interventionist – though short-lived and ephemeral – medium for local and translocal dialogue, community and network building, and exchange of experience and knowledge. In the context of the riot grrrl movement, which emerged in the 1990s out of the post-punk music scene in the United States, zinester Mimi Nguyen (2000) speaks of an informal educational project as a "punk rock teaching machine", whose basic principle is that every reader is potentially a producer who can play all positions from the production to the distribution of her/his cultural artefacts. The focus of the social practices of the DIY culture is not on success in terms of the number of zine readers. The heterogeneity of voices, which is expressed in a variety of media, is crucial, as well as becoming an agent of social change by engaging in and producing media that is interventionist.

2 Negotiating feminism as a discursive space

> "Feminist identities are usually achieved, not given.
> [. . .] Feminist identities are created and reinforced when feminists get together, act together, and read what other feminists have written" (Mansbridge 1995: 29).

How do feminist media producers in Europe relate to feminist theories and activism? And which feminist discourses, standpoints and identities do they develop with their interventionist and activist practices? Drawing upon theoretical concepts of third wave feminism and our empirical findings, we will introduce in this section three interrelated discourses arti-

---

6 See the visual contribution by Elke Zobl in this volume.

culated by feminist media producers in Europe: do-it-yourself feminism, intersectional perspectives of feminism, and pop feminism in the context of the German-speaking "new feminisms" debate.

Third wave feminism is a neologism coined in 1992 by Rebecca Walker, the daughter of literary feminist Alice Walker, in an article published in the US *Ms. magazine* heralding a new generation of feminist activists who are not "postfeminist feminists" (Heywood 2006; for a discussion on postfeminism, see Genz and Brabon 2009). However, there is no easy agreement that a third wave feminism actually exists, not least because activists and scholars have been divided about the usefulness of heralding a new wave. While some see "third wave" as a useful label for a new generation's feminism (Baumgardner and Richards 2000; Dicker and Piepmeier 2003; Heywood 2006), others consider it as a false distinction further promoting division between different generations and subsuming differences/nuances under epochal monoliths (Berger 2006). Agnieszka Graff (2007) argues that in the national, geo-political and historical context of Poland feminism resists the Anglo-American wave chronology but is also in part conditioned by Western and third wave feminism's influences (such as its preoccupation with pop culture). According to Genz and Brabon (2009) third wave feminism situates itself in the field of popular culture and continues to understand a critical engagement with pop culture as a component of political struggle. Feminist youth (sub)cultures and networks, such as riot grrrl, began using the internet for networking, organising local music events and producing websites, e-zines and blogs; such networks are generally considered an expression of third wave feminism (Reitsamer 2012). In the course of her investigation of riot grrrl in the United States, Garrison (2000) argues that the use of new media technologies for communication, cultural production and political activism, as well networking between women of different age cohorts are defining features of third wave feminism.

Whilst links can be made to the consciousness-raising strategies of the previous feminist generations, the rhetorical style of self-disclosure and personal politics has led many critics to label contemporary feminists as a "weakened form of feminism", too individualistic and lacking systemic critiques: "There are hints of good old second wave collective activity in the websites, the zines and the concerts such as Ladyfest . . . but [third-wave feminism] has a more individualist edge, reflecting among other things a radical suspicion of the politics of identity, and a marked shift to 'lifestyle politics'" (Pilcher and Whelehan 2004: 171). Tracking the path of the "personal is political" brand of feminist politics in North American, Deborah Siegel positions the latest "wave" of confessional testimony-based feminist publishing – found in zines, magazines, books, and online – as "light on the details for a program for external change" (Siegel 2007: 150–151).

The overwhelming majority of the media producers interviewed in the course of this study position themselves and their media projects in relation to second wave feminism. The publisher of the *AMIW – All My Independent Women* blog (since 2005), talks about her encounter with and (re)appropriation of the book *Novas Cartas Portuguesas* ("New Portuguese

Letters") by Maria Isabel Barreno, Maria Teresa Horta and Maria Velho da Costa (the "Three Marias"), which is considered to be a landmark text of 1970s Portuguese feminism.

> I knew about the importance of this book, that it was very radical, very sexual, but I had no idea about the content. This is pretty much what every Portuguese knows about the book but they have never read it. Finally I read the book and it was an absolute wonder. I've never imagined that it is really a piece of literature which manages to cross times. It is not so much rooted in the 70s, but it talks a lot of Portugal in the 21st century. How women still construct their identity and their sexuality, their relationship to their family, their friends and to political institutions. It had such an impact on me. I emailed everyone in the *AMIW* network and said: Guys, Girls, let's read this book collectively, let's talk about it, let's produce work that relates to it.

The *AMIW* editor further explains how tiring it sometimes is to convince people that feminism is not an outdated and anachronistic ideology. Feminists today, she argues, deal with different issues; they have a different agenda and use different strategies than did the feminists of the 1970s.

Several feminist media producers develop strategies to relate their media projects to second wave feminism such as the reference to key thinkers of the women's movements. The Belgian blog *De Tweede Sekse* named their publication after Simone de Beauvoir's groundbreaking book "The Second Sex" (*Le Deuxième Sexe*, 1949); the Belgian magazine *Scumgrrrls* refers to Valerie Solana's *SCUM Manifesto* (1967–68); and the Swiss magazine *l'émiliE* is named after the suffragette Emilie Gourd who founded the magazine in 1912.

A further strategy for media producers to underline the necessity of feminist politics and to express one's own standpoint is the publication of manifestos and manifesto-like declarations. The French activist group La Barbe note in *Le Manifeste de la Barbe* that "it's time to revive feminism and to set out to conquer all fields of power, in all its different forms" (2008, authors' translation)[7]. Similarly, the French activist network *Osez le féminisme* (2009) speak about the aims achieved by the women's movements and argue for the need of feminist activism, especially in time of economic crisis and instability. In the declaration "Why Pro Feminism" (Za Feminizm n. d.) the Russian activist group *ЗА ФЕМИНИЗМ – Za Feminizm (Pro Feminism)* situate themselves in the tradition of feminist struggles for equal rights and the advancement of women's living conditions worldwide. The author of the Russian blog *Feminisn'ts* takes up the common phrase "I' m not a feminist, but . . ." to reflect upon feminist writing, including a variety of texts dealing with feminist history and theories in Russia (Feminisn'ts n. d.).

However, the media producers interviewed also explain that second wave feminism should be "updated" due to neoliberal changes in society. While in North American the term "third wave feminism" is frequently discussed in feminist media, the feminist media producers in our study

---

7 In the french original: "Il est temps de remettre le féminisme en selle, et de partir à la conquête des territoires de pouvoir, sous toutes ses formes."

(with a focus on Europe) hardly mentioned this expression. As a result, they frequently use the adjectives "new", "queer", "postcolonial", "pop" or "do-it-yourself" to specify their feminist self-understanding.

2.1 Do-It-Yourself Feminism

The beginnings of do-it-yourself culture are rooted in the avant-garde art movements of the 1950s and the emerging new social movements of the 1960s. In the late 1970s, punk rock, media and style revolved around the DIY ethos with self-produced fanzines, independent record labels and alternative distribution networks, with the result that DIY as an organizing principle gained a greater currency in alternative cultures. George McKay defines the 1990s DIY culture as a "youth-centred and -directed cluster of interests and practices around green radicalism, direct action politics, new musical sounds and experiences" (McKay 1998: 2). Marc Calmbach sees DIY culture as characterized by "self-empowerment, self-organization, improvisation and initiative" (Calmbach 2007: 17). DIY culture participants evidence a dedicated interest in the use of new technologies (computers, video, the internet, etc.); they position themselves against hegemonic ideologies through, among other things, art and music production; and they try to produce and market their cultural productions as independent from commercial structures as possible (Kearney 1998; McKay 1998 and 2010; Spencer 2005). DIY culture and its networks place value on varied, processual social relations and communication processes with respect to established standards of professionalization, the acquisition of expertise and intellectual property (anti-copyright) (Atton 2002: 27). In the context of feminism, the 1990s riot grrrl scenes and the subsequent feminist-queer Ladyfest music and arts festivals developed a cultural activism based on doing-it-yourself, whereby music and skill-sharing is fused with political resistance and celebration, and the boundaries between organizer, participant and audience are blurred (Chidgey 2009b; Kearney 1998; Reitsamer 2008; Schilt and Zobl 2008; Zobl 2011c). Doreen Piano (2002) notes that women as cultural producers often act within a community that functions as a learning environment for teaching DIY practices, as trading of information has always been a part of (sub)cultural production. In the UK, in activist contexts and among feminist zine producers we have noted an increase in the use of the term "DIY feminism". Red Chidgey has stated that DIY feminism is used as "an umbrella term fusing together different types of feminism" which draws "on genealogies of punk cultures, grassroots movements, and the technologies of late capitalism" (Chidgey 2009b). The Belgian maker of the *Flapper Gathering* (among many others) zine describes DIY feminism as follows:

> DIY feminism is about everyone doing feminism ourselves and making changes, however small they may seem at first sight. It means not waiting for others, for "professionals" or politicians, to make the world more women-friendly and to solve problems related to sexism.

Most often, DIY feminist actions in their many forms take an anti-capitalist stance: "self/collective produced culture, politics, entertainment, and work are held as ideals, and not-for-profit voluntary/activist labour is the movement's lifeblood" (Chidgey 2009b: n. p.). This is illustrated by the Berlin-based *Make Out Magazine* (MOM), which acknowledges in its first issue (November 2011) their contextualisation in anti-capitalist DIY culture and feminism:

> We don't exactly identify as capitalists. That's why you might notice our publication isn't polluted with ads. D.I.Y. zine culture was an integral part of queer politics and third-wave feminism in the 90s, but now that blogs have become the weapon of choice for spreading propaganda, we wanted to revisit this tactical, timeless format with international relevance a bit of grown-up sheen. Not too polished, though – we like it rough! (Sona, Krusche, Spilker and Hansom 2011: n. p.)

Similarly, *Emancypunx* – an anarchist feminist group running a record label, festival organizer, tour manager and host of a zine library – was founded in the mid 1990s in Warsaw to promote feminism and women's issues within an underground DIY distribution network. They also point to their strong anti-corporate and alternative DIY stance:

> One of the main goals is to foster the diy hc punk network and to keep our creativity, spaces, creative products far from corporate business. [. . .] Emancypunx is and always was a non-profit, non-commercial initiative run on voluntary and D.I.Y. basis. (Emancypunx n. d.)

Media producers who sympathize with a DIY ethos and understand their media projects as "independent" and "autonomous" often revert to discourses that are critical of society and its established and continuously reinforced gender relations. They build "alternative economies" (Atton 2002; Chidgey 2009b) or a "DIY industry" (Peterson and Bennett 2004: 5) which are based on small collectives, fans-turned-entrepreneurs and volunteer labour for the non-commercial exchange of their media and as alternatives to commercial media corporations. Feminist media is circulated in the "DIY industry" in the context of a feminist and anti-commercial agency as well as in the wider alternative (sub)cultural feminist scenes and networks. This process of media production (and networking) aims to establish horizontal, non-hierarchical structures. As a result, for the overwhelming majority of feminist media producers who describe themselves as "DIY feminists", social change can only take place through a radical critique of a neoliberal system and through alternative economies outside of neoliberal exploitation logic.

2.2 Intersectional perspectives of feminism

The development of intersectional feminist discourses is directly related to the debates about the difference between women since the 1980s, which were initiated by lesbian women, "women of colour" and postcolonial feminists. They question the category of "woman" as the universal guiding category for the creation of feminist theory and call attention to the interconnections of the various axes of difference that inequalities can construct. An initial critique of the patriarchal concept of white middle class feminists and the idea of "global sisterhood" was formulated by the Combahee River Collective (1982), a coalition of black lesbian women. The collective drew attention to their life realities, including how they had faced discrimination on the basis of race, class, gender and sexuality, and carved out alliances between women on the basis of their different social positions. Patricia Hill Collins explores the discrimination of women of colour; she draws on the concept of intersectionality and proposes understanding race, class and gender as "interlocking systems of oppression" (Hill Collins 1990: 221) and analysing the resulting social inequalities as part of an overall "matrix of domination" (ibid.) in order to avoid an additive analysis for the explanation of complex forms of oppression. Additive models of inequality research focus on gender category and add additional categories such as age, sexuality, race, class and religion; moreover, the dichotomy of being black or white, male or female, etc., in these models have their basis in Western thought. Following the critique by black women, postcolonial feminists also began to question the feminist theory project on the basis of its "Euro-centric universalism" (Mohanty 1988). They held that white Western feminists, without any regard for the particularities of race, class and the geopolitical situatedness of women, construct representations of the "Third World woman" as a victim (Trinh 1989; Mohanty 1988) while the experiences, struggles and theories of women from the global South and minority women in Western societies are suppressed (Gümen 1998). Only through these discourses and negations could the white Western woman be constructed as a modern emancipated subject.

Several of the media producers interviewed embrace the critique raised by women of colour of the homogenisation of the category "woman" by white feminists of the second wave and acknowledge the anti-essentialism and multiculturalism associated with postmodernism.

The British zine *Race Revolt*, for example, describes itself as "an intervention into the silences around race in the queer, feminist and activist communities" (Saeed n. d.) and as a result, it focuses on issues of racism, ethnicity and identity. In the introduction of the first issue, *Race Revolt's* editor notes: "This is a beginning. A beginning of a much needed conversation that considers and addresses race within feminist, queer and diy communities and beyond. That considers the whiteness of these communities, that finds ways for us to move forward" (Saeed 2007: n. p.). The editor points to the fact that in feminist media projects, whiteness often appears to be unmarked, invisible and a dominant construction of identity (for critical whiteness studies, see e. g. Frankenberg 1993).

One blog in particular pursues a broader focus in its themes and content. The Italian activist collective Fikasicula, which runs the blog *Femminismo a Sud*, aims to create a virtual space to share experiences and opinions and to write openly about the Italian conservative government. After the blog was set up, one of their very first steps was to provide a so-called "ABC of technological feminism" (Fikasicula 2008), which is a manual on how to use the internet in general and weblogs in particular for feminist, anti-racist and anti-fascist action. In their self-description, Femminismo a Sud espouses a postcolonial and an intersectional perspective towards society, culture and politics in order to understand how sexism, racism and fascism are related to one another:

> Our blog is called *Femminismo a Sud* because the whole blog has a postcolonial view on reality. We locate ourselves at the South of the hegemonic bio-territoriality. We think that in our society, particularly in Italy, there is a use of power which controls women, immigrants and all persons who don't want this type of system and its use of power. We think that sexism, racism and fascism are different aspects of the same hegemonic situation. And therefore we can't fight against sexism if we don't understand how sexism is interwoven with racism and fascism.

Although the term intersectionality is not mentioned in the quote, the collective sees a necessity in engaging with the many different forms of oppression that people experience in their daily lives, including violence against women and children. Therefore, their blog offers many personal stories about experienced violence, complemented by a variety of advice and strategies for self-empowerment.

A much nuanced standpoint is articulated by the editors of the multilingual Austrian e-zine *Migrazine. Online Magazine by Female Migrants for All* (German: *Migrazine. Online Magazin von Migrantinnen für alle*), which has been published by MAIZ, an autonomous migrant organisation in Linz, since 2006. The initial idea of *Migrazine* is to produce a feminist alternative online media in which women with migrant backgrounds are responsible for the whole process of production. According to their website, *Migrazine* is "self-organised participation in the media landscape, intrusion into the dominant discourse, democratisation of information" (n. d.). In the centre of their feminist and anti-racist self-conception stands the category "female migrant", which is understood as a political identity taking an oppositional position in society and pointing to feminist and anti-racist partiality. This self-conception, however, does not necessarily mean that all articles published on the website discuss migrant-specific issues; nor does it suggest that *Migrazine* aims to speak for women with migrant backgrounds. Rather the editors of *Migrazine* position the experiences and knowledge production of women with migrant backgrounds at the centre of their alternative online media. In the February 2011 issue, the term "Second Generation" ("Secondo"/"Seconda") is taken up to refer to the life realities of people "who are not migrants, but are constructed as 'the Other' by members of majority societies" (Migrazine 2011). Several writers address the self-understanding of a "post-migrant" generation which calls traditional identity conceptions into question and introduces a new vocabulary of belonging. Hence, *Migrazine* can be understood as an elaborated response to the hegemonic discourses on the "First" and "Second Generation" of migrants in

Western societies by demanding political rights for migrants, such as the right to vote, and by intervening in the violent stereotypical representations through which people with migrant backgrounds are construed as "the Other". *Femminismo a Sud* and *Migrazine* question traditional identity constructions and national identity, especially with regard to the strict European immigration laws, and propose how one's individual identity exists at the intersection of multiple identity categories.

In addition to these intersectional feminist discourses of media producers, which have set their focus on racism and "whiteness" in feminist-queer communities *(Race Revolt)*, the conservative policies of their country *(Femminismo a Sud)* or European migration policy *(Migrazine)*, some media producers also make use of the term queer and queer theory in the context of intersectionality. Queer theory postulates that gender and sexuality should be understood as social and cultural constructions, without biological determinism. Hence, "queer" should not be conceptualized as an identity, but instead as a critique of identity and an "identity under construction, a site of constant becoming" (Jagose 1996: 165). As a critique of identity, queer theory does not relate representations and social practices of gender and sexuality to the hierarchical gender differences and heteronormativity, nor does it seek the dissolution or the duplication of the sexes (Engel 2002).

A queer-feminist intersectional standpoint is represented, for example, by the editor of the webmagazine *Trikster – Nordic Queer Journal*:

> Definitely we try to promote an intersectional perspective of queer feminism. I think some of the most important thinkers working in feminist and queer and critical race studies today are those who are able to see the ways in which gender, sexuality and race are folded into each other in different ways. Especially in our current political situation, I think the ability to work intersectionally with these different terms is so crucial if we are to formulate a kind of coalition politics that could really, really work. We are talking about intersectionality and the need of to continue to develop queer and feminist and anti-racist politics that looks sideways and not only towards one vector of suppression.

The editor of *Trikster* opposes a reception of queer theory, gender and sexuality that sees itself as the central axis of difference, and thus loses sight of other categories of social stratification. For an intersectional perspective of queer feminism, the impetus of the critique of racism by women and queers of colour is important, because these critiques point to the entanglement of sexuality with other categories such as gender, race, class and age.

2.3 Pop Feminism in the context of the German-speaking new feminisms debate

While in the US, the term third wave feminism dominates the discussion about a new generation of feminist actors, the term "new feminism" sparked similar debates about the feminist self-understanding of a younger generation of women in German-speaking countries. The starting point for this "new" discussion of feminism was the "demography debate" (Klaus

2008), as well as the moment when the debate that arose when the "third" wave of feminism swept over (however with much less public reception) from the US to Germany. This was followed by the publication of numerous popular books under the buzzword "New Feminism", such as *Die neue F-Klasse* ("The New F Class", 2006) by the novelist Thea Dorn; *Wir Alphamädchen* ("We Alpha Girls", 2008) by the journalists Meredith Haaf, Susanne Klingner, and Barbara Streidl; *Neue Deutsche Mädchen* ("New German Girls", 2008) by novelist Jana Hensel and journalist Elisabeth Raether; the edited collection *Das F-Wort* ("The F-Word", 2007) by Mirja Stöcker; as well as the novel *Feuchtgebiete* ("Wetlands", 2008) by Charlotte Roche. Among them were several publications that explicitly speak of a "Popfeminismus" ("pop feminism") or were connected with it in some way, like *Hot Topic. Popfeminismus heute* ("Pop Feminism Today", edited by Sonja Eismann, 2007); the novel *Zuckerbabies* ("Sugar Babies") by Kerstin Grether (2004); or the academic treatise *Popfeminismus! Fragezeichen!* ("Pop Feminism! Question Mark!", Kauer 2009).

But why the talk about "new" feminisms? While there are different viewpoints, researchers "concur that the new feminisms represent the views of a homogeneous and privileged group of women (most authors are white, well-educated and heterosexual), are neoliberal in outlook and characterised by a fierce repudiation of second-wave feminism, which is dubbed the 'old' women's movement" (Scharff 2011: n. p.). Only a few publications take a more critical and reflective stand towards this repudiation of second wave feminism and incorporate academic work and queer perspectives, such as the edited collections *Hot Topic* (Eismann 2007), *Female Consequences. Feminismus. Antirassismus. Popmusik* (Reitsamer and Weinzierl 2006) and *New Feminism: Worlds of Feminism, Queer and Networking Conditions* (Gržinić and Reitsamer 2008). In particular, the *New Feminism* anthology takes a distinctive approach to the term "new feminism" compared to the mainstream rejection of 1970s feminism and critical feminist and queer theory and politics: here it is used to revitalize the continuity of the women's movement by making new opportunities for action through various perspectives and viewpoints visible. In stark contrast to the mainstream neoliberal popular approach, the term "new" is taken up in order to address the effects of casualization, migration and the exploitation of the post-communist countries and the countries to address the South, which leads to a new type of social inequality between those who live within the "new Europe" and those outside this territory. The aim is to open up a productive field to describe, discuss and critique contemporary feminist debates around diverse living conditions and cultural and theoretical production by women from various parts of the world, as well as to strengthen political agency. However, such a critical and intersectional standpoint represents a lonely perspective in the mainstream reification, homogenisation and stereotypical portrayal of feminism with underlying homophobia, sexism and exclusionary norms (see Scharff 2011). In fact, Elisabeth Klaus found that nonfiction "new feminism" publications reveal a "strong conservatism that borders on and sometimes touches antifeminist positions" and are characterized "first by distancing itself from an older and presumably outdated feminism, secondly by a neoliberal self-celebration, thirdly by the lack of a critical social analysis and finally by an invariably heterosexual orientation" (Klaus 2008: 328). This begs the questions: Who can be, is allowed to, and should be an "alpha girl"? And who is extending this invitation? (See Hark and Villa 2010: 11). In *The Aftermath of Feminism* (2009), Angela McRobbie suggests an "undoing of feminism" in that feminist elements are taken up and are integrated into society and politics and a well-informed and well-intended approach to feminism appears to take place. However, by using the tropes of freedom, choice and empowerment in new ways in media and popular culture as an (empty) replacement for feminism, the real aim is to prevent the development of a new women's movement, and instead today we find "movements of women", she argues (see Hark and Villa 2010: 13). This can be clearly seen in the German debate on "new feminisms", as Hark and Villa indicate in the introduction to the German translation of McRobbie's book (entitled "Top Girls", 2010).

As has been mentioned, in the context of this "new feminisms" debate the term "pop feminism" is claimed by a few – such as Sonja Eismann or Kerstin Grether – who also have been criticized for its use. The term has also been used in connection with actors in the field of popular culture, such as Peaches or Lady Bitch Ray. Additionally, we have also found in our research that some feminist media producers in the German-speaking Europe make use of and see their projects in connection with a "pop feminism", such as *Missy Magazine* (since 2008). In the academic book *Popfeminismus! Fragezeichen!*, Katja Kauer argues that "pop feminism has to be considered as a new manifestation of feminism, which not only carries derogatory categorisations such as *feminism light*, but also such labels as 'postfeminism'" (Kauer 2009: 133, authors' translation). In *Hot Topic* the term "Popfeminismus" is used to describe a critique of popular culture using feminism as an instrument; furthermore, Eismann argues that the current generation has been socialized with popular culture to a much greater extent than previous generations. This, however, does not mean that (popular) culture is not a negotiated field; popular music, TV or advertising needs to be criticized with feminist methods just as much as laws legislation (Eismann 2007).

The blog *Mädchenmannschaft* is an example for "pop feminism" and a call for an update of a second wave feminism. Run by a collective of eight women and two men, who are all based in Germany, the blog was founded by the three authors of the book *Wir Alphamädchen*. In this book, we find a particular feminist self-conception of the *Mädchenmannschaft* collective. As one of the interviewed editors explains:

> Our aim is not to complain about the status quo in society; rather we want to point out to particular developments in society, no matter if they are positive or negative. But certainly, pop feminism is very important for us. [. . .] Second Wave Feminism really made things better for us as a younger generation but there is far too much the attitude of being a victim and of complaining and excluding men. Men are not perpetrators in general, they can be also feminists. We are very positive and we think that feminism makes life more beautiful.

The feminist self-conception of *Mädchenmannschaft* acknowledges that their feminism stands on the shoulders of the second wave feminist movement but that it cannot be based on separatism. Rather their feminism has to adopt what Genz and Brabon (2009, 158) call a "politics of ambiguity" that embraces tolerance, diversity and difference, breaking free from the identity politics of second wave feminism and rejecting any notion of a so called "victim feminism" which is attributed to second wave feminists. For Genz and Brabon a "politics of ambiguity" challenges the identity politics and the anti-popular and anti-feminine agenda of second wave feminism and so, they argue, it is one of the characteristics of third wave feminism. The bloggers of *Mädchenmannschaft* adopt some of the manners of third wave feminism, but they have not discarded the discourses of the second wave (for a discussion of further examples see Reitsamer 2012). They strongly locate themselves in the field of popular culture and understand themselves as powerful young actors who make feminism "more beautiful".

Conclusion: Feminist media thriving towards social change

In this article we have presented an overview of our empirical findings from the research project "Feminist Media Production in Europe". Taking Lievrouw's genre framework for alternative and activist new media as a guideline, we have analysed feminist media projects that are produced in on- and offline, grassroots and alternative contexts in relation to scope, stance, agency and action as well as to three discourses of feminism (see table 4). We have expanded her framework and applied it to feminist media produced specifically in a European context. In general, our study confirms previous research on alternative media and feminist media in particular in that they aim to challenge power structures and to transform social roles by producing "alternative" content and by reverting to a DIY-organized, alternative economy. While we were able to confirm the features of alternative and activist new media in Lievrouw's model in relation to feminist media in print and online – in that they are mostly small-scale, collaboratively produced, heterotopic, based on subcultural literacy, ironic, interventionist and perishable – we have added a particular *feminist* perspective and *European* perspective to this model and generally to the discussion on alternative and feminist media. While in our study most feminist media producers today position themselves in relation to second wave feminism, their strategies and the discourses they are involved in have changed: On the one hand networking occurs now on a much more virtual – and therefore transnational – level with the use of new and social media, which marks a major difference to the more local networks during second wave feminism. On the other hand, we have found that in the European context feminist media producers rarely refer to a third wave feminism – as it is widely discussed in the US – but are engaged in discourses on do-it-yourself feminism, in-

Table 4: Features of feminist media
Leah Lievrouw's genre framework for alternative and activist new media (2011) extended to feminist media production on- and offline

Scope	small scale:	collaborative:	
	• media types: mostly print media, blogs, electronic magazines; notable: use of various media types simultaneously and changes of medium • media by country: most published in Germany, UK, Spain, Poland, Italy, Austria, Belgium, France, Sweden • publishing frequency: Most print media quarterly, followed by irregular and biannual; online media irregular updates or frequent publishing mode • language: most monolingual, followed by bilingual, a few trilingual or more languages • use of social media platforms: most often Facebook, followed by Twitter and MySpace	• publishers: most published by collectives and groups, NGOs and independent women's organizations, individuals • tendency towards "new collectivism"	
Stance	heterotopic:	subcultural literacy:	ironic:
	• feminist media as counter-sites to the mainstream based on solidarity, exchange of ideas and experiences otherwise ignored by mainstream media	• feminist media producers require certain access to and knowledge of (sub)cultural codes, language and symbols • certain awareness and self-critical reflection of limitations in terms of access, distribution and audience	• especially in visuals (bricolages, collages) use of humour and irony • transportation of political messages and subversion of original meaning (often in zines and culture jamming)

Action & agency	interventionist: • interventionist aim either within the project itself or by encouraging interventions by others • media production as activist practice and "productive interventions" into social power relations • interventions on content and visual level and in relation to non-commercial DIY culture with a focus on bottom-up processes through "learning by doing" and "skill-sharing"	perishable: • short-lived, temporary, ephemeral	
Discourses on feminism	DIY feminism: • discourse esp. in English-speaking countries and among zine makers • feminist cultural activism based on doing-it-yourself and self-empowerment • central: anti-capitalist stance, building of an "alternative economy" with the aim of establishing horizontal, non-hierarchical structures; social change should be achieved through a radical critique of the neoliberal system and through alternative economies outside of a neoliberal exploitation logic	Intersectional perspectives of feminism: • taking up critique by women of colour and postcolonial feminists on the homogenisation of the category "woman" by white feminists of the second wave; acknowledgement of the anti-essentialism and multiculturalism associated with postmodernism • frequent drawing on the term "queer" and on queer theory in connection with intersectionality	Pop feminism ("Popfeminismus"): • specific discourse in German-speaking countries in the context of a "new feminisms" debate • situating feminist media in the field of popular culture

tersectional perspectives of feminism, and pop feminism (in the context of the German-speaking "new feminisms" debate). In their negotiation of (interrelated) feminisms, feminist media production becomes a discursive, interventionist space that is constantly re-negotiated, re-invented, and re-appropriated under neoliberal social, cultural and economic circumstances. Hence, in sum the most important contributions of our study to the field are (a) to provide a comprehensive overview on the diversity of feminist media production in Europe, (b) to give insights into how a younger generation of feminist media producers negotiate neoliberal changes in society and (c) how they take up existing feminist discourses and practices and connect them with their own experiences in different geographic contexts. (Table 4)

In this conclusion, we would like to take up the questions we have raised in the introduction: How does a younger generation of feminist media producers in Europe participate in society by producing print magazines, blogs and e-zines in grassroots, alternative contexts relating to new social movements? How do they engage in discourses on feminism(s), challenge the status-quo and effect social change?

Zine maker Nina Nijsten thinks that "zines are significant on both the individual level (for example a girl who finds empowerment in reading a grrrl zine or expresses herself in making one) and for social movements. They can and do play important roles in DIY feminist and anti-capitalist movements." In the context of media production, scholar Annabelle Sreberny-Mohammadi has found that "almost by dint of their existence alone, autonomous media controlled by women with women-defined output offer a challenge to existing hierarchies of power; when these media take up specific issues and campaigns, and align themselves with larger social movements, their political potential is significant" (1996: 234). Herein lies the biggest potential but also the biggest challenge for the larger feminist movement: feminist media (and activism) represent one of the most direct attempts "to change fundamentally the way people think" (Young 1997: 3). As Young has argued "Feminist publications seek to effect social change through propagating feminist discourse" (1997: 12–13). The aim of social transformation is well illustrated by Tea Hvala, blogger, zine maker and co-organizer of the Red Dawns festival in Slovenia:

> Whether you speak about individual acts of resistance, about organised struggles, about art projects, about self-managed social experiments, even about the invisible day and night dreaming that expand the mental space, all these things, in my view, are re-envisioning and transforming society (quoted in Chidgey 2009b).

We argue that feminist media need to be considered in a larger socio-economic and cultural context as they are an intricate part of feminist movements as new social movements. In the articulation of experiences and the struggle over symbolic control and maintenance of independence, a collective consciousness and identity can grow and emerge around common projects, as has been the case with the Love Kills collective in Romania:

By advocating revolution, by raising awareness, by questioning authority, by breaking the silence, I think that zines can have a meaningful effect. And maybe it has to be first in the individual, the one who is holding the zines in her/his own hands and starts rebelling her/himself against the oppressors; later on you can find other individuals who are rebelling and can "ally" and plot together. We started, for example, by publishing a zine a few years ago; later on the editorial group formed itself into an anarcha-feminist collective, and we were able, together, to put ideas into practice.

Such a process of personal and collective consciousness-raising and critical opinion-building can be a step toward community and political involvement and, ultimately, can initiate and lead towards cultural and social change. As Stephen Duncombe has pointed out, "the very activity of producing culture has political meaning. In a society built around the principle that we should consume what others have produced for us, [. . .] creating your own culture [. . .] takes on a rebellious resonance. The first act of politics is simply to act" (2002: 7). This takes us back to the strong interventionist aim of feminist media projects. As we have shown in relation to queer-feminist comics, they can be considered "productive interventions" in social power relationships thriving for a transformation of society.

Overall, feminist media production online and offline is characterized by a critical reflection of mainstream culture and society as much as an intervention into them. Feminist media is strongly embedded in the feminist movement as a new social movement, on the one hand, through its actors: the well-educated and creative participants as well as a collective, shared identity and meaning and symbolic production; and on the other hand through its action: informal, anti-hierarchical, social networks, the integration into everyday life, the widespread use of media and ICTs and "unconventional", creative, small-scale, decentralized action repertoires, and permanent, transnational campaigns (see Lievrouw's overview of characteristics of new social movements 2011: 48–49). While the key problem of translating feminist concerns from the micro, individual level to the meso and macro level of wider society – and specifically the enabling of broader social participation (e. g. due to a lack of available resources) – remains, truly, as Chandra Talpade Mohanty has said: "everyday feminist, antiracist, anticapitalist practices are as important as larger, organized political movements" (2003: 4).

References

Atkinson, J. D., 2010. *Alternative Media and Politics of Resistance. A Communication Perspective*. New York: Peter Lang.

Atton, C., 2002. *Alternative Media*. London: Sage.

Baumgardner, J. and Richards, A., 2000. *Manifesta: Young Women, Feminism and the Future*. New York: Farrar, Straus and Giroux.

Berger, M., ed., 2006. *We Don't Need Another Wave: Dispatches from the Next Generation of Feminists*. Emeryville: Seal Press.

Calmbach, M., 2007. *More Than Music. Einblicke in die Jugendkultur Hardcore*. Bielefeld: Transcript.

Chidgey R., Gunnarsson Payne J., and Zobl, E., 2009. Rumours from around the bloc. Gossip, Rhizomatic Media, and the Plotki Femzine. *Feminist Media Studies* 9(4), pp. 477–491.

Chidgey, R., 2009a. Free, Trade. Distribution Economies in Feminist Zine Networks. *Signs: Journal of Women in Culture and Society* 35(1), pp. 28–37.

Chidgey, R., 2009b. DIY Feminist Networks in Europe. Personal and Collective Acts of Resistance. *Transform! European Journal of Alternative Thinking and Political Dialogue* 5, pp. 159–165.

Collins, J., 1995. *Architectures of excess: Cultural life in the information age*. London: Routledge.

Combahee River Collective, 1982. A Black Feminist Statement. In: Hull, G. T., ed. *All the Women are White, All the Blacks are Men, But Some of Us are Brave. Black Women's Studies*. Old Westbury N. Y.: Feminist Press, pp. 13–22.

Dicker, R. and Piepmeier A., eds., 2003. *Catching a Wave: Reclaiming Feminism for the 21st Century*. Boston: Northeastern University Press.

Dorn, T., 2007. *Die neue F-Klasse. Wie die Zukunft von Frauen gemacht wird*. Piper: München, 2007.

Duncombe, S., 2002. *Cultural Resistance Reader*. London: Verso.

Eismann, S., ed., 2007. *Hot Topic: Popfeminismus heute*. Mainz: Ventil Verlag.

Emancypunx, n. d. About Emancypunx Records. *Emancypunx Records* [online] Available at: <http://www.emancypunx.scenaonline.org/index.php?option=com_content&view=article&id=154&Itemid=118&lang=en> [Accessed 24 May 2012]

Engel, A., 2002. *Wider die Eindeutigkeit. Sexualität und Geschlecht im Fokus queerer Politik der Repräsentation*. Frankfurt am Main: Campus.

Feminisn'ts, n. d. Феминизм в датах и картинках ["Feminism in dates and pictures"]. *Feminisn'ts* [blog] Available at: <http://www.feminisnts.ru/феминизм> [Accessed 24 May 2012]

Fikasicula, 2008. Abc della femminista teknologica. *Femminismo a Sud*, [blog] 22 March. Available at: <http://femminismo-a-sud.noblogs.org/post/2008/03/22/abc-della-femminista-teknologica/> [Accessed 24 May 2012]

Frankenberg, R., 1993. *The Social Construction of Whiteness. White Women, Race Matters*. Minneapolis: University of Minnesota Press.

Garcia, D. and Lovink, G., 1997. *The ABC of tactical media* [online]. Available at: <http://subsol.c3.hu/subsol_2/contributors2/garcia-lovinktext.html> [Accessed 8 May 2012].

Garrison, E. K., 2000. U. S. Feminism: Grrrl Style! Youth (Sub)Cultures and the Technologies of the Third Wave. *Feminist Studies*, Spring 2000, pp. 141–170.

Genz, S. and Brabon, B., 2009. *Postfeminism. Cultural Texts and Theories.* Edinburgh: Edinburgh University Press.

Glaser; B. G. and Strauss, A. L. 1967. *The Discovery of Grounded Theory. Strategies for Qualitative Research.* Chicago: Aldine.

Graff, A., 2007. A Different Chronology. Reflections on Feminism in Contemporary Poland. In: Gillis, S., Howie G. and Munford R., ed. *Third Wave Feminism. A Critical Exploration.* Expanded Second Edition. Houndmills and New York: Palgrave Macmillian, pp. 142–155.

Grether, K., 2004. *Zuckerbabies.* Mainz: Ventil Verlag.

Gržinić, M. and Reitsamer, R., eds., 2008. *New Feminism: Worlds of Feminism, Queer and Networking Conditions.* Vienna: Löcker.

Gümen, S., 1998. Das Soziale des Geschlechts. Frauenforschung und die Kategorie "Ethnizität". *Das Argument. Zeitschrift für Philosophie und Sozialwissenschaften* 40(1–2), pp. 187–202.

Haaf, M., Klingner, S. and Streidl, B., 2008. *Wir Alphamädchen: Warum Feminismus das Leben schöner macht.* Hamburg: Hoffmann und Campe.

Hamilton, J., 2000. Alternative media: Conceptual difficulties, critical possibilities. *Journal of Communication Inquiry* 24 (4); pp. 357–378.

Hark, S. and Villa, P.-I., 2010. Ambivalenzen der Sichtbarkeit – Einleitung zur deutschen Ausgabe. In: McRobbie, A., ed. *Top Girls. Feminismus und der Aufstieg des neoliberalen Geschlechterregimes.* Wiesbaden: VS Verlag für Sozialwissenschaften, pp. 7–15.

Hensel, J. and Raether, E., 2008. *Neue deutsche Mädchen.* Rowohlt: Hamburg.

Hine, C., 2000. *Virtual Ethnography.* Thousand Oaks: Sage.

Heywood, L., ed., 2006. *The Women's Movement Today: An Encyclopedia of Third Wave Feminism.* Westport: Greenwood.

Hill Collins, P., 1990. *Black feminist thought: knowledge, consciousness, and the politics of empowerment.* New York: Routledge.

Jagose, A., 2001. *Queer Theory. Eine Einführung.* Berlin: Querverlag.

Kauer, K., 2009. *Popfeminismus! Fragezeichen! Eine Einführung.* Leipzig: Frank & Timme.

Kearney, M. C., 1998. Producing Girls: Rethinking the Study of Female Youth Culture. In: Inness, S., ed. *Delinquents and Debutantes: Twentieth-Century Girls' Cultures.* New York: New York University Press, pp. 285–310.

Klaus, E., 2008. Antifeminismus und Elitefeminismus – Eine Intervention. *Feministische Studien* 26(2): pp. 176–186 (English abstract: p. 328).

La Barbe, 2008. Le Manifeste de la Barbe. *La Barbe* [online] Available at: <http://labarbelabarbe.org/La_Barbe/Manifeste.html> [Accessed 24 May 2012]

Lievrouw, L., 2011. *Alternative and Activist New Media.* Cambridge: Polity Press.

Mansbridge, J. 1995. What is the Feminist Movement?. In: Ferree, M. M. and Martin, P. Y., eds. *Feminist Organizations: Harvest of the new women's movement*. Philadelphia: Temple University Press, pp. 27–34.

McKay, G., 1998. *DiY culture: party & protest in Nineties Britain*. New York: Verso.

McKay, G., 2010. Community Arts and Music, Community Media: Cultural Politics and Policy in Britain since the 1960s. In: Howley, K., ed. *Understanding Community Media*. Los Angeles: Sage, pp. 41–52.

Migrazine, n. d. Über uns. *Migrazine* [online] Available at: <http://www.migrazine.at/content/ber-uns> [Accessed 21 March 2012]

Migrazine, 2011. Zweite Generation und Postmigration. *Migrazine*, 2, [online] Available at: <http://www.migrazine.at/ausgabe/2011/2> [Accessed 21 March 2012]

McRobbie, A., 2009. *The Aftermath of Feminism: Gender, Culture and Social Change*. London: Sage.

McRobbie, A., 2010. *Top Girls. Feminismus und der Aufstieg des neoliberalen Geschlechterregimes*. Wiesbaden: VS Verlag für Sozialwissenschaften.

Mohanty, C. T., 1988. Under Western Eyes. Feminist Scholarship and Colonial Discourses. In: Back, L. and Solomos, J., eds. *Theories of Race and Racism. A Reader*. London: Routledge, pp. 302–323.

Mohanty, C. T. 2003. *Feminism without Borders: Decolonizing Theory, Practicing Solidarity*. Durham: Duke University Press.

Nguyen, M. 2000. Ohne Titel. *Punk Planet* 40 [online]. Available at: <http://www.worsethanqueer.com/slander/pp40.html> [Accessed April 2010]

Osez le féminisme, 2009. Texte de lancement du réseau. *Osez le féminisme* [online] Available at: <www.osezlefeminisme.fr/article/texte-de-lancement-du-reseau> [Accessed 24 May 2012]

Peterson, R. A. and Bennett, A. 2004. Introducing Music Scenes. In: Bennett, A., and Peterson, R. A., eds. *Music Scenes. Local, Translocal, and Virtual*. Nashville: Vanderbilt University Press, pp. 1–16.

Peretti, J., 2001. Culture jamming, memes, social networks, and the emerging media ecology: The "Nike Sweatshop Email" as object-to-think-with [online]. Available at: <http://depts.washington.edu/ccce/polcommcampaigns/peretti.html> [Accessed 8 May 2012]

Piano, D., 2002. Congregating Women: Reading 3rd Wave Feminist Practices in Subcultural Production. *Rhizomes* 4 (Spring) [online]. Available at: <http://www.rhizomes.net/issue4/piano.html> [Accessed 30 May 2012]

Pilcher, J. and Whelehan, I., 2004. Third Wave Feminism. In: Pilcher, J. and Whelehan, I., eds. *50 Key Concepts in Gender Studies*. London: Sage, pp. 169–172.

Radway, J. A., 2002. Girls, Reading, and Narrative Gleaning: Crafting Repertoires for Self-Fashioning Within Everyday Life. In: Brock, T., Green, M. and Strange, J., eds. *Narrative Impact: Social and Cognitive Foundations*. Mahwah, N. J.: LEA Press, pp. 176–208.

Reitsamer, R. and Weinzierl, R., eds., 2006. *Female Consequences. Feminismus. Antirassismus. Popmusik.* Vienna: Löcker

Reitsamer, R., 2008. These Islands Where We Come From. Notes on Gender and Generation in the Viennese Lesbian-Queer Subculture. In: Grzinic, M. and Reitsamer, R., eds. *New Feminism. Worlds of Feminism, Queer and Networking Conditions.* Vienna: Löcker, pp. 215–229

Reitsamer, R., 2012. Female Pressure: A translocal feminist youth-oriented cultural network. *Continuum. Journal of Media & Cultural Studies* 26(3), pp. 399–408.

Reitsamer, R. and Zobl, E., 2010. Youth Citizenship und politische Bildung am Beispiel der Ladyfeste. *Magazin Erwachsenenbildung.at. Das Fachmedium für Forschung, Praxis und Diskurs* 11 [online]. Available at: <http://www.erwachsenenbildung.at/magazin/10-11/meb10-11.pdf> [Accessed 25 June 2012].

Reitsamer, R. and Zobl, E., 2011. Queer-feministische Comics. Produktive Interventionen im Kontext der Do-It-Yourself Kultur. In: Eder, B., Klar, E. and Reichert, R., eds. *Theorien des Comics.* Bielefeld: Transcript, pp. 365–382.

Reitsamer, R. and Zobl, E., 2012. Alternative Media Production, Feminism, and Citizenship Practices. In: Boler, M. and Ratto, M., eds. *DIY Citizenship: Critical Making and Social Media.* Cambridge Mass.: MIT Press (forthcoming).

Riaño, P., 2000. MEDIA: Grassroots. In: Kramarae, C., and Spender, D., eds. *Routledge International Encyclopedia of Women: Global Women's Issues and Knowledge.* New York: Routledge, pp. 1333–1336.

Roche, C., 2008. *Feuchtgebiete.* Cologne: DuMont Verlag.

Saeed, H. n. d. About. *Race Revolt* [online] Available at: <http://www.racerevolt.org.uk/about/home.html> [Accessed 24 May 2012]

Saeed, H. 2007. Introduction. *Race Revolt*, 1, n. p. Available at: <http://www.racerevolt.org.uk/issues/issue%20one/introduction%20humaira%20saeed.htm> [Accessed 24 May 2012]

Scharff, C., 2011. The new German Feminisms: Of Wetlands and Alpha-Girls. In: Gill, R., and Scharff, C., eds. *New feminities: Postfeminism, neoliberalism and subjectivity.* Basingstoke: Palgarve Macmillian, pp. 265–278.

Schilt, K. and Zobl, E., 2008. Connecting the Dots: Riot Grrrls, Ladyfests, and the International Grrrl Zine Network. In: Harris, A., ed. *Next Wave Cultures: Feminism, Subcultures, Activism.* New York: Routledge, pp. 171–192.

Siegel, D. L., 2007. *Sisterhood, Interrupted: From Radical Women to Grrls Gone Wild.* New York: Palgrave Macmillan.

Sona, Z., Krusche, D., Spilker, V. and Hansom, J., 2011. Editorial. *Make Out Magazine*, 1, n. p. Available at: <http://www.makeoutmagazine.net/pics/mom_01_leseprobe.pdf> [Accessed 24 May 2012]

Spencer, A., 2005. *DIY: The Rise of Lo-Fi Culture.* London: Marion Boyars.

Srberny-Mohammadi, A., 1996. Women Communicating Globally: Mediating International Feminism. In: Ellen, D., Rush, R. R., and Kaufman, S. J., eds. *Women Transforming Communications: Global Intersections.* London: Sage, pp. 233–242.

Staggenborg, S., 1995. Can feminist movements be successful? In: Ferree, M. M., and Martin, P. Y., eds. *Feminist Organizations: Harvest of the new women's movement.* Philadelphia: Temple University Press, pp. 339–355.

Steiner, L., 2000. MEDIA: Alternative. In: Kramarae, C. and Spender, D., eds. *Routledge International Encyclopedia of Women*, Vol. 3. New York: Routledge.

Stöcker, M., ed., 2007. *Das F-Wort. Feminimus ist sexy.* Ulrike Helmer: Königstein.

Thornton, S., 1995. *Club Cultures: Music, Media, and Subcultural Capital.* Cambridge: Polity Press.

Trinh, M. T., 1989. *Woman Native Other. Writing Postcoloniality and Feminism.* Bloomington: Indiana University Press.

Young, S., 1997. *Changing the Wor(l)d: Discourse, Politics, and the Feminist Movement.* New York: Routledge.

Za Feminizm, n. d. Почему ЗА ФЕМИНИЗМ ["Why Pro Feminism"]. *Za Feminizm – ЗА ФЕМИНИЗМ* [blog] Available at: <http://www.zafeminizm.ru/why-feminism.html> [Accessed 24 May 2012]

Zobl, E. 2009. Cultural Production, Transnational Networking, and Critical Reflection in Feminist Zines. *Signs* 35(1), Autumn, pp. 1–12.

Zobl, E. 2010. Zehn Jahre Ladyfest: Rhizomatische Netzwerke einer lokalen, translokale und virtuellen queer-feministischen Szene. In: Reitsamer, R. and Fichna, W., eds. *'They Say I' m Different . . .' Popularmusik, Szenen und ihre AkteurInnen.* Vienna: Löcker, pp. 208–227.

Zobl, E., 2011a: 'A kind of punk rock 'teaching machine'. Queer-feministische Zines im Kunstunterricht. *Art Education Research: Queer und DIY im Kunstunterricht* 2(3) [online]. Available at: <http://entrepreneurship.zhdk.ch/fileadmin/data/iae/documents/Zobl-A_kind_of_punk_rock_teaching_machine_2011.pdf> [Accessed 25 June 2012].

Zobl, E., 2011b: Grrrl Zines: Fanzines mit feministischem Anspruch. In: Hüttner, B., Leidinger, C. and Oy, G., eds. *Handbuch der ALTERNATIVmedien 2011/2012.* Neu-Ulm: Verlag AG SPAK, pp. 88–97.

Quoted feminist media (see details in the list in the annex of this book).

Acknowledgement:
Work on this report was funded as part of the stand-alone-project of the Austrian Science Fund (P 21187).

Feminist Media as Alternative Media?
Theorising Feminist Media from the Perspective of Alternative Media Studies

Jenny Gunnarsson Payne

Introduction: Feminist movements and feminist media

Forms of media – in the broadest sense of this term – are an invaluable part in furthering the determinate goals and specific demands of a given political movement. This might seem a harmless enough contention; for what would a political movement be without any means of dissemination and circulating its ideas to a wider political constituency? If winning support and forging alliances are necessary prerequisites for a movement to gain what is colloquially regarded as "critical mass", then with what means is political momentum (which a movement thrives off) possible other than through the effective (meaning the *affective*) transmissibility of ideas between a movement and what is outside of that movement? At its most basic level, the delivery of a political message between the sender and recipient entails a "medium" that shuttles between addresser and addressee. Consider the array of possible media forms that function as a transmitter of political content: more often than not the forms of delivery are associated with strictly textual output (newspapers, bulletins, zines, flyers, leaflets, etc.). This, however, is not exclusively the case. The mode of delivery could just as well be "performative", including street theatre or musical performance, graffiti or other art forms. Today, with the development of Information and Communication Technologies (ICTs), the platforms open for the transmission and dissemination of political agendas have multiplied greatly (for example, e-zines, blogs, Facebook, Twitter, etc.), providing the possibility for more immediate and responsive media output, which are in a synergetic relation with a movement that changes in accordance with the changing times and terrains of its struggles.

This chapter takes as its starting point two related observations about feminist political struggles:[1] First, the history of women's and feminist

---

1 This chapter is a slightly reworked version of the article "Feminist media as alternative media? A literature review", originally published in *Interface: A Journal for and About Social Movements* volume 1(2), pp. 190–211. It has been reprinted with the kind permission of *Interface*. Work on the original version of this chapter was conducted as part of

struggles have demonstrated time and again the central role that media production has played in the dissemination of political ideas, political mobilisation and the constitution of political identities. Second, this essential connection remains largely under-theorised.

Historicising feminist media: From *cartes-de-visite* to newspapers to Twitter

Already since the latter half of the previous century, suffragist and anti-slavery activist Sojourner Truth (born Isabella Baumfree) sold photographic cartes-de-visite of herself as a way of disseminating her politics and supporting herself financially (Irvin Painter 1994: 482–488; Downing 2001: vivii). More generally, the suffrage movements in various countries were known to be avid producers of their own press, cartoons, postcards, and posters (cf. Israels Perry 1993; Di Cenzo 2003; Di Cenzo & Ryan 2007). This rich and multifaceted feminist publishing tradition was to continue well into the twenty-first century, and has over the years taken on multiple formats, genres, modes of expression and political agendas.

Publications such as the British *Votes for Women* and Swedish *Tidevarvet* both constitute notable examples of print media in the decades around the turn of the twentieth century – and feminist publication was to peak once again during the so-called "second wave of feminism" which in many countries prospered in the spirit of 1968, with titles such as the North American news journal *Off Our Backs* (since 1970) and the long-lived and influential UK feminist magazine *Spare Rib* (1972–1993). The 1980s witnessed the birth of significant media contributions: the internationalist UK feminist newspaper *Outwrite* (1982–1988) and the self-proclaimed first ever feminist radio station *RadiOrakel* (since 1982) in Norway. In the mid 1980s, the world's first known unlicensed women's radio, *Radio Pirate Women* had its inaugural broadcast in Ireland. The 1990s saw the emergence of Nicaraguan feminist quarterly *La Boletina* (since 1991; also available online since 2005) and the Iranian independent feminist journal *Zanan* (subsequently banned in 2008). The decade of the 1990s also witnessed what has often been referred to as the transnational "girl zine revolution" – young women becoming involved in feminist politics through the development of feminist zines (see for example Harris 2003; Zobl 2004a; 2004b; Schilt and Zobl 2008; Kearney 2006; Chidgey 2007). Today, feminist media continue to flourish. New titles of magazines (such as the Norwegian *FETT* and Swedish *FUL_*, both since 2004) and broadcast media such as the Swedish community and online television programme *HallonTV* (2008–2009) and *an.schläge tv* – the sister project (since 2005) of the long-established Austrian feminist maga-

the project *Feminist Media Production in Europe* (supported by the Austrian Science Fund, P211-G20). For feedback and support, I would like to thank my colleagues within the project, Elke Zobl and Red Chidgey. Many thanks go also to David Payne for his thorough in-depth commentary on the essay.

zine with the same name appear alongside "new media" and hybrid genres such as the UK e-zine *The F-Word* (since 2001), such blogs as the Romanian *F.I.A.* (since 2005) and the extension of the queer feminist *FUL* magazine with a monthly podcast (Sweden since 2008).

Given this rich history of feminist media production, it is surprising that – despite the recently growing interest in the phenomenon – the terrain is still somewhat uncharted, both empirically and theoretically (cf. Riaño 1994; Steiner 1992; Byerly and Ross 2006). Specifically, this chapter shall attempt to rectify the theoretical inattention to the *constitutive* role that media production has for feminist and women's movements more generally. To this end, my particular focus for this chapter will in the first instance be a trend in media research captured under the appellation "alternative media studies". The purpose of this intervention is to examine the existing literature in this field and to offer an assessment of the tools that this literature makes available for the specific treatment of feminist media production.

With these broad intentions outlined, the structure of this intervention shall take the following form: I will first begin by addressing the strand of theorisation which emphasises alternative media mainly as oppositional, or counter-hegemonic, in their relationship to the state and the market. This strand of alternative media theory shall mainly be represented by media scholars John Downing and Chris Atton. Second, I will discuss a number of critiques that have been raised against these former approaches, and via these introduce alternative conceptualisations such as the notion of "citizens' media" (Clemencia Rodriguez) and the more recent idea of "rhizomatic media" (Olga Bailey, Bart Cammaerts and Nico Carpentier).

Defining alternative media: Between formal specificity and historical complexity

Still suffering from being largely under-researched, the field of alternative media can be characterised by the continuous attempts made by researchers to find and refine suitable frameworks as a way of, first, complementing existing media theories which have proven insufficient at understanding the specificity of these media forms in opposition to dominant mass media, and, second, in a way that takes into account the vast complexity within this subset of media production. These overarching – and occasionally conflicting – aims often pose a dilemma in distinguishing "dominant" or "hegemonic" from "alternative" media, while at the same time avoiding the reductive and inflexible binary oppositions drawn between "mainstream" and "alternative". The field is characterised by what I see as a somewhat problematic tension between formal specificity and historical complexity.

At its most anodyne, alternative media is defined as *any form of media which constitutes an alternative to, or positions itself in opposition to, widely available and consumed mass media products* (Waltz 2005: 2). A very general and formal definition, the inclusivity of it is only a strength for as long as it is used as an intuitive, "commonsensical", umbrella term. Here, the problem is that the terminology contributes very little to any sustained and rigorous study of these phenomena (cf. Comedia 1984: 95). Indeed, at this, the most basic definitional level, many have questioned the utility of the appellation "alternative", claiming that its nebulous nature means that what counts as an instance of "alternative" media is easily abused by personal predilection and self-definition (see Abel 1997). John Downing – who is known to prefer the term "radical media" – has argued that "alternative media" is a term that is nearly oxymoronic: "Everything, at some point, is alternative to something else" (Downing 2001: ix).

The most commonly deployed solution within alternative media scholarship to the vagueness of the term has been to denounce vague definitions and conceive of "alternative media" not only as "alternative", but more specifically as media positioned in opposition to dominant mass media – as *counter hegemonic*. This has the merit of excluding "apolitical" media forms such as niche special interest media such as sport club newsletters) (see Downing 2001: xx). More specific still, Michael Traber defines alternative media as media which aims to effectuate "change towards a more equitable social, cultural and economic whole in which the individual is not reduced to an object (of the media or the political powers) but is able to find fulfilment as a total human being" (Traber 1985: 3; also in Atton 2002: 16).[2]

The definitions so far surveyed all make the same assumption, namely that "alternative media" breaks free from the status quo, presenting alternative resources antagonistic toward "mainstream" and "official" channels. The work of James Hamilton is in this regard conspicuous in the attempt he makes to complexify the prevailing way that "alternative media" is understood. Notably, Hamilton sees congruence in the *ends* of media production, whether alternative or mainstream. Both tend to educate and mobilise a general public in the sense of a particular movement or political cause.

If seen simply as a technological process of manufacture, distribution and consumption, Hamilton argues, media/communication then simply names the *use* of media products. The resulting implications are that communication is functionally equivalent to any other consumerist practice and that it is an optional add-on to society – at best, a means of conveying ideas about more basic and important processes – rather than essential to it (Hamilton 2000: 361). Instead, he wishes to make a distinction between "media" and "communication", defining the former as "physical techniques of amplifying and making durable the expressions of individuals, thereby making them available to many more people than would other-

---

2 Within the category of alternative media Traber advances a further distinction between *advocacy media* and *grassroots media*. Alternative *advocacy* media is any media project and product embodying values other than the established ones and which in the process introduces "new" social actors (such as the poor, the oppressed, the marginalised etc), but is nevertheless produced "professionally". *Grassroots media* is a more "thorough" version of alternative media, according to which the media is produced by the people whom it aims to represent. Professionals may (or may not) be involved in these publications, but if so, only as advisers to support non-professionals to produce their own independent media (Traber 1985: 3; ibid., Atton).

wise be the case" (ibid.). The latter, he argues, is "related to and dependent on technical processes of reproduction, amplification and fixing (making durable)", but not equivalent to them. Instead, communication is described in terms of cultural processes, as the "creative making of a social order" (ibid.). Hamilton thus argues that alternative media must *enable* "alternative communication" that, in turn, facilitates "an articulation of a social order different from and often opposed to the dominant" (ibid. 362).

The work of Downing, more contextual and descriptive than Hamilton, offers instead an improved definition of "alternative media" which avoids both the risk of vacuous generality on the one hand and a specifiable purity as to what "alternative media" ought to be on the other, which rarely if ever exists in reality other than in the books of normative theorising. Thus, and in an attempt to offer a more workable terminology, Downing defines "alternative *radical* media" as any "media, generally small-scale and in many different forms, that express an alternative vision to *hegemonic* policies, priorities, and perspectives" (2001: v, emphasis added).[3] Apart from this definition, which positions radical media (or, radical alternative media) as distinctive from the merely "alternative", Downing steers clear of any clear-cut definitions. Instead, he argues that:

> There is no instantaneous alchemy, no uncontested sociochemical procedure, that will divine in a flash or with definite results truly radical media from the apparently radical or even the non-radical (Downing 2001: vii).

This is already a step further than Hamilton and other alternative media theorists. Instead of resorting to simple binaries, Downing argues that *context* and *consequences* should be the key to demarcating the radicality of a specific medium (Downing 2001: x). To give an example, Downing highlights the contextual importance of Truth's *cartes-de-visite* depicting her as a "lady", a respectable women of her times, most often sitting down with her knitting placed on her lap, and often dressed in glasses and with a book strategically placed on her side table (Downing: vi-vii; Irvin Painter 1994; Israels Perry 1994). While, when measured by contemporary standards, this representation of femininity could hardly be considered revolutionary, in the context of the mid to late nineteenth century, it is to be read as a radical refusal to identify with her previous status of enslavement. This historical example, therefore, represents a potential rearticulation of black femininity.

---

3 In a related manner, Waltz has stressed the need for further terminologies to complement the notion of alternative media, using instead the overlapping (but not equivalent) distinction between "alternative" and "activist" media. The latter would, she argues, involve encouraging readers to "get actively involved in social change" (Waltz 2005: 3). Similarly to Downing's definition of radical media, activist media can include media promoting any ideological strand, ranging over the whole scale from "left of left" to far right extremism (ibid.). In addition to this, however, Waltz's concept of activist media can – when the additional label of "alternative" is left out – also include media which advocates views that support what would generally be understood as "mainstream" (such as voting) (ibid.).

Chris Atton, author of the book *Alternative Media* (2002), has celebrated Downing for his nuanced and theoretically eclectic approach of drawing together theories of counter-hegemony, counter-publics and resistance, but sees at the same time his approach as overemphasising the collective dimension of radical alternative media production, thereby constructing a theory suitable mainly for the study of the media production of social movements. By doing so, Atton argues that Downing ignores the fact that

> hybridity and purity as problematics of alternative media are certainly accessible through an examination of new social movement media, but they can also be approached through media that accommodate themselves rather more cosily with mass media and mass consumption (Atton 2002: 21).

Atton (2002), therefore, proposes a theory of alternative media that is considerably more far reaching than those assessed thus far. Building and expanding upon the work of Downing (1984; 2001), Stephen Duncombe (1997) and Robert Dickinson (1997), Atton constructs a theory which includes not only the more politically radical variants (or the so-called "resistance media"), but one which includes also media forms such as zines, video, mail-art and creative writing, and "hybrid forms of electronic communication" – forms of media production which are not necessarily in themselves aiming at any radical social change. This theoretical perspective stresses "the transformatory potential of the media as reflexive instruments of communication practices in social networks" and focuses therefore on the *processual* and *relational* aspects of these media forms (Atton 2002: 7–8). Drawing on a wide range of discussions on alternative and radical media, Atton has constructed a "typology of alternative and radical media" (reproduced below):

1. Content – politically radical, socially/culturally radical; news values
2. Form – graphics, visual language; varieties of presentation and binding; aesthetics
3. Reprographic innovations/adaptations – use of mimeographs, IBM typesetting, offset litho, photocopiers
4. "Distributive use" (Atton 1999b) – alternative sites for distribution, clandestine/indivisible distribution networks, anti-copyright
5. Transformed social relations, roles and responsibilities – reader-writers, collective organisation, de-professionalisation of e.g. journalism, printing, publishing
6. Transformed communication processes – horizontal linkages, networks (Atton 2002: 27)

These six elements form the basis of Atton's model, with each element representing a dimension of alternative media. The first three elements in this typology specify "products"; the last three specify processes of communication (i. e. distributing, writing, printing) (Atton 2002: 27).

Atton's procedures allow, in principle, for a more refined study, sensitive to the inconsistencies of a given media project. Broken down into its composite dimensions, various aspects of a specific media form can be judged specifically as to the extent to which its constituent dimensions break with established practices, modes of representation and organisational relations respectively. For example, there could be inter-dimensional discord: the same medium can be "radical" in terms of its distribution, but "conservative" with regards to political contents. There could also be intra-dimensional ambivalences, so that *within* each dimension there are complexities to take into account that preclude easy categorisation: if, for example, a media form only allowed professionals to write, but had a collective process of decision making (2003: 28). One also needs to weigh up both historical and geographical contingencies, and appreciate that the absence of radicality (at least according to the properties listed in the typology) need not necessarily prevent its overall radical/revolutionary potential. For a certain dimension might not be available for radicalisation in certain cultural and historical contexts.

Attention to all this would enable an analysis of the "mixed radicalisation" of alternative media – looking at hybridity rather than a set of characteristics to determine "purity" of these publications (2003: 29). Atton's model thus tries to capture the *contents* of these media, as well as their *sociocultural contexts* and *modes of organisation*. In this manner, he wishes to provide a definition which includes not only their critical reactions against cultural stereotypes circulating in the mainstream, but also to create an alternative space which builds on different values (Atton 2002: 10). These media, he argues, provide forums for the "direct voices" of "subjugated knowledges" in the Foucauldian sense (cf. 1980: 81–82), offering spaces for what Raymond Williams would call *democratic communication*, the "origins" of which are "genuinely multiple", affording the possibility of "true" communication and "active response" between all participants (Atton 2002: 9; Williams 1963: 304). In the context of feminist media production, such a possibility might hold true for media forms using easily accessible and cheap technologies such as zine production and blogging. However, it would be more difficult to sustain the argument for, for example, non-commercial but established feminist cultural magazines (e.g. the Swedish *Bang*) that might, which might not be free of a certain exclusionary agenda-setting (even if, indeed, this "agenda" might be based on different, and perhaps even more democratic, principles than the ones generally found in the mainstream media).

Atton states that the ultimate "test" of a theory of alternative media would, in addition to its explanatory value, be its aptitude to capture diversity in the phenomena under study (Atton 2002: 9). The question is whether Atton's theory itself passes this test: Despite its break away from a *rigid* dichotomisation, Atton remains faithful to the basic grammar of "alternative media studies", which as a consequence imposes certain restrictions on both the plasticity and durability of his proposed theory vis-à-vis concrete instances of media production. Focussed, still, on normative judgements and evaluative criteria between radicality and non-radicality, Atton himself reintroduces the binary opposition he wishes to avoid, preventing, ultimately, the analysis of the complex relationships of interconnectedness between various media forms. Even though much feminist media has indeed managed to fill the various criteria as stated by above mentioned authored (see DiCenzo and Ryan 2007), such a dichotomous logic cannot capture the diversity of these practices. Instead, study of feminist media production needs to take into account a varied range of practices. In other words, analyses of feminist media production needs to show an ability to capture media which, to paraphrase Clemencia Rodriguez, are:

> ... legal, a-legal ... illegal, pirate, commercial, amateur, local, regional, diasporic, moni-lingual, bilingual, daily, weekly, monthly, once-in-a-while (1992: 64).

Connecting feminist media: The rhizomatic alternative

Instead of, and in a response to, the aforementioned attempts to distinguish between more oppositional, radical or activist media forms, Olga Bailey, Bart Cammaerts and Nico Carpentier have formulated a theoretical framework that seeks to further the move from a rigid economy of oppositions. Building on Gilles Deleuze and Felix Guattari's conceptualisation of the rhizome, which juxtaposes the *rhizomatic* (non-linear, nomadic, connective) with the hierarchical tendencies of the *arbolic*, or tree-like, systems (linear, unitary, with fixed points of origin and sub-divisions) (Deleuze and Guattari 1988: 3–25), Bailey, Cammaerts and Carpentier argue that this metaphor does better justice to "alternative" media systems by accenting their contingent character in contrast to the more "arbolic" and rigidly organised mainstream media (Bailey et al. 2008: 29). Similarly, the notion of the rhizome has previously been employed as a perspective to shed light on the riot grrrl movement, arguing that their zine networks, websites and distros are typically rhizomatic, stressing their character of an "underground culture multiplying via lines of connection that are not controlled from a primary location", but rather as a polymorphous de-centralised movement without leaders, spokeswomen or a unified political agenda attached to its name (Leonard 2007; see also Piano 2002). In Bailey, Cammaerts and Carpentier's understanding of rhizomatic media, however, the emphasis lays not primarily in the "subterranean" nature such rhizomatic networks. Rather, I would argue that its analytical strength lies in its ability to explore their elusiveness and contingency *as well as* possible interconnections and linkages with the state and the market (2008: 27). As such, this approach has proven useful to understand also alternative media which do not easily fit into models of counter-hegemony (such as certain zines or blogs, for example).

Feminist zines and rhizomatics

Although the majority of existing feminist zines may subscribe to the antagonistic ethos of anti-commercialism, anti-elitism and anti-professionalism, far from all of them do. A recent case study by the Central and Eastern

European *Plotki Femzine* provides an instructive example of a media project which, while motivated partly by the knowledge of existing "grrrl zines", also have employed non-prototypical strategies of media production. While the first edition of *Plotki Femzine* was a cheaply produced photocopied zine, the editorial team later successfully applied for funding from the German-Polish Youth Foundation in order to print a somewhat more magazine-like second edition, thereby negating the widespread assumption that zine production is inherently anarchist and anti-state (Chidgey et al. 2009). Similarly, the Swedish feminist magazine *Bleck* initially employed the DIY format of the zine, only later to be re-launched as a more costly magazine, which in turn assisted the editor Linna Johansson in establishing herself as a well-known columnist in one of the major national tabloid newspapers (cf. Gunnarsson Payne 2006).

In light of these ambivalences, the concept of rhizomatic media has the asset of steering clear of simple oppositions between "mainstream" and "alternative". As Deleuze and Guattari argue, the relationship between the rhizomatic and the arbolic is not one of mutual exclusiveness, but,

> A new rhizome may form in the heart of a tree, the hollow of a root, the crook of a branch. Or else it is a microscopic element of the root-tree, a radicle, that gets rhizome production going (Deleuze and Guattari 1988: 15).

The analytical value of this statement is one which should not be under-estimated – but one which has yet been downplayed in both the work of Leonard and in the alternative media theory of Bailey, Cammaerts and Carpentier. This calls for further investigation, as it offers a much-needed analytical possibility which manages to avoid romanticised ideas of alternative media as *inherently* democratic and radical, as well as demonising and simplified meanings of the "mainstream" as completely devoid of any potential for the production of counter narratives. Thereby, the rhizomatic approach may offer a potentially fruitful solution to the aforementioned tension between specificity an historical complexity in alternative media theory. Although I agree that the former *tend* to be more rhizomatic in character, and the latter more arbolic, this impasse allows for analyses of, for example, the ways in which arbolic hierarchies can and do form also within alternative media frameworks and, subsequently, how journalistic practices occasionally manage to subvert meanings and instigate social change.

Tactical media and hegemonic appropriations: Culture jamming as rhizomatic media

The term *tactical media* has been coined as a way of expressing a position outside of both mainstream and alternative media, or, as David Garcia calls it,

> . . . a no-man's land on the border of experimental media – art, journalism and political activism – a zone that was, in part, made possible by the mass availability of a powerful and flexible new generation of media tools (2007: 6).

As such, the recent developments of tactical media have been inextricably linked to the expansion of new ICTs. The growth of tactical media should, however, not be understood as a simple adaptation of movement strategies into the "information age". Instead, their positioning is one of refutation in relation to not only the presumed objectivity of journalist practices and the elitism and personality cults of the art world, but also of the disciplinary an instrumentalist strategies of traditional social movements (Garcia 2007: 6). Importantly, the term *tactical* alludes to Michel de Certeau's distinction between strategy and tactics, the latter referring to the art of the subordinated, as opposed to strategies being implemented from a locus of domination. Tactics, in this sense, consists of parasitic appropriations, subversing the meaning of signifiers, which makes techniques such as "subvertising" – the practice of parodying commercial or political advertisements by for example altering their texts or images – prime examples of tactical media.

Exemplary of feminist tactical media would be the work of Princess Hijab, whose provocative street art includes "hijabising" adverts – painting black hijabs on commercial adverts for products such as jewellery and make-up. In her manifesto she states, albeit obliquely, what could be interpreted as a feminist statement:

> Princess Hijab knows that *L'Oréal* and *Dark&Lovely* have been killing her little by little. She feels that the veil is no longer that white. She feels contaminated. (Princesshijab.org, quote no longer accessible online, archived at "Princess Hijab: Hijabizing Advertising", Grassroots feminism)

She declares her influence by "movements such as Adbusters", but argues also that "since 9/11, things have changed" and that she therefore has chosen to subvert images in a non-American way. She claims to "know all about *visual* terrorism" (emphasis added), and rearticulates thereby the dominant cultural stereotypes of the Muslim terrorist, as well as the hijab, which so often in Western contexts has served as the signified of women's oppression per se. Her street art manifesto subverts the meaning of the capitalist beauty industry by pointing its messages out as "lethal", as a threat to her life in a symbolic sense ("killing her little by little"), as well as the epithet used by dominant culture to demonise the Muslim Other. Despite these strong political statements, Princess Hijab does not position herself within any political or religious movement, but states quite clearly her independence and dedication to art only.

> And don't forget, she acts upon her own free will. She is not involved in any lobby or movement be it political, religious or to do with advertising. In fact, the Princess is an insomniac-punk. She is the leader of an artistic fight, nothing else. (Princesshijab.org, quote no longer accessible online, archived at "Princess Hijab: Hijabizing Advertising", Grassroots feminism)

The brief example of "hijabising" makes a strong case for the rhizomatic approach to tactical media, particularly with its use of the Deleuzo-Guattarian concept of *deterritorialisation*, shedding light on the process of undermining the authority of corporate advertising by tactically turning its own rhetorical tropes and imagery against it, and thereby destabilising their meaning.

Cultural and political jamming, however, should not be understood as inherently radical modes of operating.[4] On the contrary, what is used as tactics of subordinated groups and oppositional movements can also be used as "strategies" of the dominant. Processes of deterritorialisation, in this sense, are always inextricably tied to *reterritorialisation*, a process demonstrated by Bailey, Cammaerts and Carpentier's discussion of the ways in which corporate companies deploy jamming techniques for marketing purposes, and political parties appropriate techniques of jamming in their election campaigns as a way of mocking their political competition – in a way that presumably functions as an effective strategy in appealing to younger and "trendier" sections of the electorate (2008: 143–147).[5] In a feminist context, the conceptualisation of de- and reterritorialisation would be particularly useful in understanding the reciprocity between would-be "alternative" and "mainstream" socio-political messages. To give some brief examples: the ways in which the Riot Grrrl slogan "Girl Power!" has been reterritorialised by postfeminist commercial products such as women's magazines and popular music (e.g. the Spice Girls) and feminist jamming tactics such as "Revolution. Because you're worth it!" (an adaptation of the cosmetics company *L'Oréal's* slogan employed by Swedish zine *Radarka*).

I argue that a rhizomatic approach to alternative media shows a flexibility in its theoretical apparatus that is otherwise lacking in much of the literature that comprises the field of alternative media studies. The perspective offers a compelling framework for the study of the tactics, processes and connections within and between feminist media production. However, this is not to say that the approach is without its limitations. Its strength resides in its understanding of the processual dimension of media production – and an understanding that furthermore does not reduce the complexity of such processes. It is therefore particularly informative in obviating the "how" of these connections. What it does *not* offer is an explanatory purchase on the "whys" of these connections and processes.

Devoid of any notion of the subject as it is, this mode of theorisation consequently also lacks any notion of political subjectivity and the more "strategic" aspects of the building of alliances between struggles. It might even be said, then, that the gains of expunging "alternative media stud-

---

4 Although tactical media is predominantly discussed as a 1990s phenomenon, the tactics of cultural and political "jamming" are not entirely new. Their genealogy can be traced back to, for example, techniques of *détournement* (Debord 1959/2006) and the radical bricolages (Hebdige 1979: 103) of the Situationist and punk movements, both of which involve re-using and re-articulating elements of the dominant culture so as to subvert their meanings, thereby rendering their contingent character visible and showing how "things could be otherwise" (see Bailey et al. 2008: 138–9).

5 Åsa Wettergren has defined culture jamming as a "symbolic form of protest located within a field of anti-corporate activism where tensions between democratic principles and the undemocratic principles of the 'free' market are articulated as pivotal contemporary political conflicts" (Wettergren 2009: 2).

ies" of the dichotomies implicitly or explicitly present in the more counter hegemonic approaches has carried with it the loss of explanatory value as to how these media function as crucial sites for the constitution of political identification. In the study of feminist media production, this latter aspect cannot be underestimated. On the contrary, any rigorous analysis of feminist media production needs to take seriously the ways in which gendered identities are transformed into *feminist* identities. I would now like to sketch out a further contribution to the field that at least begins to make incursions into these questions.

Feminist media and political identification: From citizens' media to sites of antagonism

Rodriguez's starting point is the supposition that social subjects identify in multiple, contingent and heterogeneous ways, constituted by an assembly of subject positions (Mouffe 1992: 372). Social categories such as "women" are produced through complex intersections of various discourses and institutions, and the subordination of women cannot be understood to be constituted by a single cause or underlying essence. From this destabilised notion of the subject it follows that one can no longer view any member of a historically subordinated group as belonging to a certain "interest group" with predetermined interests and needs (Rodriguez 1992: 18). Media representations therefore cannot be said to represent the "true" interests of any certain groups. Rather, from this perspective, *interests do not precede political action, but are constituted in political acts*. As such, alternative media plays a crucial role in the constitution and negotiation of political interests and collective identities.

Mediated representations of "interest groups", then, are seen as a *constitutive practice*, actually producing the very interests that they claim to represent. Instead of risking to reproduce essentialist notions of "women's writing", this perspective allows for feminist identities not to be revealed by feminist media production, but the latter to be part of producing them. It is telling that Rodriguez dismisses the terminology of "alternative media" altogether, arguing that it problematically predetermines these media as necessarily in opposition to the mainstream media, and thereby "limits the potential of these media to their ability to resist the alienating power of mainstream media" and claims that this "approach blinds our understanding of all other instances of change and transformation brought about by these media" (Rodriguez 1992: 20). In its place Rodriguez proposes the formulation of *citizens' media*, an idea entailing three fundamental properties: i.) that it would be a collective enactment of citizenship through active interventions and transformations of dominant media; ii.) that these collective practices of citizenship take place through the contestation of social codes, legitimised identities and institutionalised social relations; and, iii.) that these interventions have an empowering – and, as a result of this empowerment, transformative – effect on the community in which they are located (2001: 20). In her notion of citizens' media, Rodriguez stresses Chantal Mouffe and Kirstie McClure's extensive understanding of "the political", extending the political from the narrow definition of "juridical demands upon the state" to also include a

> quotidian politics – a politics which extends the terrain of political contestation to the everyday enactment of social practices and routine reiterations of cultural representations (McClure 1992: 123).

In feminist terms, this "everydayness" of politics have been long known and articulated in the famous slogan "The personal is political!", so often reiterated in feminist political manifestations, relating to crucial feminist issues such as sexual violence, heteronormativity, reproductive rights and issues concerning body images.

Contemporary feminist media production can be said to embrace this quotidian dimension of politics, not least in relation to media forms such as zines and blogs. The value of feminist media production such as zine writing and blogs would not *necessarily* lie in its potential to affect political policy, but rather in the contestation of symbolic codes and rearticulation of everyday experiences. Many feminist zines, for example, offer personal accounts of negative feelings towards one's own body, thereby de-naturalising the beauty standards of commercial girls' and women's magazines.

> why do i cry when i look in the mirror? why do i look at stupid magazine ads wish that i look like that? why is there so much fucken emphasis placed on looking "pretty" and i dont know what i want to be. just don't want to hate myself anymore for not being the delicate little flower that i am told to be. why does the media try so hard to dictate to us what is and what isnt beautiful . . . I am so sick of hating myself. i don't want to cry in the mirror anymore. (*Revolution Rising* #1, in Kearney 2006: 181, spelling in the original)

This quote demonstrates a tendency displayed by many feminist zines, namely that capitalist and patriarchal mainstream media is articulated as the constitutive outside of feminist zine culture. That is, this "outside" would not only be different from feminist media, but it would constitute its "radical other" and thereby be positioned in an *antagonistic* relationship to feminism as such.

I argue that this antagonistic relationship takes us back somewhat, showing us, as it were, the loss of an analytical strength of the counter hegemonic approaches surveyed in the first part of this chapter. From the post-Marxist approach of Chantal Mouffe and Ernesto Laclau, there is no *inherent* opposition between even the most unequal subject positions (e. g. "men", "women"). Rather, the *antagonistic* relationship *occurs* only if the subordinated group *opposes* the unequal relationship by construing it *as* a relationship of domination and subordination (Laclau 1990: 6; Laclau and Mouffe 1985: 122; Mouffe 1993: 77). With its strong anti-essentialist ontology, Laclau and Mouffe's perspective avoids any pitfalls of reproducing any metaphysical ideals of any inherent "female" way of writing, or of any determinist idea of universal interests of "all women" (cf. Rhodes 2005: 10–23). Instead their theoretical approach makes possible theorisation of the ways in which feminist identities are actually constituted through the practice of media production, and how these identities – on both an individual and a collective level – are necessarily contextual, relational and processual. The explanatory value of this is that it offers a way to study not only the "hows" but also the "whys", the conditions of emergence for feminist identification and the construction of "chains of equivalence" between collective identities that are articulated in opposition to one another, between a collective identity and its "oppressive other" (e.g. "sisterhood" vs. "patriarchy") (cf. Gunnarsson Payne 2006; 2012). Understanding this process is crucial in order to understand the role that feminist media production plays in producing spaces where gendered identities and relations are transformed into sites of antagonistic struggle.

Concluding reflections: Current developments and future challenges

There has been something of a blind spot in alternative media studies to date. The limited numbers of sustained engagements with the rich and variegated history of feminist media is surprising given its historical prominence over the last two centuries. The question that I wished to raise in this chapter was that given the lack of attention to feminist media production, can it be said of the conceptual tools available that there is an essential difficulty in teasing out the specificities and nuances of instances of feminist media? The intention was not necessarily to propose that there is something "different" about feminist initiatives, which set them apart from other modes of media production, as if an engagement with feminist media projects requires a specifically feminist theoretical perspective. Rather, the aim was to move away from theorisations of alternative media with too broad and formal conceptions, under which too many concrete examples can be subsumed and made identical to one another, to the detriment of paying attention to the differences between instances of alternative media as well as the tensions and inconsistencies internal to a particular media project. A more dynamic (less static) understanding of media production was sought.

An assessment of alternative media theories reveals a wide ranging set of theoretical engagements. Ultimately, each can be brought back to a common denominator wishing to give the idea of "alternative media" a conceptual and phenomenal specificity that overdraws the distinction between alternative and mainstream forms of media. The vicissitudes and complexities of actually existing feminist media are not best served by such hard-edged analytical distinctions. Examples abound within the feminist movement itself that would caution against the use of such metaphysically infused distinctions. Both Deleuze and Guattarian and the Mouffe and Laclauian insights might be better harnessed to provide a more durable, a more empirically responsive theory, far more sensitive to the contingencies of media production. The work of Bailey, Cammaerts and Carpentier as well as Rodriguez was referred to as examples that have actively developed these insights into theories of media production beyond hegemonic mass media. Each departs from the attempt to define what constitutes an instance of "alternative media" (and whether or not we should even use this term) from outside of its particular manifestations, but at the same time brings to bear with it a set of theoretical tools that do not merely set out to describe a particular case of media production but seek to explain the processes by which media comes to be produced in a given socio-political situation.

What each of these scholars advance can only be just the start, however. As far as the successes of their operationalisations of certain post-structuralist presuppositions, further advances need to be made to fully meet the requirements of rigorous study of feminist media production. Importantly, I would suggest attention needs to be paid to the constitution of feminist identities, furthering particularly not only the ways in which alliances and coalitions are made, but also the role feminist media production plays in the constitution of collective feminist identities. A significant but hitherto overlooked dimension of alternative and/or feminist media production is the central role of media production for affective investments in certain feminist vocabularies, aesthetics and political prioritisations. Such explorations would need to combine theoretical insights of post-structuralist approaches to alternative media and nuanced conceptualisations of political subjectivity with thorough empirical investigation of both audiences and producers (to the extent such a distinction can at all be made) of feminist media.

References

Abel, R., 1997. An Alternative Press. Why? *Publishing Research Quarterly* 12(4), Winter issue, pp. 78–84.

Atton, C., 2002. *Alternative Media*. London: SAGE.

Atton, C., 2004. *An Alternative Internet*. Edinburgh: Edinburgh University Press.

Bailey, O., Cammaerts, B. and Carpentier, N., 2007. *Understanding Alternative Media*. Open University Press.

Byerly, K. and Ross, C., 2006. *Women and Media: A Critical Introduction*. London: Wiley-Blackwell.

de Certeau, M., 1984. *The Practice of Everyday Life*. Los Angeles: University of California Press.

di Cenzo, M. & Ryan, L., 2007. Neglected news: Women and print media, 1890–1928. In: Acland, ed. *Residual Media*. Minnesota: University of Minnesota Press.

di Cenzo, M., 2003. Gutter politics: Women newsies and the suffrage press. *Women's History Review* 12 (1), pp 15–33.

Chidgey, R. and Gunnarsson Payne, J. and Zobl, E., 2009. Rumours from around the bloc: Gossip, rhizomatic media and the *Plotki Femzine. Feminist Media Studies* 9 (4).

Chidgey, R., 2007. Riot Grrrl writing. In: N. Monem, ed. *Riot Grrrl: Revolution Girl Style Now!* London: Black Dog Publishing, pp. 100–141.

Chidgey, R., 2006. The resisting subject: Per-zines as life story data, *University of Sussex Journal of Contemporary History* 10 [online]. Available at: <http://www.sussex.ac.uk/history/documents/10_a_chidgey_perzines_final.pdf>

Comedia, 1984. The alternative press: The development of underdevelopment. *Media, Culture and Society,* 1984; 6; pp. 95–102.

Coyer, K. and Downmunt, T. and Fountain, A., 2007. *The Alternative Media Handbook.* London & New York: Routledge.

Curran, J. and Couldry N., 2003. *Contesting Media Power: Alternative Media in a Networked World.* Rowman and Littlefield.

Debord, G., 1959/2006. A user's guide to détournement. In: *The Situationist International Anthology.* Berkeley: Bureau of Public Secrets.

Deleuze, G. and Guattari, F., 1988. *A Thousand Plateaus. Capitalism and Schizophrenia.* London: Athlone.

Dickinson, R., 1997. *Imprinting the sticks: The alternative press outside London.* London: Aldershot Arena.

Downing, J.D.H., 2001. *Radical Media. Rebellious Communication and Social Movements.* SAGE.

Downing, J.D.H., 1984. *Radical Media. The Political Organization of Alternative Communication.* Boston: South End Press.

Duncombe, S., 1997. *Notes from Underground: Zines and the Politics of Alternative Culture.* Verso.

Foucault, M., 1980. *Power/Knowledge: Selected Interviews and Other Writings 1972–1977.* In: C. Gordon, ed. New York: Pantheon Books.

Grassroots feminism, n.d. Princess Hijab: Hijabizing Advertising. [online]. Available at: <http://www.grassrootsfeminism.net/cms/node/177>

Gunnarsson Payne, J., 2006. *Systerskapets logiker. En etnologisk studie av feministiska fanzines.* Umeå: Umeå University.

Gunnarsson Payne, J., 2012. The logics of sisterhood: Intra-feminist debates in Swedish feminist zines. *European Journal of Women's Studies,* 19 (2), pp. 187–202.

Hamilton, J., 2000. Alternative media: Conceptual difficulties, critical possibilities. *Journal of Communication Inquiry,* 2000; 24; pp. 357.

Harris, A. 2003. gURL scenes and grrrl zines: the regulation and resistance of girls in late modernity. *Feminist Review* 75, pp. 38–56.

Hebdige, D., 1979. *Subculture: The Meaning of Style.* London: Methuen.

Irvin Painter, N., 1994. Representing Truth: Sojourner Truth's knowing and becoming known. *The Journal of American History* 81 (2), pp. 461–492.

Israels Perry, E., 1994. Image, rhetoric, and the historical memory of women. In: A. Sheppard, ed., *Cartooning for Suffrage*. Albuquerque: University of New Mexico Press.

Kearney, M-C., 2006. *Girls Make Media*. London and New York: Routledge.

Kearney, M-C., 1997. The missing links: Riot grrrl-feminism-lesbian culture. In: S. Whiteley, ed., *Sexing the Groove: Popular Music and Gender*. London and New York: Routledge.

Laclau, E., 1990. *New Reflections on the Revolution of Our Time*. London and New York: Verso.

Laclau, E. and Mouffe, C., 1985. *Hegemony and Social Strategy: Towards a Radical Democratic Politics*. London and New York: Verso.

Leonard, M., 2007. *Gender in the Music Industry. Rock, Discourse and Girl Power*. Farnham: Ashgate Publishing.

Leonard, M., 1997. Rebel girl, you are the queen of my world. In: S. Whiteley, ed., *Sexing the Groove: Popular Music and Gender*. London and New York: Routledge.

Leonard, M., 1998. Paper planes: Travelling the new grrrl geographies. In: T. Skelton and G. Valentine, eds. *Cool Places: Geographies of Youth Cultures*. London and New York: Routledge.

McClure, K., 1992. On the subject of rights: Pluralism, plurality and political identity. In: C. Mouffe, ed., *Dimensions of Radical Democracy: Pluralism, Citizenship, Community*. London: Verso, pp. 108–125.

Mouffe, C., 1993. *The Return of the Political*. London and New York: Verso.

Ó Sullivan, T.,1994. Alternative Media. In: T. Ó Sullivan, Dutton and Rayner, eds. *Key Concepts in Communication and Cultural Studies*. London: Routledge.

Piano, D., 2002. Congregating women: Reading 3rd wave feminist practices in subcultural production, *Rhizomes* 2004, p. 4.

Rhodes, J., 2005. *Radical Feminism, Writing, and Critical Agency: From Manifesto to Modem*. New York: State University of New York Press.

Riaño, P., 1994. *Women in Grassroots Communication. Furthering Social Change*. SAGE.

Rodriguez, C., 2001. *Fissures in the Media Scape: An International Study of Citizen's Media*. Hampton Press.

Steiner, L., 1992. The history and structure of women's alternative media. In: L. Rakow ed. *Women Making Meaning: New Feminist Directions in Communication*. New York: Routledge.

Traber, M., 1985. Alternative journalism, alternative media. *Communication Resource* 7 (October 1985). London: World Association for Christian Communication.

Waltz, M., 2005. *Alternative and Activist Media*. Edinburgh: Edinburgh University Press.

Wettergren, Å., 2009. Fun and laughter: Culture jamming and the emotional regime of late capitalism. *Social Movement Studies* 8 (1), January 2009, pp. 1–15.

Williams, R., 1963. *Culture and Society: 1780–1950.* Harmondsworth: Penguin.

Zobl, E., 2004a. Persephone is pissed! Grrrl zine reading, making and distributing across the globe. *Hecate: An Interdisciplinary Journal of Women's Liberation,* 2004.

Zobl, E., 2004b. Revolution grrrl and lady style, now! *Peace Review: A Journal of Social Justice* 16 (4).

Zobl, E., 2003. *The Global Zine Network: A DIY Feminist Revolution for Social Change.* Ph.D. Dissertation, Academy of Fine Arts Vienna.

Archiving Feminist Grassroots Media[1]

Brigitte Geiger and Margit Hauser

Introduction: Documenting women's history

Feminist archives have an important task in passing on women's history, particularly in documenting and increasing the visibility of the women's movement and lesbian history and politics. From the 1970s on, a broad infrastructure of feminist archives and libraries has emerged which were designed to be both centers for up-to-date information within the women's movement as well as an infrastructure to support academic feminist research.[2] To do this, feminist media, especially magazines, are an important part of the collections of feminist archives and libraries because they are a substantial and dynamic source of current issues, political practices, and theoretical discussions.

As staff members of STICHWORT – the Archives of Women's and Lesbians' Movements in Vienna, which manages an extensive collection of "independent" feminist media – we will provide an overview of feminist grassroots media in Austria, focusing in particular on the accessibility and preservation of feminist media in feminist archives. We will analyze structures and developments within feminist media production in Austria from its beginnings in the 1970s up to now and give an insight into the thematic developments of the first two decades of the women's movement. We will also set a special focus on lesbian media. As only a few distinctly lesbian magazines have been published in Austria over the years, we will consider a wider range of lesbian media from German-speaking countries.

Feminist grassroots media in women's and lesbian archive collections

Feminist media, particularly magazines, are an important part of the collections of feminist archives and libraries. From the perspective of women's archives, feminist media are a substantial and dynamic source of informa-

---

1 An earlier and extended version of this paper has been published in *Interface: a journal for and about social movements*, volume 2 (2) (November 2010) in English and German (www.interfacejournal.net). The data have been updated in 2011 for this article.
2 The umbrella organization of women's/lesbian archives, libraries, and documentation centers, i.d.a <www.ida-dachverband.de>, provides an overview of these feminist archives and libraries, their special collections, and services.

tion on current issues, political practices, and theoretical discussions. They reflect the differentiation and developments of feminist movements, strategies, and concepts as well as the different societal, political, and cultural contexts. Because of this, feminist media are important as sources of up-to-date information in women's archives, on one hand, and as valuable historical resources for research on the Women's Movement on the other. Thus, their preservation and accessibility is a crucial task for feminist archives. (Geiger and Hauser 2008)

With the international abundance of feminist magazines and newsletters since the beginning of the second-wave women's movements, feminist movements have been forming spaces and structures of (counter) public spheres. Places for communication and action offer space for the unfolding of feminist discourses while building frameworks for discussions between women, for processing experiences and developing theories, for collective learning processes and self-directed development of feminist strategies and perspectives for action.[3] Feminist media serve as both a means to information, communication, and discussion within the movement, as well as a means to self-determined expression to the "outside."[4]

The diversity, difference, and international circulation of feminist print media make it difficult to establish a clear definition of the "feminist magazine" genre. The spectrum of feminist magazines reaches from the small group media of individual projects and initiatives for a limited target audience to feminist "mass media" with a relatively high circulation and a stronger commercial orientation (such as *Emma* in Germany or *Ms.* in the USA), from basic informational pamphlets to sophisticated magazines and extensive scholarly periodicals, from short-lived attempts lasting only a few issues to well-established magazines with over twenty years of history. It includes both the local women's newspaper and the international newsletter, thematically broad and specialist magazines with a narrow focus, and a wide array of lesbian media. In addition to that, newsletters distributed via e-mail – published solely online or in parallel to a print version – and online ezines have been included since the end of the nineties.

Their accessibility and preservation is essential to retracing feminist discourses and developments in the movement's history. At the same time, the documentation of feminist newspapers is highly demanding due to the magazines' diversity, decentralized organization, high fluctuation, and often independently organized production methods.

Only the larger Austrian feminist media – *AUF, An.schläge, [sic!]* – are archived at the national libraries, while smaller, regional pamphlets are often missing, despite the principle of legal deposit. Foreign feminist magazines, including "large" ones like *Emma, Courage,* or *Ms.,* are only sporadically present.[5] In Germany the situation appears to be slightly different.

---

3 See: Gruppe feministischer Öffentlichkeit 1992, Klaus 1994, Geiger 2002a.
4 On the functions of feminist magazines see Geiger 2001, 2002b, Susemichel et al. 2008.
5 The situation of scholarly periodicals is different; here the university establishment of women's and gender research has also been reflected in the acquisition policy of academic libraries.

Smaller local media from the autonomous women's movement are at least partially included in German university libraries. Feminist archives and libraries, however, map the entire spectrum of women's and lesbian movement magazine production in German-speaking countries in their holdings and also maintain the most important titles from other countries.

STICHWORT maintains the most extensive collection of independent women's and lesbian magazines in Austria. The archive of the women's and lesbian movement currently encompasses a total of over 730 titles and over 60 current subscriptions. The goal of the collection is to maintain the most complete documentation possible of independent feminist magazine production in Austria from the beginning of the 1970s to the present. This also includes small informational pamphlets and periodicals of which only one issue was published. Presently the index holds 204 Austrian titles, 49 of which are current. The international collection (more than 500 titles from 47 countries, 200 of which are from German-speaking countries) provides insight into the diversity of feminist and lesbian magazine production worldwide, in spite of its necessarily cursory character. Gaps in the collection are constantly being filled through active exchange between feminist archives and private donations. One of the special characteristics of the STICHWORT collection, as well as independent feminist archives in general, lies in the value attributed to "small" media. In order to maintain the most complete movement documentation possible, spontaneous publications and those produced with simple means are also documented. As many of them were published by short-lived women's groups active in a small field, they may have only come out once or twice. *Significance* is defined here through the focus on movement documentation according to criteria different from that of the state facilities.

Other feminist publication collectors in Austria are the *AUF* magazine archives (with almost 50 titles, about half of which are in German, including many older collections), the *ArchFem* archives in Innsbruck, and the *FEMAIL* archives in Feldkirch, all of which are limited to Austrian and German-language titles. The *AEP* library in Innsbruck and *DOKU Graz* maintain smaller collections.[6] *Frauensolidarität* has been collecting and documenting magazines and newsletters as a library and documentation center for women and the "third world" since 1993–94. It primarily focuses on countries in the global south, with more publications being produced in Asia and Latin America than in Africa, but also material from the "north" that deals with issues relating to women from the south and international women's issues. They are recorded in an online database (www.centrum3.at/bibliothek/) and also partially in the catalogue of the Österreichische Bibliotheksverbund, a network of Austrian libraries.

The larger Austrian feminist magazines, such as *AUF, an.schläge, [sic!], Frauensolidarität* or *fiber* are also found in feminist archives outside the country.

---

6 In 2011 the *AUF* magazine archive was given to STICHWORT; the magazine collections of *ArchFem* and *DOKU Graz* went to STICHWORT and other (feminist) archives and libraries at the end of 2011.

The largest collections of feminist publications in Germany are at the *Women's Research, Education, and Information Center – FFBIZ* in Berlin (with 924 titles), the *Archiv der deutschen Frauenbewegung* in Kassel (1,140), the *FrauenMediaTurm* in Cologne (976), the feminist archive *ausZeiten* in Bochum (816), and the *Spinnboden* in Berlin (over 1,600), which is focused on lesbian publications. In Switzerland the *schema f* library in Zurich holds the most significant collection. *Cid-femmes* in Luxembourg possesses all of the country-specific and regional titles.[7]

In order to make magazine collections of the lesbian/women's archives and libraries in German-speaking countries visible and also to document them in traditional catalogues, the data are being gradually entered into the ZDB, the world's largest magazine database, located at the Berlin State Library, through a collaborative project from *i.d.a. Dachverband*.[8] Many titles are being introduced to a broader public for the first time through this. At the same time, attention is being drawn to feminist archives and libraries as collection centers. In October 2009 more than 2,000 different feminist titles from the first-wave and second-wave women's movements were recorded in the ZDB, including both grassroots and scholarly publications. Currently over half of the magazine collections from the 20 facilities participating in the project have been documented in the ZDB.

The plan for the future is that all magazine titles in the *i.d.a.* facilities will be presented together on the organization's website. No solution is currently in sight to deal with the growing importance of online media and web 2.0 technologies; both the personnel and technological resources of these feminist archives have failed to meet this challenge. In this field, the central national libraries have to take the lead.

Feminist grassroots media in Austria: Structures and developments

STICHWORT'S extensive publication database allows a detailed look at the structures and developments in Austria's feminist magazine landscape. The database includes (as of late 2010) 198 Austrian magazine titles that were founded after 1970, the beginning of the second-wave women's movement in Austria, which thereby form the basis for the analysis that follows.[9] Originally a collection of print media, today the database also comprises electronic newsletters. In addition to collection data, the database also includes information on the periodicals' founding and in some cases discontinuation, publishers, former names, publishing location, frequency of publication, thematic focus, and type of magazine. However, not all details

---

7   Links to the aforementioned facilities can be found at: www.ida-dachverband.de.
8   www.zdb-opac.de. The holdings can be searched by individual archive in the ZDB under interlibrary loan region "ida".
9   Six older titles not included here are magazines with a long history published by political or church-related women's organizations.

are available for all titles; for example, the exact duration of publication is only known for 88 titles. This should be considered below.

The first independent feminist magazines begin in the 1970s as organs of the first working groups on women's liberation and autonomous women's organizations in Austria. The two oldest feminist magazines in German-speaking countries that still exist in 2010, both founded in 1974, should be highlighted here: *AUF – Eine Frauenzeitschrift* in Vienna[10] and *AEP Informationen* in Innsbruck, Tyrol. Altogether these beginnings of feminist media production in Austria are still very modest with an average of five titles published simultaneously per year and one to two new publications annually, most of which only existed for one to two years.

It is only in the 1980s, as the women's movement spread and the first women's projects were founded, that the continuous development of a feminist (print) media landscape in Austria began, lasting until the turn of the century. The number of new projects grew annually from five in the 1980s to more than eight in the 1990s; the number of existing titles increased from an average of 17 in the first half of the 1980s to an average of 72 in the second half of the 1990s. The high point was reached in 1997 with 76 documented magazine titles (Figure 1). As of 2000 the total number and the annual number of new projects receded again, leveling out at around 50 titles and three to four new projects per year. At the end of 2010 the STICHWORT magazine collection documented 46 current titles. Whether this slight recent decline indicates further reductions in the feminist media landscape or just illustrates delays in the archive's collection process will become clear in due course. In any case, an exact determination of the current number is difficult due to rapid changes and occasionally unclear classifications.[11] However, it is worrying that in recent years the balance between new projects and discontinuations was mostly negative, while in the 1980s and 90s an average of two new titles emerged for each existing title that was discontinued.

The expansion was accompanied by an internal differentiation of the magazine landscape, as shown in Figure 2, in which title development is broken down according to the type of publication. The development of titles is relatively stable for general feminist magazines directed toward "all" feminist/lesbian readers with broad subject matter; these play an important role in cross-group multidisciplinary feminist discussion. After the

---

10   *AUF* was discontinued in 2011.

11   Thus *AUF* is still included among the current magazines because it only discontinued its publication in 2011, whereas *LesbenFrauenNachrichten* and [sic!] *Forum für feministische Gangarten* are not included. Neither of these has announced an official halt to publication, but their most recent issues appeared in 2007 and 2009, respectively. For technical archiving reasons, electronic newsletters (eight current titles) are included in the database, but online news portals like *ceiberweiber.at* (since 1999) or *die.Standard.at* (since 2000) are not. For comparison, using a very narrow definition of independent feminist magazines, Horak (2003) arrives at 18 current titles; Well (2007) lists 44 media in her work, applying a broad definition that includes online media and titles associated with institutions and political parties.

Figure 1: Feminist grassroots media in Austria 1970-2010:
Title development (all titles/new projects - average)

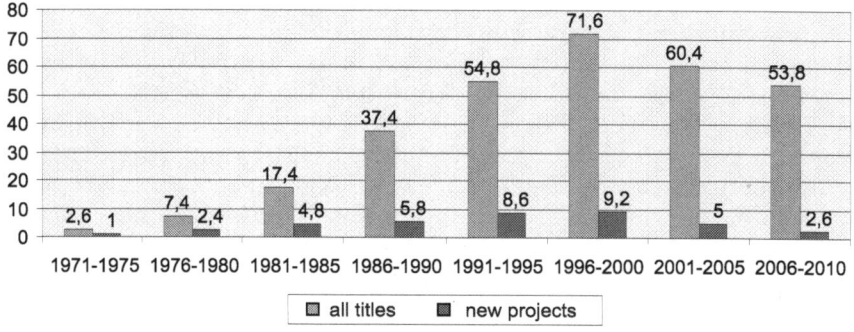

Source: STICHWORT database, authors' statistics

Figure 2: Title development according to type of publication

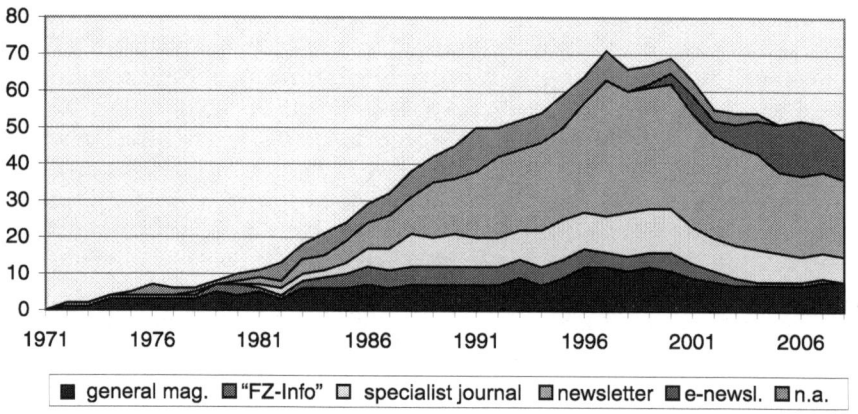

Source: STICHWORT database, authors' statistics

modest start in the 1970s, their number fluctuates between six and twelve titles. The general growth in titles is mainly due to the increasing number of newsletters, which have accompanied the expansion of the broader infrastructure of specialized women's projects as well as the facilities and mergers of women's and gender research since the 1980s. Since 2000 these have been increasingly in electronic form. The number of newsletters has escalated from an average of seven in the 1980s to 30 in the 90s and an average of 39 in the 2000s. The latter rise is mainly due to electronic newsletters, whereas the number of printed newsletters has sunk slightly, most recently to just 24 titles.

The emergence of the first specialist journals in the 1980s was connected to the thematic specialization and differentiation of activities in the women's movement. This type of magazine has been represented by an average of nine titles since the 1990s, for example the art magazine *Eva & Co* (Graz,

1981–1992); the development policy magazine *Frauensolidarität* (Vienna, 1982–present), which still exists today and is also widely received in other German-speaking countries; the newsletter of the Austrian Women's Forum for Feminist Theology, *Der Apfel* (Vienna, 1986–present); *Koryphäe. Medium für feministische Naturwissenschaften und Technik* (Vienna, 1986–2008); the literary studies magazine for the Alps-Adriatic region *Script* (Klagenfurt, 1992–2001); or the most well-established academic magazine, *L'Homme. Zeitschrift für feministische Geschichtswissenschaft* (Vienna, 1990–present).

The women's center newsletters ("FrauenZentrums[FZ]-Infos") were of great importance to the feminist information exchange, particularly during the 1980s and 90s. Published by the women's culture and communication centers and ranging from informational pamphlets to general feminist magazines, publications like *Zyklotron* in Innsbruck (1983–2003), *Infam* in Linz (1984–2000), *Zarah lustra* in Salzburg (1985–2001) and *Belladonna* in Klagenfurt (1986–1996) contributed to the decentralization of the media landscape. All in all, feminist magazine production is heavily concentrated in Vienna. About two thirds of both the total titles and the currently published titles are based in Vienna. State capitals are the other "centers," especially Graz and Innsbruck with more than ten titles each. Less than 5% of all documented titles are published outside of these urban centers.

When looking at feminist magazine production in terms of length of existence and frequency of publication, a high level of fluctuation can be seen. Almost a fifth of the titles exist for only one to two years, a further 14% last between three and five years, and almost a quarter of the titles are published irregularly or only once. On the one hand, this structure is surely a result of the difficult production circumstances of independent feminist media due to limited resources. However, the large rate of fluctuation also expresses how dynamic and lively grassroots, self-organized media production can be. Despite difficult conditions (only a few of the feminist magazine editorial departments are adequately financed or even have paid positions; see Geiger 1996, Horak 2003, Well 2007) many of the media projects nevertheless have managed to maintain an impressive continuity. Over a quarter of the current magazines have been in existence for more than 20 years, and 35% between 10 and 20 years. In other words, 63% of the current magazines and 43% of the total documented titles have been published for at least ten years.

However, limitations in the issue frequency can affect the timeliness of the information. Only 15% of the current titles are published more than six times a year. Currently these publications are *Laufschritte* (Graz, 1986–present) and *Insel Zeitung* (Scharnstein 1992–present) as well as the electronic publications *Fiftitu%-Newsletter* and *AEP-Newsletter*. *an.schläge* (Vienna, 1983–present) is the only magazine that has been published monthly since 1994 (with two double issues). Before that it appeared quarterly, like the bulk of feminist media. In total, one third of the documented feminist titles and half of the general feminist magazines are published three to six times per year. The preferred publication schedule for specialist journals is one to three times per year, whereas newsletters often appear irregularly.

Figure 3: Thematic orientation and fields of activity of Austrian feminist grassroots media (n = 150; multiple selections)

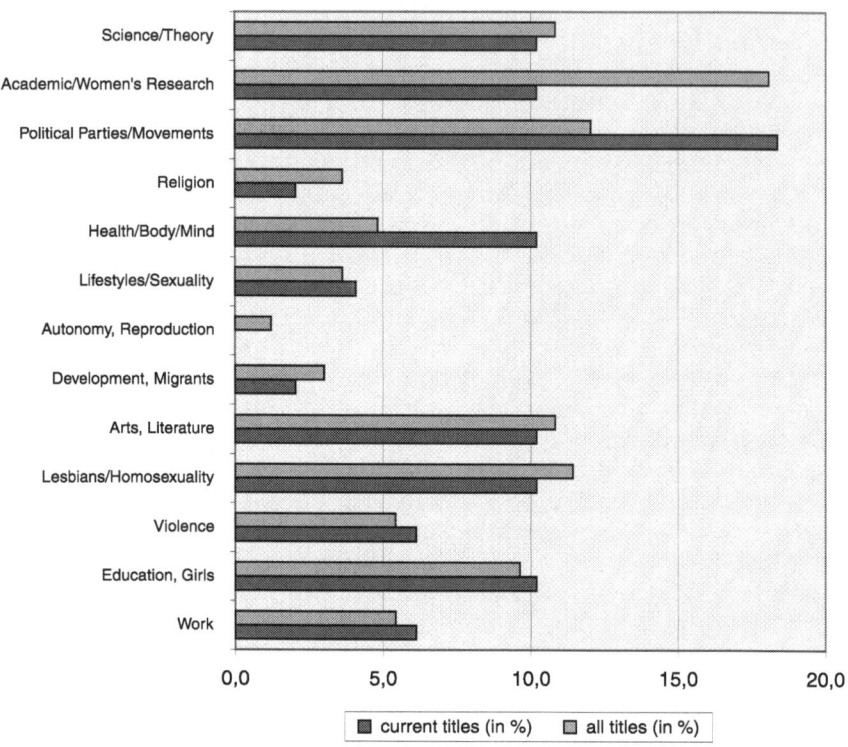

Source: STICHWORT database, authors' statistics

Figure 3 provides an overview of the thematic orientation of the publications. In such a predominately sophisticated and thematically specialized infrastructure as the women's movement, three quarters of the recorded titles (over 80% of current publications) fall into one or two subject areas or fields of activity. One focus is clearly academic and scientific, which make up over 15% of the current publications. Included under university and women's research are mainly student media and information from co-ordination centers and project centers for women's and gender research at Austrian universities.[12] In addition to general gender theory titles, the fields of history, natural science/technology, philosophy, and law are represented.[13] The media represented heavily among political parties or movements include the activities of institutionalized gender equality policy and

---

12 The noticeable decline in current publications may be due to the fact that the material from women and gender-specific courses in the Austrian states included here is only sporadically accounted for.

13 For scholarly periodicals in German-speaking countries, see Hauser and Geiger, 2008.

several titles associated with political parties (such as *Brot & Rosen* from Vienna's Green Party). Women's counseling centers and counseling centers specializing in health, education, work, or violence are very active in media, especially with printed or electronic newsletters and occasionally professional journals. It is striking that migrant (counseling) projects are scarcely represented. The topic of development policy is almost exclusively covered by the magazine *Frauensolidarität*. The subject areas of art and literature are significantly represented. In addition to the aforementioned art magazine *Eva & Co* and the literary magazine *Entladungen* (Vienna, 1985–present), the pop culture magazine projects from recent years such as *female sequences* (Vienna, 1999–2002), *nylon* (Vienna, 2000–2001), and *fiber* (Vienna, 2002–present) particularly stand out. Lesbian or gay and lesbian publications make up 10% of the total.

Looking back: Feminist discussions and issue development in the 1970s and 80s

As part of the research project *Die neue Frauenbewegung im Spiegel ihrer Medien* (1990, Geiger et al. 1992), the first two decades of feminist media production (newspapers, flyers, and posters) in Austria were analyzed by means of the STICHWORT archive holdings. This allows a detailed look at the developments in the thematic structure of feminist publications and medial discussions of the second-wave women's movement in Austria from 1972 to 1990, because the individual articles were entered into a database and indexed according to the STICHWORT system.[14]

A comparison of the structure and development of issues in the independent women's and lesbian publications in Austria during that period with the current thematic orientations of publications reveals both similarities and shifts. In the 1970s and 80s the key issues were coverage of the women's movement, literature and language, art, work, and violence against women, followed by the subject areas of political parties and movements, lesbians and the lesbian movement, and reproduction policy/abortion. The issues of bodies, environment, religion, sexuality, and theory were at the lower end of the scale.

The fact that communication within the movement (coverage of the women's movement in a narrow sense) is decentralized, and not institutionally or hierarchically organized, is key to the women's and lesbian movement. Therefore, it is the task of movement media to guarantee a self-determined (self-)portrayal and a constant exchange of information and experiences, and to convey a cross-regional discussion on the movement's organization, structure, and strategy. Conversely, movement media are received in order to learn the news about groups, activities, and dis-

---

14 The data pool comprises 4,800 articles and is accessible online through the STICHWORT website, www.stichwort.or.at. Unfortunately, a lack of resources has impeded the continuation of this bibliographical and systematic indexing.

cussions, as well as the latest gossip. (Geiger 1987: 380 ff., 351 ff.) Content covers events, conferences, operations, demonstrations, and other activities. Self-criticism and conflicts within the movement are frequent issues and reached an initial peak at the end of the 1970s; discussions on political strategies and programs are less frequent, and utopian plans and visions are extremely rare. Instead, the image cultivation of individual groups and projects dominate coverage of the movement. Reporting on group activities and events is still important today and mainly occurs through the growing number of newsletters from individual women's organizations.

The thematic focus of the publications shifted noticeably from the 1970s to the 80s. In the beginning, abortion issues and violence against women were in the forefront; by the end of the 80s cultural issues took the lead. As in other countries, the fight to legalize abortion played an important role in Austria at the beginning of the second-wave women's movement. After the legalization of abortion within the first twelve weeks in 1975 the issue quickly lost importance. The issue of violence was dealt with differently. Triggered by an international tribunal on violence against women (1976 in Brussels) as well as the fight for the first women's shelters, concern over sexual assault and domestic violence moved into the spotlight in the middle of the seventies. The issue remains relevant but subsequently became less important. In the mid 1990s the discussion partially moved over to specialized media and newsletters from the facilities providing protection against violence (*Gewaltlos*, a leaflet from the Austrian women's shelters since 1995, or *Zeitung der Plattform gegen die Gewalt in der Familie*, since 1998).[15]

It was only at the end of the 1970s that the surprisingly minimal debate on sexuality in Austrian feminist media reached a small peak, focusing on gynecological self-help as a means to the re-appropriation of one's own body. Traditional women's issues like health or religion were also hardly raised in the period before 1990. Interestingly enough, the psychology boom and the turn toward spirituality in the 1980s are only visible in a few select publications. However, the field of health/body/mind is of growing importance in the current media (about 6% of current publications are dedicated to the subject). The field of reproduction – i. e. heterosexual relationships and marriage, family and children, which are classic issues for conventional women's magazines – occupied little space in feminist magazines during the first two decades. Readers who were mothers, when surveyed during the 1980s, definitely considered this a deficit (Geiger 1987). In the second half of the 1990s one initiative attempted to take the matter into its own hands with the publication *Mutter.mund* (Vienna, 1996–1999).

The focus of the debate on party politics regarding women's issues in the beginning of the 1980s was the ambivalent relationship of the independent women's movement to the new State Secretariat for Women's Issues[16].

---

15 For more on the violence debate in the media, see Geiger 2008.
16 Established in 1979. State Secretary Johanna Dohnal was promoted to Minister of Women's Affairs in 1990. Austria has had a Minister of Women's Affairs since then, with interruptions.

At the same time, the failing economy and rising unemployment led to a focus on the subject of work. Budget cuts and slashed social services beginning in the mid 80s pushed the debate on social and labor market policy and the growing poverty among women.

The development of women's research within and outside of universities and the differentiated women's culture and art scene in Vienna, in particular, pushed new issues into the forefront. In the mid 1980s a significant growth in book reviews and the subjects of literature and language, art, education, history, feminist research, and the critique of science becomes visible. This new focus is still seen today in numerous publications from the field.

In the mid 1980s, lesbian issues also become more present; one third of this presence is borne by *Lesbenrundbrief* (1983–1993). The subject appears to be non-existent for the western Austrian publications *Orgon* and *AEP Informationen*; Viennese titles are in the middle of the scale. Above average numbers appear in the publications of some women's centers, thanks to a strong local lesbian presence.

Lesbian publications

The term "lesbian publications" includes magazines that are clearly directed toward a lesbian readership and those that define their target group as "gay-lesbian" or feminist with a lesbian slant.[17] "Queer" titles also belong to this group. STICHWORT verifies 21 titles for Austria, five of which are current. Because this is a relatively low number, and German and Swiss lesbian magazines were and continue to be of great importance to Austrian readers, we include them in this section.

It is not possible to determine the total number of lesbian magazines in German-speaking countries – at least at this point. The holdings of the *i.d.a.* facilities, searchable through ZDB, can be consulted for an overview of the German speaking countries.[18] At present, there are about 150 lesbian magazines included, but data from archives with large holdings, for example the lesbian archive in Berlin, *Spinnboden*, are still largely missing. Furthermore, magazine data in the ZDB often lacks the magazines' exact publishing duration due to incomplete records. An additional problem is that only an extremely limited amount of electronic media, most of which are irregular e-mail newsletters, appears in the ZDB, because they are hardly archived in any facility.

17 Beginning in the mid 1980s, terms like "FrauenLesben" (WomenLesbians) were common in the course of the discussion on the perception of lesbians in feminist contexts. This was also expressed with a conjunction or slash and in many other provocative and humorous heavily debated forms, for example, "women and other lesbians". Around 1990, Austrian groups and periodicals underwent some name changes. One example is the magazine *Frauen-Nachrichten des Frauenzentrums Wien*, which was called *Lesben/ Frauen-Nachrichten* as of the issue 13/1993.

18 Magazines that do not include lesbians in their titles were added from STICHWORT data as much as possible to provide a better overview.

The following can be deduced from the available data: Most of the magazines were started between 1986 and 2000, when the direction shifted from "lesbian" to "gay and lesbian". Approximately three quarters of the lesbian magazines have a regional focus (62% for Austria); lesbian magazines and gay and lesbian magazines are equally represented among the cross-regional publications. Of the former, we include titles such as *Lesbenpresse, Lesbenfront/Frau ohne Herz/Die.Lesbenzeitschrift, Lesbenstich, Ihrsinn, Unsere kleine Zeitung (UKZ)*, the Austrian *Lesbenrundbrief, Infoblatt des Deutschen Lesbenring e. V.* and others.

The first lesbian magazines after the beginning of the second-wave women's movement appeared in 1975: *Lesbenfront* (Zurich), *Lesbenpresse, Partnerin* and *Unsere kleine Zeitung* (all in Berlin). By the end of the 70s, eight more distinctly lesbian magazines had started; these are joined by a gay and lesbian title, *Rosa Revue,* from Hamburg. Most of the distinctly lesbian magazines emerged in the second half of the 1990s (10); a total of 47 lesbian-focused titles were found. In Austria there are only four: *Lesbenrundbrief,* which was published from 1983 to 1993 by different groups; *Lila Schriften* (1995–1999); the magazine from the lesbian student organization at the University of Graz *Sappho,* which has been documented from 1996 to 1998; and the e-mail newsletter *Lebenszeichen* (2001–2008).

In 1984 the term "Women/Lesbians" appeared, both in the magazine title and the name of the publishing group. Efforts toward the integration of lesbian perspectives and content into the feminist debate are reflected in this name choice. These politics are visible in the available data on new publications prior to the year 2000; after that, no new titles with such names are found. It is assumed that after that point, lesbian-focused material was still being integrated into the magazines' editorial concepts, but no longer named as such. The Austrian magazines *[sic!]. Forum für feministische Gangarten* and *an.schläge* are examples of this.

In the first half of the 1980s an increased number of magazines defining their target group as "gay and lesbian" can be found. The number of newly founded publications jumped from five in the early 1980s to 21 in the first half of the 90s. With a total of 71, the number of gay and lesbian titles is approximately as high as the categories of lesbian and women/lesbians combined. In Austria these include *Lambda-Nachrichten* from HOSI Vienna, *Pride* from HOSI Linz, *RosaLila Buschtrommel* from Graz and the gay and lesbian scene publication *Bussi.* The balance between the representation of gay and lesbian issues present in these magazines as well as the degree of divergence between the editorial stance and the perception of the lesbian audiences of feeling spoken to could be the subject of further research.

The Zurich lesbian magazine serves as an example of the changes in political orientation and aesthetic design, and thereby also as an illustration of three decades of lesbian feminism. Founded in 1975 as *Lesbenfront,* typeset and illustrated with drawings and some photos, it provided typical content for self-organized magazines, such as reports on events and political activities, copies of leaflets, open letters and other political texts, field reports, interviews with authors and activists, and reviews. From the 4/1977 issue it was also distributed in Germany by the Frauenbuchvertrieb in Berlin. In 1985 the name was changed to *Frau ohne Herz. Zeitschrift für Frauen und andere Lesben* (Woman without a heart. Magazine for women and other lesbians). Over the course of its ten-year existence, it became increasingly "professional" in its design, for example, regarding typesetting and continuous use of photos as well as paper quality and, lastly, color covers. A complete relaunch took place in 1996 when its name was changed to *die. Lesbenzeitschrift*. The new version was introduced with the line, "The era of the woman without a heart is over."[19] The literary content became more important. In 2004 it was replaced by *Skipper*, which, as a *magazine for lesbian vitality*, served the queer generation with its association to recreation, sports, and games and a seriously questionable image of women – after all, "Skipper" is Barbie's little sister. This was clearly meant to reach the "young lesbians"; reports on gay and lesbian events, organizations, and other matters (e. g. partnerships) were in the forefront of the lifestyle and gossip sections. The individual articles did not extend beyond a double-page spread and were heavily illustrated. *Skipper* was discontinued after only three issues.

Conclusion: The feminist (print) media landscape

In summary, a vivid feminist media landscape is as important for the information needs of all actually interested and engaged in feminist debates and activism as their accessibility and preservation is for historical research. Feminist archives guarantee this accessibility through their collecting and their background knowledge of the movement. The heyday of independent feminist (print) media seems to have ended with the millennium – the discontinuation of one of the oldest existing independent feminist magazines, *AUF*, in 2011 may be considered as symptomatic – but the quality of the current media shows that there is still a readership. Furthermore, new media projects are currently being planned, as represented by the Austrian *Platform 20,000women*, which, inspired by the centennial anniversary of the International Women's Day, initiated new feminist politicization and networking processes. Finally, the future feminist media landscape will depend on the further development of feminist activities as well as the local and global politics and challenges.

Translation: Emily Lemon

References

Geiger, B., 1987. *Weibliche Identität und Frauenöffentlichkeit am Beispiel autonomer Frauenzeitschriften*. Ph. D. Thesis, University of Vienna.

Geiger, B., 1996. Feministische Presse zwischen Autonomie, Markt und Förderung. In: C. Mast et al., eds. *Markt – Macht – Medien*. Konstanz: UVK Medien, pp. 353–362.

---

19 *die. lesbenzeitschrift* 1/1996, Editorial, p. 5.

Geiger, B., 2001. Feministische Zeitschriften. In: H. Klösch-Melliwa, et al., eds. *kolloquiA. Frauenbezogene/feministische Dokumentation und Informationsarbeit in Österreich. Forschungs- und Lehrmaterialien,* Vienna: Ministry of Education, Science, and Culture – Verlag Österreich, pp. 385–404.

Geiger, B., 2002a. Feministische Öffentlichkeiten. Ansätze, Strukturen und aktuelle Herausforderungen. In: J. Dorer and B. Geiger, eds. *Feministische Kommunikations- und Medienwissenschaft. Ansätze, Befunde und Perspektiven der aktuellen Entwicklung.* Wiesbaden: Westdeutscher Verlag, pp. 80–97.

Geiger, B., 2002b. Mediale Vermittlung feministischer Öffentlichkeiten. In: J. Neissl, ed. *der/die journalismus. Geschlechterperspektiven in den Medien.* Innsbruck: StudienVerlag, pp. 91–111.

Geiger, B., 2008. Die Herstellung von Öffentlichkeit für Gewalt an Frauen. In: J. Dorer, B. Geiger and R. Köpl, eds. *Medien – Politik – Geschlecht. Feministische Befunde zur politischen Kommunikationsforschung.* Wiesbaden: VS Verlag für Sozialwissenschaften, pp. 204–17.

Geiger, B., M. Hauser, L. Hirl, R. Rosmanith and R. Zechner., 1991. Frauen-/lesbenbewegte Praxis in feministischen Printmedien. *beiträge zur feministischen theorie und praxis* 30/31, pp. 85–94.

Geiger, B. and M. Hauser., 2008. Schmökern, Nachlesen, Recherchieren: Feministische Zeitschriften in Frauenarchiven. In: L. Susemichel, S. Rudigier and G. Horak, eds. *Feministische Medien. Öffentlichkeiten jenseits des Malestreams.* Königstein im Taunus: Helmer, pp. 115–123.

Gruppe Feministische Öffentlichkeit, eds., 1992. *Femina Publica. Frauen – Öffentlichkeit – Feminismus.* Cologne: PapyRossa.

Hauser, M. and B. Geiger., 2008. Feminismus denken. Ein Blick auf feministische Theorie- und Wissenschaftszeitschriften. In: L. Susemichel, S. Rudigier and G. Horak, eds. *Feministische Medien. Öffentlichkeiten jenseits des Malestreams.* Königstein im Taunus: Helmer, pp. 151–160.

Horak, G., 2003. *Feministische Printmedien in Österreich: Bestandsaufnahme und Diskussion von Qualitätskriterien und Überlebensstrategien.* Diploma Thesis, University of Vienna.

Klaus, E., 1994. Von der heimlichen Öffentlichkeit der Frauen, In: K. Pühl, ed. *Geschlechterverhältnisse und Politik.* Frankfurt am Main: Institut für Sozialforschung, pp. 72–97.

Susemichel, L., S. Rudigier and G. Horak, eds., 2008. *Feministische Medien. Öffentlichkeiten jenseits des Malestreams.* Königstein im Taunus: Helmer.

Well, J., 2007. *Bestandsaufnahme feministischer Print- und Online-Medien in Österreich 2006/2007.* Diploma Thesis, University of Salzburg.

Hand-Made Memories: Remediating Cultural Memory in DIY Feminist Networks

Red Chidgey

> [A]mnesia about political movements is not only an inno-
> cent effect of general forgetfulness, but is socially produced,
> packaged, promulgated, and perpetuated.
> Rachel Blau DuPlessis and Ann Snitow, *The Feminist Memoir*
> *Project*

Introduction: Feminist Cultural Memory in Grassroots Media

As DuPlessis and Snitow (1998) recount in no uncertain terms in *The Feminist Memoir Project: Voices from Women's Liberation*, the State and mainstream
media do not typically guarantee collective memories of social justice movements, but subject them to distortion, domestication and erasure. Part of
feminism's cultural battle is thus to secure the role of women's movements
in popular memory (Heller 2002). Feminist media can become discursive
'weapons' in this struggle: to contest hostile framings and to put forward
counter-understandings of what feminism is, what feminism can do, and
who a feminist can be.

This chapter considers the practices and mediations of feminist cultural
memory within the micro-political sphere of DIY feminist media networks.
DIY (do-it-yourself) feminism refers to a loose network of cultural producers who draw their political coordinates from anarchism, anti-capitalism,
Riot Grrrl, animal rights and queer cultures. Deploying both residual and
emerging media forms, such as analogue and digital technologies, these
feminists mobilize low-budget resources to create participatory political
cultures and to preserve activist memory. The memory work that they establish – documenting their own social movements, critiquing dominant
media representations, and making links to broader feminist praxis – creates much-needed *counter-memories* (Foucault 1977) and sites of feminist
identification. Furthermore, these media channels (such as blogs, zines,
videos, and podcasts) enact an archival function: they move feminist memory out of the realm of the institutional and create grassroots memory texts
that are mobile, shared and networked.

Remediating Feminist Memory

I define feminist cultural memory here as the ways in which past feminist movements are discussed and understood in the present moment, through the making and consuming of cultural artefacts. In considering cultural memory it is crucial to think about the practices and contexts of *remediation*. As conceptualized by David Jay Bolter and Richard Grusin (2000), remediation analyzes how media content is shaped as it moves across medial forms, and how emerging and residual media and networks historically refashion each other. The web, for example, refashions the book, magazine, radio, film, television, diary and personal letter. As remediation is multi-directional, these analogue forms and practices are also remediated by the digital. These refashionings happen through a double logic. As media forms multiply and are linked together, a *logic of hypermediacy* heightens the forms' materiality (for example, the user is made aware they are interacting with an interface). Where traces of mediation are erased in order to give a sense of real-time presence, the *logic of immediacy* is at play (such as in the use of a webcam). Whilst hypermediacy dominates the web – with its audio-visual possibilities and hyperlinked information – both logics coexist in digital media.

Remediation is an important part of cultural memory practices. As Marianne Hirsch and Valerie Smith (2002: 9) put it, "Unlike the traditional archives of history, the archives of cultural memory consist not only of the stories, images, or documents of the past but also of the 'acts of transfer' without which we would have no access to them". How cultural memories are transmitted play an intrinsic role in how these memories are fashioned: cultural memory is socially, culturally, and medially produced. As Astrid Erll and Ann Rigney clarify, "Just as there is no cultural memory prior to mediation there is no mediation without remediation: all representations of the past draw on available media technologies, on existing media products, on patterns of representation and media aesthetics" (2009: 4).

In this chapter I explore the concept of feminist cultural memory in relation to two empirical examples: First, through a scrapbook produced by Riot Grrrl Pittsburgh member Nicole Emmenegger in 1996, which was digitized and published on her UK blog, *Jenny Woolworth's Women in Punk Blog*, in 2010. Emmenegger's cut-and-paste scrapbook is a visual record of mainstream, subcultural and personal framings of the youth feminist Riot Grrrl movement and highlights how remediation plays a key role in DIY feminist media production. My second example is the short animated video *We Are Connected by Words and Wires* (2009) by Belgian feminist Nina Nijsten. Through articulating feminist identification and action in the "here and now", I argue, this video breaks with post-feminist logics indicating the aftermath of feminism, and re-imagines a historicized and still active feminist movement on a local and transnational level.

Riot Grrrl: Disputed Memories

An important trajectory within DIY feminism, Riot Grrrl is commonly seen as "a '90s third-wave-feminist punk subculture" that "spat out the image of girlhood in raw experiments in political activism, music, art, and self-invention" (Fateman 2010). Emerging in the United States in Washington D. C. and Olympia, Washington – and soon spreading to other cities and countries – Riot Grrrl was a decentralized youth feminist movement based around punk rock. Riot Grrrls organized conferences, consciousness-raising groups and street protests, dealing with issues such as sexuality, abortion, rape, harassment, body image, eating disorders, self-harm, sexual abuse, and domestic violence. Beyond mainstream media coverage, Riot Grrrls communicated through their own media and music channels. These independent networks became even more significant once prominent figures within the movement called for a "media blackout" at the end of 1992, following inaccurate and offensive coverage of Riot Grrrl within the mainstream press (Downes 2007; Marcus 2010). Riot Grrrl reclaimed feminism and fostered a girl-positive network that was both personal and political, introducing thousands of young women, men and queers to feminism.

Whilst the network's music output has received the bulk of the journalistic and scholarly attention, Riot Grrrl was also a scene of writing, art, protest, organizing and creativity, with isolated individuals often finding new groups and support. As Emmenegger tells me, "Riot Grrrl was all about DIY and singular experience within a collective shared moment" (2011). However, multiple instances of unexamined class and race privilege – and blatant classism and racism – wore out the appeal of 'girl love' for many by the mid 1990s. As Riot Grrrl historian Julia Downes notes, "Riot grrrl has been understood as a fashion, a phase, as punk, as dead, as violent, as man-hate, and ultimately, as failure" (2007: 12). The movement is commonly assumed to have fizzled out or been abandoned by the mid 1990s.[1] From Emmenegger's perspective, "There was a time after the 'movement' died out, say from 1998–2008, when there was hardly any mention of it [in the public sphere] except in ghostly remnants such as on a Spice Girls T-shirt or as a Halloween costume" (2011).

This metaphor of "ghostly remnants" seems particularly apt when thinking about the workings of cultural memory more generally: how historical moments are cited in increasingly stereotypical, fragmented, divorced traces, to the point where media representations, historical truth and cultural fantasy become utterly entangled. The commercially produced 'Riot Grrrl' Halloween costume that Emmenegger mentions, for example, is testament to how Riot Grrrl entered public consciousness in North America and how stereotypical assumptions of the "Riot Grrrl look" perpetuated within media accounts helped produce and calcify this awareness. Similarly, 'Girl Power,' the radical slogan of girls' agency and politicization that appeared

---

1   For an overview of transnational and more recent Riot Grrrl practices in relation to zines, see the *Grrrl Zine Network* (http://grrrlzines.net).

in a Bikini Kill zine in 1991, became internationally popularized as the (commercial) slogan of the manufactured mid-1990s British girl pop band, The Spice Girls. As Downes notes, "Riot grrrls have had their messages and slogans co-opted, diluted and sold back in the form of girl-powered commodities and all-girl pop groups" (2007: 12).

Despite its underground or subcultural appeal, Riot Grrrl has not been altogether forgotten as a political movement. A renewed journalistic, commercial and archival interest in Riot Grrrl has erupted in recent years, signalled by the movement's twenty-year anniversary and its increasing institution-alization.[2] This public discourse has prompted reflection, documentation, interventions and counter-memories by Riot Grrrls and ex-Riot Grrrls. Women of colour activists have deconstructed and revisited the raced investments of whiteness and nostalgia surrounding Riot Grrrl appeals (Nguyen 2010).[3] Individual disputes concerning the 'official writing of Riot Grrrl' continue to take place on blogs, book review sites, and in newspaper articles (Fateman 2010; Wolfe 2010). And participants have deployed Web 2.0 sites to solicit a range of personal memories from others: to coincide with her Riot Grrrl historiography *Girls to the Front* (2010) Sara Marcus invited people to contribute short videos about the influence Riot Grrrl on their lives (http://www. girlstothefront.com/video.html). Similarly, members of the band Bikini Kill launched a blogging platform to collect and document multiple stories and rare ephemera of their DIY musical career with the help of their fans (http:// bikinikillarchive.wordpress.com).

My Riot Grrrl Notebook: Remediating Feminist Artefacts

Inspired by this renewed public interest in Riot Grrrl, Emmenegger created a three-part retrospective on her *Jenny Woolworth's Women in Punk Blog*, finding it "the opportune time to dig into my own archives and digitize a few lost bits of my personal riot grrl journey" (Emmenegger 2011). Her three posts include a list of Riot Grrrl archives and her digitized scraptbook (2010a); a digital version of an unfinished zine from 1996 ("with the aid of modern technology, here at last is the *Beri-Beri* lost edition!" [2010b]); and an interview with Riot Grrrl historian Sara Marcus (who was also Emmenegger's pen pal during the mid 1990s [2010c]). These posts document a vibrant, personal and mediatized legacy of Riot Grrrl, which still resonates for Emmenegger today. On uploading (and remediating) her teenage zine, she writes: "Embarrassing as it is for me to share this now,

---

2   Whilst there are too many instances of newspaper articles, films, exhibitions and books to mention here, see *Feminist Memory* (http://feministmemory.wordpress.com/2010/10/25/ riot-grrrl-media-timeline) for an ongoing, interactive chronology. Riot Grrrl has also enjoyed renewed interest in connection with Ladyfest events – transnational arts and activism festivals launched in 2000 by some of the key players of the early 1990s U. S. Riot Grrrl scene.
3   For an analysis of race and class dynamics in DIY feminist networks, see *Race Revolt* (http://www.racerevolt.org.uk), *Thread and Circuits* (http://threadandcircuits. wordpress. com), and *make/shift* (http://www.makeshiftmag.com).

Figure 1: 'Talking back' to mainstream media discourses in "my riot grrrl notebook"

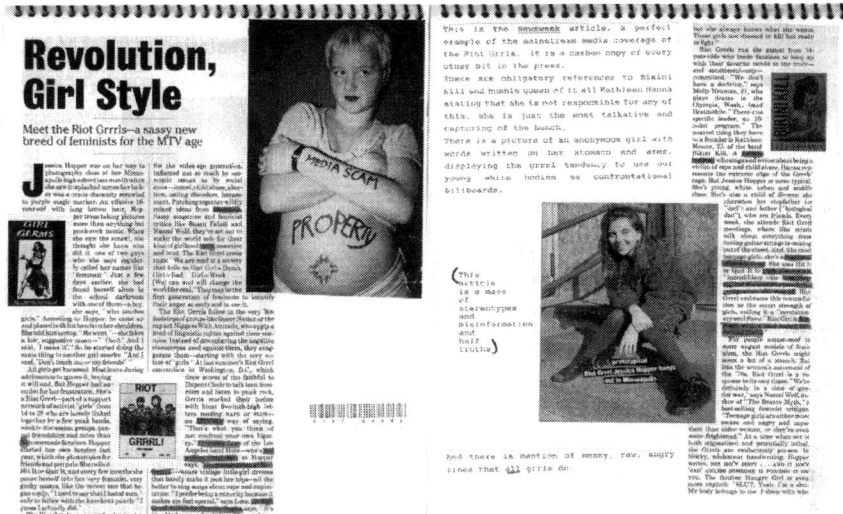

Image courtesy of Nicole Emmenegger

some fifteen years later, I have to say I am proud of what I accomplished then and still carry myself with that riot grrrl empowerment in everything I do" (Emmenegger 2010b).

Emmenegger created her Riot Grrrl notebook when she was nineteen years old, "to preserve and catalog all these various scraps" (Emmenegger 2011). A thirty-one paged spiral bound scrapbook, the front cover has "my riot grrrl notebook" doodled over strips of white masking tape and is decorated with Riot Grrrl aesthetic codes such as stars, female paper-chain characters, and the women's symbol (♀). Produced as part of Emmenegger's 'Feminist Presses' course at Antioch College in Ohio, this document enacts a personal 'talking back' to dominant discourses, and was originally shared with Emmenegger's professor, classmates and friends in its analogue form.[4]

This document is a rich historical resource: articles clipped from mainstream publications such as *Newsweek, Spin,* and *New York Times* sit alongside underground magazine offerings like *Your Flesh* and feminist coverage from *Ms Magazine* and *Off Our Backs.* All the articles are deconstructed, with sensationalist and sexist comments highlighted. The *Newsweek* article, for instance, is discussed as "a carbon copy of every other bit in the press. There are obligatory references to Bikini Kill [. . .] There is a picture of an anonymous girl with words written on her stomach and arms, displaying the grrrl tendency to use our young white bodies as confrontational billboards. And there is mention of messy, raw, angry zines that *all* grrls do. This article is a mass of stereotypes and misinformation and half truths" (see Figure 1).

---

4 See Piepmeier (2009: 29–32) for an analysis of suffragette scrapbooks in relation to DIY feminist publications.

To counteract the inaccurate, sensationalized (and deradicalized) coverage in these collected media clippings, Riot Grrrl flyers, manifestos and images were also included in the scrapbook, with Emmenegger adding clarifications to the off-page context and resonance of this cultural ephemera.[5] Like zines, which also document 'the movement', Emmenegger's scrapbook acts as an important counter-memory to mainstream media accounts by contesting patronizing frames of teenage rebellion and providing narratives against trend-orientated approaches in the press. As Emmenegger comments, "The mainstream press needed a leader, a manifesto, a clear path and that is just not what it was about" (2011).

As a form of feminist memory, it is not only the content of the scrapbook that is significant here, but also the process of digitization. Whilst Alison Piepmeier notes that "zine creators don't necessarily view blogs as a replacement for zines but, instead, as a supplement, a format that's doing something slightly different" (2009: 14), I want to emphasize how DIY feminists are using strategies of remediation to bring their hand-made artefacts online, in ways which maintain (to some extent) the 'feel' of their cut-and-paste culture.

When digitizing her scrapbook, Emmenegger scanned the document in full colour including the visual trace of the spiral binding holding the notebook together. She then uploaded her file onto the digital publishing platform *Issuu* (http://issuu.com) in a format which allows the pages to be flipped through in a codex form, mimicking, as far as possible, the experience of holding the scrapbook in one's hand. This process enacts logics of immediacy and hypermediacy: the digitization of the scrapbook is muted in the interface (the flip-book feel of the viewing medium providing a different reading experience to a rigid, downloaded PDF file, for example) whilst the juxtaposition between the yellowing pages of the document and the de-temporalized internet platform hosting it (where documents do not physically age or deteriorate) serves to emphasize the historical materiality and 'aura' of the original artefact.[6]

Through choosing a process of digital remediation which draws on the DIY impulse towards sharing documents and creating embodied media forms (Piepmeier 2009), this act of archiving and transmission is embedded within the "perceptual frames, affective attachments, [and] ideological pregivens" (Straw 2007: 3) of the hands-on maker culture from which it originates, whilst also embracing the representational and archiving possibilities of the digital.[7] Such strategies lend legitimacy to the counter-memories being archived on Emmenegger's blog.

---

5   Such texts need to be contextualized, interpreted and triangulated with other sources to ensure their historical veracity.

6   Websites can show signs of aging, however, through pages or items no longer accessible to the server, as flagged by 'page not found' or 'image not available' messages.

7   Such remediation techniques illustrate peer-led methods for capturing, storing and transmitting feminist ephemera online, reflecting the embodied, cultural economies behind the artefacts' production and reception. PDFs (Portable Document Format) also have important transmission and archiving roles. As my correspondence with Nijsten

We are connected by Words and Wires: Re-Imagining Feminist Histories

Figure 2. Remediating cultural memory to activate feminist participation. Slides from We Are Connected by Words and Wires

Image courtesy of Nina Nijsten

Nina Nijsten's short animated film, *We Are Connected by Words and Wires*, similarly takes the themes of legacies and participation as its core message. Consisting of sixteen illustrated slides edited to a self-made soundtrack, this three minute film provides a definition of DIY feminism ("We can do, make, and organise anything. We don't have to be 'professionals'"), alongside a visualization of the maker's personal history within the scene and references to 'sister' feminist history actions past and present.

This is also a story of activation. The filmmaker is shown surrounded by zines and books, believing "the diy feminist movement was active long ago and far away" (see Figure 2). New media is then depicted as helping to forge cross-border connections between the still thriving movement, as the filmmaker-protagonist finds feminist groups and publications via the internet and starts local actions of her own – learning that she too "can participate". Residual (that is, 'old-fashioned' and analogue) media forms such as letters, zines, cassettes and hand-drawn comics are also shown as communication tools between feminists, demonstrating some low-cost entry points for producing feminist media. To rally counter-memories against the myth of post-feminism, Nijsten illustrates an annotated map of the contemporary feminist network, citing a range of zines, groups and events such as Ladyfest (South Africa), *Fallopian Falafel* (Israel), *Jawbreaker* (Philippines), *cyber-femin-club* (Russia), *Mujeres Creando* (Bolivia), and *Cherry Bomb Comics* (New Zealand) as examples of a new transnational feminist movement (see Figure 3).

---

attests to, PDFs can be considered "closer to hand-made/printed zines," being "easier to print and easier to save on a computer," and therefore "more tangible" (Nijsten 2011b). Digital archiving projects might do well to combine both formats: the presentation aspect of flipbooks and the archival and circulatory strengths of downloadable PDFs.

Figure 3. Emerging and residual media are used in DIY feminist networks to communicate globally. Slides from We Are Connected by Words and Wires

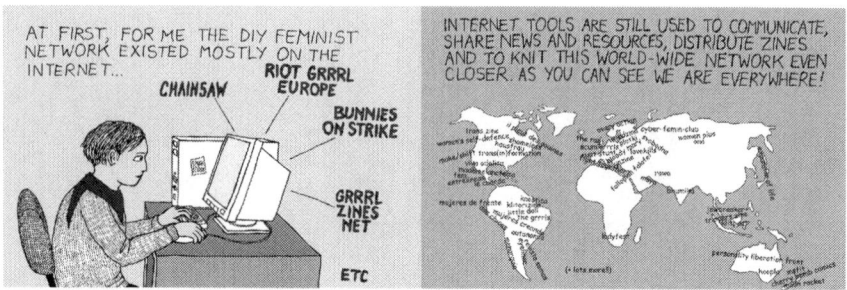

Image courtesy of Nina Nijsten

An amateur production, Nijsten's video documents cultural reference points that opened up DIY feminism for her personally. By citing little known groups and publications, the filmmaker also creates the seeds of a feminist memory consciousness. This is not straightforward representation, however. The animation showing Nijsten sitting amongst her books (Figure 2), name-checks publications like *Girl Germs* (an early Riot Grrrl zine), *Suffragettes To She-Devils: Women's Liberation and Beyond* (a visual history of feminist graphic design), *Notes from Underground: Zines and the Politics of Alternative Culture* (an academic study of zine networks), *The Power of Feminist Art* (an analysis of 1970s feminist art in the United States), and "Dolle Mina," which refers to the *Het Rode Boekje Van De Vrouw(en)* ("The Little Red Book of Women/Woman", a liberationist text by the Belgian feminist group Dolle Mina published in the early 1970s). The slide also shows a book about anarchist-feminist Emma Goldman (1869–1940) that was not itself based on any text that Nijsten had read or come across, but was included to pay homage to an inspiring historical figure and to underscore the anarcha-feminist roots of today's DIY political cultures (Nijsten 2011a).

Furthermore, the oversized "Riot Grrrl Herstory" book shown in this slide may have been influenced by a recent publication at the time (Monem 2007), but the title and cover is pure fabrication (Nijsten 2011a). To interpret this further, the "herstory" title (which does not appear on any mainstream books on Riot Grrrl) links Riot Grrrl to radical feminists of the late 60s onwards, who re-inscribed "history" as "her story" to draw attention to the male bias of the historical record. Furthermore, the cover image of a woman of colour tacitly draws attention to hegemonic and repetitive accounts of Riot Grrrl in which women of colour's voices and participation are routinely marginalized or erased. For example, in the handful of books related to Riot Grrrl that have been commercially published in recent years, many sideline the voices and input of women of colour, and all depict only white women (predominately from the band Bikini Kill) on their covers – evoking Emmenegger's 1996 scrapbook commentary on the *Newsweek* article, cited above, about the whiteness of Riot Grrrl in its tactics and in the media imagination; a critique long-held by women of colour within the Riot Grrrl movement yet still not secured within Riot Grrrl historiography.

We Are Connected by Words and Wires is a mobile text. Nijsten's video has received close to 800 hits on YouTube at the time of writing and has been screened internationally at grassroots and institutional settings such as the Civil Media UnConference (Austria), Ladyfest Liège (Belgium), Gender Fuck Festival (Czech Republic), London Lesbian Gay Film Festival (U. K.) and the Elles Tournent feminist film festival (Belgium) (Nijsten 2011a). Its title, "We Are Connected by Words and Wires," not only reflects the techno-logics increasingly associated with third wave feminism (Garrison 2000), but also speaks to the logic of immediacy. As Bolter and Grusin (2000: 226) note with regards to remediation, "the promise of 'connecting to other people' suggests transparency – breaking through the medium to achieve human contact". By foregrounding the "happening here and now" aspect of do-it-yourself culture, Nijsten deploys this logic of immediacy as a source of activation, alongside the hypermediality of a mediatized activist culture. This double logic works to promote contemporary feminist identification, participation, and cultural production in the present moment, whilst creating links to an international politicized and historicized feminist past.

Concluding Remarks: Feminist Cultural Memory as Political Consequence

Activists have greater possibilities for researching, producing, and disseminating their own memory texts with Web 2.0 innovations. By deploying emerging and residual media forms via the internet, for example, DIY feminists create personal and remediated cultural memories that serve to reinvigorate feminist engagement in the present through providing links to historical-based resources around suffrage, civil rights, women's liberation, anarchism and riot grrrl. By sharing personal stories of feminist activation and creativity, DIY feminists also narrate the cultural reference points that signal 'inclusion,' 'authenticity' and 'participation' in these networks.

In Nijsten's video, Emmenegger's scrapbook, and countless other feminist zines, blogs, and grassroots projects, tentative counter-memories are therefore produced, cited, and circulated, creating new archives of meaning whilst also revisiting residual investments. These counter-memories draw on mainstream media accounts, challenge them, and further appropriate commercial platforms such as YouTube and Issuu to popularize and disseminate personal narratives held in a collectivity.

While this chapter has considered the techniques and implications of remediation, it is important to sound a broader note in this chapter's conclusion. An uneven terrain, feminist cultural memory embraces the experiences, artefacts, stories and also silences – from the personal to the institutional, and always mediated – that shape identities, structures of belonging, and affective economies. As such, memories have political consequences.

As third wave feminist histories are still in the making, further documentation and assessment is needed to account for *what versions of the feminist past, present and future are being circulated, by which actors, for what purposes, and with what resources.* As feminist cultural memory is a site of contestation, it is important to consider how conflicts are narrated and legitimated within these networks, especially when these narratives pass into institutions and are further secured. Challenges ought to be made to DIY feminist narratives around *empowerment* and *participation*, for example, whenever celebratory story arcs risk muting antagonism from within.

As to the role of feminist cultural memory in activist networks more broadly, mediated memory can help map resistance struggles and offer feminists much needed resources to imagine alternative possibilities. Remediating political memory can also help alleviate strains of amnesia and déjà vu under late capitalism, forces which threaten present day mobilizations for social justice by robbing us of our feminist heritage and diverse connections to the past.

References

Bolter, J. D. and Grusin, R., 2000. *Remediation: Understanding New Media.* Cambridge, MA: The MIT Press.

Downes, J., 2007. Riot Grrrl: The Legacy and Contemporary Landscape of DIY Feminist Cultural Activism. In: N. Monem, ed. 2007. *Riot Grrrl: Revolution Girl Style Now!* London: Black Dog Publishing, pp. 12–49.

DuPlessis, R. B. and Snitow, A. eds., 1998. *The Feminist Memoir Project: Voices from Women's Liberation.* New York: Three Rivers Press.

Emmenegger, N., 2011. [email] (Personal communication, 27 September 2011).

Emmenegger, N., 2010a. Riot grrrl, part 1: Archives, *Jenny Woolworth's Women in Punk Blog* [online]. 30 September 2010. Available at: <http://www.jennywoolworth.ch/deardiary/2010/09/riot-grrrl-part-1> [Accessed 1 November 2011].

Emmenegger, N., 2010b. Riot grrrl, part 2: Me and the 'Zines, *Jenny Woolworth's Women in Punk Blog* [online]. 19 October 2010. Available at: <http://www.jennywoolworth.ch/deardiary/2010/10/riot-grrrl-part-2-me-and-the-zines> [Accessed 1 November 2011].

Emmenegger, N., 2010c. Riot grrrl, part 3: Sara Marcus Interview, *Jenny Woolworth's Women in Punk Blog* [online]. 27 October 2010. Available at: <http://www.jennywoolworth.ch/deardiary/2010/10/riot-grrrl-part-3-sara-marcus-interview> [Accessed 1 November 2011].

Erll, A. and Rigney, A., 2009. Cultural Memory and its Dynamics. In: A. Erll and A. Rigney, eds. 2009. *Mediation, Remediation, and the Dynamics of Cultural Memory.* Berlin: Walter de Gruyter, pp. 1–11.

Fateman, J., 2010. Her Jazz, *Bookforum* [online]. September/October/November 2010. Available at: <http://www.bookforum.com/inprint/017_03/6325> [Accessed 1 November 2011].Foucault, M., 1977. *Language, Counter-memory, Practice: Selected Essays and Interviews.* Translated and edited from French by D. F. Bouchard and S. Simon. Ithaca, NY: Cornell University Press.

Garrison, E. K., 2000. US Feminism-Grrrl style! Youth (Sub)cultures and the Technologics of the Third Wave. *Feminist Studies,* 26(1), pp. 141–170.

Heller, D., 2002. Found Footage: Feminism Lost in Time. *Tulsa Studies in Women's Literature,* 21(1), pp. 85–98.

Hirsch, M. and Smith, V., 2002. Feminism and Cultural Memory: An Introduction. *Signs: Journal of Women in Culture and Society,* 28(1), pp. 1–19.

Marcus, S., 2010. *Girls to the Front. The True Story of the Riot Grrrl Revolution.* New York: Harper Perennial.

Monem, N. ed., 2007. *Riot Grrrl: Revolution Girl Style Now!* London: Blackdog Publishing.

Nguyen, M. T., 2010. Punk Planet 40 (Nov/Dec 2000), *Thread and Circuits: an archive of wayward Youth* [online]. 28 March 2010. Available at: <http://threadandcircuits.wordpress.com/2010/03/28/58> [Accessed 1 November 2011].

Nijsten, N., 2011a. [email] (Personal communication, 23 September 2011).

Nijsten, N., 2011b. [email] (Personal communication, 22 October 2011).

Nijsten, N., 2009. *We Are Connected by Words and Wires* [online]. 6 March 2009. Available at: <http://www.youtube.com/user/ninanijsten#p/u/16/yoa _0WydUZQ> [Accessed 1 November 2011].

Piepmeier, A., 2009. *Girl Zines: Making Media, Doing Feminism.* New York: New York University Press.

Straw, W., 2007. Embedded Memories. In: C. R. Acland, ed. 2007. *Residual Media.* London: University of Minnesota Press, pp. 3–15.

Wolfe, A., 2010. Reconsidering Riot Grrrl, *New York Press* [online]. 28 September 2010. Available at: <http://www.nypress.com/article-21671-reconsidering-riot-grrrl.html> [Accessed 1 November 2011].

GENDER JAMMING. Or: Yes, We Are.
Culture Jamming and Feminism

Verena Kuni

"We're Not Feminists" (Lasn 1999)

Imagine: A video. A man in his kitchen, being interviewed. He's showing us a jar with jam: "My breakfast consists of a slice of bread, butter, and cyberfeminist marmalade. That's how I connect art and life." However, if this is the answer, what was the question?

Imagine: A billboard poster. A woman reclined. She's naked. Very reminiscent of well-known paintings, female nudes from art history. However, why is her face covered by a gorilla mask?

Imagine: A magazine ad. A model posing with a cigarette. Young, attractive, her eyes meeting ours with a perky look. However, is this really – as the text of the advertisement tells us – Ljubica Gerovac, the Yugoslavian revolutionary heroine?

We will come back to the magazine ad, the billboard poster, the video later – and of course to the questions as well. But first of all, let us start with jam.

1   Why Jam – And What Is It Good For

If we want to think about "Culture Jamming and Feminism", we must indeed first of all take a closer look at what "culture jamming" means, and how culture jamming works. The term "culture jamming" is generally associated with strategies, tactics and practices directed at the dominant politics of representation, in order to subvert and thereby fight the latter. More specifically, it is often used to denote anti-consumerist and/or anti-corporate critical action against advertisements in mass media and public spaces. Both the closer and the broader definition may already seem quite appropriate for bringing feminist critique into practice: Not only have practices – as well as theoretical reflexions – directed at the dominant politics of representation always played a considerable role in feminism, from its early beginnings up until today; we may also assume that, within this framework, critical involvement with commercial imagery in general and especially with advertisments should have its stance as well.

So how come we have to read from a guy named Kalle Lasn that culture jammers are "not feminists"?

To answer this question, it makes sense to dig a little deeper: to further trace back the history of the term and its interpretations. While Kalle Lasn's book *Culture Jam*, published in 1999, may have contributed to make culture jamming – both the term and practices it represents – even more prominent in today's media and pop culture, its first accounts go back to the 1980s, or more precisely: to a record released in 1985 by the U. S. band Negativland. A major part of the release, titled *JamCon '84*, is devoted to interviews and recordings from the titular "Jammer Convention", and the term is not only dropped in the audio itself, but also featured in the second track, "Crosley Bendix Reviews JamArt and Cultural Jamming" (Negativland 1985). Negativland, which began as an experimental band working with sounds appropriated from different sources – in its early years, to a considerable amount from radio broadcasts – and, together with live performances, also producing its own related radio broadcasts, had drawn the term from an "info-war" practice known as "radio jamming": a technique for disturbing transmissions from undesired sources, i. e. "enemy stations" or political opponents.

Of course at that time the very practices coined with "culture jamming" had neither been limited to audio, nor were they generally unknown. Strategies and techniques of "mixing original materials . . . with things taken from corporately owned mass culture and the world around" (Negativland 2012) can be easily traced back to the beginnings of early corporate capitalism and early popular mass media culture. Among the more prominent examples are pieces by artists affiliated with the Dada movement (i. e. Hannah Höch, Kurt Schwitters) or political photo-montages like those John Heartfield created for the *Arbeiter Internationale Zeitung*, as well as many of the media productions of the Situationist International, and for the following period from the late 1960s onwards, we can point to activists and groups later subsumed under umbrella terms like "Yippies" (Hofmann 1980; Krassner 2003), "Kommunikationsguerilla" (autonome a.f.r.i.k.a.-gruppe, Blissett and Brünzels 1997), and others.

Seen from this background, we may rightly ask what led to the new career of both the term and the related practices in the late 1990s up until today. Obviously Kalle Lasn's book has contributed to this career – yet it would be naive to think of it as a main cause. Rather, we will have to look at developments in the economical, technological and socio-political field: Not only had this period seen a rise in what is usually subsumed under the umbrella term "globalization" – the expansive strategies of corporate capitalism fuelled for example by the fall of Soviet Union and other political transformations in communist and now post-communist countries – but also the rise of digital media and information network technologies. In fact, the latter particularly contributed in many ways to bringing a good amount of both the tools and the materials decisive for contemporary practices of culture jamming to those involved.

2   The F-word, Again

Indeed, Lasn too was looking back rather than forward when he published his book *Culture Jam* in 1999, which is to a large extent based upon his own experiences as a communication designer and creative director having undergone a Saul-to-Paul transformation, leaving the corporate market to found his own "culture jamming agency", the now-famous *Adbusters* magazine. Together with a more general definition of culture jamming, the first paragraphs introduce the imaginary community of culture jammers as a "diverse tribe" consisting of

> "born-again Lefties to Green entrepreneurs to fundamentalist Christians who don't like what television is doing to their kids; from punk anarchists to communications professors to advertising executives searching for a new role in life. Many of us are longtime activists who in the midst of our best efforts suddenly felt spiritually winded. For us feminism had run out of steam, the environmental movement no longer excited, the fire no longer burned in the belly of the Left, and youth rebellion was looking more and more like an empty gesture inspired by Nike. We were losing." (Lasn 1999: xii)

The statement – mainly conceived as a background to let the light of culture jamming shine even brighter ("Then we had an idea") – contains already much of what we'll later be confronted with whenever Lasn mentions the f-word. While the eager reader will also find an acknowledgement of the merits of 1970s feminism, this is only the reverse side of the very same coin: for Lasn, feminism is something outdated – an attitude to be overcome if we seriously want to look towards positive future perspectives. The smart cultural jammer is already ahead in terms of socio-political consciousness as well as in creating more appropriate tools for fighting the "real enemy", global corporate capitalism.

Yet, there is one notable exception Lasn is mentioning in the very chapter starting with the already quoted bland statement, "we're not feminists" (Lasn 1999: 117) – which is for reasons to which we shall come back later also worth mentioning here: the "insightful audacity of a few eco- and cyberfeminists – Suzi Gablik, Donna Haraway and Sadie Plant among them" (Lasn 1999: 117–18). It may be added that this is perhaps also because his writings seem to owe more than the author may admit to these three.

However, when digging his book for related perspectives brought into practice, our basket will remain empty. Neither the case studies nor the *Adbusters* campaigns introduced give any hint of a conscious acknowledgement of gender-sensitive issues or strategies for fighting for example ongoing sexisms in marketing and advertisements.

Bad enough perhaps, but it gets even worse. For while we may or may not consider Lasn's book as a reliable source, we can hardly ignore that it is kind of representative indeed of most of the prominent resources usually recommended to those interested in the field. This includes some of the more prominent books dealing with similar matters and looking at strategies of resistance against global brands – such as Naomi Klein's *No Logo*

(2000), Paul Kingsnorth's *One No, Many Yeses* (2004), or Matt Mason's *The Pirate's Dilemma. How Youth Culture is Reinventing Capitalism* (2008), in none of which can we find "feminism", "feminist" or "gender" as issues worth mentioning in the index. Which does not necessarily mean feminism and gender would remain untouched throughout; however, they are not closely examined as forces of cultural jamming practice. Also tracing several of the prominent websites and blogs featuring news about and examples of cultural jamming – i. e. *Rebel Art* or *Wooster Collective* – will likewise lead to poor results: "feminism", "feminist" or "gender" are not to be found in the tag list, so to speak.

Yet, as so often, it would be wrong to conclude from these prominent publications that gender issues are not on cultural jammer's agendas, or that there is no feminism in cultural jamming. What remains invisible is not necessarily "not there".

3   ~~Why~~ Have There Been No Great Feminist Culture Jammers?

A rhetorical question, of course, because there have been, and there are quite a few examples worth mentioning here. Nevertheless, the question is chosen not only to kick the indeed somewhat strange ignorance of gender issues in the sourcebooks and sites mentioned above in the ass, but also to point out there are structural reasons for the later, which are at least partially similar to those discussed by feminist art historians like Linda Nochlin, and others (Nochlin 1971; Jones 2003). At the same time, it should also be acknowledged that in the case of culture jamming there is another, more general reason why heroes and heroines alike are difficult to be tracked and listed in books: first of all, many of the practices and actions are, at least in part, illegal – and thus it is not really adequate to carry them out under one's real name, for simple reasons of unnecessary personal risk. Secondly, a critique against the politics of branding and labelling can for good reasons also include "personal brands", heroism and the sanctuaries of authorship.

However, if we want to put some meat on the bones, it is of course possible to mention exemplary positions and examples of culture jamming that can be rightly coined as feminist – and, at the same time, also to point at publications dealing with issues of culture jamming and hereby including feminism in their discussion as well, like Joseph Heath and Andrew Potter's generally recommendable book *Nation of Rebels: Why Counterculture Became Consumer Culture* (2004). Plus, there are also other sources, such as zines, webzines and blogs, usually run by groups or individuals affiliated and/or sympathizing with feminist ideas, where examples of feminist culture jamming may pop up from time to time. And last but not least, there are also a few websites with related information about artists and groups who might indeed be related to the fem jam we're looking for.

But before going into details, we should perhaps first ask for criteria: what would we expect from a project to be subsumed under a category such as "feminist culture jamming"?

While a focus on critical action against misogynist advertisements in mass media and public spaces may be a precise match, we might claim that – seen from a feminist standpoint – it would be all too narrow as well. This is for the very reasons that feminist critique of visual culture and predominant politics of representation (Jones 2003) has shown: misogynous, derogative or "simply" misleading politics of representation and perception are generally woven so neatly into the texture of our culture that fighting against the obvious can only be one issue among others. Thus when watching out for feminist cultural jamming we will also have to include projects and strategies directed toward other areas of visual culture and other aspects of politics of representation as well.

Considering this broader scope the probability of encountering artistic projects is likely to rise: Together with art directors and other creative professionals working inside the visual and media industries, artists are certainly among the best educated and are prepared not only to analyze existing visual languages, but also to bring adequate strategies of critique into visual and media practice. In contrast to the former, who are likely to work for corporate clients rather than to start campaigns biting the hands that feed them, the latter are perhaps more likely to get involved into critical engagement – simply because the ideology of (post-)modern art includes the expectation of artists-as-critics and thus usually rewards a related attitude, at least when kept within the framework of what society usually would accept as "art." Plus (and also for the last reason) we will usually get to know simpler and more reliable information about artistic interventions, for these are more likely to be covered by the media in a professional way – and in contrast to activist's interventions, they are also in the majority of cases connectable to a real person with a real name.

If this applies to cultural jamming projects (and their authors) in general, it is even more important when it comes to feminist culture jamming, because of its generally low visibility in public media, for the very reasons stated above. At the same time, we should not feel tempted to shift our attention from feminist critique to female actors – not every person of female gender (and/or sex) engaged in culture jamming is necessarily into feminist culture jamming. Likewise, not every action dealing with representational critique – and again this is true for representational critique in general as well as for feminist representational critique – should be automatically dubbed "culture jamming". Rather, one will have to decide from case to case.

4 Fem Jam, Getting a Taste of

This being said, it may be the right time to take a look at some of the very few practical examples. If advertisements on billboards or posters in public spaces, in magazines, and in other media from TV to the internet, global acting corporate companies and major brand could be considered as core targets of culture jamming, keeping these targets in focus will of course be most appropriate. However, as argued above, widening the angle from time to time should be allowed as well.

Thus, why not start with the images we invited to imagine in the first paragraphs of our text – like the magazine ad, showing a young, attractive model posing with a cigarette? As soon as we translate the text lines accompanying the picture translated, we will realize there's been a shift. Otherwise we might ask our preferred search engine about the name Ljubica Gerovac. We learn from the text, however, that Gerovac was "charged with anti-fascist activities. Committed suicide while being arrested. Died at the age of 22." The piece is part of a series of similar "ads" launched in magazines, each combining the reproduction of a top-model shot with the dry record of Yugoslavian women who were active in the anti-fascist movement and killed, died or held in prison and who later become recognized as heroines in communist times. The name is not only placed where in the original ad the brand's name would appear, but also set in the appropriate typeface (Eiblmayr 2001).

When the Croatian artist Sanja Ivecović published her series *Gen XX* (1997) for the first time, she could be sure that the ex-Yugoslavian public would recognize both the models (all of them at that time appearing often in fashion magazines) and the names (all of them known as national heroines, closely associated with the country's communist past). However, due to the aesthetic strategy chosen, the intended shift can be easily understood by nearly anyone familiar with the visual language of fashion advertisements – indeed, it is also reported that the fashion industry itself reacted against what was initially perceived as appropriation by a Croatian "concurrent agency". Even if we consider the latter is obviously a misinterpretation failing the main intention of the artist, it may still prove the visual reading of the series as an example of successful culture jamming. It might be added that Ivecović is not the only artist from the former Yugoslavia making use of related strategies and producing works that can be aptly read under the auspices of culture jamming. Serbian artist Milica Tomic, for example, placed manipulated photos showing her in attractive clothes and make-up on the covers of glossy magazines. Only a closer look at the details will reveal she was not standing under a lamppost, but hanging from it, just as members of the anti-fascist resistance who were hung in public spaces in the 1940s (*Belgrade Remembers* 2001). Indeed, the work is not only considered to be a memory of German soldiers' cruelties, but also of Belgrade's citizens who would try to ignore these in order to proceed with their daily lives (Stokić 2006). Yet if we're looking for a clear feminist standpoint, Ivecović – who already in 1975 produced a series based on appropriated magazine ads, in this case juxtaposed with private photographs of herself sporting the same poses, and presented as unconscious mimicking of a set of learned (female) behaviour rather than as a conscious re-enactment of role models – is sincerely among those literally standing in.

From here let us switch to the next image we were invited to imagine: the billboard poster showing a reclined nude with a gorilla mask. In this case, the rather dreadful animal's head combined with what seems to be a scene all too familiar from art history – an educated visual memory will even identify the famous source, Jean Auguste Dominique Ingres' *Grand Odalisque* (1814) – is rightly pointing us to a critical reading. The same goes for the text, with its bold black and pink letters on the poster's yellow background yelling at our eyes the question: "Do women have to be naked to get into the Met.Museum?" Below what can be read as a telling answer: "Less than 5% of the artists in the Modern Art sections are women, but 85% of the nudes are female" – accomplished with the signature: "Guerrilla Girls. Conscience of the Art World" (Guerrilla Girls 1995). The precision of the piece may be debatable (Ingres' *Odalisque* is not in the Met's collection, but is owned by the Louvre; the quota may be put in doubt for it is relating of a portion of the artworks – those depicting nudes – with the sex of the artists), yet both the juxtaposition and the strong visual rhetoric are convincing. The language is for sure not sublime, but we get the message – and that's what is important here. Plus the piece has its own precision indeed, considering the fact that art museums themselves actively use very similar marketing strategies to advertise their collections and their blockbuster exhibitions, and the agencies handling this are indeed likely to propose (and realize) campaigns building upon the very mechanisms proven to be successful in consumer ads. This means that "attractive women" and female nudes are, if appropriate, among the favoured motifs – and if it's too risky to choose a photo work from the contemporary collection, the "cultured nudity" of historical paintings is always a good solution. While the billboard poster is not sincerely in the first instance a jam of museum marketing campaigns, its impact can be rightly read as hitting this target as well. Yet it is likewise fine to stay with the basic intentions of the piece: today's large museums are – in certain parts even literally – global brands, and so is the system behind it as well as its main product: the traditional concept of Western art history, including an implicit or even explicit misogyny that is still part of its "big sells" in our consumerist culture.

5   FF: Gender Jamming. Another turn of the screw

If both the magazine ad and the billboard poster turned out to be almost classical examples from the history of feminist culture jamming, then what about the video clip?

At least at a first glance, it seems likewise to operate within the familiar framework of appropriating the language and the media of commercial advertising – in this case of TV ads for household consumer products and food. The latter being presented by a male actor is not at all unusual, at least whenever it's about dairy products, cereals, jam and other breakfast food that does not need to be prepared in any complicated manner but is simply

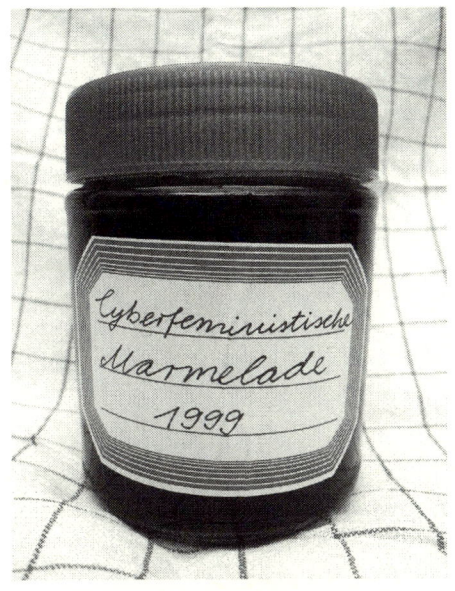

Cornelia Sollfrank:
Cyberfeminist Jam (1999)

A verbatim example of a cyberfeminist jam, featured in
Sollfrank's video clip from the
same year. It is disguised insofar
as the video's English subtitles
translating the German "Cyber-
feministische Marmelade" into
"cyberfeminist marmalade" are
somewhat misleading – for in
the jar and on the bread is tasty
raspberry-redcurrant spread.

eaten (which does not necessarily mean a presumed gender equality among
target customers – rather, it would tell the housewife buying the jam and
serving it will make the husband and herself happy without any additional
efforts needed, and the single male, just as the exceptional 'houseman', will
know the same will apply to himself as well).

However, listening to the guy telling us about his breakfast consisting
"of a slice of bread, butter, and cyberfeminist marmalade" should make us
wonder, shouldn't it? Has feminism – or a particular kind of feminism with
a strange appendix – become consumable and even tasty for men? Something to enjoy and, at least in this case, something capable of reconciling
"art and life"?

Indeed, we may rightly ask about the very special brand he is marketing here. The answer is of course in the jam – or maybe more precisely, it's
the cyberfeminist ingredients that make the jam special.

As it turns out, the clip is just an excerpt of a longer piece featuring
statements from a variety of people of different ages, genders and nation-
alities, all answering a question posed by the author of the clip: "How has
cyberfeminism changed your life?" The answers to this question are generally positive (except for one, a ". . . dunno . . . has not really changed anything . . ."), and the interviewees all seem to be serious – only that in the
majority of cases their answers point to results sounding somewhat ab-
surd. Thus, if we consider the clip as an advertisement for cyberfeminism,
we might wonder even more.

The solution to this riddle is still to be found in the jam – and of course
in the special brand combining feminism with its strange appendix. Yet
perhaps this is not exactly the way Kalle Lasn would have put it, claim-

ing instead that cyberfeminists (together with eco-feminists) could refresh the "old feminism" he preferred to sneeze at (in contrast to his positively mentioned authorities by the way, none of whom has ever dropped arguments against feminism – rather all of them relate to "old feminism(s)" as something that laid the groundwork for further developments).

When Cornelia Sollfrank produced the clip in 1999 to become part of a small series of media productions to bring the message of cyberfeminist diversity to the people, cyberfeminism itself had already a history – and consisted of a network of people (indeed of different age, gender, nationality and profession) including a far broader variety of positions than those of the two authors mentioned by Lasn, Donna Haraway (coined as cyberfeminist for her famous "Manifesto for Cyborgs," 1989/1991) and Sadie Plant (who coined the term cyberfeminist in her book *zeros + ones*, 1997).

Accordingly, a broad variety of approaches and methods had been brought into theory and practice – among these those favoured by the members of the Old Boys Network, "the first cyberferminist international", of which Sollfrank was a founding member (OBN 1998; 1999; 2002). Indeed, already the name (Old Boys Network) and one of its first manifestations, the *100 anti-theses* published on the occasion of the First Cyberfeminist International Conference that took place in the context of *documenta X* in Kassel, can provide a hint to its relation with feminist culture jamming: first, the programmatic appropriating and queering of the name, traditional format and strategy of old boys' networks (usually known for their implicit and/ or explicit misogyny). Second, there is the appropriation and queering of one of the most prominent formats of the political and artistic movement's public manifestations, the manifesto. While an example the latter, the *100 anti-theses* explicitly avoids any serious definition of cyberfeminism(s) in order to list one hundred statements about what cyberfeminism is not (from "1. cyberfeminism is not a fragrance", through "7. cyberfeminism ist kein gruenes haekeldeckchen", "20. sajbrfeminizm nige nesto sto znam da je", and "65. cyberfeminismo no es una banana", to "100. cyberfeminism has not only one language"; OBN 1997), thus pointing to the necessity of diversity and difference. The Old Boys Network has tried to develop methods and formats to bring this idea of diversity and difference into practice within the framework of a society in transformation under the impact of digital network technologies and media (including problems and potentials), and by using as well as reflecting digital network technologies and media.

But how far may we speak of "gender jamming", as the title of this chapter would suggest, as a further development or "turn-of-the-screw(s)" of feminist culture jamming? More generally, we should assume gender jamming to slightly shift the perspective of both target(s) and strategies not only by looking at the multiple relationships between (the politics of) sex(ing) and gender(ing) – for these are on the feminist agenda, and are thus also on the agenda of feminist cultural jamming already. Rather, we will think of perspectives more specifically brought in by and with the more recent developments of gender studies, queer studies and "post-gender studies" (the latter related to what has been coined as "postgenderism", yet not necessarily identifying with a trans-humanist position, as claimed for example by Dvorsky and Hughes 2008).

More specifically, however, at least the gender jamming brought into practice by the Old Boys Network and its members for good purposes built upon feminist culture jamming to implement another turn of the screw indeed. While rejecting (and jamming) the high expectations against cyberfeminism as a theory, practice and "high art" of transforming feminism into a cultured consumable for a post-feminist digerati generation, at the same time gender issues were addressed in an unmistakable openness towards people of all genders, but with one rule clearly defined: everybody could become a member of OBN and take part in the network, as long as s/he calls herself a woman ("bearded or not", her sex, sexual preferences, etc., notwithstanding; see i. e. Kuni 2003). Which is, to sum up the jam, not just another example for feminist cultural jamming or cyberfeminist gender jamming, but should be one of the (if not "the") most important ingredients for any kind of feminist culture'n'gender jam.

References

autonome a.f.r.i.k.a.-gruppe, Blissett, L. and Brünzels, S., 1997. *Handbuch der Kommunikationsguerilla.* Berlin: Assoziation A.

Dvorsky, G., and Hughes, J., 2008. Postgenderism: Beyond the Gender Binary[online]. Available at: <http://ieet.org/archive/IEET-03-PostGender.pdf> [accessed 12 February 2012].

Eiblmayr, S. ed., 2001. *Sanja Ivecović. Personal Cuts.* Vienna: Triton.

Guerrilla Girls, 1995. *Confessions of the Guerrilla Girls.* New York: HarperCollins.

Haraway, D., 1989. A Manifesto for Cyborgs. Science, Technology, and Socialist Feminism in the 1980s. *Socialist Review* 80, pp. 65–108. Reprinted in: D. Haraway, , 1991. *Simians, Cyborgs and Women. The Reinvention of Nature.* New York: Routledge, pp. 149–181.

Heath, J. and Potter, A., 2004. *Nation of Rebels: Why Counterculture Became Consumer Culture.* New York: HarperCollins.

Hofmann, A., 1980. *Soon to be a Major Motion Picture.* New York: Perigee Books.

Jones, A. ed., 2003. *The feminism and visual culture reader.* London and New York: Routledge.

Kingsnorth, P, 2004. *One No, Many Yeses: A Journey to the Heart of the Global Resistance Movement.* London: Simon & Schuster.

Klein, N., 2000. *No Logo.* London: Flamingo.

Krassner, P., 2003. *Confessions of a raving, unconfined nut: misadventures in the counter-culture.* London: Simon & Schuster.

Kuni, V., 2003. 'Are There Any Women Here Today?' Beyond the Stone Butch Blues: Fe/Male Troubles Revisited from a (Cyber)Feminist Point of View. In: N. Höchtl and S. Van Rossenberg, S., eds. *trans/gender*. Rotterdam: Piet Zwart Institute, pp. 10–20.

Lasn, K., 1999. *Culture Jam. The Uncooling of America*. New York: Eagle Brook.

Liebl, F. and Düllo, T., 2005. *Cultural Hacking. Kunst des Strategischen Handelns*. Wien and New York: Springer.

Negativland, 1985. *JamCon '84. Over the Edge, Vol. I*. Taylor/Tx.: SST.

Negativland, n. d. *Negativland Bio* [online]. Available at: <http://negativland.com/index.php?opt=bio&subopt=neglandbio> [Accessed 12 February 2012].

Nochlin, L., 1971. Why Have There Been No Great Women Artists? *ARTnews*, January, pp. 22–39 and 67–71.

Old Boys Network, ed., 1998. *First Cyberfeminist International. A Reader*. Hamburg: OBN.

Old Boys Network, ed., *Next Cyberfeminist International. A Reader*. Hamburg: OBN.1999.

Old Boys Network, 1997. 100 anti-theses [online]. Available at: <http://www.obn.org/reading_room/manifestos/html/anti.html> [Accessed 12 February 2012].

Plant, S., 1997. *zeros + ones. digital women + the new technoculture*. New York and London: Doubleday.

Stokić, J., 2006. Un-Doing Monoculture. Women Artists from the "Blind Spot of Europe" – the Former Yugoslavia. *ARTmargins*, March 10 [online]. Available at: <http://www.artmargins.com/index.php/archive/532-undoing-monoculture-women-artists-from-the-blind-spot-of-europe-the-former-yugoslavia> [Accessed 12 February 2012].

Websites*

Adbusters
http://www.adbusters.org
Bitch Magazine
http://bitchmagazine.org
Culture Jam (The Film)
http://www.culturejamthefilm.com
Culture Jamming
http://www.culture-jamming.de
Grassroots Feminism
http://www.grassrootsfeminism.net
Grrrl Zine Network
http://grrrlzines.net
Guerrilla Girls
http://www.guerrillagirls.com

Jammin' Ladies
    http://jamming.wordpress.com
Negativland
    http://www.negativland.com
Old Boys Network
    http://www.obn.org
Rebel:Art
    http://www.rebelart.net
SubRosa
    http://www.cyberfeminism.net
Wooster Collective
    http://www.woostercollective.com

* Accessed 12 February 2012

Making Feminist Media: Feminist Media Activists Share their Views

with Jessica Hoffmann/Daria Yudacufski (*make/shift*, USA), Sonja Eismann (*Missy Magazine*, Germany), Jeanna Krömer (*AMPHI magazine*, Belarus), and Jenni (*Emancypunx*, Poland/international)

Compiled by Stefanie Grünangerl

Women's media production has played and still plays a crucial role for the feminist movement(s) by questioning given social orders, discussing gender regimes and opening up new spaces of engagement. But how do feminist media makers themselves see their commitment, the obstacles they face, and the questions of social change, participation, networking and feminist activism? The following compilation presents the views of activists involved in four different feminist media projects from Europe and the USA: Jessica Hoffmann and Daria Yudacufski are editors of *make/shift* magazine. Based in Los Angeles and launched in 2007 it aims to be a platform for contemporary feminist culture and activism by presenting all its manifold and vivid facets, by network building and by encouraging feminist engagement and participation in these multiple feminist communities. Sonja Eismann answered the questions on behalf of the German *Missy Magazine*, which was founded in 2008 to close a gap in the German-speaking magazine landscape by providing a feminist perspective on popular culture, politics and style especially addressing younger women and inspiring their interest in feminist ideas. Jeanna Krömer, founder and editor of the Belarusian web magazine *AMPHI* – which since 2008 has sought to spread discussions about gender equality and feminist thinking among a wider Russian-speaking community – talks about feminist (media) activism in post-Soviet countries. Finally, Jenni is a member of *Emancypunx Records* which started in Poland in the mid 1990s as a distro and today runs a record label, a distro and a zine library, organizes festivals (*Noc Walpurgii, Ladyfest Warsaw*, etc.) and tours, and above all is active in building and fostering DIY hc punk and anarcha-feminist activism and networks.

What kind of issues do you think need to be urgently discussed and taken up in the feminist movement(s) and in feminist media?

make/shift: We believe that feminist analysis and action needs to be applied to everything, including things like prisons, food, health, militarism, climate change, immigration struggles, education, poverty . . . on and on and on.

Image 1: Cover of Missy Magazine issue 02/12

Missy: The question of involvement of younger women – why do they so often think that feminism is something of the past and not needed by them? The gap between different feminist generations, branches and classes (older and younger feminists, feminists of colour and feminists with white privilege, queer feminists and straight feminists, feminists with or without children, working class feminists and economically privileged feminists) – we all need to reach out to each other in order to become a stronger, more visible movement again, and we need to argue with each other in a constructive way. The distribution of care work. The pay gap between men and women. Why traditionally "feminine" professions are still paid less than traditionally "male" professions. Why everybody is always talking about "die Frauenquote" [women's quota], but nobody talks about the fact that these highly paid positions are impenetrable for the vast majority of women. The question of sexism, sex work and pornography, the exploitation of (female) bodies, and why there are no simple answers like Alice Schwarzer's *PorNo* Campaign.[1] New beauty regimes and their effects on (young) women. The marginalization of Hijab-wearing women as mute "victims". The continuing oppression of women worldwide. And much, much more.

AMPHI: I think it is important to realize that feminism in Western countries and feminism in the states of the former Soviet Union have different historical backgrounds. While American and Western European women still struggled for example to be allowed to work, women in the Soviet countries not only had been working for quite a long time, but already were overburdened with it (the same can be said for issues like the right to vote or reproductive rights like legal abortion, which had already come true for Soviet women while women in Western countries only could dream of it). The Belarusian women have already been profiting from a lot of rights for a long time, but it's the duties that are still unequally distributed. Western feminist activists who want to deal with and engage in post-Soviet states must take this into account. Unfortunately quite often this doesn't happen and that's why a lot of good ideas and projects already fail at the beginning.

Another important issue which I would like to address is the issue of solidarity among women. Unfortunately, this solidarity – or rather lack of solidarity – still remains a problem, even among feminist communities: everybody is fighting on her own and not together.

Emancypunx Rec: As mentioned above, there are a lot of issues that need to be debated. It also depends much on the scenes, countries, etc. For example, within feminist environments based in Poland the issues of racism or ableism get almost no attention. Personally I would love to hear more debates about our own responsibilities. How we ourselves strengthen the status quo and what is our role in maintaining patriarchal and other oppressive regimes and social orders. I also miss a broader view on society's constructions and interdependency. Some people treat feminism as a way of self-realization only. There is this fear on my side that the feminist movement will end up as a "movement" of individuals and that the professionalization and "NGOization" will go further. I also see that a part of the feminist movement is highly competitive, as it's often linked to workplaces. So the ones who are getting access to those resources or/and to power positions (for example as representatives of a minority group) are becoming elitist and are sometimes not interested in involving others if they don't need them for some reason (for example as clients or a resource). Academic feminism is no exception.

---

1   Alice Schwarzer is the founder and editor of the German feminist magazine *Emma* (since 1977) which is also known for its campaigns including the aforementioned *PorNO* campaign promoting a strict anti-pornography agenda (see http://www.emma.de/kampagnen/grosse-themen-pornografie/).

It would also be great to sometimes have a more international perspective and communication within feminist movements, but without the assumption that the situations or movement principles and beliefs are everywhere the same.

What are the biggest challenges in producing alternative feminist media (e. g. in relation to collaboration, self-organization, alternative economies, participation in terms of inclusion/exclusion)?

make/shift: We feel really lucky to be able to work in a partnership where we have similar sensibilities around process, what we want to represent, and everything. For us, the real challenge is time – balancing this volunteer/after-hours work with everything else our lives contain (work, family, etc.).

Missy: The lack of money. This is truly the most adverse issue that we are dealing with on a daily basis. Collaboration with other women is fine, sometimes nearly perfect; feedback from other media is a lot of times overwhelmingly positive, but there is never enough money or enough time to really devote yourself to your feminist media project, because you have to earn part of your money elsewhere. Big companies still do not want to place ads in a magazine that tells women they are beautiful in all colours and sizes, just as they are, instead of telling them to be insecure and to buy lots of commodities that will make them feel less imperfect.

AMPHI: The biggest challenge for us is the lack of money and also the need to arrange our feminist media activism with earning our living and our personal living circumstances. If my partner weren't an activist and feminist himself who supports me financially but also in having the time for the project and thus enabling me to work on our magazine, it would have died a long time ago. And of course this project is only possible because of various funds which from time to time have supported it financially – thanks to them.

Image 2: Logo of Emancypunx Records

© Emancypunx Records

Emancypunx Rec: Networks are the core of independent publishing. Distribution networks like in DIY hc punk do not really exist in feminist environments. Also trades are not common; that's why money plays a much bigger role. This is definitely an excluding factor. The publishing houses usually use commercial channels or they distribute themselves, which means being a "center" with a group of "clients". Networking with similar projects is not that common. That also means that in the end those initiatives are mostly known rather locally, and interaction is limited and rather service oriented. A dream would be a DIY feminist network with a thin line between the ones creating, publishing, "consuming" and distributing. It would be great to have more sort of alternative models, where access to financial resources would play a smaller role. But of course it's a question of our goals: if we want to simply integrate feminism into the existing structures or if we want to create different sorts of economies and relationships among people.

Which role do you think feminist media do/should play in creating and negotiating participatory spaces and networks? Which strategies do you think would be most effective to create, maintain and strengthen these participatory spaces and networks? And in respect to your own project(s): how important is it for you to enable participation and to build up networks with others (media makers, activists, etc.)?

Image 3: Cover of make/shift issue 11, spring-summer 2012

make/shift: We feel that relationships and relationship-building are crucial. We started the magazine already having multiple kinds of relationships in different feminist communities, and have built more intentional relationships through the process of making the magazine. We hope we are providing a space for different feminist voices to be in conversation and to connect, and also to offer readers opportunities to engage in feminist action and to connect with each other through things like our "Participate" column, where we post many different forms of opportunities for involvement, from calls for submission to invitations to volunteer or join a feminist activity group. We don't see ourselves as playing any kind of lead or expert role in building up networks, but we do try to document and connect networks that do exist, and to constantly participate in building relationships with readers, contributors, people and projects profiled in the magazine, and the many feminist communities of which we are all part.

Missy: This depends on the kind of media. As for *Missy Magazine*, with its focus on pop culture and DIY politics, it deems us extremely import to interact with our readers, to create (new) networks and spaces for feminist women, and to empower them to become (politically) active themselves. But I also believe in the power of reading theory, and forming the "bond of reading".

AMPHI: Having the chance to get feedback from and to exchange experiences with other feminist media producers and activists about our project would be very important to us. We already do have this sort of exchange with other media producers from the Caucasian region and Russia, but the exchange with colleagues from Europe and America is still missing and not working so well. I would be interested in attending and also recommending to others conferences, workshops or training courses which enable such an exchange and networking with others and which promote and talk about feminist media production, and I wish I would have more opportunities (and time) to do all of this.

Emancypunx Rec: Concerning music and culture, one of the main attempts of *Emancypunx* was the creation of participatory spaces for feminist/queer voices, self-organizing, and networking. Such spaces are/were temporal like festivals and shows, but also continuing like the creation of a cultural center in Warsaw. Sharing knowledge is an important strategy to start and maintain change. For example, a lot of contacts and knowledge developed within *Emancypunx Rec* activities were transferred by cooperating with new people and also by establishing a cultural center in Warsaw, where people with no experience in those fields of activity could engage and work in new areas, as the responsibilities were rotating. It's interesting to see new initiatives which use that knowledge. A precondition for development through knowledge sharing is of course that the people who get access to that shared knowledge do not privatize it again for one's own sake.

Work sharing is another useful strategy that can be helpful when there are missing capacities. An example of a work-sharing strategy is the organization of touring events, like for example the *FAQ! Festival* we organized in 2007. Through that it was possible to share a cultural program, artists with other places and organizing groups in Poland. The organizers only had to provide space and everything was mostly financed by the Warsaw event which was bigger and had more resources as the feminist scene is larger there.

The publishing of media is especially important in order to access people who we can't reach physically. *Emancypunx* as a label is pretty much international and reaches people from almost all over the world – from small villages to big towns. It's part of a worldwide DIY network. Music is not that much dependent on language, so that makes things easier. I also think it's important to publish music on records in order to keep a historical memory and to give a value to DIY cultural activities done by women/queers/feminists. Through all the years I can see that at least in the case of Poland there is a huge difference and the promotion of feminist culture was really successful.

How can feminist media production challenge and intervene into the status-quo and initiate and effect social change? Which strategies have you developed in your own project(s) to do so?

make/shift: One thing we are doing is documenting the challenges and interventions people are making in many places and in many ways. Also, radical, feminist media production in and of itself is an intervention, as we share and amplify voices and stories not found in dominant media – and the fact that we do it collaboratively, with a lot of skill-sharing and an emphasis on collective process and relationships, as well as a multiplicity of voices and perspectives.

Missy: By presenting alternative images of women/queers and empowering readers to look at their surroundings critically and to take action themselves. But we have to be realistic – we're publishers of a feminist magazine first, not activists or politicians, so the scope of our impact is somewhat limited by our job description.

AMPHI: We try to provide our readers with information and material that they otherwise couldn't get, either because it is ignored in other media (because it is too subversive, feminist, etc.) or because it had been published in foreign languages. In fact, 80% of the content of *AMPHI* are translations and 20% are self-produced texts. One example which may illustrate to you why this is important: when we worked on our issue about contraception we realized that all the information we found on Russian websites dealing with this topic was at least 3 or 4 years older than on English or German websites. We also try 1) to write as clearly and simply as possible in order that people who don't have any former knowledge about these issues still can understand what we are talking about; 2) to inform our readers, and not to judge certain developments; 3) if it's possible, to present more than one view on a specific topic; and 4) also to keep the magazine "attractive" in terms of layout and aesthetics. Our influence is rather limited, as for the moment the magazine is only subscribed to by a rather small community on a regular basis (a little bit more than 1,000 readers). But our aim and also our dream is to publish *AMPHI* as a printed and free magazine that gets distributed in waiting rooms of gynecologists, at universities, in public spaces, etc. Unfortunately this is not possible at the moment, not only because it is too expensive, but also because in Belarus every independent activity is prohibited and threatened (with penalties, prison, and in some cases even with death). Not only political activists get persecuted, but also independent journalists.

Image 4: Screenshot of AMPHI magazine

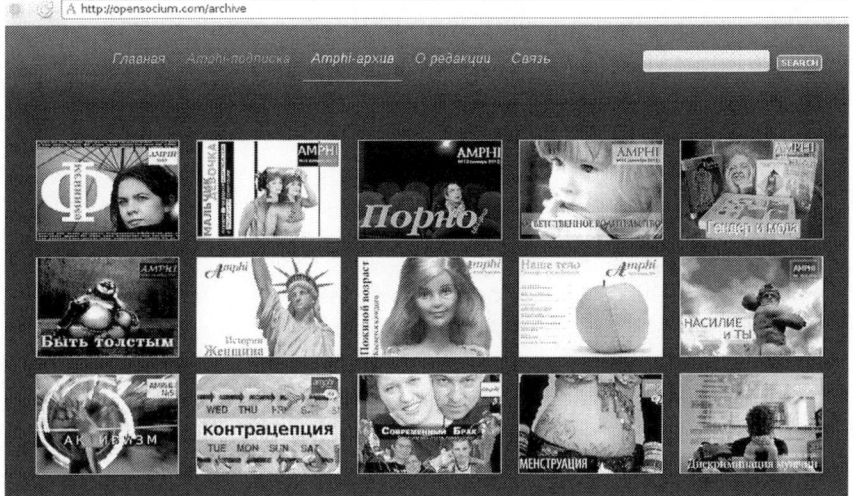

© AMPHI magazine

Emancypunx Rec: Emancypunx Records is and was involved in really many projects, so I won't be able to mention all strategies. Also some of them were successful in certain times and contexts and would not have been successful in others. To put it short: one of the main strategies is to live and give examples of how life and society could work differently. In the case of record publishing *Emancypunx* tries to promote bands and cultural performances which break with traditional gender roles and transport political messages. It all goes step by step.

How do you see the relationship between political feminist activism and alternative feminist media production? How would you describe this relationship regarding to your own project(s)?

make/shift: We think they have to be in relationship – they work together. Feminist media is a form of feminist activism, and media made *about* feminist activism while not being connected to it doesn't feel like feminist media.

Missy: Especially in German-speaking countries, there is probably not a close enough relationship as of yet. Feminist media makers and feminist activists tend to work side by side a lot of times instead of together. If you are talking about the work of political parties, then it is a different story, since there are always attempts to embrace us and we are quite wary of being instrumentalized, as no party in Germany, Austria or Switzerland qualifies as being truly feminist in our view.

AMPHI: About a year ago some (former) editors, writers and active and interested readers of *AMPHI* formed a feminist activist group called *Krapiva Belaruskaya* ("Belarusian Nettle"), which aims to foster awareness and discussion about gender issues, violence, discrimination, sexism, etc. So there definitely has been a development from a "mere" media-project into a more activist and political project. This year, for instance, we awarded prizes for the development of civil society and for the fight against discrimination and sexism in Belarus, but at the same time contrasted these positive examples by awarding anti-prizes for exceedingly sexist, macho, discriminatory and homophobic behavior.

Emancypunx Rec: I agree that feminist media production usually is a form of political activism. *Emancypunx* was from the start a political project. The idea was to cause change, while at the same time avoiding the methods and language used by typical political activist environments. *Emancypunx* rather tries to document or create facts and communicate through cultural production, performances, emotions, images or music.

Links

AMPHI magazine
     <http://www.opensocium.com>
Emancypunx
     <http://www.emancypunx.scenaonline.org>
Fem.fm
     <http://www.fem.fm>
gender_by
     <http://gender-by.livejournal.com>
Krapiva Belaruskaya
     <http://krapiva-belarus.livejournal.com>
     <http://www.facebook.com/groups/193158994062914>
     <http://krapiva.org>
LOUDmouth
     <http://calstatelausu.org/ccc/loudmouth>
make/shift magazine
     <http://www.makeshiftmag.com>
Missy Magazine
     <http://missy-magazine.de>
Noc Walpurgii Festival
     <http://nocwalpurgii.worldpress.com>

Biographies

Sonja Eismann is a journalist, a cultural theorist and university lecturer. She is one of the founders and editors of *Missy Magazine* and lives in Berlin with her partner and her daughter. She is also the editor of the book *Hot Topic. Popfeminismus heute* (2007).

Emancypunx was formed in the mid 1990s initially as a distro run by the anarchist feminist group *KDP* (later transformed into *Emancypunx group*, which ceased to exist in 2002). The idea was (and still is) to promote feminism, women's sexual and reproductive rights and sexual education, and to raise anti-homophobic consciousness in Poland. The record label was initiated in order to promote females and a feminist consciousness within a still male dominated hc punk scene. Today *Emancypunx Records* is not just a distro and record label; it's also active in many other areas such as festival organization (art, music, movies, performance), tour managing, running a zine archive and flying zine library, etc. *Emancypunx* participated and continues to participate in various feminist and anarchist feminist groups and projects. *Emancypunx* is and always was a non-profit, non-commercial initiative run on a voluntary and DIY basis.

Jessica Hoffmann is co-editor/co-publisher of *make/shift* magazine. She has contributed to numerous publications, including *ColorLines*, *AlterNet*, *Scholar and Feminist*, and the anthologies *We Don't Need Another Wave: Dispatches from the Next Generation of Feminists* and *Nobody Passes: Rejecting the Rules of Gender and Conformity*. She is also a member of the *POOR Magazine* Solidarity Family. She has been engaged in activism around various issues since she helped organize a student walkout against the first Gulf War at her junior high.

Jeanna Krömer (Yamaykina) is co-founder and editor of the Belarusian e-zine *AMPHI*. She was born in 1980 in Belarus. At a young age (19) she married for the first time and became a mother, and thus experienced all of the inconveniences of living in the pro-patriarchal society of a post-Soviet country. She studied German (Minsk), journalism (Warsaw, Berlin) and sociology (Vienna). Since 2010 she has been living in Berlin, but as an activist she is still involved in projects in Belarus and in other countries of the former Soviet Union, including the Belarusian LJ blog *gender_by*, building up a Russian-speaking women's radio program *(Fem.fm)* and the feminist activist group *Krapiva Belaruskaya*.

Daria Yudacufski is co-editor/co-publisher of *make/shift* magazine. She is also the managing director of Visions and Voices, an arts and humanities initiative at the University of Southern California in Los Angeles. She has worked at universities for almost 20 years, focusing on cross-cultural education and arts administration. She was formerly the publisher of *LOUDmouth* and director of the Cross Cultural Centers at Cal State L. A.

Chapter 2:
Participatory Spaces, Networks and Technology

"Zine making is a pleasure, it's getting to know people from all over the world and from my own country, it's to share ideas and opinions, it's to learn and teach, it's to open my mind and help others to open their minds."
Editor of *Pink Punkies* E-Zine
(Argentina)

"One of the primary strengths of the current feminist movement is that there is this global network of young women who are able and eager to help each other succeed, promote each others projects".
Ladyfriend Zine (USA)

Drawing by Nina Nijsten (Belgium)

"For me, women making zines, or art, or anything else creative is about taking the media back – challenging the bullshit that goes on in the mainstream media, reclaiming public media space, and above all, expressing ourselves creatively. It's about creating our own spaces where this creative expression is possible, on our own terms."
Editor of *Good Girl Magazine*
(Canada)

Streetwise Politics: Feminist and Lesbian Grassroots Activism in Ljubljana

Tea Hvala

Introduction: Feminist and Lesbian Counterpublics

In 1990, the American political theorist Nancy Fraser argued for the neces-sity of theorizing non-liberal, non-bourgeois and competing public spheres that were excluded from Jürgen Habermas's influential theory on *The Structural Transformation of the Public Sphere* (1962). Her argument rested on the growing body of feminist and postcolonial revisionist historiogra-phies which, among other things, demonstrated that members of subordi-nated social groups "repeatedly found it advantageous to constitute alter-native publics" (Fraser 1990: 67). Fraser's main point was that "subaltern counterpublics" contested the exclusionary norms of the bourgeois public sphere by elaborating alternative styles of political behaviour and alterna-tive norms of public speech. In these parallel discursive sites, subordinated people could "invent and circulate counterdiscourses, which in turn per-mitted them to formulate oppositional interpretations of their identities, in-terests and needs" (ibid.). Consequently they could enter the official public sphere on their own terms by representing themselves. The proliferation of counterpublics therefore lessens the chance of informal exclusion and leads towards greater democracy.

For Fraser, "participation means being able to speak 'in one's own voice', thereby simultaneously constructing and expressing one's cultural identity through idiom and style" (69). Counterpublics have the power to articulate an issue in their own way – or in dialogue with other counterpublics – and insist on it until it is recognized as an issue of general concern. Fraser men-tions "domestic violence" or "date rape" as terms that have entered the list of general concerns and legislature because of feminist efforts that origi-nally started in weak counterpublics that possessed only opinion-making power.[1] In societies where legal equality does not guarantee actual equality, feminist and lesbian counterpublics continue to fulfil two functions: the

---

1 These examples confirm that Nancy Fraser was referring to feminist groups, rather than individual women who would fit Gayatri Spivak's definition of subalterns as "sub-jects of exploitation" who "cannot know and speak the text of female exploitation even if the absurdity of the nonrepresenting intellectual making space for her [them] to speak is achieved" (Spivak 1988: 84). Since my essay is concerned with feminist and lesbian activ-

internal and the external. In Fraser's terms, counterpublics function internally as "spaces of withdrawal or regroupment" (68). The external function comes into play when members of feminist or lesbian counterpublics seek to convince society as a whole of the validity of their claims by challenging existing structures of authority through political activity and theoretical critique. In this sense, counterpublics function as "bases and training grounds for agitational activities directed towards wider publics" (ibid.).

Grassroots activism offers a variety of accessible communication and agitation tools to (mainly) young progressive feminists and lesbians who want to address wider publics. Since the concept of public sphere presupposes a plurality of perspectives among those who participate in it, the expression of conflicting views within (as well as between) political groups which strive for political recognition can be perceived as an advantage rather than a disadvantage. Knowing how vulnerable grassroots groups can be, I argue that some form of appeal to collective identity or solidarity has to prevail if a group wants to communicate with other counterpublics. In addition, there is always a disparity between the internal and external perception of specific counterpublics; between its self-understanding as a representative forum for a variety of (often conflictual) political identities, and the image of unity the group has to present to the public in order to be "taken seriously" – to be able to communicate with other (counter) publics. For Nancy Fraser, this communication is vital. She claims that the public orientation of oppositional spheres allows people's participation in more than one sphere, which makes both "intercultural and interpublic discussions possible" (70). Since the concept of counterpublics assumes an orientation towards wider publics, it – in the long run – also works against separatism: no matter how limited they are in their numbers or outreach, members of counterpublics see themselves as part of a potentially wider public. That is why counterpublics are not separatist enclaves by definition even if they might be "involuntarily enclaved" (67).

Due to historical and sociopolitical circumstances, discussed below, feminist and lesbian politics in Slovenia after 1991 have been marginalized to the extent that there is a great need for (grassroots) activism to defend already existing rights, demand new rights and most importantly, create new counterpublics where alternative norms of public speech can be developed. I applied Fraser's insistence on the necessity of proliferating forms of political expression to the tactical significance of what I call "streetwise politics" (local feminist and lesbian grassroots activism) because the institutionalized understanding of political participation and public matters of general concern in Slovenia continues to exclude such gender-related and sexuality-related issues as personal, private and apolitical. I am therefore not interested in "assigning abstract political value to particular techniques" (Felski 1989: 164), but in reviewing a selection of local feminist and lesbian street actions, street art and graffiti of the last two decades in order to see

---

ism in Slovenia, where counterpublic organizing is possible and indeed taking place, I have refrained from using the term "subaltern".

how and why activists reacted to current political issues and/or addressed new ones. I am going to focus on the external function of local feminist and lesbian counterpublics – not because I would be merely interested in the immediately visible effects of their interventions in the official public sphere but because the length of this essay prevents me from examining their internal function. I have written about it elsewhere (Hvala 2010).

In what follows, I am going to review the historical and sociopolitical conditions that have contributed to the gradual disappearance of feminist and lesbian politics from the official public sphere in Slovenia. I am going to continue – and conclude – with the analysis of sporadic, fleeting, illegal and anonymous forms of political agitation in public space such as graffiti, stencils, posters, paste-ups and street performances that "take the space nobody offered" (Fajt and Velikonja 2006: 23).

(In)visibility of Feminist and Lesbian Politics

The participation of grassroots feminist and lesbian groups in Ljubljana's "new social movements" of the 1980s and their increasing public visibility at the end of that decade has been lessened by the 1991 disintegration of Yugoslavia, the subsequent wars in Croatia and Bosnia, nationalist and antifeminist historical revisionism, and finally, by the NGO-ization and the institutionalization of the relatively small movement. Whereas many feminist activists who protested against nationalism and war in 1991 were, especially in Croatia, demonized as "betrayers of the nation" and "witches", feminists in Slovenia were not ostracised to the same extent. Nevertheless, the movement *was* pacified as many groups shifted their focus from educational, agitational, and mobilizing activities to humanitarian, social and cultural work.

According to the feminists who helped shape the politics of "new feminism" of the 1980s, the feminist and (to a lesser extent) the lesbian movement of that period have "become part of everyday life" (Plahuta Simčič 2006: 15) after 1991 when former activists entered educational, cultural and social institutions, and – in humble proportions – parliamentary politics. While the simultaneous introduction of Gender Studies and feminist academic publishing has enabled the (re)production of feminist knowledge, it has – paradoxically, due to historic revisionism and the immediate discursive colonisation of Gender Studies programmes by British, American and French sources – produced a generation of highly educated women and men who are not aware of local feminist activist history and are unable to relate their academic knowledge about "women's issues" and "gender issues" to contemporary feminist and lesbian activism.

In the new, neoliberal setting, feminism in Slovenia was late to react to "the rise of the Church, the rise of the Right, the rise of hate speech" (Kuhar 2007: 11). It was also late to react to "an incredible wave of patriarchal and sexist views" (Plahuta Simčič 2006: 15) on one hand and "pop values, pop identities, with less and less immersion into things, apolitical standpoints"

(Kuhar 2007: 11) on the other. While it is true that women have not lost any of the legal rights achieved in socialism, the reintroduction of "private patriarchy" (Burcar 2011), the increasingly precarious conditions on the labour market and repeated attacks on women's reproductive and sexual rights call for a strong opposition. Prominent feminist scholars like Svetlana Slapšak agree that "the situation is ripe for feminist activism" (Plahuta Simčič 2006: 15). In 2006, when the Ministry of Labour, Family and Social Affairs intended to limit abortion rights, graffiti from 1991 (the year when abortion rights were threatened as well) appeared with renewed urgency. "Women against nation – for abortion rights" (Photo 1) they called, signed by the feminist symbol and a clenched fist. More graffiti from 2006 cynically remarked that in Slovenia, "A foetus has more rights than a woman".

Photo 1: "Women against nation – for abortion rights"

Photo by Barbara Berce, 1991. This graffiti reappeared near the (old) Pediatric Clinic in Ljubljana in 2006.

Since 1993, when a large alliance of political groups and artists occupied the former military base on Metelkova Street in Ljubljana, most of the grassroots feminist and lesbian groups have been based there, in the Autonomous Cultural Centre (ACC) Metelkova mesto. Because feminist and lesbian counterpublics in Metelkova were shaped by so many individuals, groups and events, and because these groups collaborated, disbanded and later joined forces on different political grounds, their knowledge production has to be theorized as a discontinuous and site-specific practice, defined by a variety of non-dominant and non-hegemonic views. Today, collaborations between academic, non-governmental and grassroots initiatives do exist; however these groups cooperate only in response to particularly dangerous threats or cases of discrimination and usually disband when the goals of the struggle have been achieved. This defensive position is one of the reasons for their political invisibility.

The temporary and provisional nature of cooperative actions in Ljubljana reflects other problems that are specific to feminisms from postsocialist countries and only partly coincide with the problems of Western feminisms: the reluctance to identify and be recognized as feminists due to the general stigmatization of feminism as a separatist and misandrist ideology; the depoliticized attitude towards a number of issues including class differences within the traditional (unified) political subject of women; and the lack of solidarity between feminists and other social movements, their potential allies. I believe those are the main reasons why a feminist counterpublic with "the potential to build alliances and collaborations across divisive boundaries" (Mohanty 1991: 196) is, at this stage, still very vulnerable and loose. Nevertheless, the existing alliances are important agents of both continuity and change within the fragmented feminist map of Ljubljana; they can serve as a platform for the development of stronger feminist and lesbian movement.

It is interesting to note that in the last twenty years, lesbian activism has been more visible than feminist activism. There is a tendency to explain this disparity by the greater stigmatization of LGBTI people who are, supposedly because of their greater exposure to verbal and physical violence, more committed to activism. A more reasonable answer relates to the fact that "the state does not need professional lesbians and gays" (Kuhar 2007: 11). That is how Suzana Tratnik, lesbian activist and award-winning fiction writer, replied to the question of why the lesbian movement, unlike feminism, was not institutionalized in the 1990s. It might also be the reason why the new generation of politically engaged lesbians in the 1990s and 2000s regularly frequented the "streetwise school" of activism and wrote its own "graffiti textbook". Lesbian activist and theorist Nataša Velikonja wrote: "In the late 1990s, when the level of homophobia in Slovenia rose and the educative tools against intolerance were entirely insufficient, a library wall in Maribor was sprayed with the slogan 'Where are all the lesbian books?'" (Velikonja 2004: 125).

In the next section, I am going to review the metaphorical textbook of grassroots activism that has been – and continues to be – "written" by and for young progressive feminists and lesbians who are forming their political identity through practice. I will focus on several examples that represent some of the most frequent themes and tactical approaches, used in streetwise politics. However, due to the methodological difficulties related to the research of anonymous actions (such as the lack of sources), my essay should not be read as the only possible history of feminist and lesbian grassroots activism in Ljubljana.

Feminist and Lesbian Grassroots Activism in Ljubljana

Graffiti and public interventions are sporadic, fleeting, mostly anonymous and illegal forms of political agitation using artistic means. Especially for young feminist and lesbian activists, they represent the most accessible and visible medium of resistance. The case of feminist graffiti from 1995 ("Goddammit, Ivan! Make that damn coffee yourself! – Mother Francka") indicates that these actions can have very provocative effects.

"Ivan's graffiti" was written on 25 November 1995 as part of activities organized for the International Days for the Elimination of Violence against Women by groups from the (now defunct) Women's Centre in Metelkova: Kasandra, Women's Counselling Service, Modra and Prenner Club. The alliance carried out an impressive action with slogans addressing domestic violence, rape, incest and several other issues. From a feminist point of view, the graffiti parodying Ivan Cankar's *Skodelica kave* (1920),[2] a short story that had been "nationalized" to serve the Slovenian literary establishment long before 1991, was protesting against the gendered division of labour. Gregor Tomc, a prominent sociologist specialized in subcultures, responded with an article published in the largest daily in Slovenia. He claimed that graffiti written by "Ljubljana's Amazons" dealt with obsolete issues, since "contemporary Slovenian family has overcome the traditional division of labour a long time ago" (Tomc 1996: 39), thus referring to the indeed obsolete state-socialist views on feminism as a superfluous ideology. Similarly, graffiti that addressed women's sexual rights were accused of animosity and separatism while lesbian graffiti like "No more fear – Thelma and Louise", "No more shame – Mojca and Metka" or "Lesbians for peace – Peace to lesbians" were denied both peace and equality by his statement that "a heterosexual relationship and homosexual sexuality, after all, cannot be equal" (ibid.). Gregor Tomc tried to discredit the activists with antifeminist views that continue to dominate the public sphere in Slovenia. Of course, from a feminist and lesbian point of view, the article discredited its author.[3]

In 1997, *Lesbo* magazine documented a series of lesbian graffiti written on the river banks of Ljubljanica. Graffiti such as "Eva + Adama" and "My grandfather is bisexual" ridiculed compulsory heterosexuality; others like "Sorry mum, no grandchildren" kept the same humorous spirit as the action carried out in the night before Independence Day (25 June) when activists "appropriated" the national holiday by postering the center of town with *Lesbo* covers. Ten years later, lesbian graffiti continue to be more visible than

---

2 Ivan Cankar's autobiographical short story *Cup of Coffee* [my translation] is about young Ivan who visits his poor mother and asks her for a cup of coffee, knowing that she cannot even afford to buy bread. To his surprise, his mother manages to find and prepare coffee for him but he refuses to drink it and tells her to stop bothering him. The narrator deeply regrets young Ivan's reaction and speaks of his lasting feeling of guilt.
3 "Ivan's graffiti" was also printed on promotional postcards of the Women's Group within Združena lista, a coalition that later restructured into a centre-left political party. Also, journalist Agata Tomažič used it in her 2004 critique of the nationalist appropriation and ideological exploitation of Ivan Cankar's literature in Slovene schools.

feminist ones. Slogans like "Homophobes are human, too" and "Step out of the heterosexual matrix" are among the few that directly address heterosexuals. The idea that it is possible to "step out of the matrix" has received an interestingly utopian (or queer) answer in January 2008 when the order of construction site fences on which it was originally sprayed was changed so that the new constellation read "trix ual ma heterosex Step out".

In the new millennium, several feminist actions were inspired by UZI (Urad za intervencije or Bureau for Interventions), an informal network of local groups, founded after the protests against the World Trade Organization meeting in Seattle in 1999. For example, "in Interspar [shop], a group of female activists 'advertised' Heidersil; a new washing powder that cleans historic stains and contains 'adolfils'" (Zadnikar 2004: 15). On 8 March 2001, the Women's Section of UZI temporarily squatted in two cosmetics and women's apparel shops in Ljubljana in order to address the commercialization of International Women's Day and the privatization of public space. When the dancing activists were asked to leave, they continued the action on public grounds (outside the shop's entrance). On the same day, Nada Hass, an improvised all-female activist choir, performed at Klub Gromka in ACC Metelkova mesto. Dressed up as cleaners and housekeepers, they sang: "Let's set things straight with our past, let's wipe away the borders, let's make our relationships work and wipe away the violence" (Ozmec 2001: 14). (Photo 2)

Photo 2: Spontaneous street action in the centre of Ljubljana during 9th Rdeče zore festival

Photo by Rüzgar, 9 March 2008.

In Slovenia, the country where lesbians and gays are still denied the legal rights provided by the institution of marriage ("Registration = discrimination" sums up the issue in graffiti on Roška street), reproductive rights have been discussed primarily in relation to heterosexual women. However, in 2000 when the right-wing government attempted to implement legislation that would make artificial insemination available only to heterosexual couples who are married or cohabiting, this serious violation of women's reproductive choices faced severe opposition from a wide array of feminist, lesbian and other progressive groups. Four years later, on 8 March 2005, an anonymous letter entitled *Do you remember March 8th?* claimed that the new governmental program for positive demographic growth used hate speech and discriminatory measures. The letter was handed out by a small activist group that staged a burlesque portrayal of patriarchal family roles in Park Zvezda and managed to ridicule the (former) Minister of Labour, Family and Social Affairs Janez Drobnič personally by calling itself The Janez Drobnič Folklore Group.

On 15 November 2006, the same minister proposed a "fertility raising strategy" which, among many other discriminatory measures, tried to limit access to abortion. The strategy proposed a 400 euro fee for certain procedures, thus ensuring that abortion would become inaccessible for a large number of poor women and girls. The strategy, like the successfully opposed proposition from 1991, was to instrumentalize women for the state's "nation-building" goals. Furthermore, the new legislation used Catholic discourse that equates the beginning of life with conception. Feminists responded with graffiti declaring "Let's abort Drobnič!", "I'd rather be a test-tube baby than Drobnič's child" and a slogan which connected the discriminatory proposal about artificial insemination from 2000 with the same type of demographic policy by sarcastically offering "the perfect solution": "To raise fertility – inseminate single women and lesbians". On 17 November, Feminist Initiative in Support of Abortion Rights entered ministry bureaus early in the morning and met the employees with statements objecting to the proposed strategy. The activists used posters and banners to surround the bureaus and expose them to the public as violators of women's rights. The slogans ("Women = birth machines", "Defend abortion rights now – tomorrow it is going to be too late", "Yesterday migrants and Erased citizens, today Roma people and women; who is next?") connected discriminatory policies against women with institutionalized violence against sexual and ethnic minorities.

On the eve of large trade union demonstrations of 17 November 2007, Ljubljana's streets were sprayed with several different examples of feminist graffiti. Older graffiti ("Fuck better wages, I don't even have one – Housewife", "New! Housework workshops for men", "Boys, who's gonna do the dishes?") were accompanied by a series of new protests. Perhaps the most memorable was the stencil of a young woman with a clenched fist, shouting "Because we are not a commodity!" (photo 3) An ambiguous stencil designed to look like a construction site traffic sign (the official sign "Workers on the street" includes an image of a male worker with a shovel in his hands) claimed "Female workers on the street – 17.11." and replaced the male worker with an image of three women and a small girl holding hands. It could be read in several ways: as a call for joining the trade union demonstrations, as a comment on the growing rates of unemployment among women and the discrimination of mothers on the labour market or as an indirect reminder that sex work is an illegal and dangerous yet possible source of income for impoverished women. The workers' demonstrations were supported by Avtonomna tribuna, a students' alliance which included an explicitly feminist initiative (The Feminist Initiative for Social Rights) and a lesbian-feminist group called The Lesbian Insurrection.[4] Their members carried anarchofeminist flags, cynical banners like "I am a woman, therefore I work for free" and the classic slogan "We are lesbians and we are everywhere".

Photo 3: "Because we are not a commodity!"

Photo by Tea Hvala, 17 November 2007, the eve of large trade union protests in Ljubljana.

Very little graffiti in Ljubljana concerned sex work (with the exception of "Prostitutes of the world, unite!"). A few days before 8 March 2007, a series of posters appeared that problematized the relation between economy and the regulation of sexuality. Troubling questions like "Do money and love exclude each other?" were written in the headers of large blank sheets of paper, intended for comments of people who passed by. Somebody replied: "Not really". The question "Is marriage an institution of legal prostitution?" was reformulated in barely legible handwriting as "Legal prostitution is the institution of marriage. Complicated, huh?" while somebody

---

4   Vstaja Lezbosov or The Lesbian Insurrection was formed after 10 October 2007, when two lesbians were forced to leave Orto bar, a rock bar in Ljubljana, because of "explicitly showing their lesbian identity" (Tratnik 2007: 14) by kissing in public.

else simply confessed that s/he "Wouldn't know". Comments to the question "What do you expect from sex after marriage?" were hilarious: "Nothing, I' m already married" and "Sex with a relative". The poster series also included questions like "What do artists and sex workers have in common?" and "Are sex workers the last street fighters?". The postering action was organised by a Viennese feminist art collective which was invited to Ljubljana by the International Feminist and Queer Festival Rdeče zore as part of the *Sex, Work and Society* art exhibition in Alkatraz Gallery.

Photo 4: "Street of Feminist Movements"

Photo by Nada Žgank, 2007.

In the night of 8–9 March 2007, several feminist activist groups renamed around fifty streets in Ljubljana. Like the street-renaming actions in Zagreb (2006), Sarajevo (2006) and Kutina (2007), the action in Ljubljana was based on the statistical fact that the majority of streets are named after men and the feminist fact that women need to contest versions of history that exclude them. New street names paid homage to The International Women's Day, Simone de Beauvoir, local and international women artists, female pop icons, women political organizers and activists, important events from feminist history, fictional female characters, etc. (Photo 4) In November 2007, a similar action was carried out in Maribor where The Lesbian Insurrection group introduced the Square of Lesbian Revolution (including house number 69), the Lesbian Path and the Road to the Lesbian. These signs were left on display for several weeks. However, Path to the Lesbian Peak and Square of Lesbian Brigades (Photo 5) disappeared immediately: probably because they renamed the official address of the Roman Catholic Diocese and Archdiocese in Maribor.

Photo 5: "Square of Lesbian Brigades" at the seat of the Roman Catholic Archdiocese in Maribor

Photo by Mojca Rugelj, 2007.

In the night of 8 March 2012, two anonymous actions took place in the centre of Ljubljana. The first included graffiti and stickers with slogans such as "Proud Feminist" and "Up with Feminism!"; the other action was strategically placed in front of the local Museum of Contemporary History, which hosted an exhibition about Slovene women's struggles for emancipation between 1848 and 1945. The activists spray-painted the tank in front of the museum a pink colour, ridiculing the militarist symbol of Slovene independence and commenting on the fact that an exhibition dedicated to feminist history was symbolically threatened by a tank from the ten-day war in 1991 (and the implied historical revisionism). The director of the museum failed to see or publicly mention the action's connection to the exhibition, to International Women's Day or to LGBTI couples whose right to adopt a child was rejected in a referendum on 25 March 2012. The director said: "Since we don't know how we are going to restore the tank, we thank the guerillas or the vandals for at least choosing a colour that matches the museum's façade" (Svenšek 2012). The third feminist action on 8 March 2012 was organised by the international arts collective Bring In Take Out – Living Archive, who co-organised the visual arts programme of the 13th Rdeče zore festival. Its members joined the 15O (15 October or Occupy!) demonstrations against austerity measures and blocked the entrance to several banks in the centre of Ljubljana. The feminist art collective protested against "all forms of social repression and economic exploitation" (Crvena 2012) and paid homage to the women textile workers' strike in Lawrence, Massachusetts, on 8 March 1912 by chanting "We want bread, and roses too."

Conclusion

The grassroots actions discussed in this essay by no means represent the entire thematic and tactical scope of feminist and lesbian streetwise politics in Ljubljana. However, I tried to select examples that represent the most frequently addressed issues and the most common tactics. To summarize: in the past twenty years, feminist and lesbian activists criticized the gendered division of labour (women's unpaid reproductive labour vs. men's paid productive work), the growing rates of unemployment among (older) women, discrimination of mothers on the labour market, precarious labour conditions in general, double measures regarding the (lack of) regulation of sex work, the instrumentalization of women's reproductive and sexual freedom by the state, domestic violence, rape, incest, institutionalized violence against sexual and ethnic minorities, compulsory heterosexuality, legal discrimination of same-sex couples, conservative revisions of history, commodification of International Women's Day and the privatization of public space. They advocated pacifism, lesbian visibility, women's sexual freedom, reproductive rights of LGBTI people and single women, the destigmatization of sex work and the general visibility of feminist politics. In doing so, the activists have employed the following tactics and tools: graffiti, stencils, posters, paste-ups, demonstrations and street art (performance, theatre, singing).

I interpreted feminist and lesbian grassroots actions in Ljubljana as sporadic, fleeting and mostly anonymous interventions in the public sphere and in the sphere of institutionalized knowledge (re)production. I argued that they represent an important chapter in the metaphorical textbook "written" by and for young progressive feminists and lesbians who are forming their political identity through practice. Since most of these actions were illegal, the activists had to learn to cope with the stress of (probable) harassment by their political opponents or the police. They were strengthened in the process. The activists were additionally strengthened by the chance to articulate their own political identity, needs and demands in ways that suited them. As such, grassroots activism can be theorized as one of the communication tools available to young activists who want to develop their own counterpublics and alternative norms of public speech. Finally, I argued for the necessity of expanding the notions of political and public beyond those prevalent in the official public sphere in Slovenia. My essay can be therefore read as an internal critique of the latter and as a contribution to the diversification of (counter)public feminist and lesbian discourses. As the actions described in this paper suggest, one of the places where these discourses can be tested publicly is the streets.

References

Burcar, L., 2011. What is Left of the Feminist Left? [online]. Available at: <http://bringintakeout.wordpress.com/video-booth/audio-interviews/> [Accessed 27 October 2011].

Crvena, 2012. We want Bread, and Roses Too [online]. Available at: <http://bringintakeout.wordpress.com/2012/03/12/we-want-bread-and-roses-too/> [Accessed 15 March 2012].

Fajt, M. and Velikonja, M., 2006. Ulice govorijo/Streets are Saying Things. *Časopis za kritiko znanosti* 223, pp. 22–29.

Fraser, N., 1990. Rethinking the Public Sphere: A Contribution to the Critique of Actually Existing Democracy. *Social Text* 25–26, pp. 56–80.

Hvala, T., 2010. The Red Dawns Festival as a Feminist-Queer Counterpublic. *Monitor ISH* (1/XII), pp. 7–107.

Kuhar, R., 2007. Prečuta noč za lezbični manifest. Intervju z Natašo Sukič in Suzano Tratnik. *Narobe* 4, pp. 9–12.

Mohanty, C. T., 1991. Cartographies of Struggle: Third World Women and the Politics of Feminism. In: P. Essed, ed., 1991. *Race Critical Theories: Text and Context*. Oxford: Blackwell Publishing, pp. 195–219.

Ozmec, S., 2001. Osmi marec: dan, ko se pretvarjamo, da je vse v redu. *Mladina* [online], 19 March. Available at: <http://www.mladina.si/tednik/200111/clanek/m-osmi/> [Accessed 27 October 2011].

Plahuta Simčič, V., 2006. Ne smemo se slepiti, patriarhat je povsod! *Delo* (48/74), p. 15.

Svenšek, A., 2012. Rožnati tank pred muzejem: vsak ima svojo interpretacijo akcije. *Multimedijski center RTV SLO* [online], 8 March. Available at: <http://www.rtvslo.si/slovenija/roznati-tank-pred-muzejem-vsak-ima-svojo-interpretacijo-akcije/278467> [Accessed 20 March 2012].

Tomc, G., 1996. Je ženska brez moškega kot riba brez bicikla? *Delo – Sobotna priloga* (38/28), p. 39.

Tratnik, S. 2007. Ne vstopaj s svojimi sendviči! *Narobe* 4, pp. 14–15.

Velikonja, N., 2004. Grafiti: poulično revolucionarno branje. In: L. Stepančič and B. Zrinski, eds. *Grafitarji/Graffitists*. Ljubljana: MGLC, pp. 124–130.

Zadnikar, D., 2004. Kronika radostnega uporništva. In: J. Holloway, ed. *Spreminjamo svet brez boja za oblast: pomen revolucije danes*. Ljubljana: Študentska založba, pp. 201–225.

"It's a Hard Job Being an Indian Feminist"
Mapping Girls' Feminist Identities and "Close Encounters" on the Feminist Blogosphere

Jessalynn Keller

Introduction: Finding Feminism Online

You won't find anyone writing, "I'm not a feminist, but . . ." on the *FBomb* (http://thefbomb.org) website. In fact, the online community is a meeting ground for teen feminists who embrace the "f bomb" – or feminist – identity. While we are often told that today's girls are not interested in "their mother's movement," websites like *FBomb* prove otherwise.

The *FBomb* represents one of the most active spaces for feminist activism over the past five years: the internet. The feminist blogosphere, a loose affiliation of blogs dedicated to discussing feminism and gender inequality, has become an important space for women to connect with likeminded women, speak their thoughts on feminism, and organize feminist events. While girls can access these blogs, the target demographic is usually adult women, and consequently, girls may feel marginalized by their age and educational status. Blogs like *FBomb* serve to shift power instead to teen feminists, providing a forum for them to discuss gender issues relevant to their lives as adolescent girls.

While the feminist blogosphere is globally accessible to anyone with a computer and an internet connection (as well as a working knowledge of English, the primary language used), many of the websites are based in Europe and North America, often resulting in conversations focusing on Western-centric feminist issues. While there are many women reading these blogs, little research has examined how non-Western women navigate their identities, both as feminists and as non-Westerners, within a feminist blogosphere often dominated by Western feminist discourses. This chapter then will make two important interventions into this topic: first, by focusing on *girls'* participation in the feminist blogosphere, and second, by addressing the specific issues facing *non-Western* girls' in these spaces.

I will focus my analysis on the *FBomb* website, drawing on theoretical discussions of third wave feminism, postcolonial feminism, and critical Internet studies, and using a discursive textual analysis of fifteen blog posts to determine how feminism as a transnational movement is talked about through postings by non-Western[1] girls and the conversations that these postings produce. Additionally, I will draw on the comments of two non-Western *FBomb* bloggers from India and Jordan in order to better contextualize my textual analysis. These comments are taken from qualitative, open-ended interviews, which I conducted with each blogger via email in April 2011.

Reimagining a Transnational Third Wave: Intersectionality, Close Encounters, and the Internet

I am positioning the contemporary feminist blogosphere as part of the third wave of feminism, which developed in the early 1990s out of young women's desire to articulate feminism according to their own lives.[2] The third wave is typically understood as racially and sexually inclusive, global and ecological in perspective, influenced by poststructural notions of identity and subjectivity, an interest in popular culture as a site of resistance, and a focus on sexuality and pleasure (Karlyn 2003). The third wave's privileging of a multiplicity of issues and, as Rory Dicker and Alison Piepmeier (2003) note, an understanding that "identity is multifaceted and layered", means that the monolithic category of "woman" is problematized, making the third wave a rich site for thinking about diversity and difference within feminism (10).

This approach is based upon an intersectional understanding of identity, a perspective that views race, class, gender, sexuality, nationality, age, ethnicity and other identities as mutually constructing systems of power (Collins 2005). Thus, intersectional paradigms do not attempt to privilege one identity over another, but grapple with the ways that multiple identities intersect to position individuals in varying relationships to social power. Coined by U. S. Third World feminists who critiqued the women's liberation movement for their assumption of an unproblematic "global sisterhood," intersectionality has since become a significant concept for both feminist scholars and activists and a foundational concept for the third wave's "politics of hybridity and coalition" (Heywood and Drake 1997: 9).

Despite the third wave's emphasis on intersectionality and diversity, several scholars have critiqued third wave practices as reinforcing the dominance of white, Western middle-class feminists and equating the First World with the *whole world* (Woodhull 2004). Denise deCaires Narain (2004) argues that the third wave must do more to build coalitions with Third World women, arguing that the third wave's emphasis on individ-

---

1   The term non-Western is not entirely unproblematic. I employ it as an analytic and political category, representing those outside of the white, Anglo-Saxon, middle-class, Western feminist movement, similar to Mohanty's (2003) use of "Third World." I do not mean to enforce a Western/non-Western binary here and I utilize these terms while recognizing them as being potentially problematic.

2   While I agree that the wave metaphor does not capture the rich complexity of feminist movements, I utilize third wave feminism as demarcating a cultural context, rather than a narrowly defined generational marker in opposition to the second wave.

ualism and pleasure risks difference "being articulated entirely in terms of a consumable, chic, metropolitan hybridity, rather than an engagement with 'other' contexts and representations" (243). Her critique exists as part of a lengthy history of feminist postcolonial theory, which has made important interventions into the ways in which Western feminists think and write about women in non-Western nations since the mid 1980s.

Chandra Talpade Mohanty (1988) argues that some Western feminist writers have promoted a "third world difference," a universalist discourse that positions non-Western women as traditional, oppressed, uneducated, devoutly religious, and possessing little control over their bodies. Mohanty notes that this image of the "oppressed woman" simultaneously constructs Western women as modern, free, educated, secular, agential, and thus able to "save" their non-Western "sisters." Thus, instead of employing the universalizing "woman" as a category of analysis, Mohanty advocates for a contextual analysis that understands women as located within specific local, historical, and social conditions as a way to find productive spaces for a coalitional politics that do not rob women in non-Western nations of their agency.

Mohanty's critiques remain significant, particularly in the context of the "war on terror" and the mainstream attention given to Muslim women over the past decade. Thus, we must ask: how might contemporary feminists build transnational coalitions that avoid universalizing, simplifying, and commodifying the experiences of non-Western women? Sara Ahmed (2000) suggests that transnational collective politics be formed through what she calls "close encounters." She describes these close encounters as a "politics that is premised on closer encounters, on encounters with those who are other than 'the other' or 'the stranger' . . . The differences between us necessitate the dialogue, rather than disallow it – a dialogue must take place, precisely because we don't speak the same language" (180).

According to Ahmed (2000), close encounters avoid common universalist approaches whereby Western feminism assumes the ability "to get inside the skin of the other," adopting the position of speaking for her (166). But stepping back in the name of cultural relativism, assuming that the best way to avoid speaking for others is to avoid speaking at all, is also problematic as it confirms the very privilege that it seeks to disavow. *Not* encountering then becomes an active choice that can stall the development of a transnational feminist network, while ignoring the necessity of this network within a globalized world (Ahmed, 2000). I want to suggest that the internet may offer new potential for global networks where close encounters as articulated by Ahmed can take place, and I will now turn to a discussion of this possibility.

Technological advances such as the internet have provided new spaces for feminist activism within popular culture. Ednie Kaeh Garrison (2010) argues, "Technology is a major discursive repertoire in the cultural geography of third wave feminism, [as] 'democratized technologies' have played a significant role in the feminist political consciousness of many young women today" (396). While feminism has always relied on networks of people to sustain it as a movement, networking within the context of third wave internet culture takes on new meanings and opportunities. Garrison describes third wave networks as being "technologic", signaling a particular practice of communicating information over space and time, the creation of temporary unified political groups made up of unlikely collectivities, the combining of diverse technologies to construct oppositional cultural expressions, and the construction of feminist politics of location that "weav[es] between and among the spaces of race, class, sexuality, gender, that we all inhabit" (187). Third wave networks imply a kind of "messiness" that complicates the notion of a unified social movement with a clear agenda and boundaries and in this sense, may serve as a useful way to think about intersectional identities and transnational feminist coalitions online.

However, Stacy Gillis (2004) argues that while the Internet has been promoted as a "global consciousness-raising tool" for third wave feminists, "the myth of cyberfeminism – that women are using cyberspace in powerful and transgressive ways – far exceeds what is actually taking place online" (185). Gillis maintains that this is primarily because feminism's transgressive potential in an online space is limited by the specificities of embodied identities, including those of race, ethnicity, and class, within online experiences. Likewise, Winifred Woodhull (2004) argues that the third wave's use of new media technologies often reproduces divisions by prescribing Western models of feminism for women worldwide. According to these scholars, third wave feminists must conscientiously work to build coalitions online that can recognize and challenge inherent power relations, rather than reinforce them.

Performing Feminist Identities In Flux

Much of the existing research on girls and internet use focuses on the use of social media by girls for identity exploration and navigation (Mazzarella 2005). danah boyd (2007) notes that without the physical body to guide others' perceptions of us, "people must learn to *write themselves into being*" (12). This articulation of a virtual presence can present an opportunity for girls perform and experiment with identities, including *feminist identities*. While blogging is viewed as a "new" form of media production, finding one's feminist identity through the craft of writing has a lengthy history amongst women from all over the world (Muaddi Darraj 2003). This is especially true for non-Western *Fbomb* bloggers who seem to often specifically state their identity upfront, and in several cases, describe how their geographic location, informed by their national, ethnic, religious, or racial identity, shapes their feminist identity.

In a post dated 28 April 2010, Mumbai, India native Jasmin,[3] grapples with her own feminist identity, which is situated within the tensions between India and the West. She writes,

---

3 All names are pseudonyms.

> I am an Indian and I live in India. How convenient. At the same time, I'm not really sure what an Indian feminist is . . .. Most Indian teenagers have to negotiate their Indian identity into either blending in with Western values and immediately being liberal or retaining their Indian-ness and try to re-negotiate what norms they accept, for what purpose etc. To add to this existential burden, if the teenager is also (unfortunately) a feminist, then said teenager has to again see what norms of Western feminism to pick and which ones to leave out . . .. it's a hard job being an Indian feminist.

This post gestures to the complexity of identity issues, where being a feminist is only part of one's identity, and must often be navigated with other aspects, which can include national, ethnic, racial, religious, or sexual identity. This intersectional approach is indicative of the influence of third wave feminism that informs many of the blog posts and discussions on the site, and forms the standpoint from which many bloggers "write themselves into being" (boyd 2007).

boyd's description of writing oneself into being is particularly useful here, as the authors of many of the blog posts I analyzed use the space of their post and the practice of writing to work through their own hesitations about their feminist identity. In the same April 28, 2010 post, Jasmin writes,

> So just because I talk of Nora Ephron instead of Gurinder Chadha . . . Margaret Atwood instead of Arundhati Roy, harp praises about P. J. Harvey instead of Kavita Krishamurthy, bring up Gilmore Girls instead of Ladies Special – the list never ends – *my Indian-ness* doesn't fade away in the Western hoo-ha. If I talk using 'Indian' terminology (case in point: rotis, chai and dhobis) I'm not being any more Indian than I am now.

Here, Jasmin articulates her feminist identity using her own framework through writing, calling out the fallacy of the West/rest binary that often structures talk about global feminisms. In doing so, she carves a space within the *FBomb* to talk about feminist identities as being more than just about gender, but about the different power structures that operate on the lives of girls around the world, while also recognizing that these identities do not fit into neatly established binary of Western/non-Western feminism. This arguably globalized perspective also points to the influence of the third wave and globalization itself on this younger generation of girls.

It is often this tension over identity that spurs girls to participate within the feminist blogosphere. Nyssa, a seventeen-year-old blogger from Amman, Jordan tells me that being a *Middle Eastern feminist* was an important reason as to why she wanted to contribute to the *FBomb*. She explains that, "I've been on the feminist blogosphere as a reader for awhile now, but I thought that I had a different perspective because most of what I've read is from the U. S. or other Western countries. I've seen very little coverage on feminism in the Middle East and the perspective of a young person in the Middle East – and so I wanted to write from my own perspective."

Like all identities, the feminist identities of the *FBomb* bloggers are far from static, and instead are constantly shifting through blogging, dialogue, and new experiences. Jasmin tells me that many of her opinions have changed since she posted and that I shouldn't regard her posts as her take on feminism right now. She explains,

> I find that I've become more nuanced in my understanding of feminism – if you see my earliest posts they're still a part of Oh Yay We Are All Fighting Sexism/ Misogyny Together And Everything Is So Freaking Perfect to now where I am no longer appalled when white feminists ask me to prioritise my race and body over gender . . . so my feminist identity is fissured today. . . . I need a feminism that goes from the local to the global, so to speak – writing these thoughts out week after week has build me up to what I am today.

While Jasmin acknowledges that her views have changed dramatically through her blogging experience, this doesn't make her previous posts invalid or no longer important. Instead, they can be read as documenting a feminist identity *in flux*, a position that many other girls (and women) can relate to and a position that really exemplifies what sites like the *FBomb* are all about.

Similarly, Nyssa describes herself as "indecisive" about many feminist issues, and that the *FBomb* comments section serve as a productive space to hear about other's perspectives, which sometimes shift her own. "The comments section is a testament to how layered feminist issues are, it's definitely made me more aware of how feminism is in the West and challenged some of the perspectives I've developed about feminism from living in the Middle East, reading blogs has definitely helped fill in the layers in between." In this sense, the process of blogging is a practice that helps girls make sense of their thoughts, try out different perspectives, and to shift their feminist identities as they grow. Thus, the *FBomb* must be read as a space that is in constant motion, recording identities in flux rather than documenting static "truths" about contemporary feminisms or how teen feminists *really* are.

Renegotiating Space: Close Encounters and Closed Borders

I am labeling the *FBomb* as "in-between space" based upon Nyssa's comments that, "reading [feminist] blogs has definitely helped fill in the layers *in between*." This comment speaks to the ways that online spaces like the *FBomb* can be thought of as physical space occupying a *location in-between geographies*, and thus, has the potential to serve as an "in-between space" where close encounters can occur (Ahmed 2000). An 11 October 2010 post by Iraqi citizen Sheena serves as a useful example of what I'm calling a close encounter on the *FBomb*:

> Before we go about judging those women who dress in loose, black clothing and click their tongues at our skinny jeans, we have to remember that they can't help their beliefs, in that this is how they were brought up. The people who are performing [female genital mutilation] don't do so to hurt the girls, they just want

to protect them. The procedure, although backwards, is thought to ensure mar-
riageabilty and cleanliness. The only way to stop this is through education.

> When there are things like this going on, who really cares if Hannah Montana
> isn't completely coherent with feminist standards? We're so wrapped up in the
> issues that directly involve us that we forget to consider the bigger things.

Sheena's posting generated seventeen comments, expressing a variety of
thoughts, including readers who identify as an Orthodox Jewish feminist,
an Indian American girl, a Muslim American currently living in Saudi Ara-
bia, and a British Muslim girl.

For example, Courtney writes in the comments section,

> As an Indian-American girl, I often find myself flabbergasted at some of the
> things that white feminists find SO important . . . I mean, yeah, it is necessary to
> scrutinize pop culture. But don't do it so much that it overshadows other issues.
> I barely see international women's rights issues or issues explicitly pertaining to
> American women of color on fbomb, and it really upsets me. Women of color
> and their stories are hardly represented here.

Another poster, Kirsten, responds writing,

> I totally agree that transnational and global feminist issues are important, but it's
> also important not to trivialize more local issues. It's not just about whether or
> not Hannah Montana is a feminist. The fact is, young women are being brought
> up on this media and therefore, it is shaping a new generation. The problem of
> patriarchy and the sexualization of young girls is systemic and it is communi-
> cated through media, i. e. television, music, movies . . .

> I'm glad that you showed that this issue [FGM] is extremely important, but it
> doesn't need to be done at the expense of other issues.

I'll refrain from discussing the potential problems with the arguments being put forward and instead focus on the discursive in-between space that
they produce, a site for potential close encounters.

Ahmed (2000) writes that, "Close encounters work with what is *missing from or in the formation of collectives* . . . Alliances are not guaranteed by
the pre-existing form of a social group or community, where that form is
understood as commonality or uncommonality. The collective then is not
simply about what 'we' have in common – or what 'we' do not have in
common. Collectivities are formed through the *very work that we need to do*
in order to get closer to others, without simply repeating the appropriation
of 'them' as labour, or as a sign of difference" (179–180). Sheena's post and
the resulting discussion does not provide solutions or simple agreements.
However, this rich example makes visible the *work to be done*, complicating
notions of differences and commonalities and working through these issues within the space of the blog, what I would characterize as productive
close encounter.

Despite the ways in which sites like the *FBomb* have the potential to
function as an in-between space, they do not always do so. Jasmin was the
most outspoken about the ways in which borders function to homogenize
the feminist blogosphere. She says,

> Most – if not all – discussions in the feminist blogosphere end with western bor-
> ders. I'm not asking people to write about things they don't know . . . I'd just like
> to see borders in their writing, acknowledging that everything they write about
> exist within specific borders . . .

This comment confirms some of the critiques made by scholars such as
Woodhull (2004), and reveals the ways that the geographic borders that get
inscribed within the online world often go unacknowledged, perhaps because of the incorrect assumption that the internet is borderless.

This logic also affirms Mohanty's critiques, such as the notion of the
white, Western feminist as the unmarked norm, the assumed center of feminism. *FBomb* bloggers are often assumed as white and Western – unless
they overtly identify themselves as "other". Jasmin argues that because of
this assumed white, Western norm, girls who do not fit this identity are
legitimated only through talking about their *difference from* Western feminists. She tells me that Western feminists often,

> Don't see my body as beyond brown, where my location in India is an "interest"
> for them because of how "different" the cultures are – so I notice people 'listen-
> ing' to me, or re-blogging whenever I rant – but in day-to-day interactions, there
> is still an invisible, unequal dichotomy . . . when I'm not directly addressing
> them or pointing out their fails, very few have any interest in what I have to
> say.

Jasmin's comments point to the complexity of dialogue within an online
space, and reveal the ongoing tension between creating open space for
close encounters and closed borders that limit these close encounters from
occurring.

Conclusions: Creating Transnational Feminisms?

The *FBomb's* diverse community hints at the formation of a transnational
feminism, fostered by online global coalitions. For example, Nyssa is optimistic that the feminist blogosphere is an avenue for the development of
a transnational feminism. She says that, "The Internet has definitely really
opened up the scope, allowing people from virtually everywhere to chip
in. I think it's opening eyes everywhere – you can read poems by a Saudi
Arabian feminist or a Jamaican LGBT activist or the thoughts of an American woman in Afghanistan and a bunch of other scenarios . . . and while it
might not be perfect, it's definitely great to have that access."

Nyssa's comment points to the ability of sites like the *FBomb* to facilitate
dialogue where everyone is encouraged to have a voice and participate by
both speaking and listening to others. This is especially significant for girls,
whose voices are rarely present within mainstream media and public institutions, unless incorporated into an adult-directed initiative (Harris 2004). The
ability for girls around the world to exercise agency online through identity
exploration and connections with other girls, may suggest as to why girls are
increasingly active online, especially as bloggers (Lenhart et al. 2008).

But Jasmin's comments remind us that borders, geographies, and bodies still exist in this space, privileging a normative white, Western feminist lens with which to view issues both within Western borders – and outside them. While having girls from different countries write their own posts is a good first step, it does not necessarily negate the power dynamics present within the feminist blogosphere or dismantle the West/rest binary that has long marked transnational feminisms. Thus, Jasmin often says she feels like the "token brown" on many Western-based feminist sites. It is telling when Jasmin confides that, "I've experienced more racism online than I have in my non-online life."

The feminist blogosphere, and the *FBomb* in particular, cannot then be regarded as indicative of an unproblematic transnational feminism. However, based on my analysis and interviews, I argue that it *can* be seen as an *activist space that both makes visible the work that needs to be done, while working towards making more close encounters possible.* This is not an easy task, and leads to a space that at times appears messy, contradictory, and fraught with tensions – a position that aligns it with the feminist activism of the third wave.

Girls' blogging on the *FBomb* can be viewed as a form of feminist activism in progress, with the practice of writing constituting a way to develop, perform, and explore one's shifting feminist identity and make space for close encounters with girls from around the world. This does not always happen, as borders, bodies, and nations often get reaffirmed through the blogging process, however, as the *FBomb* and other feminist sites continually shift and change, we can hope that these shifts continue to make more space for future transnational feminisms.

References

Ahmed, S., 2000. *Strange Encounters: Embodied Others in Post-Coloniality.* New York: Routledge.

boyd, d., 2007. Why Youth (Heart) Social Network Sites: The Role of Networked Publics in Teenage Social Life. In: D. Buckingham, ed. *Youth, Identity, and Digital Media.* Cambridge, MA: MIT Press, pp. 119–142.

Collins, P., 2005. *Black Sexual Politics.* New York: Routledge.

deCaires Narain, D., 2004. What Happened to Global Sisterhood? Writing and Reading 'the' Postcolonial Woman. In: S. Gillis, G. Howie, R. Munford, eds. *Third Wave Feminism: A Critical Exploration.* New York: Palgrave MacMillan, pp. 240–251.

Dicker, R. and Piepmeier, A., 2003. *Catching a Wave: Reclaiming Feminism for the 21st Century.* Boston: Northeastern University Press.

FBomb. (2009–). http://thefbomb.org.

Garrison, E. K., 2000. U. S. Feminism – Grrrl Style! Youth (Sub) Cultures and the Technologies of the Third Wave. In: N. Hewitt, ed. *No Permanent Waves: Recasting Histories of US Feminism.* New Jersey: Rutgers University Press, pp. 379–402.

Gillis, S., 2004. Neither Cyborg Nor Goddess: The (Im)Possibilities of Cyberfeminism. In: S. Gillis, G. Howie, R. Munford, eds. *Third Wave Feminism: A Critical Exploration*. New York: Palgrave MacMillan, pp. 185–196.

Harris, A., 2004. *Future Girl: Young Women in the Twenty-first Century*. New York: Routledge.

Heywood, L. and Drake, J., 1997. *Third Wave Agenda: Being Feminist, Doing Feminism*. Minneapolis: University of Minnesota Press.

Karlyn, K. R., 2003. *Scream*, Popular Culture, and Feminism's Third Wave: 'I'm Not My Mother'. *Genders*, 38 [online]. Available at: <http://www. genders.org/g38/g38_rowe_karalyn.html/> [Accessed 25 February 2011].

Lenhart, A., Arafeh, S., Smith, A., and Macgill, A., 2008. Writing, Technology, and Teens. *Pew Internet & American Life Project* [online]. Available at: <http://www.pewinternet.org> [Accessed 20 September 2011].

Mazzarella, S., 2005. *Girl Wide Web: Girls, the Internet, and the Negotiation of Identity*. New York: Peter Lang.

Miller, T., 2007. *Cultural Citizenship: Cosmopolitanism, Consumerism, and Television in a Neoliberal Age*. Philadelphia: Temple University Press.

Mohanty, C., 1988. Under Western Eyes: Feminist Scholarship and Colonial Discourses. *Feminist Review*, 30, pp. 65–88.

Mohanty, C., 2003. *Feminism Without Borders*. Durham: Duke University Press.

Muaddi Darraj, S., 2003. Third World, Third Wave Feminism(s): The Evolution of Arab American Feminism. In: R. Dicker, and A. Piepmeier, eds. *Catching a Wave: Reclaiming Feminism for the 21st Century*. Boston: Northeastern University Press, pp. 188–205.

Woodhull, W., 2004. Global Feminisms, Transnational Political Economies, Third World Cultural Production. In: S. Gillis, G. Howie, R. Munford, eds. *Third Wave Feminism: A Critical Exploration*. New York: Palgrave MacMillan, pp. 252–262.

Choreographing Coalition in Cyber-Space: Post *Natyam's* Politico-Aesthetic Negotiations

Sandra Chatterjee and Cynthia Ling Lee[1]

Introduction

This practice-based essay unpacks the collaborative process of the Post *Natyam* Collective, a transnational, internet-based group of women artists working on critical approaches to South Asian dance. The essay aims to reveal the sticky politico-aesthetic negotiations of choreographing coalition and to discuss how the internet, used "as a grass-roots medium" (Wulff 2004: 190), initiates a re-visioning of collaborative, (feminist)[2] choreographic processes. As Polly Carl and Vijay Mathew, directors of the American Voices New Play Institute, state, "the 'we' potential in Internet technologies" allows "build[ing] our knowledge commons" through "idiosyncratic, alternative, or 'off-label' uses that serve the particular needs of our community" (Carl and Mathew 2011).

The Post *Natyam* Collective is firmly committed to collaboration. Structured as a horizontal network, rather than a vertical hierarchy with an artistic director, the collective honors multiple perspectives, geographic locations, cultural contexts and movement forms, while refusing a signature dance-vocabulary "brand." Collective members Sandra Chatterjee, Cynthia Ling Lee, Shyamala Moorty, and Anjali Tata, located between Los Angeles, Kansas City, Munich, and India, stay in regular artistic and political dialogue utilizing free internet technologies.

Committing to collaboration requires making room for each other's perspectives and stepping outside individual comfort zones to support each other's art-based political action. Such grassroots art making, to borrow contemporary art theorist Grant Kester's words, requires "the artist to surrender the security of self-expression for the risk of inter-subjective engagement" (2004: 8). As collective members, we have different political stances that map onto distinct aesthetic preferences. Our stances range from community-based art activism to deconstructing dance histories, questioning classical dance's gender constructs, challenging the audience's sexualiz-

---

1 The article has been co-written by Chatterjee and Lee. Authorship is equal.
2 Not every collective member self-identifies as activist or feminist. But we all engage with activist and feminist approaches (see also Mohanty 2003: 50).

ing/exotifying gaze, and connecting the political and the spiritual. These stances overlap, yet they can also contradict each other, producing conflict. Similarly, our differing politics manifest themselves through different aesthetics: while some of us favor creating images of healing and empowerment, others insist on highlighting multiple contradictory meanings and tensions; simultaneously others engage in the deconstruction of culturally diverse movement forms.

Working through our politico-aesthetic conflicts towards a progressive South Asian choreographic coalition brings deep feminist disagreements to the surface. In a critical discussion of women and "women of color" as a social category, feminist theorist of color Chandra Talpade Mohanty states that "there is no logical and necessary connection between being female and becoming feminist" (2003: 49). She critiques the term "feminism" from the perspective of women of color:

> Feminist movements have been challenged on the grounds of cultural imperialism and of shortsightedness in defining the meaning of gender in terms of middle-class, white experiences, internal racism, classism, and homophobia. All of these factors, as well as the falsely homogenous representation of the movement by the media, have led to a very real suspicion of "feminism" as a productive ground for struggle. (49–50)

Drawing on Mohanty's framework, then, a coalition of women of color would be effective as a "viable oppositional alliance [based on] a common context of struggle rather than color or racial identifications" (2003: 49). Critiquing unity as "a potentially repressive fiction," Mohanty and Biddy Martin (2003: 99) write:

> It is at the moment at which groups and individuals are conceived as agents, as social actors, as desiring subjects that unity, in the sense of coherent group identity, commonality, and shared experience, becomes difficult. Individuals do not fit neatly into unidimensional, self-identical categories (ibid).

Similarly, gender theorist Judith Butler states: "No one stands within a definition of feminism that remains uncontested." (2004: 174) She continues:

> I approach feminism with the presumption that no undisputed premises are to be agreed upon in the global context. And so, for practical and political reasons, there is no value to be derived in silencing disputes. The questions are: how best to have them, how most productively to stage them, and how to act in ways that acknowledge the irreversible complexity of who we are? (Butler 2004: 176)

Consistent with our internet-based process, the "disputes" of the collective are largely "staged" on a blog, where the individual members' local processes intersect.[3] The blog illustrates what Grant Kester, following Bakhtin, describes as "dialogical art practice" (2004: 10), which replaces the art object with "a cumulative process of exchange and dialogue" (2004: 12). In this sense, the collective's sustained online "conversations" bring together "a locus of differing meanings, interpretations, and points of view" (Kes-

---

3 See www.postnatyam.blogspot.com

ter 2004: 10) aiming to "imagine beyond the limits of fixed identities, official discourse, and the perceived inevitability of partisan political conflict" (Kester 2004: 8).

The artistic works discussed here reflect the politics of process (grassroots internet choreography) and the process of choreographing coalition. How does our internet-based choreographic coalition enact dialogue among difference? How should we re-envision choreography in light of our border-crossing, hyperlinked attempts at a democratic, many-headed voicing of feminist, postcolonial, contemporary South Asian dance? What are the most promising practical strategies for negotiating the tension between our political stances, between the individual and the group, and between the local and the long-distance?

Shifting Sites: The Politics of Process

Since late 2008, the collective has largely transitioned from studio-based to internet-based collaboration – not because of an aesthetic interest in cutting-edge technology and globalized intercultural networks, but out of a lack of resources. We utilize free and inexpensive internet tools such as blogging, video posting, conference calls, and online documents to stay connected across the distance despite a lack of funding, the high costs of travel and visas, and time constraints due to responsibilities of motherhood and earning a living. The internet, in dance anthropologist Helena Wulff's terms, functions here "as a grass-roots medium connecting people of lesser means and political agendas on a global level" (2004: 190). This runs contrary to seemingly related dance-media work like dance telematics, where networked performers in different locales simultaneously perform together. While such work is usually sited in well-funded institutions with high internet bandwidth, our work aesthetically reflects a DIY sensibility: our technology seldom looks slick and can be rough around the edges.

Our shift to internet-based collaboration grew out of a process of generating material for a live performance project, SUNOH! Tell Me, Sister.[4] Collective members rotated to give monthly assignments,[5] posting video responses and providing feedback to each other through blog comments. As such our online creative process encourages multiple voices, creates a structure of supportive feedback, and puts democratic dialogue about our sometimes conflicting (feminist) approaches, political methods, and aes-

---

4 Our online creative process was initially devised to generate movement material for SUNOH! Tell me, Sister, a joint performance inspired by the artistic legacy of Indian courtesans, to be compiled during two short residencies and premiered as a live performance. The performance's thematic focus widened and did not materialize with the four collective members as planned. The show, containing long-distance contributions from all members, has been mostly performed by Cynthia and Shyamala, with one run with Anjali as a trio.
5 Our process has shifted to accommodate a wider range of choreographic and research methodologies, as themes, ideas, and threads emerged that required longer development.

Picture 1: "Cyber Chat"

Clockwise from upper left: Anjali Tata, Cynthia Ling Lee, Shyamala Moorty, Sandra Chatterjee

thetic manifestations into the public sphere, opening up our process to outside intervention.[6] This shift of making our online collaborative process transparent to the public undoes the hermeticism of choreographic process, where creation usually takes place in private with only polished products made public through performance. As such, it democratizes and demystifies artistic practice, in line with the feminist visual/conceptual art practice of approaching documentation of process as an artistic end in itself (McDowell 2009).

The gradual shift to an internet-based process has had profound, unforeseen effects on the collective's overall work:

(1) Change of choreographic process: transforming each other's material into multiple, independent, and local manifestations instead of working towards one common, stable, and finished product.

(2) Mediatization of artistic product: online cultural production (video, text, sound design, art-books) supplants live dance; and change of presentation format: online sharing and art installations as alternatives to theatrical performance.

---

6   While it is rare for total outsiders to give feedback (and we do moderate comments by outsiders), in our recent project, local collaborators outside of the four-person collective regularly consulted the blog and made comments.

(3) Change of relationship to audience: (a) making a blog-based creative process transparent to the public (b) cultivating participatory structures that invite local audiences and artists to contribute to live artistic productions.[7]

Situated in a liminal space between online and live performance, our dance-work edges towards what dance scholar Harmony Bench calls "social dance-media," a hybrid form of screen-dance and social media, i. e. "the subset of Web 2.0 technologies through which internet users share and comment upon others' posted content" (2010b). Typified by an "agenda of accessibility," social dance media refers to "choreographies that elaborate upon social media's ideologies of participation. . . . dance should be shared, copied, embodied, manipulated, and recirculated rather than preserved for the professional and elite dancer . . . to create new grounds upon which to establish movement communities" (ibid). Between 2009 and 2011, we developed an "open source" policy within the collective, encouraging each other to "borrow, steal, appropriate, translate" and "creatively recycle" (Chatterjee, Lee, Moorty, and Tata 2011) each other's ideas to build our "movement community". While we have not yet centralized public participation in our process, social dance-media's emphasis on participation, sharing, and circulation facilitates a crucial transnational exchange about feminist, choreographic and activist approaches within the collective.

An artistic by-product of our shift to internet-based collaboration is an ongoing series of dance-for-camera pieces, the *Cyber Chats*. Created in collaboration with filmmakers Sangita Shresthova and Prumsodun Ok, these dance-for-camera pieces evolved unexpectedly out of our creative assignments and make extensive use of sampling and remixing. They illustrate a politics of process, negotiating between individual and collective authorial voices.

The first *Cyber Chat* – "Cyber Chat, Cyber Spat" – emerged organically from a series of Skype-inspired responses to assignments between January and November 2009, without an artistic director or aesthetic restrictions on each member's contribution. Cynthia created a sound-score to evoke the bad reception and overlapping voices of our online administrative meetings, to which Shyamala and Sandra created mock-Skype call videos that re-contextualize Indian gestures and facial expression for a webcam. Building on what had emerged by chance, Cynthia and Anjali created Skype-inspired videos as well. Though initially envisioned as live group choreography, the distance caused us to translate it into video form, cementing our shift towards online cultural production. Sangita Shresthova edited all four videos into "Cyber Chat, Cyber Spat," a loop of humorous combinations of solos, duets and a quartet,[8] which playfully strips Indian classical dance of its timeless, spiritual veneer by placing us in the context of the Skype call and our quotidian lives: trying to communicate with each other

---

7 Examples include "Make-Your-Own-Padam," "Rasa Rerouted," and *SUNOH! Tell Me Sister*'s pre-show installation (documented on www.postnatyam.blogspot.com)
8 Screened at an art installation, TRACE, in Los Angeles. See http://postnatyam.blogspot.com/2010/01/remembering-trace.html

while quieting noisy babies or drinking coffee bleary-eyed, our art-making is interlaced with domesticity. Locating us in our individual homes, the piece provides geographical context rather than placing us in the "no-place" (Bench 2010a: 54) of the black box or green screen that typifies many dance-media works.

However, many of us felt that the individual parts of "Cyber Chat, Cyber Spat" were effective as solos but too chaotic and unrelated as a quartet: the individual voices were strong, but the collective voice was less coherent. We revised "Cyber Chat, Cyber Spat," translating an artistic idea that had emerged organically into a tightly controlled choreographic process with an intricate timeline. Consciously utilizing our assignment process to co-create a dance-for-camera piece across distance rather than letting chance elements emerging from our process determine the artistic outcome, Sangita and Cynthia, co-facilitators of "Cyber Chat Revisted," specified rules to create clear relationships, encourage more stylistic consistency (fixed camera, no editing), and ensure all elements of the sound-score were addressed: "Cyber Chat Revisted" was created through an "iterative sequence wherein each member created their own cyber chat set to their own sub-track of the audio while watching previous members' interpretations" (Shreshtova 2010).[9]

The making of "Cyber Chat Revisted" reflected a new understanding gleaned from an organizational restructuring process. Realizing that it was not always empowering or efficient for all collective members to be equally involved in every decision, the collective was changing toward a clearer division of roles and responsibilities to empower individuals to take initiative to facilitate a project/process. The resulting video-solos were not as interesting as stand-alone works, but the quartet emphasized the relationships between us while maintaining a sense of multivocality: the collective voice was crafted to become stronger than each individual voice.

The Process of Choreographing Coalition: SUNOH! Tell Me, Sister

The *Cyber Chat* series exemplifies a shifting politics of process, negotiating between individual and collective authorial voices. By contrast, the politico-aesthetic conflicts between members when creating the live performance, *SUNOH! Tell Me, Sister,*[10] exemplify the choreographic process of coalitional politics. As an example, we will dissect the negotiations behind making a section of *SUNOH!*, which catalyzed tension between creating images of empowerment through community activism and portraying politico-aesthetic complexity for a theatrical context.

Community activism was introduced to the project in accordance with the community partnership requirement of *SUNOH!*'s producer, TeAda Pro-

9   See http://postnatyam.blogspot.com/2010/09/cyber-chat-revisited.html
10   From here on identified as *SUNOH!*

Picture 2: "My Silent Cry"/"The Thorn, the Leaf, and the Butterfly"

performer: Shyamala Moorty
photo by Andrei Andreev; multimedia design by Carole Kim

ductions, with Shyamala's community-based work expanded to the larger collective.[11] Based on her work with AWAZ, the Southern California-based South Asian Network's (SAN) support group for survivors of domestic violence, Shyamala created a short choreography, "My Silent Cry," in collaboration with survivor Uma Singh, who had asked Shyamala to interview her about surviving a thirty-year abusive marriage. Their duet was a variation on "verbatim theater," where interviews with usually marginalized subjects serve as a foundation for a script performed by professional actors (Heddon 2008: 127). Their joint performance at a SAN community event, where Uma spoke her story while Shyamala, bound in forty feet of white cloth, struggled, broke free, and transformed into a butterfly, was Uma's coming out as a survivor to her community. According to Shyamala, the performance was deeply transformative for Uma, herself, and the SAN community.

Nevertheless, incorporating the community-based performance, "My Silent Cry," into the collective's project led to politico-aesthetic disputes. For Cynthia, "My Silent Cry," while effective in a community context, had a script too blatant for the theater and was aesthetically disconnected from the project's investment in India's historical dancer-courtesans. Cynthia therefore drew from Uma's interview to rewrite a courtesan poem by the seventeenth-century poet Ksettraya. Highlighting resonances between the poem's refrain, "I

Picture 3: "The Thorn, the Leaf, and the Butterfly"

performer: Shyamala Moorty
photo by Andrei Andreev; multimedia design by Carole Kim

didn't say a word," and an incident where Uma refused "to tell her husband that she love[d] him when he [came] home, drunk, and demand[ed] that she profess her love," Cynthia aimed to "capitaliz[e] on the ambiguity of a woman's silence, which can be both passivity and resistance" (Lee 2010a).

A politico-aesthetic disagreement unfolded on the blog between Shyamala and Cynthia: Shyamala was interested in a clear arc from oppression to empowerment, while Cynthia wanted to evoke complex, emotional nuances. While excited "about the potential connection to the poetic tradition of the courtesans and the SAN women's experience" (Moorty 2010), Shyamala articulated concern that the ambiguous ending of Cynthia's poem was "tragic" (ibid.), suggesting that the poem end on an empowering note of resistance instead. For Cynthia, however, this change rendered the husband "flatter and more evil," "romanticizing the moment of transformation" when "acts of resistance are contingent, momentary, provisional and . . . you never fully escape" (Lee 2010b). Together with collective member Anjali and multimedia collaborator Carole Kim, they revised the piece during a residency in Los Angeles, integrating the two conflicting politico-aesthetic approaches and incorporating South Asian aesthetics such as live video feed of *abhinaya* (facial expression) and *mudras* (hand gestures), visual references to Mughal miniatures, and the rewritten Ksettraya poem. Ultimately, we created two versions of the piece: "My Silent Cry," a standalone piece suitable for survivors' groups and women's shelters, and "The Thorn, the Leaf, and the Butterfly," which related clearly to the aesthetic themes of *SUNOH!* and targeted a theatrical audience.

Throughout the revision process from a community-based performance to an abstracted choreography, Shyamala was concerned whether the increased abstraction created too much distance from Uma's story. The ethics of verbatim theater are indeed complex, for as performance scholar Deirdre Heddon explains, these projects aim to give "voice to the voiceless" (2008: 129) but run the risk of appropriating the voice of the other, giving the appearance of an authentic retelling when they are actually highly mediated by the artists' agendas (2008: 133). Whereas Uma's performative presence in "My Silent Cry" authenticates the story without foregrounding Shyamala's authorial hand, the abstraction of "The Thorn, the Leaf, and the Butterfly" de-emphasizes Uma's voice but makes no claims to literal truth. It remains debatable whether "aestheticizing" the work made it less accessible to the community from which it emerged. While Uma enjoyed our show, an activist felt the work was too abstract to be readable to working-class domestic violence survivors.

Shyamala remained in constant conversation with Uma throughout the revision process because, importantly, "[e]thical practice is located not only in the finished 'product', but also in the process" (Heddon 2008: 155). This accords with philosopher Margaret Urban Walker's "'expressive-collaborative' model" as a feminist model of ethics that "plac[es] at its centre the practice of negotiation between people in deciding appropriate ethical behavior," as opposed to the "juridical-theoretical model" (Walker in Heddon 2008: 152), a masculinist ethical model that emphasizes abstract, universal principles of justice (Garlough, in press).

These politico-aesthetic negotiations surrounding "My Silent Cry"/"The Thorn, the Leaf, and the Butterfly" largely transpired locally in Los Angeles, but disagreement about relating "courtesan" material to domestic violence also created rockiness in the long-distance process. Sandra, far away in Munich, had less opportunity to articulate her position in favor of a complex exploration of the courtesan as artist, not only victim. Simultaneously, Shyamala was worried about creating more shame for the survivors by associating them with courtesans.

This disagreement, exacerbated by an imbalance between local and long-distance engagement, put the collective into a moment of "crisis." The aesthetic requirements of the evening-length theatrical performance, which demand a dramatic arc and through line, do not allow for the same unruly fragmentation of a blog or art installation with multiple voices co-existing in the same space. Some of us wondered whether it was even viable to work collaboratively when our politico-aesthetic differences were so strong:

- How can we bring all of those streams together and still make a project that holds together?
- Do we sacrifice depth for breadth?
- By combining this material, can we do justice to the histories of the courtesans and to the stories of the women in the community based support group?
- As activists, do we need to speak from a "unified" position to make an argument?

As a collective of women choreographers of color, we are not unified in our aesthetics or our relationships to feminism and activism. At the same time, by working through our disagreements politically and aesthetically, we hope to enrich our work and extend its reach. In order to choreograph our coalition, our artistic negotiations have to make room for and actively support each other's individual political investments while being unafraid to bring our politico-aesthetic disagreements to the forefront. We sought to build a "viable oppositional alliance" of women of color while acknowledging our individual differences by identifying a "common context of struggle" (Mohanty 2003: 49) for *SUNOH!* as resistances to patriarchal structures in diverse contexts and registers. We expanded our initial focus from the courtesan's legacy to "women's stories of being silenced, finding voice, and the importance of sisterly[12] community" (Chatterjee, Lee, Moorty, and Tata 2011a). Weaving together courtesan histories, stories of domestic violence survivors, and our own personal struggles with tradition, we hoped to create "political links . . . among and between struggles" (Mohanty 2003: 46) without compromising the historical and sociocultural specificity of any specific perspective. The autobiographical stories further served to reveal our personal investment in the material and in our distinct politico-aesthetic approaches.

Lastly, in line with Butler (2004), we chose to integrate our disagreements into the performance rather than cover up tensions. The premiere included "meta-theatrical" (Heddon 2008: 153) moments such as a Skype-style video of Sandra critiquing the lack of the "radiant," erotically powerful courtesan in *SUNOH!*[13] Shyamala integrated her "self-reflexive" (ibid) perspective while performing an autobiographical section, "I see, but . . .":

> They don't know that [the courtesans] were the bearers of our dance traditions, economically independent artists, powerful business women, landowners, even revolutionaries! No, all people think about courtesans is (slaps butt). But Uma and the other survivors already feel so much (arms wrap around body in shame). . . .
>
> I can't help but see the connections, but I'm afraid of putting them together. But if I don't, then I' m not interested in the courtesans, or even in Indian dance, unless I can relate it to the world I'm living in, to the women I'm working with, and to the things I care about. Tell me sisters, what should we do? (Moorty 2011)

---

12 "Sisterly" in this piece is drawn from an ethnographic interview with a courtesan in Lucknow, India in the 1980s (Oldenburg 1990: 268 and 285). In a South Asian context, "sister" resonates differently than the feminist idea of "global sisterhood," which can be seen as contradicting the idea of coalition (Mohanty 2003: 106–123). Sociologist Patricia Jeffrey writes: "Sister' comes to mind not primarily because of a Western feminist rhetoric, but because the sister-sister can be used in South Asia to to express fictive kinship, even across caste and other boundaries" (1998: 228). Individual collective members relate to the term sister differently.

13 Screened in the premiere but removed later for dramaturgical reasons.

Conclusion: "Yes to Process," "Yes to Each Other"[14]

In conclusion, the collective's online assignment process has transformed Post *Natyam's* collaboration from live performance to internet-based cultural production. The assignment process strongly brings out the individual aesthetic/political voices of the four members, which come together on our blog. Online, media-based projects seeded from this process negotiate the power dynamics of collaboration, striking a balance between individual leadership and collective voice. Members also translate the materials created online into live performance interventions. During collaboration, our different feminist politico-aesthetic stances often require negotiation, for bringing together our voices can both enrich and undermine each other's political efficacy. The conflicts between the members' intertwined politics and artistic practices are partially resolved online and partially in person without always affecting the entire collective.

After *SUNOH!*, we evaluated the creation process to identify best practices for negotiating between the individual and the collective, between working long-distance and live. How might we cultivate multiple voices while strengthening our shared politics and pushing the envelope as artists? How might we reconsider our modes of choreographic production to suit our increasingly internet-based, transnational nature? To address and catalyze these concerns, we co-wrote and are co-choreographing a manifesto (Chatterjee, Lee, Moorty and Tata 2011), which has confirmed our desire to elevate process over product. As opposed to a dance company dedicated to performing together live, the main purpose of our transnational collective is to share an online creative process, where we translate each other's material into our own individual, localized products. We are also discussing alternative ways of presenting our work through online sharing, web-streaming, and using Web 2.0 tools to draw in public participation – formats more suitable to our internet-based communication. The staging of our process in the product itself is a technique that has served us well in both *SUNOH! Tell Me, Sister* and in the *Cyber Chats*. We believe that performing our negotiations, dis/agreements and questions strengthens, rather than undercuts, the solidarity of our collective voice.

References

Bench, H., 2010a. Anti-Gravitational Choreographies: Strategies of Mobility in Screendance, *The International Journal of Screendance* [online]. Available at <http://journals.library.wisc.edu/index.php/ screendance/ article/viewFile/312/305> [Accessed 1 March 2012]

Bench, H., 2010b. "Screendance 2.0: Dance and Social Media." *Participations: Journal of Audience and Reception Studies*, special edition Screen Dance Audiences, 7.2. Available at: <http://www.participations.org/ Volume%207/Issue%202/special/bench.htm> [Accessed 5 March 2012]

---

14 Chatterjee, S., Lee, C. L., Moorty, S. and Tata, A., 2011

Butler, J., 2004. *Undoing Gender.* New York: Routledge.

Carl, P. and Mathew, V., 2011. Building a New American Theater of the Commons. *Shareable: Sharing by Design* Community blog [blog], 4 December. Available at <http://www.shareable.net/blog/the-theater-at-a-crossroads-seeking-a-sustainable-model-for-creativity> [Accessed 12 February 2012].

Chatterjee, S., Lee, C. L., Moorty, S. and Tata, A., 2011a. SUNOH! Tell Me, Sister [online video channel]. Available at: <https://vimeo.com/channels/sunoh> [Accessed 2 March 2012].

Chatterjee, S., Lee, C. L., Moorty, S. and Tata, A., 2011b. Post *Natyam* Collective Manifesto 2.2. *Post Natyam Collective blog* [blog], 6 October. Available at: <http://www.postnatyam.blogspot.com/2011/10/post-natyam-collective-manifesto-22.html> [Accessed 7 March 2012]

Garlough, C., (in press). *Desi Divas: Activism and Acknowledgment in Diasporic Performances.* Jackson: University Press of Mississippi. (Accepted for publication 2012).

Heddon, D., 2008. *Autobiography and Performance.* New York: Palgrave Macmillan.

Hollins, Q., 2011. *Re: your feedback please* [Email]. Message to S.Moorty, Tuesday, 12 April 2011, 11:42 PM.

Jeffrey, P., 1998. Agency, Activism, and Agendas. In: P. Jeffrey and A. Basu, eds. *Appropriating Gender: Women's Activism and Politicized Religion in South Asia.* New York and London: Routledge, pp. 221–243.

Kester, G., 2004. *Conversation Pieces: Community and Communication in Modern Art.* Berkeley: University of California Press.

Lee, C. L., 2010a. Uma's padam, or Rewriting Ksettraya. *Post Natyam Collective blog* [blog], 29 November. Avalilable at <http://postnatyam.blogspot.com/2010/11/umas-padam-or-rewriting-ksettraya.html>. [Accessed 25 October 2011].

Lee, C. L., 2010b. Uma's padam, or Rewriting Ksettraya (comment). *Post Natyam Collective blog* [blog], 7 December. Available at <http://postnatyam.blogspot.com/2010/11/umas-padam-or-rewriting-ksettraya.html?showComment=1291737095985#c2684252623991594695> [Accessed 25 October 2011].

Martin, B. and Mohanty, C. T., 2003. "What's Home Got to Do With It?" in Mohanty, C. T., *Feminism Without Borders: Decolonizing Theory, Practicing Solidarity.* Durham, N. C.; London: Duke University Press, pp. 85–105.

McDowell, C., 2009. Personal communication [conversation], 29 October.

Mohanty, C. T., 2003. *Feminism Without Borders: Decolonizing Theory, Practicing Solidarity.* Durham, N. C.; London: Duke University Press.

Moorty, S., 2010. Uma's padam, or Rewriting Ksettraya (comment). *Post Natyam Collective blog* [blog], 7 December. Available at: <http://postnatyam.blogspot.com/2010/11/umas-padam-or-rewriting-ksettraya.>

html?showComment=1291723577164#c6722444679244587107>, [Accessed 30 October 2011].

Moorty, S., 2011. I see, but ... In: *SUNOH! Tell Me, Sister* [performance script]. Performed Santa Monica CA, Miles Memorial Playhouse. Post Natyam Collective. 1 April – 3 April 2011.

Ramanujan, A. K., Velcheru N. R., and David Schulman, eds. and trans., 1994. *When God is a Customer: Telugu Courtesan Songs by Ksetrayya and Others*. Berkeley: University of California Press.

Shresthova, S., 2010. Cyber Chat Rough Cut. *Post Natyam Collective blog* [blog], 6 July. Available at <http://www.postnatyam.blogspot.com/2010/07/cyber-chat-rough-cut.html> [Accessed 8 March 2012].

Wulff, H., 2004. Steps on Screen: Technoscapes, Visualization, and Globalization in Dance. In: C. Garsten and H. Wulff, eds., *New Technologies at Work: People, Screens, and Social Virtuality*. Oxford and New York: Berg, pp. 187–204.

On the Aesthetics of Self-Representation: Mustached "Female" Youth on Flickr.com

Marcus Recht and Birgit Richard

1   Introduction: Youth Culture & Web 2.0

In what follows, an attempt will be undertaken to shed light on a phenomenon that appears within the contents of the Web 2.0 platform Flickr.com that takes as its starting point the medium of the music video clip as "shifting image" (Richard 2003): the image of the woman with a mustache. If the mustache is staged plausibly enough, this image functions as a "gender bender," but the credibility of the performance can also have both intentionally and unintentionally humorous associations.

Before this particular phenomenon can be delved into, a brief overview of the changes that Web 2.0 has effected on young people should first be given. For many young people, Web 2.0 has taken over the function of an examination of their environment, of questions of worldview, of fashion, love, sexuality, violence and death, where positions are relative and a reaction is called for. Here not every ironic twist is discussed, ironically acted, always appropriately classified, satirized or simply just hated (Richard, Recht, Grünwald and Metz 2010).

In addition to the classic "real existing" locations of youth interaction, the internet in particular, in its form as "Social Web 2.0," presents itself as a space that, if nothing else, is oriented towards youth culture. In a different form, the idea of the "Street Corner Society" (Whyte 1996) can be transferred to Web 2.0 and its communities. In 1943, the term "Street Corner Society" was coined in the course of the Chicago School's groundbreaking gang study, and it has profoundly influenced the subsequent historical research on youth culture. Whyte's observation that street corners constituted congregation and meeting places for young people from marginalized social milieus due to the lack of alternatives would later be addressed by British cultural studies in the course of subsequent youth studies. The lack of representation spaces is perpetuated with the internet in the age of Web 2.0, with seemingly unlimited space at its disposal, which, given the media literacy of young people, is easy to conquer. At the same time, the virtual network is comparable in quality to the original street corner, because Web 2.0 guarantees visibility and, as a place for two-way and multi-pronged interaction, offers the potential to be a provocation space, as will also be seen in the selected examples of young women with mustaches. Web 2.0 has become a new form of the virtual street corner, ensuring visibility as a meeting place for young people from marginalized social milieus or from parts of the society which have no other alternative places in "real life" (Richard, Recht, Grünwald and Metz 2010: 13). Photos shot with mobile phone cameras, webcams or with professional cameras become a stumbling block to the media. Thus, self-expression, as will be shown below using the images of women with mustaches, can exhibit exploratory traits, not least by playing with gender identities.

In addition to the level of showing oneself and being seen, the photographs take on yet another function: they become, as it will be argued, a virtual mirror instance, which allows, in contrast to the "analog street corners" of the previous generations, even the spectators to have their own self-representation which itself is assessed (through the distance granted by the medium). This procedural ambivalence has been overlooked by the previous research, in which the representation of the other has always been assumed. At the center of such a presentation is the *ego shot*, the kind of photograph in which young people capture themselves as participants in youth cultural styles.

For the young generation, media poses are natural and commonplace. Their behavior before the camera is professional and trained. The reference to previous formats is central: such precursor images originate from pop culture media and are moreover peer images. Thus synthetic image hybrids take shape out of *me* and *I* – new forms that are not comparable to "classic" images. A very common type is the so-called *mirror shot*, in which the people photograph themselves in the mirror. This category is distinguished from the aesthetic known as the *one arm length shot*, in which the subject photographs him- or herself with a reversed camera held at arm's length. In contrast, in the mirror shot, the individual person, the visible camera and possibly a visible flash are all a part of the picture.

This youth self-presentation is reflected in a *media ego*, following its own image socialization. This can be a star double (Ullrich 2002), but in any case, an image product arises that serves the requirements of media formats and, within this framework, seeks an individual access. The *media ego* in the image always moves in predetermined categories. This is complemented by an expanded "masquerade" idea (Weissberg 1994), which applies not only to the depiction of gender relations but also to the self-presentation of young people on the internet, to refute the ideology of an "authentic" youthful appearance in images as natural or genuine. The images in general are not about the "illustration" of an authentic social reality, allowing direct inferences on the life of young people to be drawn.

2 The female mustache as "shifting image"

At this point one of the phenomena of Web 2.0 on the Flickr photo platform will be examined from the gender aspect: the representation of "mustached" femininity by youthful females. This phenomenon, based on media precursor images, is thus part of a mimetic self-representation; Web 2.0 serves here in any case as a mirror instance.

Prior to this, the term "Queer Theory" has to be specified, which was first coined in 1991 by Teresa de Lauretis (1991) as a way to transcend identity politics and categorical restrictions. The groundwork was set up for example by Judith Butler (1990), however, who showed both terms "gender" and "sex" to be socially and culturally constructed. Butler offers a critique of both terms, even as they have been used by feminists. Butler argued that feminism made a mistake in trying to make "women" a discrete, ahistorical group with common characteristics. She believes this approach reinforces the binary view of gender relations because it allows for two distinct categories: men and women.

The concept of Queer Theory was heavily influenced by the work of Eve Kosofsky Sedgwick (1985), Judith Halberstam (1998) and Michel Foucault (1978). Later it was established in the U. S. as a term for political activism (for instance as Queer Politics) and a mindset (as Queer Theory and Queer Studies). Queer works with the politics of visibility, with the critique of heteronormativity and heterosexual bisexuality as the norm, as well as criticism of all gay and lesbian identity models. Queer Theory emphasizes several sexes, the notion that gender can be divided not only into men and women, girls and boys. The novelty of Queer Studies is a comprehensive critique of heteronormativity and the emphasis that there are people who are not just dividable into the strict categories of man or woman: intersexuality, transsexuality, cross-dressing, transgender, hermaphroditism, gender ambiguity and gender-corrective surgery, etc. By demonstrating the impossibility of any "natural" sexuality, Queer Studies calls into question even such apparently unproblematic terms as "man" and "woman."

The queer image of the bearded woman possesses a certain history. José Ribera's painting from 1631, titled "Magdalena Ventura," (figure 1) should be considered the "queerest" example from art history. Magdalena is defined as a woman by her bare female breast, her child in her arms and her clothing, but she wears a long and thick beard. Another example of a bearded woman is Marcel Duchamp's Ready-Made with the title "LHOOQ" from 1919. It shows Mona Lisa with a mustache and goatee. The title is pronounced in French as "Elle a chaud au cul" and means something like "she has a hot ass." As part of this sexualized alienation of arguably the most famous painting through the appended text, the woman takes on a humorous aspect, which can also be found later on the photo platform Flickr. Another painting depicting a woman with a beard is Frida Kahlo's portrait "Autorretrato con Collar de Espinas y Colibrí". Unlike with Duchamp, however, a humorous intention of the artist is not intended in this work.

A continuation of this "pop image" can be found in professional music videos. A key example is the music video "Rainbow Warrior" by CocoRosie; in this video, Bianca Casady dons a painted-on mustache. Another "biologically" female musician who wears a conspicuous mustache is JD Samson from Le Tigre, who ensures visual deviance in her videos with her tousled, characteristically male hair. JD Samson also has bushy eyebrows,

Figure 1: Jusepe de Ribera: Magdalena Ventura with Her Husband & Son, 1631

which is typically gendered masculine in our culture. As the final example, the singer known as Peaches must be singled out, who posed for her album "Fatherfucker" with another kind of beard. It should be emphasized at this point that the nature of the facial hair in each of the three examples is very different: for Peaches, it is a glued-on classic Dutch chin beard that Abraham Lincoln also wore, which in combination with her glued-on eyelashes and a typically feminine top with spaghetti straps appears rather "queer." The other examples differ even more: JD Samson's mustache is genuine, however, and in conjunction with male-connoted clothes, produces an unflamboyant image of masculinity. The same applies to the painted-on mustache of the singer CocoRosie, which, in combination with the classically male uniform, produces a playful but authentic-looking image of masculinity.

3   Female mustaches on Flickr

This study has its origins in a quantitative analysis of the tag combination "girl" and "mustache," which resulted in 6,840 hits (as of 28 April 2011), and because of its quantity, what follows provides the basis for an investigation into images of women with mustaches and results in three categories of beard-usage. A prerequisite in the research and the subsequent investigation is the analysis of the "pure visual," excluding the accompanying text, such as the comments of other users, which would clarify what the image was intended to mean or from what situation it has emerged.

Mustached women remaining women

There are many possibilities for staging mustached femininity on Flickr. One can also find a few variants of "portable mustaches," such as those painted on the finger, as with "Jay Wolf" and her photo "Mustache Girl," or the in form of letters spelling out the word "mustache" on the finger placed above the upper lip, as in the image "Mustache" posted by "the robots revenge."

Figure 2: topupthetea: non pas!

Let us therefore consider a representative photograph by the author "topupthetea" which bears the title "non pas!": The image is, first of all, a self-portrait of the photographer in landscape format, taken possibly by her own hand from an elevated angle. The cropping shows her face from the middle of the forehead to the chin. Due to the low depth of field (on closer examination, digitally generated using a filter), only a small portion of her nose is truly sharp; due to the camera angle, her visible uncovered shoulders melt into the background blur. The coloring of the image includes dark reddish-brown tones that harmonize well with her curly red-hair. The pictured Flickr user has plucked eyebrows, the viewer can see green eyes with large pupils in the middle; her face has light freckles. Her eyelashes are blackened with mascara and her eyes are framed by a discreet eye liner. On the slightly parted lips, behind which one can see a glimpse of her teeth, a subtle red lip gloss is applied. Last but not least, on her upper lip, a thin handlebar mustache drawn with kohl can be seen, which seems at first glance to cause a disruption in the construction of femininity.

The representation of femininity within the described photograph involves a classic-romantic to sensual staging. The romantic is constructed by the dark brown tones of the photograph, as well as by the cliché of the red-haired women – particularly if she is depicted out of focus to such a large degree – as a symbol for rustic naturalness. The sexualization is produced by the presentation with slightly parted lips, and especially by the large pupils, which are dilated in a state of excitement but at the same time look challenging. Furthermore, her direct glance at the observer destroys any possibility of a voyeuristic gaze, because the viewer is in this case caught in her vision (see the chapter on "Gaze" in Recht 2011). The romantic and sensual elements of the photo are classically feminine; an erotic charge is generated through the direct eye contact with the subject captured at a high camera angle. The mustache functions more like a "comical" element, because, as can be seen at first glance, it is only painted on and does not by any means effect a deconstruction of gender. The remainder of the subject, the image genre, clothing and makeup are too feminine for it. The binary gender matrix is not disrupted by such an image.

With many female members of Flickr, facial hair often functions in a similar way, emphasizing the female performance all the more as a point of contrast, so that it functions in the sense of a gender bender.

Fun enactments of mustached masculinity

It should not be neglected at this point that the representations of mustached femininity on Flickr take many forms, some of which are humorous representations of an event requiring a costume. One such example is the image bearing the title "the real janelle," (fig. 3) which shows two women with rather imprecisely glued mustaches as part of a playful American "police detective" costume. Both are wearing sunglasses and neckties which seem to have designs originating from the 1970s; the tie on the woman to the left is so wide as to support this time period. The allusion to this era in conjunction with the visual genre of the U. S. police detective seems to make mustaches indispensible to such a masculine form. As in the history of the military (Corson 2001 and Severn 1971), mustaches were not as legally regulated with the police, but seem to follow a stylistic requirement as an element of a masculine performance.

The woman on the left is wearing a kind of weapon holster around her shoulders, which emphasizes her female form slightly underneath her rugged khaki shirt. While the woman on the left is in a speaking pose with her mouth open, her upper teeth bared, she smiles self-assuredly at the camera. The woman on the right is holding a beer can in her hand and wears eye liner behind her slightly transparent glasses.

This photo seems to be a fun party performance of uniformed masculinity. Unlike the previously discussed photographs, the "biological" femininity of the subjects is not stressed directly, but there is a convincing presentation of masculinity – rather more playful and humorous.

Figure 3: the real janelle

Becoming mustached men

While a feminine appearance is still in the foreground in the previously discussed category, the women of the final category are presenting themselves as men in a convincing way and thus deconstruct their assigned gender.

Figure 4: ksen: drag – pleased

As one such example, the photo by "ksen" with the title "drag: pleased" can be presented: the self portrait is once again photographed at a high angle, as it is a "one arm length shot." The head is turned away from the body towards the camera. The nearly square photograph is cropped from the forehead to the upper fifth of the torso. Initially, the big brown eyes that are looking directly into the lens stand out. The pupils are directed to the recipient as well. Through the use of flash, the image lacks depth perspective, and the face casts small, harsh shadows on the white unpressed collar protruding from the round neck of the black sweater. She has neck-length, intensely black layered hair and, last but not least, a little short mustache, which runs with a slight curve only to the corners of the mouth and has a central gap at the middle of the upper lip. Up to there, this is a successful boyish presentation. There are no recognizable feminine body forms, no make-up around the eyes or on the rest of the face. Even the eyebrows, by their enormous thickness and size, function as classically male. Then there is the facial expression, which lies between seriousness and expressionlessness and therefore can also be read as "gendered" classically male (Mühlen Achs 1998: 80). The only irritating point, in the truest sense of the word, is the nose piercing visible in the picture: a pinpoint-sized silver stud that in our society – particularly if it is a stud and not a ring – is typically considered feminine. The author is not aware of this, as is evident from the discussion within the Flickr commentary, but it only actuates the ambiguity that a truly interesting photograph is able produce and makes the subject into a "drag king," as the title of the photo already indicates. This is the disruption that "Gender Trouble" (Butler 1990) produced and with that a deconstruction through the confusion of gender can be triggered.

4   Conclusion: three perspectives on mustaches/ three feminisms

The woman with facial hair permeates the so-called "shifting image" of classical art, "professionally"-produced music video and finally the Web 2.0 platform. The three main types of productions on Flickr in which women are staged with a mustache are also applicable to the representation of mustached femininity and can be interpreted from three different feminist perspectives. The question that now arises is what these three different mechanisms bring about and to what respect this promotes "equality."

The use of the mustache in all categories forms a parallel to the different interpretations of feminist practice in the late 1970s and 80s, which is known as "power dressing." At that time, businesswomen in particular wore masculine suits that, with the help of shoulder pads, attempted to imitate an even more "masculine figure" and simultaneously conveyed the feeling that a woman could be whatever she wants to be. This image was quickly put into perspective through the elaboration of diffuse power structures, which society imposes as gender mechanisms (Bordo 1993). Furthermore, the strategy of power dressing as a mimicry of the male form was put in a negative light particularly by third-wave feminism: women should rather imbue feminine attributes with "positive qualities" instead of blindly imitating the masculine characteristics of success or power. In the case of power dressing or the use of a mustache, the feminist subject proves itself to be discursively constituted by the very political system that makes its emancipation possible.

Especially with regard to the *first* group presented here, the bearded woman remaining a woman can be interpreted in a similar way: These women adopt the symbol of the mustache, but without taking on the associated symbolism of, for example, power, wisdom, potency, etc.; they remain, all in all, typically female. This can also be linked to the form of the mustache, as the thin, dainty French mustache fits a classic dreamy female gender performance and is anything but a potent symbol of male power.

All the more it seems surprising that the strategy of the *second* group, which uses the beard for humorous purposes, can be seen as following a feminist agenda. They follow, of course maybe without knowing it, the example of the American feminist B. Ruby Rich, who supported the female use of comedy as a powerful political weapon with a "revolutionary potential as a deflator of the patriarchal order and an extraordinary leveler" (Rich 1998: 77). It was time for the power of female laughter, which questions the symbolic and political systems that keep the woman in her classical place. To use Luce Irigaray's words: "Isn't laughter the first form of liberation from a secular oppression? Isn't the phallic tantamount to the seriousness of meaning? Perhaps woman, and the sexual relation, transcend it 'first' in laughter?" (Irigaray 1985: 163). In this form of fun staging, the mechanisms of power are brought together with a masculine presentation and adopted as a political weapon. Here also the distinction between pastiche within the first category and parody with the second group is made clear. While the first group can be seen as the imitation of a neutral practice of mimicry without laughter, the second group, with its satirical and humorous elements, stands for parody (Jameson 1998: 114).

The *third* group is a more serious presentation of masculinity, providing the viewer with a paroxysm that brings the gender-binary system to collapse, thereby creating "Gender Trouble." This is mainly due to the fact that gender is no longer identifiable in these cases because of the mustache. The question of the actual gender of the mustache wearer has already been dealt with in the section on of the third category, and points to the difference between the three distinct types of bearded representation: While the first category takes up *gender* as an issue, and the second already partially deconstructs the same, but it is in the third that *sex* undergoes a deconstruction. Following Foucault's model of emancipatory sexual politics, the overthrow of the category of biological sex brings with it the liberation of a primary sexual diversity (Foucault 1977), which is also found in the third category described here. It makes no difference whether it is a woman who gives such a convincing male performance, or whether the "true gender" is no longer recognizable. The fact that one such form of travesty imitates gender identity implicitly reveals the imitative structure of gender identity itself. This means that gender and sexual identity are de-naturalized by the performance.

References

Bordo, S., 1993. Feminism, Foucault and the politics of the body. In: C. Ramazanoglu, ed.: *Up against Foucault. Explorations of some tension between Foucault and feminism.* London: Routledge, pp. 179–202.

Butler, J., 1990. *Gender Trouble: Feminism and the Subversion of Identity.* New York: Routledge.

Corson, R., 2001. *Fashions in Hair. The First Five Thousand Years.* London: Peter Owen.

de Lauretis, T., 1991. Queer Theory: Lesbian and Gay Sexualities. *Differences: a Journal of Feminist Cultural Studies* 3.

Foucault, M., 1978. *The History of Sexuality Volume 1: An Introduction?* New York: Vintage.

Halberstam, J., 1998. *Female Masculinity.* Durham: Duke University Press.

Irigaray, L., 1985. *This Sex which is Not One,* trans. C. Porter and C. Burke. New York: Cornell University Press.

Jameson, F., 1998. Postmodernism and Consumer Society. In: Jameson, ed. *The Cultural Turn. Selected Writings on the Postmodern 1983–1998.* London: Verso.

Mühlen Achs, G., 1998. *Geschlecht bewusst gemacht. Körpersprachliche Inszenierungen. Ein Bilder- und Arbeitsbuch.* München: Frauenoffensive.

Recht, M., 2011. Der *sympathische Vampir. Visualisierungen von Männlichkeiten in der TV-Serie Buffy.* Frankfurt am Main/New York: Campus.

Rich, R., 1998. *Chick flicks: theories and memories of the feminist film movement.* Durham: Duke University Press.

Richard, B., 2003. 9–11. World Trade Center Image Complex + "shifting image". In: B. Richard and S. Drühl, ed. *Kunstforum International: Das Magische* 164, pp. 36–73.

Richard, B.,/Recht, M., Grünwald, J. and Metz, N., 2010. *Flickernde Jugend – rauschende Bilder. Netzkulturen im Web 2.0.* Frankfurt am Main: Campus.

Sedgwick, E. K., 1985. *Between Men – English Literature and Male Homosocial Desire.* New York: Columbia University Press.

Severn, B., 1971. *The Long and the Short of It. Five Thousand Years of Fun and Fury over Hair.* New York: David McKay.

Ullrich, W., 2002. Der Starkult als Verdopplung: Doubles. In: W. Ullrich and S. Schirdewahn, eds. *Stars.* Frankfurt am Main: Fischer. pp. 121–149.

Weissberg, L., ed., 1994. *Weiblichkeit als Maskerade.* Frankfurt am Main: Fischer.

Whyte, W. F., 1996. *Die Street Corner Society: Die Sozialstruktur eines Italienerviertels.* Berlin: de Gruyter.

Illustration sources

Figure 1: Jusepe de Ribera: Magdalena Ventura with Her Husband & Son, 1631. Online: http://www.kunstgeschichte.uni-mainz.de/1025.php

Figure 2: topupthetea: non pas! Online: http://www.flickr.com/photos/topupthetea/388467313/

Figure 3: the real Janelle. Online: http://www.flickr.com/photos/janelle/76457186/

Figure 4: ksen: drag – pleased. Online: http://www.flickr.com/photos/theskyeisfalling/150210699/

Struggling for Feminist Design: The Role of Users in Producing and Constructing Web 2.0 Media

Tanja Carstensen

Introduction: Users in Web 2.0 between gender stereotypes and feminist struggles

Web 2.0, with its social network sites, music- and video-sharing platforms, wikis and weblogs, is celebrated as the users' web. It is linked to hopes concerning user participation, information exchange and sharing, interoperability, user-centred design, the removal of the sender-recipient structure, and boundless participation and collaboration without hierarchies (Best 2006; critically: Reichert 2008: 8). The agency of the users is expected to increase enormously; every user is a potential sender. As bloggers, wiki participants and members of social network sites, they generate content and applications and therein contribute to the construction and production of Web 2.0 media.

The first studies on the gendered aspects of Web 2.0 show a heterogeneous picture (Carstensen 2009): While weblogs offer spaces especially for female users to express their thoughts and meanings as well as their diverse versions of femininity (Herring, Scheidt, Bonus and Wright 2004; Harders and Hesse 2006; van Doorn, van Zoonen and Wyatt 2007) or even for new subject constitutions and queer politics (Landström 2007), analyses of the scripts of the registration forms on social network sites as well as of users' self-presentations in the personal profiles show stereotypical constructions of gender identities on the sides of both the users and the designers (Wötzel-Herber 2008; Manago, Graham, Greenfield and Salimkhan 2008).

Beyond that, from a feminist viewpoint it is interesting that users have initiated a few struggles for (and against) feminist, gender-sensitive, queer or inclusive designs within Web 2.0. In the following, I discuss the questions of what agency, possibilities and restrictions users with feminist or gender-sensitive requests have to influence, contribute to or intervene in media production and the design of Web 2.0. I therefore first give a short overview of the debate on the social construction of technology and the role of the users in shaping technology within the field of Science and Technology Studies and recent internet research with a special focus on feminist perspectives. I then introduce my empirical results, which are based on considerations taken from three examples of feminist interventions: a struggle of content, a struggle of language and a struggle of forms. In the end I discuss the role of (feminist) users and the extent to which they have become active participants in producing Web 2.0 media.

From users that matter to prosumers

In the field of Science and Technology Studies (STS), it is no longer controversial that technology is a result of negotiation processes and power struggles. Mainly initiated by the research into such approaches as *Social Shaping of Technology* (SST) and *Social Construction of Technology* (SCOT) it is also uncontested that technological development does not follow its own logic, but rather is the outcome and materialisation of social power relations (MacKenzie and Wajcman 1985; Bijker, Hughes and Pinch 1987). The design process is characterized not by "one best way", but by high "interpretative flexibility" (Pinch and Bijker 1987: 40). These opportunities for different designs and meanings of one artefact are negotiated by relevant social groups in the fields of technology, science, politics, economy and the public (Bijker 1997: 269), in which the most powerful actors achieve their interests. Technological artefacts therefore represent social structures, norms, discourses and motives.

Within this conceptualisation of technology as socially constructed, users have come into view as relevant actors in recent years, too (see esp. Oudshoorn and Pinch 2003). On the one side they are considered to be 'imagined users', who play a role in the construction of technologies. Akrich (1992) suggests that "innovators 'inscribe' a specific vision about the world into the technical content of the new object". She calls the end product of this work a "script" (Akrich 1992: 208). The scripts of technological objects enable or constrain human relations as well as the relationships between people and things. These representations of the anticipated interests, skills, motives and behaviour of future users become materialised in the design, and attribute and delegate specific competencies to users and technological artefacts (Akrich 1992: 207).

Dutch and Norwegian feminist scholars have extended the script approach to gender perspectives and developed the concept of a "gender-script" (Berg and Lie 1993; van Oost 1995; Rommes, van Oost and Oudshoorn 1999). This concept follows the idea that designers (unconsciously) inscribe different views of female and male users and uses into technology. Gender is imprinted onto objects through instructions, advertisements, associations with gendered divisions of labour, and associations with gender symbols and myths. Artefacts that incorporate a gender script then construct users' gender identities (see Cockburn and Ormrod 1993; Oudshoorn, Saetnan and Lie 2002; Zorn et al. 2007) and are therefore powerful, materialized co-players in gender relations (Haraway 1991: 153).

On the other side, STS approaches emphasize that scripts are not closed; they remain flexible and cannot determine users' practices and identities completely (Oudshoorn, Saetnan and Lie 2002: 478). The domestication approach analyses how *technological objects are integrated into daily life and* how users, through their different ways of interpreting, using and talking about technologies, further contribute to the social shaping of technology (Silverstone and Hirsch 1992; Lie and *Sørenson 1996)*. Users do not necessarily have to adopt the scripts constructed by the designers. They may slightly modify the scripts, drastically transform them, or they may even completely reject or resist them, create new meanings and uses for the objects, or become non-users (Kline and Pinch 1996; Kline 2003; Oudshoorn, Saetnan and Lie 2002; Wyatt 2003). Therefore, users play a crucial role in shaping technologies.

This also opens room for manoeuvre with regard to gender: "Users define whether things are useful, or maybe fun, what things are good for and for whom, whether they experience them as gendered and whether they find them useful to articulate and perform their (gender) identities. By interpreting and using technologies, users are active participants in shaping the gendering of artifacts" (Oudshoorn, Saetnan and Lie 2002: 481). Users are conceptualised as "co-designers of their relationship to technological products" (Lie and Sørenson 1996: 3).

The domestication approach has led to a shift in the conceptualisation of users from passive recipients to active participants. It focuses on the creative agency of users, but leaves room for a critical understanding of the social constraints on user-technology relations and the differences among and between designers and users.

However, while the designer-user differentiation still remains relevant in the domestication approach, this separation erodes in current concepts of the role of users in constructing Web 2.0 technologies. No other previous technology has been constituted by users to the same extent as the internet, with homepages, Wikipedia entries, personal profiles in social network sites, the open source movement, forums and chats. Referring to Alvin Tofflers "prosumer" (1970), it is suggested that the role of producers and consumers begins to blur and merge. The consumer becomes part of the production process. Voß and Rieder (2005) point in a similar direction and describe how increasingly professional processes and functions are outsourced to private customers. They call this new type of customer a "working customer". Furthermore, Bruns (2008) shows how the collaborative content creation carried out in the open source software development and in Wikipedia is based on active users. As relevant actors, users participate in designing content and software and become producers, developers and designers of technologies.

However, at second glance, it becomes clear that Web 2.0 is by no means solely constructed by users, nor is it entirely democratic and participatory. Rather, a range of power structures and hierarchies can be identified in wikis, weblogs and social networks. Stegbauer (2009) shows how power relations and hierarchical organizational structures arose among Wikipedia users and how this restricts opportunities to participate. Herring, Scheidt, Bonus and Wright (2004) and Hesse (2008) point out that despite a female dominance among weblog writers, the so-called A-bloggers – the most-read weblog writers – are almost 70% male. Thus, traditional mechanisms of hierarchical gendered public spaces still have an impact on digital publics. Finally, recent research on social networks has shifted the focus from social networks as spaces for individual networking and self presentation to the business strategies of companies like Facebook and their effect on techno-logical infrastructures, not at least as materializations of hegemonic and governmental norms (Leistert and Röhle 2011). It becomes clear that Web 2.0, like most technologies, is a field of negotiations structured by power relations. However, the role of gender in these struggles and negotiations is still wide open.

Against the background of opportunities for user participation on the one side and hierarchical power structures on the other, it is interesting to study the feminist users' struggles in Web 2.0 to see the users' agency and restrictions on contributing to and intervening in the construction and pro-duction of Web 2.0 technologies and media.

Feminist struggles in Web 2.0

In the following I investigate some of the struggles in which users try to realise feminist and gender-sensitive design ideas in order to get some insights in the users' role in Web 2.0 media production from gender per-spectives. Feminist struggles happen at different places: at decentralized weblogs (e. g. controversies with/about trolls) as well as at central loca-tions like MySpace, studiVZ, Wikipedia, or Facebook (Carstensen 2009). The following three cases represent only examples of struggles, illustrating the variety of aims, strategies and achievements of the involved users. A systematic study of even more struggles is lacking, and would be able to complete and ground these preliminary results.

In the three investigated examples of interventions, design is criticised by feminist users, gender-sensitive and feminist design ideas are developed and discussed. Three distinct types of struggles concerning the design of Web 2.0 are carried out:

1. Struggles for content: the discussions concerning the suggested de-letions of the two feminist entries, "Ladyfest" and "riot grrrl", in the German version of Wikipedia.
2. Struggles for language: the discussion on the German social network site studiVZ on the use of gender-sensitive language within the net-work.
3. Struggles for forms: the discussion on the German social network site studiVZ about the registration form as well as the request in Facebook "For a queer positive facebook . . ." as recommendations to change the profile options.

In some senses, these examples represent different feminist strategies and can map a certain bandwidth of feminist aims: revaluating the relevance of feminist issues as well as implementing and defending feminist and gender issues in the mainstream public (1), making women visible (2), and deconstructing binary gender concepts and enabling subject positioning beyond female and male (3).

Online (deletion) requests, petitions, documented discussions within Wikipedia, Facebook and studiVZ, as well as the self presentations of the involved groups and actors, all serve as data material.

Struggles for content

The first example covers the discussions about the suggested deletion of two feminist entries, "Ladyfest" and "riot grrrl", in the German version of Wikipedia. Wikipedia is based on wiki technology, the technological script of which enables users to contribute, edit and discuss content within Wikipedia.

The explicit idea of Wikipedia is that everybody can participate.[1] At the same time Wikipedia disposes of differentiated social rules. A central principle of the Wikipedia policy is the "neutral point of view",[2] which means that all articles must represent fairly, and as far as possible without bias, all significant views that have been published by reliable sources. Every user can suggest the deletion of an entry; this can be discussed by all and a decision can be reached. The deletion itself can only be performed by administrators. Reasons for deletion (in the German version of Wikipedia) are a lack of relevance,[3] a lack of quality, or copyright problems.[4]

In August 2007 the existing entries on "Ladyfest" and "riot grrrl" in the German version of Wikipedia were suggested for deletion. The deletions of these entries were reasoned by one user as having a lack of relevance, quality and significance. Other critics who followed described the entries as "free association" which was "not objective". The fact mentioned in the entry that women and girls are underrepresented in the music industry was disputed. Furthermore, the statement of gender as a social construct was questioned. The initiator of the deletions argued "I always thought that gender is concerned with genetics." The subsequent responses fought for the relevance and the quality of the entries. It was stated that Ladyfests and riot grrrls are part of a supra-regional movement and an expression of a new feminist self-conception, and are therefore relevant. Furthermore, it was criticised that in a "male-dominated internet medium, an entry on a feminist group is censored". One user wrote that it should be noted that the entry for "riot grrrl" can be

1 http://en.wikipedia.org/wiki/About_Wikipedia
2 http://en.wikipedia.org/wiki/Wikipedia:NPOV
3 http://de.wikipedia.org/wiki/Wikipedia:Relevanzkriterien
4 http://de.wikipedia.org/wiki/Wikipedia:L%C3%B6schregeln

found in eight other Wikipedia versions in other languages. In the end, an administrator decided to keep the entries.[5]

These incidents illustrate that the question of whether feminist contributions to content production are possible and successful in Wikipedia is predominantly decided among users. Feminist users' interventions do not fail or succeed because of closed technological scripts, but because of other users who argue against feminist topics. Feminist interventions into content production can be successful but they must deal with differences, attacks, negotiations and opposing views at the same level – the users' level. In addition, the key role in these decisions is held by the administrators, so we have to take into account some important hierarchical structures.

Struggles for language

The second example covers the unsuccessful struggles within the German social network studiVZ over the use of gender-sensitive language within the network. As in other social network sites, the technological scripts allow users to construct a personal profile, connect with other users, found groups and have discussions.

For the denominations of the functions one can have within the network, such as "student", "moderator" or "administrator", only male forms are used.[6] This androcentric and discriminating script was cause for some users to found a group called "gender sensitive language in studiVZ".[7] The group formulated the aim to also use female forms like "Administratorin", "Freundin" or "Studentin". A student had expressed this concern to the responsible persons of studiVZ and posted her message and the administrator's response in the group forum. In the answer, the administrator argued that implementing gender-sensitive language would be "highly difficult". He stated that studiVZ's concern was by no means to discriminate against women through grammatical finesse. Further, he outlined that the emancipation of women, which was doubtlessly an important movement, ought to have more important things to do than to try to "change grammatical designs": "While we argue about word endings, infants are killed in other countries simply because they aren't male. I am sure that the whole team [of studiVZ] . . . would be pleased to support you if you have any ideas on

---

5 The discussions are documented under http://de.wikipedia.org/wiki/Wikipedia:L% C3%B6schkandidaten/5._August_2007#Ladyfest_.28bleibt.29; http://de.wikipedia.org/ wiki/Wikipedia:L%C3%B6schkandidaten/5._August_2007#Riot_grrrl_.28erledigt.29.

6 In the German language, there are female and male forms for nouns such as "Studentin" (a female student) and "Student" (a male student). The German feminist movement has long criticised that women are not visible in this use of language (Pusch, 1984). Feminists suggest different possibilities to make language more gender-sensitive, including the "Binnen-I" or the use of gender-neutral forms such as "Studierende." In governmental institutions, the use of non-discriminating terms has since become regulated.

7 http://www.studivz.net/Forum/Threads/df0dbc9fd58e4e34/p/1.

to fight against the real discrimination of women. Certainly, you must have proposals for that if you think about emancipation, right?"[8]

This provocative answer stirred disgust and rebellion, as well as the idea to compile a catalogue of requests to studiVZ. However, the group grew fast, and with it also the number of members who argued against gender-sensitive language. These opponents started a thread within the group called "pro preservation of the generic masculine noun!" with a range of anti-feminist reasoning. In this group, a controversial discussion of the purpose of gender-sensitive language ensued. The idea of a joint catalogue of requests therefore failed because of the controversies within the group.

This example illustrates different problems relating to feminist interventions in social network sites. The first point faces a similar problem as already discussed in the Wikipedia example: Users are different; they have different political attitudes and opinions, and are by no means united in their feminist aims. Feminist interventions as common actions and strong alliances to shape design, supported by a larger group, therefore already fail because of the controversies and differences among users.

Furthermore, the possibilities to influence the androcentric design of the social network are restricted technologically as well as socially. There are no possibilities for users to change the gendered scripts directly, because they do not have access to the level where the denominations are fixed. The member's message to the responsible persons of studiVZ illustrated the hierarchical decision structures in which no direct interventions are intended. The responsible administrators decided on the language script and now affirm it as unchangeable; feminist requests are refused, and even treated derogatively.

Nevertheless, users have – as advised by technological scripts – the possibility to found groups, open spaces to discuss, criticise the language use and launch protests against the structure of the platform. They can address the responsible persons and try to achieve changes via petitions and mails. The scripts of social network sites offer large possibilities for transporting feminist aims and concerns into a larger public. So the feminist interventions to change the androcentric language use in studiVZ did not achieve their aim, but by placing this issue on the agenda, they sensitised other users and pointed out that women are not visible in this use of language.

Struggles for forms

The third example deals with users' requests for non-binary registration forms. Most of the social network sites require the indication of diverse information to register as a member, such as name, birthday, location, nationality, etc. Gender plays a significant role in the gaps in the registration forms, and in most cases one can only choose between the two options of male or female (Wötzel-Herber 2008). This is also the case on the social network sites studiVZ and Facebook.

---

8 http://www.studivz.net/Forum/ThreadMessages/df0dbc9fd58e4e34/ce5bfaba358bd792

If users refuse to choose one of the two alternatives of gender in studiVZ, they are sent to the statement: "Only female or male entities can register with us!" In the current version of Facebook, users are asked by a dropdown menu "Select sex: Male/Female" and are requested to "Please select either Male or Female" upon refusal. Thus, in both cases the technological scripts do not allow registering without a subject positioning as male or female.

In studiVZ, the registration forms were also criticised within the "gender-sensitive language in studiVZ" group mentioned above. One user asked who in the group might also be angry about that, and suggested that studiVZ should offer a third possibility, such as "indecisive". It was suggested to formulate a common request to change the registration forms. This, however, did not happen.

In 2007, a Facebook group was founded which fights "For a queer positive facebook. . . .".[9] The members of the group are lobbying the operators of the site to make certain changes to the way user profiles are currently formatted. The users want Facebook to add new features to the user profiles which would allow a more inclusive representation of a wide range of personal self-identities. They published a statement in which they claim that "we have the right to demand that it [Facebook] be an open, inclusive and positive community, which reflects the identity of all members." They recommend different changes to profile options: the drop down menu for "sex" should be changed to "gender" and switched to a "fill in the blank" format. Further, the next category "interested in" should have extra boxes of "none" and "other", followed by a "fill in the blank", added to the selection of "men" and "women". Finally, they demand that persons who select "in a relationship" should have the option of including multiple partners. They point out that persons who do not identify with any of the above identities will still have the 'traditional' options and will simply not make use of the additional services.

Users can join the group to support their concerns, and they can also download and use an application offered by the group which supplies the requested possibilities: "Finally you can express your sexual orientation and gender identity accurately, the way it should be expressed: your way! Choose from many options, both binary and non-binary, for sex, transition status, gender identity, gender presentation, orientation, interested in, title, and pronoun, or fill in your own." Users are also pointed to the notice: "This application was *not* developed by Facebook."[10]

Just as in studiVZ, the attempts in Facebook to change the registration forms also failed. Although the group has had at its best times over 11,000 members who supported this concern and contributed to a heated discussion, Facebook did not react.

---

9 http://www.facebook.com/group.php?gid=2214484023.
10 http://calpoly.facebook.com/apps/application.php?id=2353404662.

This third example illustrates how strong the technological scripts as well as the social power relations are within social network sites. The operators of Facebook decided on a design with dichotomous gender scripts and now ignore requests to change them. Feminist users criticize these restrictions, but in the end have no possibilities to change the registration forms.

So, feminist agency to change forms in social network sites is limited, while at the same time this technology not only offers space and agency regarding discourses, protests, requests and petitions, it also enables the development of an independent supplemental application which does not influence the registration form, but at least broadens the possibilities inside the network to express oneself within the personal profile. This does not change the design, but amends it.

Conclusion: Feminist users don't matter?

Against the hopes of strong users' agency these examples show that users' possibilities to intervene in the design of Web 2.0 are restricted by social and technological barriers, differences among users, strong hierarchies (within the group of the users as well as between users and administrators) and by fixed affirmed scripts, which in most cases do not permit possibilities to change design directly. And it has been shown that it is easier to influence content than language use or forms. The prognosis for the erosion of the producer-user differentiation turned out to be inaccurate. Although users can produce a lot of media content in profiles, wikis, weblogs, etc., in questions of design it still makes a difference which side you are on.

It also has been shown that in the investigated struggles, users with feminist or gender sensitive aims have to negotiate and argue against strong anti-feminist, androcentric, and heteronormative structures, norms and attitudes, which are manifest within Web 2.0 in content, language and forms, among other things. This constellation is not specific to the internet; it also can be found in workplaces, politics, print media, etc., but it comes to a head in Web 2.0. Furthermore, it can be assumed that these current power relations and conflicts become more visible in the participatory and user-centred technological environments of Web 2.0, as if technology is produced behind closed doors.

However, it is remarkable how many rooms for feminist discourses exist within the technological scripts of Web 2.0 media technologies. Aside from the disillusioning result that (feminist) users are not able to influence site design in a far reaching way, another conclusion is that the domestication of media and technology now takes on a public dimension in Web 2.0: the negotiation, transformation, rejection, modification and reinterpretation of technological artefacts moves from households and private places into public spaces. Feminist users carry out visible struggles, raise their voices against existing design, produce trouble and develop ideas for alternative design in spaces made available by Web 2.0 technologies. Dissatisfaction with technological scripts becomes a public issue that can be verbalised and discussed directly with others, so at least self-understanding and an exchange of opinions are promoted. Whether or not these discursive struggles will have consequences for feminist media production in the long term remains to be seen.

References

Akrich, M., 1992. The de-scription of technical objects. In: W. E. Bijker and J. Law, eds. *Shaping technology/building society, studies in sociotechnical change.* Cambridge, Mass.: MIT Press, pp. 205–224.

Berg, A. J. and Lie, M., 1993. Feminism and constructivism: Do artifacts have gender? *Science, Technology and Human Values* 20(3), pp. 332–351.

Best, D., 2006. *Web 2.0 Next Big Thing or Next Big Internet Bubble? Lecture Web Information Systems.* Technische Universiteit Eindhoven.

Bijker, W. E., 1997. *Of Bycycles, Bakelites, and Bulbs. Toward a Theory of Sociotechnical Change.* Cambridge, Mass.: MIT Press.

Bijker, W. E., Hughes, T. P. and Pinch T. J. eds., 1987. *The Social Construction of Technological Systems. New Directions in the Sociology and History of Technology.* Cambridge, Mass.: MIT Press.

Bruns, A., 2008. *Blogs, Wikipedia, Second Life, and Beyond: From Production to Produsage.* New York: Peter Lang.

Carstensen, T., 2009. Gender Trouble in Web 2.0: Gender Relations in Social Network Sites, Wikis and Weblogs. *International Journal of Gender, Science and Technology* 1(1) [online]. Available at: <http://genderandset. open.ac.uk/index.php/genderandset/article/view/18> [Accessed 21 September 2011].

Cockburn, C. and Ormrod, S., 1993. *Gender and Technology in the Making.* London: Sage.

Haraway, D., 1991. *Simians, cyborgs, and women. The reinvention of nature.* New York: Routledge.

Harders, C. and Hesse, F., 2006. Partizipation und Geschlecht in der deutschen Blogosphäre. *femina politica* 19(2), pp. 90–101.

Herring, S. C., Scheidt, L. A., Bonus, S. and Wright, E., 2004. Bridging the Gap. A genre analysis of Weblogs. Paper presented at the 37th Hawaii International Conference on System Sciences [online]. Available at: <http://www.ics.uci.edu/~jpd/classes/ics234cw04/herring.pdf> [Accessed 23 April 2009].

Hesse, F., 2008. Die Geschlechterdimension von Weblogs: Inhaltsanalytische Streifzüge durch die Blogosphäre. *kommunikation@gesellschaft* 9(1) [online]. Available at: <http://www.soz.uni-frankfurt.de/K.G/B1_2008_ Hesse.pdf> [Accessed 21 September 2011].

Kline, R., 2003. Resisting consumer technology in rural America: The telephone and electrification. In: N. E. J. Oudshoorn and T. J. Pinch, eds.

How users matter: The co-construction of users. Cambridge, M. A.: MIT Press, pp. 51–66.

Kline, R. K. and Pinch, T. J., 1996. Users as agents of technological change: The social construction of the automobile in the rural United States. *Technology and Culture* 37(4), pp. 763–779.

Landström, C., 2007. Queering Space for New Subjects. *Kritikos. An international and interdisciplinary journal of postmodern cultural sound, text and image* 4, November-December [online]. Available at: <http://intertheory.org/clandstrom.htm> [Accessed 20 September 2011].

Leistert, O. and Röhle, T. eds., 2011. *Generation Facebook. Über das Leben im Social Network.* Bielefeld: transcript.

Lie, M. and Sørenson, K. H. eds., 1996. *Making technology our own? Domesticating technology into everyday life.* Oslo: Scandinavian University Press.

MacKenzie, D. and Wajcman, J. eds., 1985. *The Social Shaping of Technology. How the Refrigerator Got its Hum.* Milton Keynes/Philadelphia: Open University Press.

Manago, A. M., Graham, M. B., Greenfield, P. M. and Salimkhan, G., 2008. Self-presentation and gender on MySpace. *Journal of Applied Developmental Psychology,* 29(6), November-December, pp. 446–458.

Oudshoorn, N. E. J. and Pinch, T. J. eds., 2003. *How users matter: The co-construction of users and technologies.* Cambridge, Mass.: MIT Press.

Oudshoorn, N., Saetnan, A. R. and Lie, M., 2002. On gender and things: Reflexions on an exhibition on gendered artefacts. *Women's Studies International Forum* 25(4), pp. 471–483.

Pinch, T. and Bijker, W., 1987. The Social Construction of Facts and Artifacts: Or How the Sociology of Science and the Sociology of Technology Might Benefit Each Other. In: W. Bijker, T. Hughes and T. Pinch, eds. *The Social Construction of Technological Systems. New Directions in the Sociology and History of Technology.* Cambridge, Mass.: MIT Press, pp. 17–50.

Pusch, L. F., 1984. *Das Deutsche als Männersprache. Aufsätze und Glossen zur feministischen Linguistik.* Frankfurt am Main: Suhrkamp.

Reichert, R., 2008. *Amateure im Netz. Selbstmanagement und Wissenstechnik im Web 2.0.* Bielefeld: transcript.

Rommes, E., van Oost, E. and Oudshoorn, N., 1999. Gender and the design of a digital city. *Information Technology, Communication and Society* 4(2), pp. 476–95.

Silverstone, R. and Hirsch, E., 1992. *Consuming technologies: Media and information in domestic spaces.* London:Routledge.

Stegbauer, C., 2009. *Wikipedia. Das Rätsel der Kooperation.* Wiesbaden: VS Verlag.

Toffler, A., 1970. *Future Shock.* London: Bodley Head.

Van Doorn, N., van Zoonen, L. and Wyatt, S., 2007. Writing from experience: Presentations of Gender Identity on Weblogs. *European Journal of Women's Studies* 14(2), pp. 143–59.

van Oost, E., 1995. 'Male' and 'female' things. In: M. Brouns, M. Verloo and M. Grunell, eds. *Women's Studies in the 1990s. An introduction to the different disciplines.* Bussum: Couthinho, pp. 287–310.

Voß, G. G. and Rieder, K., 1995.*Der arbeitende Kunde. Wenn Konsumenten zu unbezahlten Mitarbeitern werden.* Frankfurt am Main: Campus.

Wötzel-Herber, H., 2008. *Doing Me and the Others. Identitätskonstruktionen in Online-Communities.* M. A. thesis, University of Hamburg [online]. Available at: <http://woetzel-herber.de/2009/02/22/doing-me-and-the-others-identitatskonstruktionen-in-online-communities/> [Accessed 20 September 2011].

Wyatt, S., 2003. Non-Users also matter: The construction of users and non-users of the internet. In: N. E. J. Oudshoorn and T. J. Pinch, eds. *How users matter: The co-construction of users.* Cambridge, M. A.: MIT Press, pp. 67–79.

Zorn, I., Maaß, S., Rommes, E., Schirmer, C. and Schelhowe, H. eds., 2007. *Gender designs IT. Construction and Deconstruction of Information Society Technology.* Wiesbaden: VS Verlag für Sozialwissenschaften.

Using New Technologies to Enter the Public Sphere, Second Wave Style

Linda Steiner

Introduction: Historical Contexts for Second Wave Production

Although some contemporary movements operate with and through mainstream media, the women's movement has long suspected mainstream media outlets of harboring sexism, so it avoids relying on mainstream media to represent women in their diversity or to disseminate relevant news and information. The internet is merely the latest and clearest example of a pattern of focusing on men as the initial, primary market for communication technologies (Wajcman 2010; Melhem and Tandon 2009). Nonetheless, feminist organizations have used each new medium in turn to carve out space in which to share women's news and feminist perspectives among themselves and with wider publics (see Chambers et al. 2004; Steiner 1992).

Apart from the content carried, each medium has a material and technological structure that may either constrain or promote social movements. Different media have advantages and disadvantages in reaching known sympathizers or unknown "masses." They facilitate (or discourage) certain ways of thinking and interacting. They require different kinds of material investment and degrees of technical skill, even if financial profit is irrelevant and if aesthetics and slick production values are low priorities. Moreover, while feminists typically emphasize disseminating principled content, information is not the only goal. Often participants want to learn complex skills, study significant issues, and form and sustain community. Therefore, in figuring out the best way to communicate, whether internally or with potential converts or policy-makers, feminists must calculate the goals and available human and financial resources against the costs and capital investment required.

The research reported here highlights the importance of the *process* of producing feminist content and thereby sustaining feminist solidarity. Given the media options available to U. S. feminists, how do both the processes of participation and the potential for developing a sense of community and group loyalty figure in the long-term success of feminist media projects? The focus here is an emphatically feminist collective that since 1994 has produced a public service show, *New Directions for Women* (NDW), available on public access channels on cable systems in three states. The collective is a New Jersey chapter of the National Organization for Women (NOW). Most of its participants have been involved since the start, and reflect a second wave sensibility. A few are members of the Veteran Feminists of America – feminists who struggled together and want to rekindle the spirit of that revolution.

The question is whether cable access continues to offer viable opportunities for public participation by feminists using feminist modes of production, given the intersection of generation with medium-specific advantages and disadvantages. NDW participants explicitly describe themselves as "not innovative or inventive." But they take the fact that their shows are archived at Smith College, an elite women's college, as evidence that NDW not only represents relevant contemporary issues, but also will last far beyond the cablecasts and YouTube, where the group also posts all shows.

Second Wave Broadcast Feminist Media

Similar to their first wave forerunners during the campaign to win the right to vote, second wave feminists were prolific in print. They published many local, regional, and national newspapers and magazines, newsletters and comic books (see Endres and Lueck 1996; Steiner 1992). Such ventures were supported by then-new feminist publishing houses and imprints, bookstores, and news distribution services. Many of these periodicals were produced by, for, and about specific niches: women with particular religious, sexual, professional/vocational, ethnic, racial or political identities. Others, of course, had more comprehensive scope and sought more general popularity, as represented most prominently in the U. S. by *Ms.* magazine. The cable show described here changed its name to *New Directions for Women* (NDW) after the cessation of a national feminist newspaper by that name founded in 1972 by Paula Kassell, who was also active in the NOW chapter. *New Directions for Women* grew from a mimeographed quarterly to a thick bimonthly with a broad healthy subscriber base and international renown.

Other "platforms" were more difficult. Yet least 33 women's groups in the U. S. produced radio programs between 1963 and 1985 (Allen 1988). Moreover, like second wave services that distributed newspaper and magazine content, the Feminist Radio Network (FRN), formed in 1974, distributed feminist radio programming nationwide. Martha Allen's point is that the FRN was typical of women's media: It enabled women to share their experiences, offered access to technology, and had a collective structure, particularly regarding decision making. It insisted: "Feminist programming can replace the passive media-audience relationship with one in which the audience and participants are synonymous, and in which we can see the strength of our own lives reflected in our programming" (quoted in Allen 1988). Feminists continue to maintain beachheads in radio; nonetheless, the structure and financial imperatives of commercial broadcasting discourage its use by social reform movements. The FRN eventually concluded that because men controlled the technology and owned the radio stations, women in broadcasting could never enjoy the same autonomy as print-oriented women.

Producing regular feminist broadcast television is even more difficult, complex, and expensive, given, inter alia, the structure of advertising. In 1974, for this very reason, a North Carolina women's group applied to the Federal Communications Commission (FCC) for permission to use a seemingly abandoned FM frequency. When the original license-holder sought to re-operate the station, the FCC rejected the women's application (Allen 1988). In Chicago, the Women's News Service Project, which served stations not normally covering women's news, began an evening news feminist show in 1974. Meanwhile, in 1980 the FCC issued a license to some Connecticut women to build a television station, but they never managed to raise the $1.5 million needed to get on air.

The History of Public Access Television

Feminists soon came to realize that commercial television would never be feasible for them. Their best chance became public access channels on cable. Multiple reports in the 1960s and 1970s (by which time utopian discourse had peaked) confidently predicted that the new "television of abundance" could deliver information, civic education, and citizen participation (Doty 1975). A blue-ribbon commission heralded the "awesome" promise of cable to revolutionize cultural life (Sloan 1971). Despite concern that "production elitism" and citizen apathy would limit its potential for decentralized participation (Gillespie 1975), public access cable television in particular was hailed for its democratic potential to revolutionize cultural life and encourage direct engagement. Public access was the "last best hope for a public sphere and for an active enlightened polity" (Devine 1992: 9). Nonetheless, implementation was slow. In 1973, some 69 women's (and mixed) organizations jointly applied for a Memphis, Tennessee cable channel that would provide serious alternative programming for and by women but not exclusively about women (Allen 1988). The city opted not to go forward with cable TV. Similar coalitions in Maryland, Kentucky, New York, Wisconsin, and Washington, D. C. failed for assorted reasons.

Meanwhile, in 1969, after experiments first in Canada and then in the U. S., the FCC endorsed cable's potential to augment community self-expression (Linder 1999). In 1972, the FCC required cable systems in the 100 largest markets to provide channels specifically for public, educational, and local government use (so-called PEG channels), which come bundled in the basic cable package. The Cable Communications Policy Act of 1984 authorized local municipalities to request channels, if they wanted, and to require cable franchise holders to provide training, equipment, and production facilities, usually for free.[1] Typically, anyone may produce programming for a public-access channel. The 1984 Act barred cable operators from

---

1 Municipalities may choose to forego PEG channels, thereby pocketing all franchise fees. Cable, including public-access television, is not subject to the same rules as broad-

exercising editorial control over PEG channel content. As of 2000, some 18 percent of cable systems provided equipment and facilities for local public programming (Aufderheide 2000). Because some states no longer require cable providers to offer public access channels, more than 100 PEG stations across the country (out of about 5,000) have closed since 2005; another 400 face extinction (Arnold 2011). A bill proposed in 2011 would protect PEG channels and restore some funding.[2]

Analysts personally involved in recent public access projects remained optimistic about public access's Do-It-Yourself aesthetic and value to democracy (Halleck 2002). Although political effectiveness presumably requires wide distribution, access television enables "ordinary people" to reframe commercial ideologies, exercise democratic free speech rights, and represent themselves to the larger community (Stein 2001). But feminist cable access shows are essentially limited to a few big cities and college towns – and are sparse and short-lived. Naysayers question the capacity of public access shows to help build community, and ridicule the programming as self-indulgent, amateur, homemade, and "pathetic" (Aufderheide 1992: 58). Meanwhile, public access can be exploited by for-profit businesses.

Internal technical constraints are not insignificant. Even producing a fairly primitive public access show necessitates a core mass of skilled people. It cannot be done on the spur of the moment, at home, or alone. This communal need for participation by and interaction among a group is perhaps an advantage of public access for feminists. Meanwhile, the technology continues to change. Community program producers have always exploited new technologies whenever possible, especially as costs drop. First, video camcorders were relatively easy for non-professionals to learn and use. Now, even cheaper, easier Web 2.0 technologies and digital equipment, including open-source or user-modifiable software, may gradually replace cable system-operated public access. On the other hand, in the short term, the open-source model discourages and reduces interaction among producers and may further exclude underserved and seniors, among other groups (Arnold 2011).

NOW Media Policy

From its birth in 1966, the National Organization for Women has been suspicious of mainstream media. Its website, among other venues, expresses NOW's pointed criticism of televised sexism (and violence). In 1999, for example, NOW complained that opponents interrupt and distort their message whenever its activists speak. This attention to television makes sense:

cast television, although people mistakenly complain to the FCC about public access programming.
2 Public-access channels operate in United Kingdom and Europe, Canada, Australia, New Zealand, and South Africa, usually on cable but occasionally through terrestrial television. Germany, Norway and Sweden have "open channels." For example, since 1985, government-financed Offener Kanal (Open Channel) Dortmund is free for use by local citizens (http://homepage.tinet.ie/~openchannel/ctvlinks.htm).

Television symbolizes and allocates status. In 1996 three women (including two women from the local NOW chapter described here) brought to NOW's national convention a resolution calling for feminist media to counter the images of women as sex objects and/or victims and to supply feminist perspectives. Their mimeographed statement claimed NOW needs "a public voice, public awareness of feminist positions, a forum for feminist thought and analysis of national policy issues, and a vehicle for recording women's herstory." Feminist television could be a powerful tool for organizing, fund raising, and potentially converting "mainstream" women into "declared feminists."

In 1999, NOW joined a coalition of foundations and nonprofits to advocate more public affairs and political programming, as well as support for public service media, community accountability, and diversity. This project quickly faded, but its separate campaign to promote "positive and diverse" portrayals of women and people of color lasted a while longer. NOW's "Watch Out, Listen Up!" project focused on television, given "its unbeatable reach into our homes and its influence on our attitudes." "Watch Out, Listen Up!" encouraged people to regard themselves as media activists – by complaining about offensive content and applauding positive content. In 2002 NOW issued a fairly damning analysis of all primetime programs on six channels, but it seems to have abandoned this series of reports.

NOW also urges people to create their own programming – for cable access shows, low-power radio stations or online radio shows. Occasionally this works. NOW members have been quoted in press accounts discussing the effectiveness of programs they made for community or access channels. More to the point, in 1999 NOW launched its own Feminist Communications Network – a TV, cable, radio and web broadcast network. The chair of the Feminist Communications Network Task Force described participants as "energized and committed to working together toward a common vision" (Grieco 1999). But this idea also died. The only cable access show nominally linked to NOW is the focus here, *New Directions for Women*. After twice appearing as a guest, I interviewed members individually and in groups several times during November 1997, February 1998, March 1998, April 1998, December 2000, July 2004 and February-March 2012. I intended to remain an observer in the field, not to turn this into a participant-observation project. Nonetheless, three times while observing, I was recruited to do camera work because someone failed to show up. Background came from interviews and documents, especially from the show's original executive producer.

New Directions for Women

NOW chapter activists in Morris County, New Jersey were inspired to consider producing their own cable television show by Florynce Kennedy, a radical lawyer, civil rights activist, and feminist whom *People* magazine called "the biggest, loudest and, indisputably, the rudest mouth on the battleground" (Martin 2000). In the late 1970s, Kennedy co-produced a feminist news analysis show in New York City for cable for the Feminist Party, which she had founded. "The Flo Kennedy Show" also aired on cable. Ironically, Flo Kennedy helped found NOW, but abandoned it after deciding it was overly geared to white, middle-class women (Martin 2000; Hoffman 1985). Meanwhile, New Jersey NOW members were tired of being vilified by right-wing extremists. "We decided it was time for us to do more than just write letters to the editor to let people know what we stood for and who we really were" (DeRise 1995). They turned to cable.

Taped at the cable system's studio, the programs themselves nearly always involve interviews with one, two or three guests. The production rate has dropped slightly, probably due to a drop in membership. Yet they persevere: By January 2012, NDW had produced 219 shows in eighteen years. The show, which is re-aired several times a month, is listed in local cable guides and on the chapter's increasingly sophisticated, content-rich website. NDW is the chapter's major activity, but the chapter's other communication mechanisms include Facebook and Twitter.

In the spirit of the newspaper's emphasis on detailed hard news, the collective insists that shows be informative. "The quality of the shows depends on the quality of the guests," the host says. Guests include nationally-known feminists, researchers, university scholars, political leaders, and professionals, as well as people whose personal experience gives them warrant. Men are rarely guests, but men have discussed male feminists, stay-at-home dads, puberty, prostitution, bi-sexuality, and pornography, among other questions. NDW wants to be "effective" so it demands topics that, in their estimation, bring the private into the public domain, resonate broadly, and interest people with all kinds of views. Several members assert that NDW programming is and should be relevant to men, as many feminists have more generally claimed about feminist content, including Kassell herself. Men may join NOW – whose preposition is 'for,' not 'of' – although no men were members of the chapter in 2012. Potential NDW topics must be approved at an open meeting of the chapter's board of directors. One NDW member explains, "Viewers need to be interested and NOW needs to be convinced there is enough interest." It's a matter of making choices among possible topics. The board rarely disapproves a proposal outright; suggestions are most likely to be denied because NDW had recently done something similar, or a guest who proposed a topic did not attend a meeting to explain it.

NDW members are satisfied with anecdotal evidence that they reach an audience, including direct responses, positive and negative. They claim to have over 32,000 views of their programming and are expanding on YouTube. A few years ago, one stalwart said, "I want to believe there is an audience. . . . Well-educated people tune into questions of importance. They are concerned with these issues." The current chapter president says: "While we don't have millions of views, we have tens of thousands and our subscriber list is slowly growing. I have been exploring all avenues of social media in an effort to spread awareness of NOW and to engage younger women. It is a philosophy of 'If you build it, they will come.'"

After carefully pondering whether to feature argument, NDW members decided that avoiding incivility or pandering was more important than being exciting or adversarial. They understand the intellectual and moral vacuity of the myth of objectivity espoused by mainstream news professionals. Noting frequent instances when the political right has manipulated journalists and misrepresented feminism, they see no responsibility to present opposing or anti-feminist viewpoints. A founding NDW member said: "We don't directly present anti-feminist content or shows that work against women." Announcements of topics often proclaim their agenda. For example, the teaser for a discussion of the impact of neoconservatives on sex education referred to "the 'civil war' between those who want to go backwards and those who understand that that will never happen."

NDW has featured several issues of particular concern to feminists, including the debate over equal rights, pay equity, feminist activism, the closing of women's prisons, prisoners' children, sexual slavery, sex crimes, domestic and dating violence, discrimination of various kinds and women in the workplace – especially in "nontraditional" fields. Deans of two women's colleges discussed pressures on women's colleges to go co-ed. Third World women occasionally come up. Not surprisingly, given that women over 50 dominate the crew, practical issues about aging (navigating the empty nest, senior care, retirement) have been featured. But breast feeding, fertility, and especially reproductive rights are more prominent. Several shows have dealt with (homo)sexuality, trans-sexuality, and same-sex marriage and partnerships. Among the historical shows, in early 2012, NDW featured Sojourner Truth, who so famously asked "Ain't I a Woman," as well as suffragist Alice Paul and journalist Margaret Fuller.

Technology somewhat constrains the potential for a specifically feminist approach to collective action in that it requires people have a certain technical literacy (although mastery of the technology is widely regarded both as an asset and part of the fun). The local cable company originally provided ten weeks of training to 18 chapter members, who learned to direct, operate cameras and lighting, and work the control panels. The crew tapes shows, two at a time, at the sponsoring cable system's facilities. Although additional people have taken the course or apprenticed with the crew, of course they have lost some of their original members. Recently the NDW chapter's newsletter – wholly online – described NDW's "dire need" in all production roles. Luckily, after doing NDW for so long, they can now get by with fewer people than before – a director, two camera operators, one audio technician, one video graphics, plus the host/interviewer. Indeed, most of the burden is on the host: She must study the topic, plan out questions, and consider how to engage with guests who might be difficult to draw out. Moreover, after years of taping on Saturdays, NDW now enjoys a "very good" mid-week time, when cable system employees are available to fix broken equipment – a chronic problem.

Like its parent organization, NDW is not obsessed with the feminist method, including the anti-hierarchical sentiment of the 1960s. It is fairly casual about power and leadership. NDW's main concern is getting the work done without glaring errors. Still, consistent with feminist action for well over a century, NDW is concerned with group processes and group learning. Taping sessions remain consistently quiet and calm. The women, who now know each other quite well, offer and accept sisterly, friendly advice. The effort survives on a shoestring. FCC law forbids advertising on PEG channels but, as with public television, corporate underwriting is acceptable. On occasion, a few businesses underwrote NDW's "thought-provoking" show. But soliciting sponsors takes time; this has fallen off. The collective still lacks the human resources necessary to apply for grants – something the newspaper did quite successfully. So they cannot build a nicer set, and must shuttle their few props (flowers, tablecloth, mugs) back and forth.

The collective largely but not exclusively expresses the voice of white, middle-class, liberal feminists. One long-time member is African American; none are Asians.[3] No men remain members of the chapter or crew. One member who teaches at a technical high school occasionally brings students to work on the crew, but the regular members are all over the age of 50. The members themselves explicitly emphasize that they are all busy with families, careers, and a host of community, volunteer and social responsibilities that they take very seriously. These women have sacrificed to carve time out of their complex, highly over-committed work and family lives to acquire the requisite technical literacy and to continue on.

Generations, Technology and Community

To promote participation, NOW's own documents list camaraderie and "a great time," along with learning new skills, personal development, and pride in accomplishment. Along with a sense of community, these virtues have been highly important to other feminist projects and to other public access collectives, as well as to contemporary internet projects. Some years ago, NDW's instrumental view of their work, their apparent disinterest in regular extra-curricular socializing and their thin sense of community seemed surprising. NDW participants describe themselves as a community and enjoy their time together (as well as, occasionally, time outside of NOW projects). They refer to NDW as a "labor of love." Not only do they come together to produce their public access show, but they also attend NOW meetings, as well as parades and protest marches. In 2011, this included an Occupy rally in Washington, D. C. and marches on behalf of peace, labor rights, and healthcare.

The sense of community is relative and its definition plastic. Mastery of skills and fun accord with research on many Web 2.0 projects, but third-wave feminist activity arguably creates an even thinner community. Although I cannot examine this here, it's worth noting briefly that third wave feminists' favorite media tools require no interpersonal interaction. Third

---

3   This is not surprising given the demographics of Morris County.

wave cyberfeminists still seek "community," albeit a mostly virtual community. The bilingual Canadian blog site Kickaction.ca, for example, often mentions its status as a "community." Feministlawprofessors.com aims for a stronger feminist law professor "community." Feministing.com has a "Community" page, where "all members of our community" can post. The mission of fourthwavefeminism.com is "to foster feminist community in our contemporary world. . . . It's up to us, as a community – as a movement – to actually orchestrate change." But the blogosphere does not offer the shared identity or nurturing enjoyed by second wave feminist communities, nor do they provide a specifically feminist structure. Producing online content facilitates self-expression in the moment but neither requires nor encourages group interaction or ongoing loyalty to a shared "cause." Feminists' new online social interactivity and networking is largely virtual, anonymous, and accomplished by individuals. In particular, personal blogs (essentially online diaries) have a libertarian essence that is arguably at odds with the feminism of the older generation.

For their part, third wavers have largely rejected second wave's condemnation of mainstream media. Second wave tactics do not speak to the "media-savvy, culturally driven generation" of the third wave (Baumgarder and Richards 2000: 77). One eponymously named third wave website proudly asserts: "This is not the second wave warmed over. We are building on what they have accomplished and taking it in new directions appropriate for the 21st century" (quoted in Karras 2002).

Conclusion: Public Sphere or Screen

Jürgen Habermas's (1989) history of the emergence and disintegration of the liberal bourgeois public sphere has been accused of multiple empirical, historical, and conceptual errors. Nancy Fraser (1997) notes that Habermas's public sphere privileged white bourgeois men, formal political issues, and rational debate, so never offered universal or equally distributed power. Proposing instead the concept of counter-publics, she says a single, comprehensive public sphere is impossible in complex multi-cultural societies (Fraser 1997). Moreover, at least initially, Habermas conceived of mass media in mass-market terms, ignoring alternative or oppositional public spheres. On the other hand, while agreeing that the concept of the public sphere remains essential, Kevin DeLuca and Jennifer Peeples (2002) criticize those trying to reform Habermas's notion of the public sphere for problematically focusing on rationality and dialogue, producing "an exclusionary and impoverished normative ideal that shuns much of the richness and turbulence of the sense-making process" (128). They propose instead the "public screen," which "highlights dissemination, images, hypermediacy, spectacular publicity, cacophony, distraction, and dissent" (145).

This debate captures on the key difference between the playfulness of third wave feminists and the second wave, exemplified by the New Jersey feminists' preference for rationality, deliberation, and civility. That is, NDW manifests two kinds of genetic ancestry: Habermas's interactive salon tradition; and the 1970s dramatistic style of feminist activism. They decidedly do not ignore difference. But they aspire to dialogue that produces consensus. They struggle together, holding firm to their long-term and explicitly shared commitment to protracted work at a variety of levels and in multiple contexts in order to produce incremental changes for women. The general claims made on behalf of public access television – that it promotes media literacy, "real" political activism, and empowerment at both the individual and group levels – continue to describe NDW. The "talking head" is, they acknowledge, old-fashioned. Indeed, more than ever, NDW members wish they could go on location and use the technology in more sophisticated and jazzy ways. Still, it actively chooses the calm, rational, moderate tone. This is not only technically easier but it also befits their general politics, inherited from liberal feminism.

While they appreciate that they don't need to confront (or solve) the economic and editorial constraints confronting commercial television, they lack the resources required for more innovative, creative work. In my view, this is not a matter of lack of time, commitment, imagination, or even money. Rather, technical and structural demands within public access channels over-determine the "product." No single medium is perfect; no single mechanism can fully support deliberation among all publics. Far greater technical resources and theatrical skills than NDW can muster are necessary to reach third wave feminists. But NDW has negotiated a partial way of serving complex and even contradictory purposes by acknowledging their own limitations and those of the form. They continue to offer for public discussion – especially audiences of their generation – genuine news from women's personal and work worlds. They have properly redefined the public not as a collection of individual consumers, but as social identity groups with real material, political, social, cultural, and intellectual needs. They have both recognized who they are, who they would like to be, and whom they want to serve. They do so without pandering or compromising their feminism.

References

Allen, M. L., 1988. The Development of Communication Networks Among Women, 1963–1983 [online]. Available at: <http://www.wifp.org/table-ofcontents.html>

Arnold, E., 2011. The Cable TV Access Crisis. *Alternet*, 7 August 2011 [online]. Available at: <http://www.alternet.org/media/151905/99_percent _300x250_flash.swf>

Aufderheide, P., 1992. Cable Television and the Public Interest. *Journal of Communication* 42(1), pp. 52–65.

Aufderheide, P., 2000. *The Daily Planet: A Critic on the Capitalist Culture Beat*. Minneapolis: University of Minnesota Press.

Baumgardner, J. and Richards, A., 2000. *Manifesta: Young Women, Feminism, and the Future*. New York: Farrar, Straus and Giroux.

Chambers, D., Steiner, L. and Fleming, C., 2004. *Women and Journalism*. London: Routledge

DeLuca, K. M. and Peeples, J., 2002. From Public Sphere to Public Screen: Democracy, Activism, and the "Violence" of Seattle. *Critical Studies in Media Communication* 19(2), pp. 125–51.

DeRise, M., 1995. Lights, Camera, Take Action. *NOW newsletter* November 1995 [online]. Available at: <http://www.now.org/nnt/11-95/morristv.html>.

Devine, R. H., 1992. Access in the 21st Century: The Future of the Public. *Community Television Review* 15(6), pp. 8–9.

Endres, K. and Lueck, T., eds., 1996. *Women's Periodicals in the United States: Social and Political Issues*. Westport, Conn.: Greenwood Press.

Doty, P., 1975. Public Access Cable Television: Who Cares? *Journal of Communication* 25, pp. 33–41.

Fraser, N., 1997. *Justice Interruptus: Critical Reflections on the 'Postsocialist' Condition*. New York: Routledge.

Gillespie, G., 1975. *Public Access Cable Television in the United States and Canada*. New York: Praeger.

Grieco, H., 1999. Media Institute Sets Sights on Feminist Network [online]. Available at: <http://www.now.org/nnt/fall-99/mediains.html>

Habermas, J., 1989. The Structural Transformation of the Public Sphere: An Inquiry into a Category of Bourgeois Society, trans. T. Burger, with F. Lawrence. Cambridge, Mass.: MIT Press.

Halleck, D., 2002. *Hand-Held Visions: The Impossible Possibilities of Community Media*. New York: Fordham University Press.

Hoffman, M., 1985. Flo Kennedy and Irene Davall: Forever Activists, *On the Issues Magazine* 5. Available at: <http://www.ontheissuesmagazine.com/1985vol5/mh_vol5_1985.php>

Karras, I., 2002. The Third Wave's Final Girl: Buffy the Vampire Slayer. *thirdspace: a journal of feminist theory & culture* 1(2) [online]. Available at: <http://www.thirdspace.ca/journal/article/viewArticle/karras/50>.

King, D. L. and Mele C., 1999. Making Public Access Television: Community Participation, Media Literacy and the Public Sphere. *Journal of Broadcasting & Electronic Media* 43(4), pp. 603–623.

Linder, L. R., 1999. *Public Access Television: America's Electronic Soapbox*. Westport, Conn.: Praeger.

Martin, D., 2000. Flo Kennedy, Feminist, Civil Rights Advocate and Flamboyant Gadfly, Is Dead at 84. *The New York Times,* December 23, 2000. Available at: http://www.nytimes.com/2000/12/23/us/flo-kennedy-feminist-civil-rights-advocate-and-flamboyant-gadfly-is-dead-at-84.html

Melhem, S. and Tandon, N., 2009. *Information and Communication Technologies for Women's Socio-Economic Empowerment*. Washington, D. C.: World Bank Working Paper Series.

Shamberg, M., 1972. *Guerilla Television.* New York: Holt, Rinehart and Winston.

Sloan Commission, 1971. *On the Cable. The Television of Abundance.* New York: McGraw-Hill.

Stein, L., 2001. Access Television and Grassroots Political Communication in the United States. In: J. D. Downing, with T. V. Ford, G. Gil and L. Stein, eds. *Radical Media: Rebellious Communication and Social Movements.* Thousand Oaks, CA: Sage, pp. 299–324.

Steiner, L., 2005. The Feminist Cable Collective as Public Sphere Activity. *Journalism* 6(3), pp. 313–334.

Steiner, L., 1992. The History and Structure of Women's Alternative Media. In: L. Rakow, ed. *Women Making Meaning: New Feminist Directions in Communication.* New York: Routledge, pp. 121–143.

Wajcman, J., 2010. Feminist Theories of Technology. *Cambridge Journal of Economics* 34(1), pp. 143–152.

Chapter 3:
Cultural Citizenship
and Social Change

BEFORE

WHY DO THEY NEVER SHOW PEOPLE LIKE US ON TV?

"Alternative and independent media is VITAL for any social change and movement. Grrl zines are especially important because we live in a world were male voices reign supreme and strong, independent, feminist women's voices are few and far between. They are out there, but we don't often get to hear them ... unless you pick up zine to read!"
Editor of *Pretty Ugly*
(Australia)

NOW

WHY DO THEY NEVER SHOW PEOPLE LIKE US ON TV?

"I've decided that I want to produce something that'll CHANGE people's mindsets, make them think and talk about it, make them angry, make them stand up and spit, scream and stomp on it. I know I can't single-handedly start a revolution and overthrow the government or anything like that. All I wanted was to start a tiny little revolution in all my reader's minds and hearts that I hope'll lead to bigger changes."
Editor of *Trippers zine*
(Singapur)

Drawing by Nina Nijsten (originally published in *ScumGrrrls*, Belgium, no. 16, 2009)

"I think zines are significant on both individual levels and for social movements. They play important roles in DIY feminist and anti-capitalist movements. Anyone can contribute to a kind of non-academic/non-professional but very valuable DIY political theory and herstory."
(Nina Nijsten, Belgium)

Cultural Citizenship. Participation by and through Media

Elisabeth Klaus and Margreth Lünenborg

1   Rethinking citizenship in the era of globalisation

In recent years the notion of citizenship has triggered many debates in the political arena as well as in different disciplines. There are a number of reasons why the concept of citizenship, largely taken for granted since the Age of Enlightenment and the bourgeois revolutions in Europe, has since the 1990s given rise to many questions (e. g. Turner 1994). Firstly, globalization has undermined the overwhelming power of the nation-states, which are closely linked to citizenship. Secondly, the emergence of multi-ethnic, multi-cultural societies and migration processes has nourished doubts as to the unambiguousness and clear meaning of the concept. Instead it is quite obvious that nation-states are more and more inhabited by social actors who are affiliated with different regions (residing in one, working in another, speaking the language of a third) and assume multiple subject positions. Thirdly, the development of popular media discourses and the increase in entertainment programmes has partially supported a de-politicisation of the public sphere, but at the same time the advent of new digital media and especially the Internet has provided new means for individual actors as well as marginalized groups to publicly voice their opinions and to become involved in politics (here understood in the wider sense of the term).

All these developments have resulted in the emergence and the greater visibility of new practices of citizenship as the different articles in this book demonstrate quite forcefully. Various scholars have tried to capture the defining characteristics and the inner workings of new modes of participating in society by qualifying citizenship in a number of ways, as cosmopolitan or transnational citizenship, diasporic citizenship, emotional citizenship, do-it-yourself citizenship (DIY citizenship), digital citizenship practiced by netizens, media citizenship and so on (e. g., Dietze 2012; Hauben and Hauben 1997; Hartley 1999; Ong 1999a; Valentine 2001). All these terms stress the diverse subject positions and identities that can be taken up by citizens and the modified practices and processes of enacting citizenship in everyday life. Although the different terms are quite distinct and highlight different aspects of what it means to be a citizen and participate in society, they do have a common ground since they all relate in some way or other to cultural identities and cultural practices. Moreover, they share a concern with participation and address questions of social inclusion and exclusion. This is what has been loosely termed as *cultural citizenship* by different scholars.

But what exactly does cultural citizenship mean? How is it related to traditional notions of citizenship? Is it just another ideal that masks processes of exclusion or can it contribute to participatory practices? In the following discussion, we will first ponder the concept of citizenship, its emergence and its shortcomings. We will then trace the origins and different meanings of the term "cultural citizenship." Our understanding of cultural citizenship is linked to theory and research on media and communication. We conceive of society as fundamentally determined by media and communication. When we claim that we live in a media society, we refer to the fact that information, knowledge, experience and participation today are mediated at all levels of identity formation, at the level of the sub-cultural community, the nation-state and the global, de-territorialized society. On these grounds we argue that cultural citizenship can function as a key concept for exploring processes of cultural meaning production and participation. Thus, we suggest integrating cultural citizenship as a contextual element in the circle – we see it as a globe – of meaning production, which is one of the central models developed by the Centre for Contemporary Cultural Studies in Birmingham. We finally ponder the complexity of the issue using the example of reality television – especially talent shows – and its portrayal of migrants and queers. These TV programmes are ambiguous in that they allow for new forms of representation and visibility that can include, lead to or stimulate participatory practices. At the same time the genre is reproducing traditional stereotypes with regards to gender, sexuality, class and ethnicity and reiterates topics that reinforce the exclusion of particular social groups.

2 Social, political and civil citizenship

For quite a long period of time the concept of citizenship has been discussed and elaborated almost exclusively within the disciplines of political sciences and sociology. Citizenship refers to the terms of belonging to a nation-state: A citizen is acknowledged as a worthy member of a nation-state or a conglomerate of nation-states like the EU. To convey or grant citizenship is linked to different rights of participation and to the obligations to assume responsibility within the political public sphere.

The British sociologist Thomas H. Marshall is credited with a widely accepted clarification and systematization of the rights citizenship confers to its members. Marshall introduced the now well-known and much-used distinction between civil, political and social citizenship in 1949. He thus highlighted three different aspects of citizenship: civil citizenship, sometimes termed with equal justification economic citizenship, addresses the individual's right to participate in the economy as a free producer and consumer. Political citizenship centres on rights and obligations to participate in the political decision making process. In a parliamentary democracy the rights to vote and to be elected are at the core. Finally social citizenship, now a highly contested area in Western European societies, acknowledges that society has a collective responsibility for the well-being of its subjects. The social welfare state, while never a heaven of justice and equality, nevertheless provided a kind of safety net for persons who were hit by illness, unemployment or infirmity and supported some of the more vulnerable members of society like children, the disabled or the elderly.

Marshall's tripartite model distinguishing civil, political and social citizenship was extremely useful in explaining different aspects of citizenship. However, he failed to see the autonomous and essential role that cultural aspects played in ascribing rights of belonging. Education for him was part of social citizenship. This is plausible when one considers the right to attend school and to gain an educational degree. But education beyond formal schooling is one of the central socializing agencies in society and entails much more than the right to attend school, since it provides the individual with the cultural means to participate in society. Thus, education to a large extent determines whether social rights can be claimed for all. Employment opportunities as well as the means to voice one's opinion all depend on educational opportunities. For example, if people cannot speak and write in their native language, they will not be entitled to full citizenship rights. Media, of course, provides the other central socializing agency, but its power goes beyond this function, and we will return to it later in our discussion.

Political theory starting from Marshall's work has almost exclusively focused on the political as well as the cognitive-rational dimension of citizenship and the public sphere. This includes the work of Jürgen Habermas (e. g. 1988), although his account of the emergence of the public sphere takes as its starting point the literary sphere and demonstrates that the cultural sphere can be an important articulator for political debates. Various scholars have pointed out that the public sphere cannot be divided and is always and at the same time created by political as well as cultural discourses (e. g. Couldry 2006; Hermes 2006; McGuigan 2006). Thus citizens operating in the public sphere are politically as well as culturally located. Newer developments which are discussed under the headline of globalization and the changes from industrial society to a society based on communication, information, knowledge and media made clear that the neglect of the cultural sphere and its relationship to power is a blind spot in Marshall's model.

Another problem concerns his lack of attention to the pre-requisites for acquiring citizenship rights and obligations, since he did not pay much attention to the workings of different power relationships in determining the terms of belonging to a nation-state. Marshall basically assumed a linear development and a continuous extension of the rights citizenship entailed. Civil rights preceded political rights and were then followed by social rights. The linearity and inflexibility of the model were precisely the reasons why a number of researchers, most of them arguing from the viewpoint of discriminated groups, have voiced criticism. Taking the perspective of critical political economy, Marshall neglected to see that not everyone was entitled to all types of citizenship at the same time. The rights of women, who in a number of European countries gained the right to vote only after the First World War and in the context of a strong suffrage movement, provide a well-researched case in point. The acknowledgement of equal rights for people of colour in the U. S. is another. Here civil rights had to be won after political rights were already granted. Both examples show that the right to belong to a nation-state was always a contested domain that marginalized groups had to fight for. Citizenship pointed to an ideal that was never truly accomplished, but granted inclusion to some members of society by excluding others (Fraser and Gordon 1994). Citizenship from the beginning was associated with white, heterosexual maleness. The concept, then, cannot be adequately understood when it is stripped of this heritage of normalizing some identities and of marginalization others. This said, it also must be acknowledged that the ideal of citizenship has proven as useful in social struggles when repressed and marginalized groups claimed the fulfilment of its accompanying norms of solidarity, equality and justice. The early labour movement, the women's movements and the civil rights movement all testify to the fact that participatory practices have emerged from the claim to be granted full citizenship.

Taken together, for a number of reasons it makes sense to build on Marshall's model by enhancing his distinction between civil, social and political citizenship by cultural citizenship in order to fill some blind spots and to do justice to the more recent social and cultural developments.

3   Cultural citizenship and its diverse meanings

Cultural citizenship extends Marshall's model by acknowledging the powerful role of culture and by capturing new aspects of belonging and participation in a globalized media society. Different authors have used the term cultural citizenship to refer to more recent social and economic developments and bring an awareness of the importance of culture to the forefront of the discussion on the terms of belonging to a specific society. However, the concept is not well defined and different authors refer to diverse aspects when using it. Accordingly, Gerard Delanty (2002), in a review of two influential volumes on cultural citizenship (Kymlicka and Wayne 2000; Stevenson 2001), has distinguished between two different conceptions. Although he is probably drawing too strict a line between the two approaches, his distinction leads to a helpful clarification of the colourful term. One approach is influenced by political theory; the other is based in cultural sociology.

The first approach, stemming from the area of political theory, was developed in the context of multiculturalism, migration and community studies (Kymlincka and Wayne 2000). These contributions demonstrate that the fulfilment of equal rights in a society needs the acknowledgement that it is structured by diversity. Demands for equal rights thus have to be complemented by the right to be different and to voice these differences. Rights of citizenship thus have to be complemented by cultural diversity, generally termed as multiculturalism, or ethnopolitics. The most prominent researcher representing this strand is Renato Rosaldo. He defines cultural citizenship as "the right to be different (in terms of race, ethnicity, or native language) without compromising one's right to belong, in the sense of participating in the nation-state's democratic processes" (Rosaldo 1994: 57). Cultural citizenship refers fundamentally to the rights of cultures and communities to be accepted as different within a given nation-state or territory. Respect is a key term for Rosaldo: "Bridging the discourses of the state and everyday life, of citizenship and culture, the demand for *respeto* is a defining demand of cultural citizenship" (Rosaldo 1999: 260). Richard Sennett, a critical sociologist stemming from the working class himself, although not concerned with citizenship per se, uses the same term when analyzing the consequences of the demise of the welfare state. In his book "Respect in a World of Unequality" (2002), he shows how inequality is accompanied by disrespect for those that are less well-off. This in turn hinders the development of self-respect by members of marginalized groups and thus reinforces their social as well as cultural exclusion from society. Delanty (2002: 64) notes that cultural citizenship in the line of thought often equated with Rosaldo's work and originating from political theory links citizenship and different (minority) cultures. Integration into society is no longer defined as an obligation to assimilate into a given culture and to give up one's own cultural identity, but as a right to be included and accepted as different, but equal. However, the concept does not really integrate cultural aspects into a radically new conception of citizenship. Delanty writes: "Culture is not divisive and can be a basis of citizenship. It is unlikely to be a basis of common citizenship in the classic liberal sense, but it is essential to the working of the democratic order" (ibid.).

The other strand, embodied in Nick Stevenson's volume (2001), relies more heavily on cultural sociology and Cultural Studies and does not equate culture with cultural diversity, migration and ethnopolitics per se. Instead it is more generally concerned with "cultural resources, identities and the cultural presuppositions of the polity. Thus citizenship as cultural citizenship is about the status of culture as discursively constructed. In this view what is at stake is cultural rights rather than minority rights" (Delanty 2002: 64). When cultural citizenship is defined as a discursive process it brings into focus the learning dimensions of citizenship and the socialization processes initiated by the different socializing agents of society. One consequence of this shift is the demise of the still-persistent dichotomies that draw strict lines between fact and fiction, information and entertainment, public/political versus private/personal discourses and rational versus emotional debates. From the perspective of cultural citizenship these dualisms mark continuums whose different sides are both involved in affirming rights of belonging and inclusion in society. Education and media in all their different facets, then, move to the forefront of the realization of citizenship rights. Media and communication are of essential importance in setting the stage for participation and belonging. For media and communication research, for determining one's place within the processes of cultural production the latter strand then seems a promising starting point in order to better understand the cultural aspects of belonging in today's societies; or phrased differently: for revealing those aspects of culture and cultural meaning production that are essential for excluding some people or groups of people from full participation in society.

Despite the different usages of the term and the different academic traditions it refers to there are some essential commonalities of cultural citizenship. As Leehyun Lim (2010: 221) summarizes: "A reaction to the limits of the legal and normative idea of citizenship, cultural citizenship locates the substantial meaning of citizenship in the everyday practices of sharing space and forming and exchanging ideas." Besides bridging the gap between the private and the political, the personal and the public, the literature on cultural citizenship also shares a concern with the relation of equality and diversity in the making of a citizen. It is linked to the earlier criticism raised against Marshall's model of citizenship for not including questions of power. For Rosaldo cultural citizenship entails the promise to overcome power relationships. While he stresses processes of empowerment, he underestimates the complexity of this issue. Aiwah Ong (1999) holds that Rosaldo's demand for "respeto" nourishes the illusion "that immigrant or minority groups can escape the cultural inscription of state power and other forms of regulation that define the different modalities of belonging" (Ong 1999: 264). Ong, who is concerned with citizenship in the context of global and transnational processes, defines cultural citizenship as "the cultural practices and beliefs produced of our negotiating the often ambivalent and contested relations with the state and its hegemonic forms that establish the criteria of belonging within a national population and territory. Cultural citizenship is a dual process of self-making and being-made within webs of power linked to the nation-state and civil society" (Ong 1999: 264).

Involved here are the terms of belonging that the granting of citizenship confers, the rights and obligations attached to it and the regulations governing it, as well as the processes of identity formation and identification. Such processes are intimately linked to the cultural resources people possess in participating in society and shaping its social, political and cultural environment. When we look at the migration debates in Europe, we see that cultural signifiers are overwhelmingly used to exclude people from full societal participation. For example, in the headscarf debates, a particular style of clothing is used to mark women as foreigners, as the "cultural others." The same holds true for religious affiliations in the case of the Islamic belief. Examples of such culturalization of social difference abound. When discussing the connection between culture and citizenship, Bourdieu's (1979) analysis of the culture of taste and the social hierarchies with which these are intimately linked could be profitably utilized. Forms of cultural and social distinction are intensively interwoven. Culture is in no way less entrenched with power relations than other realms in which citizenship rights acquire meaning and citizenship practices are acted out.

Critical contributions to the debate on cultural citizenship by Nick Couldry (2006), who points to the fuzziness of its use, and by Toby Miller (2011) necessitate some further specification of the concept. Miller argues that cultural citizenship is as much an outcome of "adjustment to economic transformation" as resulting from social movements. While his character-ization of the different origins of the concept seems rather arbitrary and hardly does justice to the research tradition mapped out in our article, he raises an awareness of the fact that addressing culture in the context of citizenship is also used by neoliberal politicians as well as by the media in establishing new forms of exclusion (see also Cho 2007: 472–474). In an Austrian case study focusing on particular persons whose entitlement to citizenship rights led to public debates, we found that the ascription of cultural characteristics such as improper behaviour, religious beliefs, ed-ucational norms, etc., was used to distinguish a worthy citizen from the so-called illegal immigrant, the ideal citizen from the undesirable one (Klaus and Drüeke 2011). The different newspapers to a large extent tied citizenship rights to the possession of the "correct" and "proper" values, attitudes or behaviours. In this way cultural factors were used to construct "the other" and exclude members of particular groups from citizenship. Cultural citizenship, then, has to avoid misinterpretation as an essential-ist concept. People do not have or possess a specified "culture", although they are all involved in cultural practices. In the media discourse culture is being used as a made of distinction, causing forms of inclusion and ex-clusion. Cultural citizenship, then, has to be understood as a dynamic and ambiguous *process* of affirming a sense of belonging embodied in and ap-propriated through *practices of citizenship*. This seems in line with Lily Cho's (2007) insistence on the performative aspects of citizenship, which is "not so much bestowed by the state once and for all but repeatedly scripted and enacted" (Cho 2007: 470).

Due to the hegemonic character of the citizenship concept and to the dominant cultural forms, cultural citizenship per se cannot serve as a con-cept for liberation and emancipation, but needs further specification. In her programmatic essay "Can the subaltern speak?" Gayatri Chakravorty Spi-vak (1988) has posed a critical question. What are the conditions of being seen and being able to raise one's own voice? Spivak analyses how cultural tradition and established systems of thought and language prevent other voices from being heard and marginalized people from becoming visible. She also criticizes a uniform conception of such a diverse group called "the subaltern" and questions the attempts of critical intellectuals to speak *for* and *about* marginalized persons or to inscribe their culturally bounded meanings into their speech. Instead she develops a model of a subversive listening and "strategic essentialism" that empowers diverse groups to speak up for themselves and raise their own distinct voices. Cultural citizenship, then, is not so much something everyone *has or should have*, but a set of strategies and practices to invoke processes of empowerment in order to subversively listen and to speak up in the public sphere. Thus the production of diverse feminist media can be understood as an engagement in participatory practices of citizenship.

4 The mediated meaning of cultural citizenship

Not surprisingly the concept of cultural citizenship has been taken up and welcomed especially in the analysis of communication and new media. In a society dominated by media, cultural resources are to a large extent media-based and mediated. Identity formation in modern society is media-drenched, i. e. linked to the distinct spaces that media provide for different identities. Graham Murdock (1999: 10) sees television as "the principal stock exchange of public discourse". Jostein Gripsrud describes today's television as the "primary source of common knowledge", "a widely shared pool of information and perspectives from which people shape their conceptions of self, world and citizenship" (1999: 2). Digital forms of online communication open up the field for new modes of citizens' participation no longer limited by national or cultural boundaries. On the internet, media users become producers themselves, production and reception here is not to be seen as distinct elements but as closely linked together. Identity as a citizen is then not primarily a matter of political participation. More relevant are discursive negotiations of the cultural practices essential for the individual and social identity.

The above considerations lead to our definition of the concept of cultural citizenship:

Cultural citizenship *is an essential dimension of citizenship in media society and unfolds under the conditions of unequal power relations. It entails all those cultural practices that allow competent participation in society and includes the rights to be represented and to speak actively. Media as a particular form of cultural production is both an engine and an actor in the processes of self-making and being-made, in which people acquire their individual, group-specific and social identities.*

Cultural citizenship is a central concept for understanding the process of societal meaning production, since it intimately links cultural production, cultural products and audiences and binds them firmly together. They denote different aspects in the process of meaning production, but fundamentally remain dependent on each other. Richard Johnson (1985) has introduced a circle to better understand the cultural production of meaning which has been further developed and specified by Paul du Gay (1997). The "circuit of culture" is framed by an intermingling of public representations and private lives, of abstract expressions and concrete and particular utterances. Johnson singles out four moments in the circle, namely production, texts, readings and lived cultures. The picture is insofar misleading as "lived cultures" is conceptually different from the other elements. It is the space and the horizon that fundamentally enables processes of encoding and decoding, of production and reception. This is why we have introduced a three-dimensional model with *cultural citizenship* taking the place of lived culture being the context in which processes of cultural meaning production are embedded (Figure 1).

Figure 1: Cultural Citizenship as part of the circuit of culture

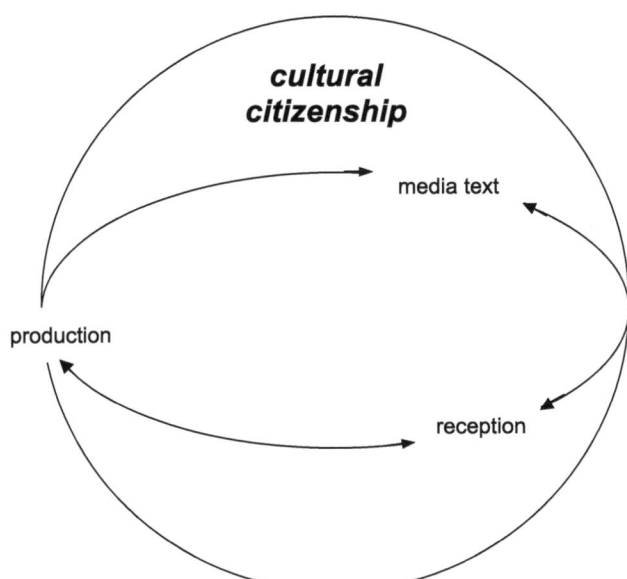

We applied the model for looking at media processes, e. g. those that are triggered by reality TV programs, and it seems well suited to do so. Cultural citizenship serves as a universe that allows meaning production and structures the terms of belonging. The conditions of media as a form of cultural production both on the side of those initiating it – journalists, bloggers. artists, counter-hegemonic movements – and on the side of audiences and users, appropriating and thus changing it, unfold within specific social and individual contexts. Though both roles are no longer necessarily distinct and separated they are regulated by the society that envelops it, but can also be reorganized and re-evaluated by the social and cultural practices of individuals and groups. Thus involvement in media practices as forms of cultural meaning production at the same time signifies cultural belonging and constructs cultural identity.[1] When arguing that cultural citizenship becomes essential for inclusion in a media society we need to think about necessary preconditions on an individual level as well as on societal.

---

1 Here we come back to specifications du Gay (1997) has worked out on the circuit of culture, including production, reception, representation, regulation and identity.

Graham Murdock (1999) has singled out four rights that he sees as necessary for the realization of cultural citizenship:

- *Rights of information,* as a basis for informed social and political decision-making.
- *Rights of experiences* that mirror the diverse ways of life and can serve as a basis for the development of the individual's conception of identity.
- *Rights of knowledge,* as a possibility for integrating information and experience, making sense of information in everyday life and generalizing one's everyday experiences and linking it to other forms of information. This implies interpretative schemes that bridge the universal and the particular, the general and the specific, the macro-level of social structure and the micro-level of everyday existence. Finally,
- *Rights of participation* that entail the possibility to make one's voice heard, to act out one's cultural practices and express one's cultural ideas; in short, to take part in the meaning production of society and be able to speak up in public.

The institutionalization of such rights and the passing of the respective legislation always has been more or less directly been the result of a social struggle that led to the acceptance of the different dimensions of citizenship. For example, the struggle for the individual's freedom to become involved in trading has resulted in individual rights of freedom of speech, action, etc., and the acceptance of civil citizenship; the struggle for representation in politics and the public sphere has resulted in the right to vote and the acceptance of political citizenship and the struggle to claim basic provisions in times of need has resulted in health care services and other social welfare rights and the acceptance of social citizenship. Cultural citizenship rights that would entail the right to be different are as yet not installed. According to Hartley cultural citizenship "is in the process of formation – being made to mean something – long before it can be institutionalized and legislated. In my view 'cultural citizenship' is at a late stage of rights-formation, moving into formal legislative existence in a number of contexts" (Hartley 1999: 161). Joke Hermes (2006) on the other hand sees cultural citizenship much less as a legal and regulatory practice, but as a sensitizing concept. In "Citizenship in the Age of the Internet" she uses the concept to explore new information and communication technologies. She concludes that "ICTs do not necessarily produce new citizens but they do provide for new and important citizen practices" (Hermes 2006: 306). This is an aspect of cultural citizenship that, apart from the legal and political questions about its realization, is most usefully employed when analyzing cultural (media) production as a process of meaning production. Engin Isin and Patricia Woods's (1999: ix) "emphasis on the process of rights-claims, rather than the rights themselves" may lead to the reconciliation of positions that advocate the institutionalization of cultural rights in parallel to the legislation meant to guarantee civil, political and social rights and those other voices that are seeing cultural citizenship in the contexts of strategies for participation and resistance.

Using the example of reality TV we will explore the issue of cultural production and its powers of representation. In this context we will raise some critical questions against the claim made that reality TV today is the site where the subaltern, members of minority groups can start to be visible and to raise their voices. This, then, leads us to rethink forms of cultural and media intervention enabling marginalized groups to speak for themselves and thus claim cultural citizenship.

5 Contested realms: Cultural citizenship and reality TV

One of the most prominent developments in television production is the success of various forms of reality TV in many Western European countries and the U. S. These genres and formats, characterized by the blurring of borders between fact and fiction, information and entertainment, privacy and public affairs, can be understood as addressing cultural aspects of citizenship. During the public service period, television had the primary duty to inform citizens enabling them to participate in democracy. So the non-fictional programme was responsible for serving citizens with *information*. The dominant function allocated to television during the paternalistic period of public service broadcasting was the provision of knowledge based on information. Elites in politics and media had to tell the audience – imagined as a passive crowd – what was relevant for them. This has changed fundamentally as a result of the commercialization of television and reality TV is an important genre for this shift from educating the public to enticing the consumer. Reality TV underscores the commercialization of popular culture by means that have ambivalent consequences for the audiences addressed. In an article focusing on popular culture and material deprivation Blackman and France (2001) have elaborated on the way commercialized popular culture supports the dominant order by incorporating forms of protest and resistance originally generated in the context of counter-hegemonic activities by young people. Thus they point to the ambivalence of commercialized media and provide some rationale for our finding that reality TV is characterized by the "exclusionary inclusion of identities" – a term we will explain later on – that do not fit into the hegemonic order.

The fictional programme offered *experience* in the sense that a variety of different ways of living where presented. These were the background to build up different cultural identities. This has always been a specific function of broadcasting, but was largely ignored during the public service period. Finally, *participation* is discussed as a quite new phenomenon that encompasses diverse forms and has multiple meanings. Participation is a common feature in all forms of reality TV. Common people participate in docu-soaps, daily talks, talent shows or real-people shows. Ib Bondebjerg (1996) describes this development as "democratisation of an old public service discourse, dominated by experts and a very official kind of talk, and the creation of a new mixed public sphere, where common knowledge and everyday experience play a much larger role". The "old" elites in politics, economy and the media loose influence in the way they are (re-)presented in these kinds of programmes. Instead everyday people with their language, their issues and their way of living become visible and relevant.

Reality TV applies narrative strategies known from fictional programmes such as personalisation, stereotyping, intimatisation and the use of cliff-hangers. Seen from the perspective of the audience the distinction between fictional and non-fictional programme loses importance. People watching television in today's media society know about the constructiveness of any kind of media product – news as well as soap opera. Reality TV is a genre where people and their everyday lives move to the forefront. Not surprisingly, then, members of marginalized groups play a more relevant role in programs and formats of reality TV then it is usually the case in television. The Berlin anthropologist Gabriele Dietze (2008, 2011) has linked the surprising success of people with migrant backgrounds in different talent shows directly to cultural citizenship. She argues that by winning the contest migrants both have become visible and are able to secure their own voice. She calls these forms of being represented on screen "emotional citizenship" (Dietze 2011: 171), offering some kind of emotional belonging to the nation state as an imagined audience.

When the winner of the Austrian talent show "Die große Chance" (The Big Chance, ORF1, finale on 11 November 2011) was pronounced, it turned out to be a lesbian singer-songwriter. She was portrayed in her home together with her partner and their baby daughter. There was also a transsexual performer among the last nine contestants, a person with a migrant background, an older singer, and some acrobats presumably with roots in Asia. Undoubtedly this is a much greater diversity than is usually to be seen on television or mentioned in the information-based 'quality media'. So we would agree that reality TV allows for more diversity, members of groups are visible in a literal sense and you can hear their voices in a literal sense. But can they also speak in the wider sense that Spivak referred to? The winner in "Die Große Chance" was placed not so much within a lesbian sub-culture, but normalized within traditional concepts of the family. Her partner was only addressed as "her wife" and she was quoted as saying that having a baby was much more important than winning the contest, writing music or performing. Thus her sexual identity was normalized by connecting her way of life to the notion of a holy family and linking her values and preferences to the idea that motherly love is universal and much more important than success or other creative work.

We conducted a qualitative content analysis of German TV programming analysing the frequency and form with which migrant women are represented in current TV (Lünenborg et al. 2012). The talent show "Germany's Next Topmodel" with Heidi Klum was the program showing the most migrant women characters within 300 hours of TV production. Looking at the format in more detail offered an ambivalent picture of these forms of representation. While it is obvious that a broad variety and diversity of candidates is essential for the format – giving us an impression of the *global* character of the models' world – at the same time these models have to fit the given norm incorporated by the host Heidi Klum. This norm based on ideological premises of neoliberalism marking those migrant models as 'others' who do not refer to the construct of a modern, successful, hard-working woman. While femininity is presented as an effect of performances, ethnic roots are shown as naturalized. Deviances from the overarching norm are marked as "exotic", "too ethnic" or "traditional". The way diversity is integrated into the concept of this talent show can be seen as a form of "post-multiculturalism" as it is called by Lentin and Titley (2011). It is a specific mode of market orientation that opens the floor for non-white models, but they need to fit into the consumerists' logic to be successful. Thus we are sceptical about the description of reality TV as a new form of self-representation of minority groups in current TV for three main reasons:

Firstly: Society frames the talent shows and other forms of the reality TV genre. It is embedded into existing cultural notions and power relationships. Talent shows are very much a product of a neoliberal ideology that claims that everyone who strives hard enough to transform his or her personal identity can win. So the winning of a contest for one migrant, one lesbian, one transsexual, one member of the working poor is not at all an indicator for making the group more visible. Sometimes the logic in effect is exactly the opposite: "See, why do they complain about discrimination and exclusion?" The winner shows successful inclusion.

Secondly: The speech about those members of marginalized groups in reality TV programmes is pre-formed and the stereotypes about members of that group frame the acceptance. All too often they do not speak, but are spoken about. There is an orchestration they have to adhere to.

Third and finally: It is not uncommon to portray members of marginalized groups that become famous via reality TV as exotic strangers or as freaks (Dovey 2000). Thus, they are exhibited as strange or as monsters for the entertainment of those who are presumably normal. The latter belongs; the first will always be the stranger.

6   Conclusion

Media and cultural production have enormous potential to change stereotypes and pave the way for members of discriminated groups to participate in society, to raise their voices and communicate. But having them on the screen and in the headlines does not necessarily mean inclusion in the socially and culturally rooted formations of power. Visibility in the neoliberal media system is mostly caused by economic interests addressing diverse target audiences, rarely by the challenge of participation. The concept of cultural citizenship offers perspectives for both the demand for participation in cultural meaning production as well as for opportunities to speak authoritatively in public. Whether this will lead to new meaning production and opens up the hegemonic cultural order is a question that needs to be addressed and can be tackled in the analysis of current media discourses. Media as cultural products will only gain momentum, when their audiences appropriate them. Audiences then will become co-producers, either explicitly by producing media discourses in forms of digital communication or implicitly by becoming active interpreters of media texts. This process of interpretative activity can be seen as chances of empowerment in media society during which cultural citizenship is appropriated. Cultural citizenship as an all-encompassing, universal and essentialist concept seems dispensable, but it has merit for those at the margins of society and for those who are interested in bringing about changes through media projects challenging the hegemonic structure. Since such a diverse and vibrant feminist media landscape, which is documented in this book, links producers, texts and audiences, it can play an important role in transforming and altering the production of meaning in society.

References

Blackman, S. and France, A., 2001. Youth Marginality Under 'Postmodernism'. In: N. Stevenson, ed. *Culture and Citizenship*. London: SAGE Publications, pp. 180–197.

Bondebjerg, I., 1996. Public discourse/private fascination: Hybridization in "true-life-story" genres. *Media, Culture and Society* 18(1), pp. 27–45.

Bourdieu, P., 1984. *Distinction. A Social Critique of the Judgement of Taste*, trans. R. Nice. Cambridge: Harvard University Press.

Cho, L., 2007. Diasporic Citizenship: Inhabiting Contradictions and Challenging Exclusions. *American Quarterly* 59(2), pp. 467–478.

Couldry, N., 2006. Culture and citizenship. The missing link? *European Journal of Cultural Studies* 9(3), pp. 321–339.

Delanty, G., 2002. Review Essay. Two Conceptions of Cultural Citizenship: A Review of Recent Literature on Culture and Citizenship. *The Global Review of Ethnopolitics* 1(3), pp. 60–66.

Dietze, G., 2008. Casting Shows und Cultural Citizenship. "Deutschland sucht den Superstar" als BONGO für Beheimatung von Migranten. *Medienjournal*, 32(3), pp. 19–30.

Dietze, G., 2011. "Against-Type-Casting" Migration – Castingshows und kulturelle Vielfalt. In: K. Knüttel and M. Seeliger, eds. *Intersektionalität und Kulturindustrie. Zum Verhältnis sozialer Kategorien und kultureller Repräsentationen*. Bielefeld: transcript, pp. 161–183.

Dovey, J., 2000. *Freakshow. First Person Media and Factual Television*. London: Pluto Press.

Du Gay, P. ed., 1996. *Production of Cultures/Cultures of Production*. London: Sage.

Fraser, N. and Gordon, L. 1994. Civil Citizenship against Social Citizenship? On the Ideology of Contract-Versus-Charity. In: B. van Steenbergen, ed. *The Condition of Citizenship*. London: SAGE, pp. 90–107.

Gripsrud, J. ed., 1999. *Television and Common Knowledge*. London: Routledge.

Habermas, J., 1991. The Structural Transformation of the Public Sphere. An Inquiry into a Category of Burgeois Society, trans. T. Burger with F. Lawrence. Cambridge, Mass: MIT Press.

Hartley, J., 1999. *Uses of Television*. London: Routledge.

Hauben, M. and Hauben, R., 1997. *Netizens: On the History and Impact of the Net*. Hoboken, N. J.: Wiley-IEEE Computer Society Press [online]. Available at: http://www.columbia.edu/~hauben/book/ [Accessed 11 May 2012].

Hermes, J., 2006. Citizenship in the Age of the Internet. *European Journal of Communication* 21(3), pp. 295–309.

Hooks, B., 1984. *Feminist Theory. From Margin to Center*. Cambridge, Mass.: South End Press.

Isin, E. F. and Wood, P. K., 1999. *Citizenship and Identity*. London: SAGE Publications.

Johnson, R., 1985. Was ist überhaupt Kulturanalyse? In: F. Januschek, ed. *Poltische Sprachwissenschaft. Zur Analyse von Sprache als kulturelle Praxis*. Opladen: Westdeutscher Verlag, pp. 23–69.

Klaus, E. and Drüeke, R., 2011. More or less desirable citizens: Mediated spaces of identity and cultural citizenship. *Global Media Journal* [online] 1(2), pp. 1–16. Available at: http://www.globalmediajournal. de/2011/12/09/more-or-less-desirable-citizens-mediated-spaces-of-identity-and-cultural-citizenship/ [Accessed 17 April 2012].

Klaus, E. and Lünenborg, M., 2004. Cultural Citizenship. Ein kommunikationswissenschaftliches Konzept zur Bestimmung kultureller Teilhabe in der Mediengesellschaft. *Medien und Kommunikationswissenschaft* 52(2), pp. 193–213.

Kymlicka, W. and Norman, W. ed., 2000. *Citizenship in Diverse Societies*. New York: Oxford University Press.

Lentin, A. and Titley, G., 2011. *The crisis of multiculturalism. Racism in a Neoliberal Age*. London: Zed Books.

Lim, J., 2010. Reimagining Citizenship through Bilingualism: The Migrant Bilingual Child in Helena María Viramontes' Under the Feet of Jesus. *Women's Studies Quarterly* 38(1 & 2), Spring/Summer 2010, pp. 221–242.

Lünenborg, M. et al., 2012. Geschlecht und Ethnizität in audiovisuellen Medien. Methodologische und methodische Herausforderungen intersektionaler Medienanalyse. In: T. Maier, M. Thiele and C. Linke, eds. *Medien, Öffentlichkeit und Geschlecht in Bewegung*. Bielefeld: transcript, in press.

Marshall, T. H., 1992. *Bürgerrechte und soziale Klassen: zur Soziologie des Wohlfahrtsstaates*. Frankfurt am Main: Campus.

Miller, T., 2011. Cultural Citizenship. *MATRIZes* 4(2), pp. 57–74.

Murdock, G., 1999. Rights and Representations: Public Discourse and Cultural Citizenship. In: J. Gripsrud, ed. *Television and Common Knowledge.* London/New York: Routledge, pp. 7–17.

Ong, A., 1999. Cultural Citizenship as Subject-Making: Immigrants Negotiate Racial and Cultural Boundaries in the United States. In: R. D. Torres, L. F. Mirón and J. X. Inda, eds. *Race, Identity, and Citizenship. A Reader.* Oxford: Blackwell, pp. 262–293.

Rosaldo, R., 1994. Cultural Citizenship in San Jose, California. *PoLAR: Political and Legal Anthropology Review* 17(2), pp. 57–64.

Rosaldo, R., 1999. Cultural Citizenship, Inequality and Multiculturalism. In: R. D. Torres, L. F. Mirón and J. X. Inda, eds. *Race, Identity and Citizenship. A Reader.* Oxford/: Blackwell, pp. 253–261.

Sennett, R., 2002. *Respect in a World of Unequality.* New York: W. W. Norton.

Spivak, G. C., 1988. Can the Subaltern Speak? In: C. Nelson and L. Grossberg, ed. *Marxism and the Interpretation of Culture.* Basingstoke: Macmillan Education, pp. 271–313.

Stevenson, N., 2001. Culture and Citizenship: an Introduction. In: N. Stevenson, ed. 2001. *Culture and Citizenship.* London: SAGE Publications, pp. 1–10.

Turner, B. S., 1994. Postmodern Culture/Modern Citizens. In: B. van Steenbergen, ed. *The Condition of Citizenship.* London: SAGE, pp. 153–168.

Valentine, G., 2001. *Social Geographies: Space and Society.* London: Prentice Hall.

Online Cultures and Future Girl Citizens[1]

Anita Harris

Introduction

This chapter explores young women's use of online DIY culture, blogs, social networking sites and related technologies to open up questions about what counts as participatory practice, and what is possible as politics for young people, and young women in particular, at the present moment. It suggests that these activities represent new directions in activism, the construction of new participatory communities, and the development of new kinds of public selves, while also telling us important things about the limits of the kinds of conventional citizen subject positions offered to young women at this time.

In the current 'crisis' of youth citizenship, young people are increasingly called upon to participate in the polity and in civil society, and to develop their civic knowledge, and yet this is in an environment of reduced opportunity for the mobilisation of a traditional citizenship identity and its associated activities. In addition, as many have argued, consumption has replaced production as a key social driver, and this has seen young people targeted as rights-bearers and decision-makers as consumers rather than in any more politically meaningful sense (Miles 2000). Thus while young people are alienated from political decision-making they are also contending with the commercialization of their civil rights, which are reconstructed as choices, freedoms and powers of consumption. Products and expressions of youth culture and youth voice are increasingly appropriated by big business, young people have less public physical space to occupy (Bessant 2000; White and Wyn 2007), and as Bauman (2001: 49) argues, what is left of the public sphere is now 'colonised by the private' and 'the public display of private affairs'; all of which leaves young people with fewer spaces for self-expression, critique and collective deliberation of political and social issues.

This context for youth participation has particular meanings for young women. As argued by McRobbie (2000; 2007) and Harris (2004a), there is an intense focus on young women as the vanguards of the late modern

---

1 This chapter is a slightly reworked version of the article "Young woman, late modern politics, and the participytory possibilities of online cultures", originally published in: Journal of Youth Studies, Volume 11 (5), 2008, pp. 481-495.

socioeconomic order that foregrounds this diminished citizenship. This has occurred through a dovetailing of feminist and neoliberal agendas resulting in a complex nexus of economic, political and social interest in the expansion of girls' education and employment and the promotion of new family, sexual and reproductive practices for a new global work order. Young women are produced as ideal consumers and skilled choice-makers who approach work, education and family as a series of personally calculated and flexible options disembedded from social structure. They are invested in as those least likely to hold onto modern identities or collective practices, especially political ones, and therefore best positioned to prevail in times that demand individualisation and the forfeit of a traditional rights-based citizenship identity. As McRobbie (2007: 733) argues, the promotion of young women as the ideal 'subjects of capacity' for the new socioeconomic order has been secured through an illusion that we live in a post-feminist time in which young women have no need for social justice politics, or indeed, any conception of themselves as political subjects. As she writes (2007: 734), 'the means by which such a role in economic life are being made available substitute notional ideas of consumer citizenship in place of political identity'.

For young women who continue to seek to insert themselves into the political sphere and to engage in feminism, it becomes necessary to manoeuvre around these biopolitics. Accordingly, their cultural and political action may take on new forms, and emerge in liminal spaces between the public and private and through strategies that are designed to both evade surveillance and containment and reach out to youth (see for example Mitchell et al. 2001: 22). Young women's involvement in online DIY cultures and in social networking can illustrate how they are using new technologies to grapple with shifting boundaries between public and private, their interpellation as consumer citizens, the contraction of a traditional public sphere and in particular the absence of spaces for critique, self-expression and peer dialogue, and a loss of faith in conventional politics and formal political institutions. Activities such as blogging, virtual community engagement and personal website maintenance can be understood as examples of a broader range of practices that young women engage in to create new kinds of politics and new meanings of participation. However, in some manifestations they also reveal the difficulties of contending with the kinds of citizens young women are rewarded for being: consumption-focused and on display. Next, I turn to an analysis of these uses of technologies to explore the ways these activities reflect the possibilities and limits of young women's participatory practices and citizenship status in late modernity.

Online DIY Cultures

The first of these activities, online DIY cultures, encompass technology-enabled practices that are socially and politically aware, but not conventionally political. These include websites that are created by young women and express political points of view on topics of relevance to young women. These often set out key ideas about girl-centred feminism and anti-racism, and direct readers to offline activities that may be activist or cultural. These sites are often, although not always, inspired by the early 1990s riotgrrrl or grrrlpower movement which saw punk and feminism come together in a new, young women-oriented scene focused on music, left wing politics, art and writing (see Harris 2004a). Many bear the hallmarks of the original medium of riot grrrl culture: zines (a comprehensive inventory of e-zines and blogs and other grrrl media can be found at Elke Zobl's site http://www.grrrlzines.net/). They include websites that combine personal points of view, political analysis, strategies for activism, artwork, links to other relevant sites and information about 'real life' activities that relate to the focus of the site. These are sometimes collectively-constructed and represent a loose affiliation of young women, or can be individually authored, in which case they are usually known as blogs; that is, websites that are individually written and narrative based. (Here I am using the term 'blog' in a fairly specific sense, to refer to self-published, regularly updated online narratives that include socially and politically engaged content. I discuss personal journals later).

While it is difficult to measure, mainly due to definitional challenges, some researchers have claimed that young women are the largest group of creators and readers of blogs (Orlowski 2003; Bortree 2006), while others contend that both women and youth are represented at least as frequently as adult men, but that young women outnumber young men (Herring et al. 2004). However, unlike blogs authored by male political pundits, women's blogs are taken less seriously, valued less within blogging culture and in the mainstream, and less likely to be ranked highly or linked to (Ratliff 2004; Gregg 2006). Similarly, girl-centred websites created by and for young women have been a significant subgenre of personal websites since the early 1990s, but have not generally received attention as a politics outside of feminism. I would suggest however that both girl-centred websites and blogs are important practices of 'counter-public' construction in that they are forums for debate and exchange of politically and socially engaged ideas by those who are marginalised within mainstream political debate. However, what is sometimes frustrating for analysts is that these forums are not necessarily outcome-oriented, or rather their end function is often simply to exist as a space for expression and debate. They tend to operate for information sharing, dialogue, consciousness raising and community building, but can also be playful, leisure-oriented and mix up personal and political material. They often focus on having a voice and building a place for speaking rather than agitating for change through appeals to political institutions, the state and its actors (see Melucci 1996). In this regard, they can be seen as just one manifestation of a wholesale shift in activism from the traditional social movements of the 1960s to a postmodern style of glocalised, decentralised and individualised politics. There is of course overlap, and some blogs, e-zines and websites connect up with more conventional political campaigns, activism or advocacy. However, they often advocate individual strategies, political practices based in youth cultural experiences and culture-industry oriented activism. These include practices like culture jamming (altering an advertising slogan or image to undermine its message), examples of which can be found on the website of the Jammin' Ladies at http://jamming.wordpress.com/, or radical cheerleading (groups gathering in public with pom-poms calling out political 'cheers'), exemplified on the website of the Dutch grrrl collective Bunnies on Strike at http://bunniesonstrike.cjb.net/.

Young women who are involved in these kinds of activities often articulate a need to act as cultural producers at a time when they feel overwhelmingly interpellated as consumers (see Stasko 2008). Many talk about the need for a new kind of feminist practice that takes into account the encroachment of the culture industry into every aspect of their lives, including politics (Harris 2004b). Using the internet as a space that exists between the public and the private enables them to negotiate a desire to organize and communicate with others with a need to avoid surveillance and appropriation of their cultures and politics. It also operates as a safer and more welcoming space for young women than traditional political forums.

However, it must be acknowledged that participation in online DIY culture, especially the creation of politically and socially engaged websites, occurs amongst only a minority of young women. Most do not have the resources, time or subcultural capital to engage with these kinds of activities. Moreover, the feminism that is drawn upon in the specifically 'grrrl' online cultures is of a specific kind that has its roots in what is often seen to be an elite, white, US-based scene. This is in spite of its international take-up. However, what is also worthy of note is the popularity with young women of youth-led internet sites that do not necessarily focus on feminist or women's issues. For example, two important Australian-based websites run for and by young people are Reach Out! and Vibewire, which focus on social services and media respectively, and are overwhelmingly used by young women (Vromen 2007). Vromen's (2008) research shows that sites such as Vibewire are valued because they offer a place in the media, which is perceived as *the* site of power in an information society, for young voices to be heard and for young people to be engaged. She has also found that participants appreciate the more open kinds of youth communities that are created through these sites, and that, in contrast to the usual argument, these are perceived to actually bring together diverse groups of youth who hold different opinions on issues rather than simply cater to the like-minded.

However, while online DIY cultures are an important, albeit minor practice in young women's technologically enabled political activities, it remains that if we want to talk about where the girls are in terms of uses of new technologies, we have to turn to much less intentionally political practices, that is, social networking.

Social Networking

'Social networking' has a specific meaning related to the creation of personal profiles on sites such as MySpace and Facebook and the engagement in online interaction with others who also have profiles. These sites feature profiles, friends and a public commenting component. Boyd (2007a: 1–2) explains:

> Once logged into one of these systems, participants are asked to create a profile to represent themselves digitally. Using text, images, video, audio, links, quizzes and surveys, teens generate a profile that expresses how they see themselves. These profiles are sewn into a large web through "Friends" lists. Participants can mark other users as "Friends" . . .. [They can then] use the different messaging tools to hang out, share cultural artefacts and ideas, and communicate with one another.

However, social networking can also be used as a catch-all phrase to mean the various ways that technology is used by people to meet up with others, often peers, and communicate about personal issues. This can include the use of organised, commercial social networking sites, the construction of independent personal websites and journals, the use of internet chatrooms or bulletin boards, photo and video sharing websites and texting and image sharing via mobile phones. In both its broad and specific definition, social networking is a very popular use of new technology by young women (Boyd 2007b). Even before the phenomena of Friendster, MySpace, Bebo, Facebook, LiveJournal, YouTube, Twitter and so on, research has shown that girls have tended to use new technologies more frequently for social purposes through email, chatting facilities and Instant Messaging, whereas boys have been more likely to play and download games and music (Lenhart et al. 2001; Tufte 2003, quoted in Mazzarella 2005: 2). Young women have also been well established as heavy users of text messaging since the early take-up of mobile phones amongst youth in pioneer countries such as Finland (Kasesniemi 2001).

Social networking technologies are often perceived as frivolous or problematic because of their association with youth and femininity, as illustrated by a debate within blogging communities about gender difference in journal-style uses of the internet (see Herring et al. 2004; Gregg 2006). Nowhere is this more evident, however, than in the broader public debate about the risks facing young women in their use of the internet. There is a growing body of literature on the dangers of social networking, wherein young women's own perspectives are not always prominent, and there is little regard for what Driscoll and Gregg (2008: 81–82) describe as 'the forms of literacy involved in being able to control and realise "what you're being" in online spaces'. Current approaches to social networking are heavily weighted towards addressing the risks that face young people, and often young women in particular, by revealing personal information that might become embarrassing, by exposing themselves to online predators, and by spending too much time away from 'real life' (see for example Dewey 2002;

Wolak et al. 2003; and for a critique, Gregg 2007). Young women's social networking is perceived as a risky behaviour that needs to be managed by responsible adults.

When their own points of view are solicited, young women widely report that they use these social networking technologies to simply stay in touch and communicate with their friends (Schofield Clark 2005; Boyd 2007b). Very early research on young women's use of bulletin boards (Kaplan and Farrell 1994) notes that these are activities perceived by young women as an extension of their immediate, offline social worlds. Australian research on young women's use of online chatrooms has found that they use chatting facilities for social interaction and to maintain connection with friends in ways that are outside of adult monitoring and free from some of the social mores they feel constrain their offline lives (Gibian 2003). UK research on mobile phones (Henderson et al. 2002: 508) supports this perspective that young women enjoy the opportunities that are offered by communication technology 'to claim greater personal and sexual freedom in a movement from the domestic to more public spheres.' In summary, research with young female users of social networking technologies shows that they enjoy creating and using a space where they can engage with friends, sometimes meet new people, and express themselves in a public forum where they are not under parental or other authoritarian control.

Profiles on social networking sites and personal webpages and blogs often reflect this peer orientation strongly through their design and discursive style. To adults they are often hard to 'read', and can appear aesthetically messy and full of banal, inconclusive exchanges. As Kaplan and Farrell (1994: 8) note in relation to bulletin boards, 'the sociability of [the] exchange seems its sole reason for being', and this is primarily a peer to peer sociability that confounds those it excludes. In this respect, there is a case that social networking is a way for young women to create new participatory communities for and by their peers. As Barnes (2007: 2) suggests, 'teenagers are learning how to use social networks by interacting with their friends, rather than learning these behaviours from their parents or teachers.' This capacity to bypass adults in the construction of public communication communities is seeing young people generating public selves in their own ways. This is qualitatively different from traditional constitution of youth cultures or subcultures, which have also operated to allow young people to create identities and spaces of their own, because of the reach offered by the global stage and the large-scale participation on the part of 'ordinary' youth that characterise online social networks.

This in turn has implications for young people's political participation in two significant ways. First, theorists such as Boyd (2007b) suggest that these kinds of youth communities ought be understood as counterpublics, even though the content of the sites is usually personal rather than related to matters of the public good. She suggests that social network sites are places where young people 'write themselves and their community into being' (ibid.: 13–14) in view of an audience, and that they do this online because they have very little access to real public spaces (Boyd 2007b: 19). She says 'their participation is deeply rooted in their desire to engage publicly.' (ibid.: 21). Social network sites are therefore an important way for young women in particular to participate in a public sphere, regardless of the fact that the nature of their public expressions is not necessarily political. Second, others have argued that social networking facilitates or can be a precursor to 'real' participation. That is, it is valued insofar as it can lead to the formation of communities or collective activities focused on civic or political practices (see for example Burgess et al. 2006: 2). This kind of analysis of social networks sits within a larger body of work on the political significance of virtual communities, where claims and counter-claims are made about their capacity to empower the marginalised and to deliver more democratic modes of communication.

Do Online DIY Cultures and Social Networking Constitute Political Participation?

I would suggest that there are several ways in which both online DIY cultures and, more controversially, social networking, ought be included in the conversation about young women's political participation, but there are some important arguments that qualify these interpretations. First, I would argue that these activities are about creating a public self, which is the first step in seeing oneself as a citizen. They give young women an opportunity to bring the private into the public in ways that were unprecedented prior to these new technologies. Whether or not these private matters can then be worked into associated publicly deliberated issues is an open question, but it is clear that many young women are attempting the work of public self-making in the counterpublics of online DIY cultures, while others are simply engaged in creating public identities that can connect with others, which may be valuable in itself. Moreover, literature that looks at social networking as a technique for young women's identity construction work demonstrates that the kinds of public selves they create can be undermining of gender expectations. New technologies facilitate young women's capacity to play with gender and to resist feminine stereotypes, for example by acting more confidently than they might face to face, and by feeling less constrained by gendered norms concerning appearance, especially in the cases of pre-video mobile phones, instant messaging and chatrooms (Henderson et al. 2002; Gibian 2003; Thiel 2005).

However, many would claim, along the lines of Bauman (2001: 106–7), that these young women are merely filling what is left of public space with personal stories and troubles, without any capacity for these to be, as he says, 'translated as public issues (such that) public solutions are sought, negotiated and agreed'. From this perspective, the kinds of communities and dialogues that occur in online DIY cultures and social networking cannot be political because they infrequently move beyond personal sharing. This is most clearly a problem in social networking, as online DIY cultures often explicitly attempt to make this move beyond the personal to a structural critique, and sometimes work towards public solutions. It can appear that even the structures of the messaging tools of social networking (with their emphasis on expression rather than listening, lack of closure or resolution, absence of moderators) seem to work against the conventions of democratic deliberation, as does the style of much interaction (see Davis 2005: 130). For example, as Kaplan and Farrell (1994: 8) note in relation to bulletin boards: 'the conversations among these young women and their contacts on the bboards often seem, at least to an outsider, driven more by the desire of the participants to keep the conversation going than by their desire to achieve understanding of or consensus about some topic or issue'.

Even so, I would argue that there is much to be gained from under-standing how young women interact online. Feminists have noted that traditional ideas about deliberation and how public conversations should look are gender biased (Tannen 1995). Sociability and the capacity for de-liberation are not necessarily inconsistent, and in fact the former may even expand the conventions of the latter. Coleman (2006: 258) has written that it is 'random sociability that makes the internet such an attractive place for young people', and to learn from this, 'policy designed to promote demo-cratic online interaction must resist the anxieties of managed communica-tion and take its chances within networks of autonomous and acephalous interaction.' In other words, online deliberative democracy and random social networks of unmanaged participation are not mutually exclusive, and to draw young people into deliberative democratic practices online requires adaptation to their preferred modes of interaction. Social net-working activities are also not cut and dried in terms of their relationship with conventional politics or activism. They do not always sit easily on the 'private' side of the divide, but negotiate this very border. For example, there is a considerable amount of activism and social justice campaigning that occurs on these sites. MySpace alone has over 33,000 'government and politics' groups. Kann et al. (2007: 4) suggest that 'this merging of social networking and online politics has the potential to integrate political dis-course into youths' everyday lives.'

Notwithstanding this issue of what kind of public conversation counts as politics, there is perhaps a thornier one of what kinds of public selves are being constructed by young women in these sites. The very project of making a self that is publicly visible is contained within the new discourses of femininity for young women that link success to image, style, and visible work on oneself rather than a more robust concept of citizenship (McRob-bie 2000; Harris 2004a). Hopkins (2002) argues that young women have become the stars of a postmodern contemporary culture obsessed with omnipresence of identity, image and celebrity. Being 'somebody', however, means living a celebrity life: looking good, having a watched and envied persona, and engaging with leisure and consumption rather than politics. Thus the public selves that young women are encouraged to create are not political subjectivities, but self-inventing celebrity selves who gain status from their take-up of consumer culture. McRobbie (2007: 734) suggests that it is through the construction of 'spectacular femininity' that a shift away from the political is made possible. For young women creating public identities online, the goals of self-expression and peer connection are bound up with being on display as a consumer citizen.

What seems indisputable, though, is that these activities allow young women to take up virtual public space at a time when physical public space for young people is diminishing. As noted by White and Wyn (2007: 240–41), there has been 'a considerable narrowing of places where young people can comfortably hang out freely', owing to the mass privatisation of public space and the intensification of the regulation of that space. If young people have few free spaces left to them, then these online activities indicate a desire to create and occupy new public spaces beyond these constraints. Bessant (2000: 117) notes that 'young people are not "moved on" in this new social space and public sphere as they have been in the streets and shopping centres. . . . Likewise, the presence of young people in most electronic space is not prohibited or subject to curfews as it is in the actual social and political space of modern industrial capitalism.'

Relatedly, both online DIY cultures and social networking signify a desire to be a cultural producer, that is, to actively engage in the construction of one's cultural world, rather than simply consume. There is considerable pleasure to be taken in the design and upkeep of personal websites and blogs, especially when youth culture artefacts are used creatively and playfully in order to attribute them with new meanings. Young women have been the primary targets of a shift to consumer citizenship for youth, and these creative uses of new technologies demonstrate how they play with, negotiate and sometimes resist the encroachment of the consumer imperative on their everyday lives. The idea of talking back to youth consumer culture is an explicit political agenda of many girl-centred websites, but even the engagement with the products of this culture as evident in the profiles and conversations on social network sites often reveals a critical agency rather than passive consumption.

However, there are concerns raised about the potential for such practices to remain free from corporate or government interests, that is, for young people to craft out truly public spaces, given the encroachment of interested parties, including corporate media, the advertising industry and also mainstream politics, upon them (see Castells 2007). There is some evidence that young people are moving away from the sites taken over by major corporations (for example, MySpace having been bought by News-Corp and YouTube by Google), and towards less commercial networking sites (see Boyd 2007b; Castells 2007). However, it remains that the internet and mobile phones have been an enormous boon for those seeking to capture the youth market, and at best young people who use them are engaged in a constant negotiation of advertising interests (Barnes 2007). But even if corporate and government interests are advancing on youth online spaces, parents and other authority figures are some distance behind, and in this regard, these activities allow young women to connect with their peers away from the prying eyes of the adults in their lives. In this sense, they contribute to the making of a whole lot of albeit 'thin' youth communities to which their members feel a commitment and in which they actively participate.

Conclusion

Online DIY cultures and social networking are important examples of the ways that young women are negotiating the absence of traditional citizenship identities and the emergence of new, somewhat problematic ones in their place. Young women engage in these activities at times to develop new modes of activism and political subjectivity, but more often to create unregulated, public spaces for peer communities and to construct public selves. These practices reveal the challenges for young women in positioning themselves within a regulatory culture that rewards them for their capacity as ideal neoliberal consumer subjects. I have suggested that the ways in which young women are using new technologies demonstrate that, in the light of the so-called crisis of youth political engagement, and in concert with the pressures to perform as particular kinds of consumer citizens, many are already doing their own kinds of participation. This is a different argument than the idea that an emergent collectivist politics or conventional civic or political activity will flow out of such practices. It is not always or even predominantly the case that conventional or activist offline participation emerges out of these. But it is important to recognise the ways that simply participating in online cultures and networking is a form of developing citizenship skills, regardless of any specific involvement in political causes.

More than this, though, I would also suggest that we need to consider the value of these practices in themselves, rather than only looking towards what 'better' or more conventional participatory practices they might turn into. Riley et al. (2010: 54) draw on the work of Maffesoli to make a case that activities of these kinds are both a sovereignty- and sociality-oriented politics that reject traditional political structures and instead invest in self-determination and social affiliations. As they say, 'for Maffesoli (1996) politics occurs in terms of survival, in the ability to create spaces to enact cultural rituals that enact sociality, solidarity, sovereignty, hedonism and vitality'. It is important to acknowledge in the face of the widespread youth citizenship panic that young people, and young women in particular, are participating in their own communities and are expressing a desire to occupy public space on their own terms.

References

Baumann, Z., 2001. *The Individualised Society.* Cambridge: Polity.

Barnes, S., 2007. A Privacy Paradox: Social Networking in the United States, *First Monday,* 11 (9) [online]. Available at: <http://www.firstmonday.org/issues/issue11_9/barnes/index.html> [Accessed 28 September 2007].

Bessant, J., 2000. Social Action and the Internet: New Forms of Political Space. *Just Policy,* September Issue, pp. 109–118.

Boyd, D., 2007a. Social Network Sites; Public, Private or What? *Knowledge Tree,* 13 [online]. Available at: <http://kt.flexiblelearning.net.au/tkt2007/?page_id = 28> [Accessed 3 November 2011].

Boyd, D., 2007b. Why Youth (Heart) Social Network Sites: The Role of Networked Publics in Teenage Social Life. In: D. Buckingham, ed. *MacArthur Foundation Series on Digital Learning – Youth, Identity and Digital Media Volume.* Cambridge, MA: MIT Press [online]. Available at: <http://www.danah.org/papers/WhyYouthHeart.pdf> [Accessed 3 November 2011].

Bortree, D., 2006. Review of Girl Wide Web. *New Media and Society,* 8(5), pp. 851–856.

Burgess, J., Foth, M. and Klaebe, H., 2006. Everyday Creativity as Civic Engagement: A Cultural Citizenship View of New Media. *Communications Policy and Research Forum,* 25–26 September 2006 Sydney. Unpublished paper.

Castells, M., 2007. Communication, Power and Counter-power in the Network Society. *International Journal of Communication* 1, pp. 238–266.

Coleman, S., 2006. Digital Voices and Analogue Citizenship: Bridging the Gap Between Young People and the Democratic Process. *Public Policy Research,* 13(4), pp. 257–261.

Davis, R., 2005. *Politics Online: Blogs, Chatrooms, and Discussion Groups in American Democracy.* New York: Routledge.

Dewey, L., 2002.Girls On Line Feeling Out of Bounds. *Camping Magazine,* 75(5), pp. 48–50.

Driscoll, C. and Gregg, M., 2008. Broadcast Yourself: Moral Panic, Youth Culture and Internet Studies. In: U. Rodrigues and B. Smaill, eds. *Youth, Media and Culture in the Asia-Pacific Region.* Newcastle: Cambridge Scholars Press, pp. 71–86.

Gibian, J., 2003. "They're All Wog Rooms": The Online Chat of Culturally Diverse Teenage Girls in Western Sydney. In: M. Butcher and M. Thomas, eds. *Ingenious: Emerging Youth Cultures in Australia.* North Melbourne: Pluto Press, pp. 47–65.

Gregg, M., 2006. Posting With Passion: Blogs and the Politics of Gender. In: J. Jacobs and A. Bruns, eds. *Uses of Blogs.* New York: Peter Lang, pp. 151–160.

Gregg, M., 2007. Thanks for the Ad(d): Neoliberalism's Compulsory Friend-ship. *Presentation at Goldsmiths College,* July 2007 London. Unpublished paper.

Harris, A., 2004a. *Future Girl: Young Women in the Twenty First Century.* New York and London: Routledge.

Harris, A., 2004b. Jamming Girl Culture: Young Women and Consumer Citizenship. In: A. Harris, ed. *All About the Girl: Culture, Power and Identity.* New York and London: Routledge, pp. 163–172.

Henderson, S., Taylor, R. and Thomson, R., 2002. In Touch: Young People, Communication and Technologies. *Information, Communication and Society,* 5(4), pp. 494–512.

Herring, S., Kouper, A., Scheidt, L. and Wright, E., 2004. Women and Children Last: The Discursive Construction of Weblogs. In: L. J. Gurak et al., eds. *Into the Blogosphere: Rhetoric, Community and Culture of Weblogs* [online]. Available at: <http://blog.lib.umn.edu/blogosphere/women_and_children.html> [Accessed 3 November 2011].

Hopkins, S., 2002. *Girl Heroes: The New Force in Popular Culture.* Annandale: Pluto Press.

Kann, M. E., Berry, J., Grant, C. And Zager, P., 2007. The Internet and Youth Political Participation. *First Monday,* 12 (8) [online]. Available at: <http://www.firstmonday.org/htbin/cgiwrap/bin/ojs/index.php/fm/article/view/1977/1852> [Accessed 4 November 2011].

Kaplan, N. and Farrell, E., 1994. Weavers of webs: A portrait of young women on the net. *The Arachnet Journal on Virtual Culture,* 2 (3) [online]. Available at: <www.ftp_byrd.mu.wvnet.edu/pub/ejvc/Kaplan.v2n3> [Accessed 17 October 2007].

Kasesniemi, E., 2001. Finnish Teenagers and Mobile Communication: Chatting and Storytelling in Text Messages. In: A. Furlong and I. Guidikova, eds. *Transitions of Youth Citizenship in Europe: Culture, Subculture and Identity.* Strasbourg: Council of Europe Publishing, pp. 157–180.

Lenhart, A., Rainie, L., and Lewis, O., 2001. *Teenage life online: The rise of the Instant message generation and the Internet's impact on friendships and family relationships.* Washington, DC: Pew internet & American Life Project [online]. Available at: <http://www.pewinternet.org/pdfs/PIP_Teens_Report.pdf> [Accessed 17 October 2007].

Mazzarella, S. R., 2005. It's a Girl Wide Web. In: S. R. Mazzarella, ed. *Girl Wide Web: Girls, the Internet and the Negotiation of Identity.* New York: Peter Lang, pp. 1–12.

McRobbie, A., 2000. *Feminism and Youth Culture.* London: Macmillan.

McRobbie, A., 2007. Top Girls? Young Women and the Post-Feminist Sexual Contract. *Cultural Studies,* 21(4), pp. 718–737.

Melucci, A., 1996. *Challenging Codes: Collective Action in the Information Age.* Cambridge: Cambridge University Press.

Miles, S., 2000. *Youth Lifestyles in a Changing World.* Buckingham: Open University Press.

Mitchell, A., Rundle, L. and Karaian, L., 2001. Introduction: A Conversation with Allyson, Lisa and Lara. In: Mitchell, A. and Rundle, L., eds. *Turbo Chicks: Talking Young Feminisms.* Toronto: Sumach Press, pp. 11–24.

Orlowski, A., 2003. Most Bloggers "Are Teenage Girls" – Survey. *The Register* [online]. Available at: <http://www.theregister.co.uk/2003/05/30/most_bloggers_are_teenage_girls/> [Accessed 3 November 2011].

Ratliff, C., 2004. Whose Voices Get Heard? Gender Politics in the Blogosphere. *CultureCat* [online]. Available at: <http://culturecat.net/> [Accessed 17 April 2007].

Riley, S., Morey, Y. and Griffin, C., 2010. The "pleasure citizen": Analyzing partying as a form of social and political participation. *Young,*18(1), pp. 33–54.

Schofield Clark, L., 2005. The Constant Contact Generation: Exploring Teen Friendship Networks Online. In: S. R. Mazzarella, ed. *Girl Wide Web: Girls, the Internet and the Negotiation of Identity.* New York: Peter Lang, pp. 203–221.

Stasko, C. 2008. (r)Evolutionary Healing: Jamming with Culture and Shifting the Power. In: A. Harris, ed. *Next Wave Cultures: Feminism, Subcultures, Activism.* New York: Routledge, pp. 193–220.

Tannen, D. 1995. *Gender and Discourse.* Oxford: Oxford University Press.

Thiel, S. M., 2005. IM ME: Identity Construction and Gender Negotiation in the world of Adolescent Girls and Instant Messaging. In: S. R. Mazzarella, ed. *Girl Wide Web: Girls, the Internet and the Negotiation of Identity.* New York: Peter Lang, pp. 179–202.

Vromen, A., 2007. Australian Young People's Participatory Practices and Internet Use. *Information, Communication and Society,* 10(1), pp. 48–68.

Vromen, A., 2008. Building Virtual Spaces: Young People, Participation and the Internet. *Australian Journal of Political Science,* 43(1), pp. 79–97.

White, R. and Wyn, J., 2007. *Youth and Society: Exploring the Social Dynamics of Youth,* 2nd ed. London: Oxford University Press.

Wolak, J., Mitchell, K. J. and Finkelhor, D., 2003. Escaping or Connecting? Characteristics of Youth Who Form Close Online Relationships. *Journal of Adolescence,* 26(1), pp. 105–119.

Acknowledgements

Thanks to Ariadne Vromen and Melissa Gregg for very helpful conversations, and to Lesley Pruitt and Lejla Voloder for research assistance.

Rethinking Political Communication and the Internet: A Perspective from Cultural Studies and Gender Studies

Ricarda Drüeke

1 Introduction: Politics and Media

Political communication is seen as a link and an intermediary between political institutions, mass media and the general public. The articulation of political interests and opinions, the identification of political problems or the finding and enacting of binding political decisions requires diverse communication processes. Politics, and therefore political communication, is transmitted and experienced mostly via the media. These days political communication in and through the internet takes on a central function in democratic societies. Faster access to information, participation opportunities for diverse actors, communication via e-mail and exchanges on on-line discussion forums all indicate that the internet is seen as a medium of political communication and means of deliberative processes. The internet is the technical infrastructure that makes social communication of any kind possible (cf. Schweiger and Weihermüller 2008: 535), but it can also be examined as a "cultural forum" (Jensen and Helles 2011: 530) in terms of the number of communicative practices – including political communication. Since the internet has changed both the formal political process as well as political communication among institutional, civic and individual actors and movements, the question of the composition and the formation of public spheres must be reexamined.

Based on a critique of the traditional view of political communication, this chapter will propose an expansion of the concept and the subject area of political communication from the standpoint of cultural studies and gender studies. This view of political communication, as will ultimately be shown, is useful for analyzing the relationship between the internet, participation and democracy.

2 Political Communication: State of Research

A systematic overview of the research on political communication is difficult to compile due to the large number of studies and the diversity of the approaches chosen. For this reason, in what follows I would like to work out primarily the central aspects of the existing research and to emphasize its inherent positions and exclusions.

In research on political communication, an analytical distinction is made particularly between the actors and content of political communication and its impact and reception (cf. Vowe and Dohle 2007). Consequently, a focus on the Laswell formula ("who says what in which channel to whom with what effect?") is initially a useful systematization in order to proceed economically with the research. Although the research process is divided into individual parts, the component phenomena of political communication can still be researched (cf. Schulz 2011: 58). Based on the varying meanings of the concept of political communication, Donges and Jarren (2005) suggest an analysis that distinguishes between the different social levels. By dividing the subject into the micro, meso and macro levels, each of the levels on which political communication takes place can be taken into account: At the micro level, individuals act as though they are not part of a special group of actors. The meso level is the action level of organizations and institutions. The macro level refers to the societal level. The political actors in this distinction are primarily the government and parliament, on the one side, and organizations, movements, parties and media on the other. Individual citizens still have no constitutive role in the political communication process, because they have hardly any agency ascribed to them on the micro level. Political communication is thus only a flow of news and information which structures the political process and plays out in two arenas: First, the parliamentary-administrative arena, and second the public arena, in which organizations and movements also operate (cf. Pfetsch 2005: 349). The participation of citizens is not considered, since the main task of political communication is to be a transmission and information service. Moreover, political communication in such approaches is often equated with public communication (cf. Marcinkowski 2001).

In addition to this distinction regarding the role and the effective power of the actors, another distinction in political communication has been established. The production of politics, which precedes a decision-making process, is distinct from the representation of politics, which is shaped in communication processes (cf. Sarcinelli 1994: 40–47). The representation of politics, according to Jarren and Donges (2006), is increasingly becoming an integral part of the political process itself. Particularly in empirical research, as Sarcinelli and Tenscher (2008: 7) also point out, the mass media's representation of politics is sliding into the foreground, while the production of politics in isolation from the public is examined far less.

Political communication is therefore seen altogether as the central mechanism for formulating, establishing and enforcing collectively binding decisions (cf. Jarren and Donges 2006: 22) – and thus as a basic component of a democratic society. The subject area of political communication is defined in various ways, however.

3 On the Relationship between Media, the Internet and Political Communication

What the approaches to the concept of political communication shown in the previous section have in common is that they view (political) communication processes between the government and citizens as a constituent part of a democracy. These days, the focus is on the connection between media, the internet and political communication.

What is central in terms of political communication, according to Funiok (2007: 92 f.), is the information function of media. Media can transmit knowledge, create discussion topics, offer identification and invite to social action. Politics appears to be transmitted mostly by way of the media, and citizens experience politics primarily via the media, since they are mostly informed about it through mass media. Media can also, according to Krotz (2007: 89 f.), modify, change and differentiate communication, which leads to a rise of new forms of interaction and communication. The media thus contribute far more than the mere provision of information or opinion; media have become fundamental for a democracy. Dahlgren (2009) sees the role of media in a democracy in the visualization of politics, in which media provide information, but also analysis as well as forums for debate. Additionally, media can stage a particular view of the world, but it also has an integration function, as it is used, received and appropriated (cf. Thomas 2010).

A change of media and technology requires a change in the political communication processes, which is accompanied by a discussion of its implications for politics, democracy and society. Particularly with the increasing penetration of the internet into so many areas of life these debates have flared up anew. For political communication, the internet serves as a medium for information, communication and participation (cf. Polat 2005). The ways of utilization related to political participation are varied and include not only the traditional forms of communication, but also informal and everyday practical forms (cf. Moy et al. 2005). In the theoretical debate over the relationship between the internet and politics, three positions are usually found: The first assumes an increase in political mobilization through the internet because it enables new forms of democracy and participation; the second posits a strengthening of existing patterns of political participation and their actors; and the third warns against the negative effects of the internet, such as a growing digital divide (cf. Norris 2001).

In order to make any statements about the relationship between the internet and political communication, however, it is crucial to consider what is generally understood as political communication. This is because, depending on the underlying conceptual and theoretical assumptions – as presented – different subject areas of political communication are defined. It is prevalent in analyses of online communication to limit the content that is considered political to an institution-based view of actors (such as political parties and government), and to focus on specific events such as election campaigns (cf. Davis 2009; Papacharissi 2010; Wright 2012). What are essential for studies of political communication on the internet are also the assumptions made concerning the forms, content and actors of political communication.

To determine the relationship between media and democracy theoretically, there are *three traditional lines* (cf. Dahlgren 2009), which are based in a similar form on analyses of the emerging political public spheres on the internet. The first traditional line comes from political science and has a strong focus on the political system and the actors within it, including political institutions, citizens and media. In the second traditional line, particularly through Jürgen Habermas and his conception of the public sphere, the perspective on media and democracy is extended to encompass deliberative processes and civil society (cf. Habermas 1995, Calhoun 1993). In the third line, the perspectives of cultural studies are offered, which deal with issues of identity, ascription of meaning and practices of culture, and interrogate them critically (cf. Dahlgren 2009).

According to each of these three traditional lines, the role of the *actors* is constructed differently. Thus today it is mostly institutions, as well as the market, the economy and civil society, that are viewed as actors that produce public spheres (cf. Winter 2010). The economy takes advantage of the new technologies for information and communication in order to sell products (e-commerce) and to generate target group-specific data. With the focus on political communication – particularly within political science – institutionalized communication has resulted in the long-popular concept of eGovernment (cf. Henman 2010). As a consequence of this, the view of certain forms of participation of government and state actors has narrowed; research has therefore come to the not-unexpected conclusion that the internet is mostly used for the dissemination of information. eGovernment is often seen as part of the measures to modernize administration and make it more efficient, but it is also part of electronic democracy and it is increasingly seen as a means of ensuring greater citizen participation (cf. Chadwick 2003 and 2009). The concept of eDemocracy expands the scope of political participation on the internet and involves the participation of civil society and its actors. In this context, Baringhorst (2010) points out that protest movements in particular strongly influence the political debate, as network-based campaigns generate feelings of political community, mobilize and show the possibilities for vertical and horizontal co-operation (ibid. 389 f.). Social movements and civil society groups in particular contribute to the emergence of counter-publics (cf. Wimmer 2007). The internet is both a medium of communication as well as a mobilization tool or sometimes the site for the rally itself (cf. Harders 2005). Altogether, according to Lang (2004), there are three aspects that form the civil-society basis for the public sphere on the internet: the facilitation of networking between actors, the production of common problem definitions as a basis for common action and the provision of mobilization opportunities for political commitment. In addition to institutions and civil societies, however, it is mostly individual actors who are on the internet

– i. e. citizens who can participate in a new kind and a new way of political communication and produce public spheres. Particularly through the development of the so-called "social web," passive recipients become active content producers (cf. Bruns 2008). These individual forms of communication are especially evident in blogs; with citizen journalism, the mass media is confronted with a powerful form of alternative journalism (cf. Allan and Thorson 2009).

The democratic-theoretical classification of media and the internet can thus be distinguished from the content and actors of political communication on the internet. From each of the underlying theoretical assumptions, a particular view of the subject area results.

4   Rethinking Political Communication

In what follows, it is proposed for research into political communication to consider the insights of cultural studies and gender studies more carefully in order to broaden the subject area of political communication conceptually. The potential of this expansion is shown by means of five central discussion threads that result from the foregoing explanations:
1.) The concept of participation and role of citizens
2.) A discussion on the content of political communication
3.) Argumentation for an expansion of the concept of politics
4.) A consideration of the contextual linkages of political communication
5.) Changes in the public sphere

1.) In an approach to the subject area of political communication, the role of citizens in processes of political communication is defined conceptually and structurally. This is closely related to the underlying concept of citizenship, as well as to the question of who is considered an active member of a political community. In the past, for example, women were excluded from voting; now, migrants who lack state citizenship are usually ineligible to vote. These aspects are closely linked to the question of what role is granted to the citizens in a democratic society, as well as to the types and forms of participation that are considered political and relevant. Voluntary engagement, for example, is usually not considered to be traditional political participation, which is only recognized as involvement in political parties and social movements. Accordingly, the "gender gap," which is often held responsible for varying political participation, is not questioned for its gender-specific connotations, nor are their causes analyzed (cf. Westle 2001).

Feminist political theory expands the concept of citizenship accordingly, and as a consequence, social movements and seemingly apolitical areas of private life are politicized (cf. Sauer 2001). Politics is thus no longer seen as only produced by certain institutions, spheres or levels of society (cf. Mouffe 2005). Varying political participation is also caused by sexually hierarchical access and an unequal distribution of speaking and listening (cf. Holland-Cunz 2006). These structural inequalities should be made available to a critical test, and the opportunities for participation that are not yet taken into account must be reflected accordingly. Coding various forms of participation as political can also lead to more opportunities for participation in a society (cf. Carpentier 2011: 47).

2.) Regarding the content of political communication, mostly political topics and forms of presenting political content are up for negotiation, as well as the question of which fields of action require a public social negotiation process. According to a central point of discussion, political communication will, through increasing tabloidization – e. g. by dealing with increasingly private connoted topics – either lose political content, or on the contrary, make groups of people who cannot be reached through traditional channels of information receptive to political content (cf. Dörner 2001).

Gender studies see the separation between information and entertainment as altogether critical. In a narrow understanding of political communication, as Zoonen criticizes (2005: 143 f.), entertainment and popular genres are marginalized and devalued on the grounds that they do not pertain to serious information and deliberation. For example it is assumed that such popular formats as soap operas cannot be political *qua* form (ibid.). However, entertainment and popular formats have an explicit political component, because these formats include diverse citizens. In this way, civil rights can be tested, even if the exercise takes place in a way that Zoonen paraphrases as to "entertain the citizen" (ibid.: 151). Saxer (2007) makes a similar argument, that "politainment" – the integration of politics and entertainment – encourages at least a temporary political inclusion of marginalized citizens, and therefore a variety of formats can be described as political. Thus viewers use the format of politainment to construct identity and meaning in the context of their current living situation, both of which are politically connoted actions (cf. Dörner, 2006). Not only is high culture relevant to this, but everyday and popular culture are also central to contemporary societies and are a part of politics (cf. Dörner 2006: 223). Likewise, the entertainment dimension can be located not merely on a symbolic level (cf. Saxer 2007).

3.) Both cultural studies and gender studies argue for a broader definition of politics. The very concept of culture employed by cultural studies is politically dimensioned, because it is not possible to separate the concept from the political and the two ideas are mutually dependent (cf. Dörner 2006: 222 f.). For the concept of political communication, this means that even supposedly "popular" communication, and not just the communication of traditional political actors such as governments or – following Habermas (1995) – civil societies, may also have a political impetus. Those forms of communication are also important for a democracy, but they are often viewed as non-political or pre-political, or even as non-informative in the traditional research on political communication. In contrast to a narrow definition of politics, a broader definition presupposes no social field to be apolitical (cf. Pelinka 2004), because the coexistence of people and any connection between them is potentially political.

The redefinition of the concept of political communication is primarily due to the insights of gender studies. Feminist communication studies works with a gender-theoretical perspective on different levels (cf. Dorer and Geiger 2002: 11 f.; Klaus 2001). Thus, to begin with, the social model that underlies the conventional view of political communication is scrutinized. Furthermore, the effects of the androcentric orientation are examined and, based on feminist theory, new concepts and models of social communication processes are developed. It should be noted that gender relations are embedded in the political culture of communication in a variety of relationships (cf. Abels and Bieringer 2006: 9), and neither politics nor the public sphere are gender-neutral terms. The "gendering" of political communication, according to Abels and Bieringer (ibid.), could be linked, from a feminist perspective, to reflections on democratic participation in order to call into question the conception of political citizenship according to its inclusions and exclusions. It is also important to reflect on what actors and forms of communication can be counted as political communication.

4.) Media as well as the internet are part of different communicative, social and societal practices that must be taken into account in any analysis of political communication processes. Cultural studies points to the contextuality of media content that cannot be considered separately from historical, social and cultural contexts (cf. Krotz 2007; Fiske 1992). Furthermore, media and the internet are influenced by organizational, economic and technical peculiarities as well (cf. Dahlgren 2009). This means that a change in the forms and the subject area of political communication has an impact on the citizens' perception of politics and political events. Cultural studies also follow an action-theoretical approach and shows that differentiated media-oriented action takes place within specific contexts of interpretation.

5.) It should also be discussed how the internet can ensure the mediated production of the public sphere in the sense of deliberation (cf. Dahlgren 2007). It is crucial that the internet has changed the production of the public sphere. Not only privileged actors, but also individual citizens can create public spheres. The public sphere cannot be regarded as a static concept, but can be found in the interplay of social and technological transformations in a constant state of change. Fraser (2005) points to a critical-theoretical approach which seeks to locate normative standards and emancipatory political possibilities precisely within the historically unfolding constellation as an alternative to participation and inclusion in the center of a concept of the public sphere. Therefore it is not just a question of what the public sphere actually is; rather, the transformation and the various forms of the public sphere must be taken into account in order to study political communication on the internet. The public sphere can in this case consist of different levels of conceptualization, as Fraser (1996) introduced and Klaus (2005) further developed. Political communication in and through the internet does not take place in only a single public sphere; the public sphere consists of a variety of publics and partial publics, all of which can have social relevance.

Furthermore, the media contributes to the fact that systematic distinctions, such as between public and private as well as the aforementioned related distinction between entertainment and information, appear fragile (cf. Lünenborg 2009). These distinctions, however, are often still part of the subject descriptions of political communication and thus also the considerations of media and democracy. Gender research has already for some time drawn attention to the productive dissolution of socially constructed dichotomies and thus has critically challenged the concept of a political (media) public sphere. Cultural studies has also worked to ensure that popularization, entertainment and politainment are counted in the realm of politics as well and can be considered politically relevant to a democracy.

These (and other) discussion threads are related to aspects of participation and representation, which are substantial for a democratic society. Representation moves between substitution and portrayal, while participation is in most cases based on a varying constructible citizenship (cf. Carpentier 2011: 16; Klaus and Lünenborg in this volume). To summarize, it can be said that the subject area of political communication is often based on implicit normative statements about what is considered to be political, or descriptive questions about the organization of the political realm, which require a reflection especially in relation to the insights of cultural studies and gender studies. This appears to be helpful in expanding the field of political communication to take a variety of participation opportunities into consideration.

5 Conclusion: A Redefinition of the Scope of Political Communication

For research on political communication, it is not sufficient to describe only the functions of media and the internet in a democracy. According to Dahlgren (2009), the value of theories can be measured by the fact that, in addition to the mere description of empirical phenomena, they can show better alternatives. With the help of a broader definition of politics, an expansion of the spectrum of actors and the renunciation of a narrow view of political content, both the concept and the subject area of political communication can be extended. Based on this, both the changed forms of communication embraced by the internet as well as dichotomies such as between private and public, or between entertainment and information, can be critically scrutinized. This expanded concept opens up perspectives that enhance the visibility and distinguishability of varied actors and in the process, feminist media production and feminist audiences can be considered as central for political communication.

References

Abels, G. and Bieringer, J., 2006. Geschlecht in der politischen Kommunikation: Einleitung. *femina politica. Zeitschrift für feministische Politik-Wissenschaft* 15(2), pp. 9–20.

Allan, S. and Thorsen, E. eds., 2009. *Citizen Journalism: Global Perspectives.* New York: Peter Lang.

Baringhorst, S., 2009. Politischer Protest im Netz – Möglichkeiten und Grenzen der Mobilisierung transnationaler Öffentlichkeit im Zeichen digitaler Kommunikation. *Politische Vierteljahresschrift* Sonderheft 42/2009, pp. 609–635.

Bruns, A., 2008. *Blogs, Wikipedia, Second Life, and Beyond: From Production to Produsage.* New York: Peter Lang.

Calhoun, C. ed., 1993. *Habermas and the Public Sphere.* Cambridge, Mass.: MIT Press.

Carpentier, N., 2011. *Media and Participation. A Site of Ideological-Democratic Struggle.* Bristol: Intellect books.

Chadwick, A., 2009. Web 2.0: New Challenges for the Study of e-Democracy in an Era of Informational Exuberance. *I/S: A Journal of Law and Policy for the Information Society* 5(1), pp. 9–41.

Chadwick, A., 2003. Bringing E-Democracy Back In. Why It Matters for Future Research on E-Governance. *Social Science Computer Review* 21(4), pp. 443–455.

Chen, P., 2010. Adoption and Use of Digital Media in Election Campaigns: Australia, Canada and New Zealand. *Public Communication Review* 1(1), pp. 3–26.

Dahlgren, P., 2005. The Internet, Public Spheres, and Political Communication: Dispersion and Deliberation. *Political Communication* 22(2), pp. 147–162.

Dahlgren, P., 2007. Civic Identity and Net Activism: The Frame of Radical Democracy. In: L. Dahlberg and E. Siapera, eds. *Radical Democracy and the Internet.* London: Palgrave MacMillan, pp. 55–72.

Dahlgren, P., 2009. *Media and Political Engagement: Citizens, Communication and Democracy.* Cambridge: Cambridge University Press.

Davis, R., 2009. *Typing Politics: The Role of Blogs in American Politics.* Oxford: Oxford University Press.

Donges, P. and Jarren, O., 2005. Politische Kommunikation – Akteure und Prozesse. In: H. Bonfadelli, O. Jarren, and G. Siegert, eds. *Einführung in die Publizistikwissenschaft.* 2nd ed. Bern: Böhlau, pp. 359–385.

Dorer, J. and Geiger, B., 2002. *Feministische Kommunikations- und Medienwissenschaft. Ansätze, Befunde und Perspektiven der aktuellen Entwicklung.* Wiesbaden: Westdeutscher Verlag.

Dörner, A., 2001. *Politainment. Politik in der medialen Erlebnisgesellschaft.* Frankfurt am Main: Suhrkamp.

Dörner, A., 2006. Medienkultur und politische Öffentlichkeit: Perspektiven und Probleme der Cultural Studies aus politikwissenschaftlicher

Sicht. In : A. Hepp and R. Winter, eds. *Kultur – Medien – Macht. Cultural Studies und Medienanalyse*. 3rd ed. Wiesbaden: VS Verlag für Sozialwissenschaften, pp. 219–236.

Fiske, J., 1992. Cultural Studies and the Culture of Everyday Life. In: L. Grossberg, C. Nelson and P. Treichler, eds. *Cultural Studies*. London: Routledge, pp. 154–173.

Fraser, N., 2005. *Transnationalizing the Public Sphere* [online] Available at: http://www.republicart.net/disc/publicum/fraser01_en.pdf [accessed 20 May 2012]

Fraser, N., 1996. *Öffentlichkeit neu denken*. Ein Beitrag zur Kritik real existierender Demokratie. In: E. Scheich, ed. *Vermittelte Weiblichkeit. Feministische Wissenschafts- und Gesell- schaftstheorie*, Hamburg: Hamburger Edition, pp. 151–182.

Funiok, R., 2007. *Medienethik. Verantwortung in der Mediengesellschaft*. Stuttgart: Kohlhammer.

Habermas, J., 1995. *Strukturwandel der Öffentlichkeit: Untersuchungen zu einer Kategorie der bürgerlichen Gesellschaft*. Frankfurt am Main: Suhrkamp.

Harders, C., 2005. Das Netz als Medium der Politik: Virtuelle Geschlechterverhältnisse zwischen neuen Öffentlichkeiten und alten Spaltungen. In: H. Kahlert and C. Kajatin, eds. *Arbeit und Vernetzung im Informationszeitalter. Wie neue Technologien die Geschlechterverhältnisse verändern*. Frankfurt am Main: Campus Verlag, pp. 215–238.

Harfoush, R., 2009. *Yes We Did! An Inside Look at How Social Media Built the Obama Brand*. New York: New Riders Press.

Holland-Cunz, B., 2006. Sprechen und Schweigen in der Demokratie: Ideale politischer Kommunikation und mediatisierte "Massendemokratien". *femina politica. Zeitschrift für feministische Politik-Wissenschaft* 15(2), pp. 21–32.

Jackson, N. and Lilleker, D., 2009. Building an architecture of participation? Political parties and Web 2.0 in Britain. *Journal of Information Technology and Politics* 6(3/4), pp. 232–250.

Jarren, O. and Donges, P., 2006. *Politische Kommunikation in der Mediengesellschaft. Eine Einführung*. Wiesbaden: VS Verlag.

Jensen, K. B. and Helles, R., 2011. The internet as a cultural forum: Implications for research. *New Media & Society* 13(4), pp. 517–533.

Klaus, E., 2001. Das Öffentliche im Privaten – Das Private im Öffentlichen. Ein kommunikationstheoretischer Ansatz. In: F. Herrmann and M. Lünenborg, eds. *Tabubruch als Programm. Privates und Intimes in den Medien*. Opladen: Leske + Budrich, pp. 15–35.

Klaus, E., 2005. *Kommunikationswissenschaftliche Geschlechterforschung. Zur Bedeutung der Frauen in den Massenmedien und im Journalismus*. 2nd ed. Vienna: Lit Verlag.

Krotz, F., 2007. *Mediatisierung: Fallstudien zum Wandel von Kommunikation*. Wiesbaden: VS-Verlag für Sozialwissenschaften.

Lang, S., 2004. Globale Öffentlichkeit, das Internet und Netzwerkbildung. In: A. Scharenberg and O. Schmidtke, eds. *Das Ende der Politik? Globalisierung und Strukturwandel des Politischen.* Münster: Westfälisches Dampfboot, pp. 302–315.

Lilleker, D. and Malagon, C., 2010. Making Elections Interactive: Online Discourse during the 2007 French Presidential Election. *European Journal of Communication* 25(1), pp. 25–42.

Lünenborg, M., 2009. Politik auf dem Boulevard? Eine Einführung aus geschlechtertheoretischer Perspektive. In: M. Lünenborg, ed. *Politik auf dem Boulevard? Die Neuordnung der Geschlechter in der Politik der Mediengesellschaft.* Bielefeld: transcript, pp. 7–21.

Marcinkowski, F., 2001. Politische Kommunikation und Politische Öffentlichkeit. Überlegungen zur Systematik einer politikwissenschaftlichen Kommunikationsforschung. In: F. Marcinkowski, ed. *Die Politik der Massenmedien. Heribert Schatz zum 65. Geburtstag.* Cologne: Herbert von Halem Verlag, pp. 237–256.

Mouffe, C., 2005 *On the Political.* Abingdon/New York: Routledge.

Moy, P., Xenos, M. A., and Hess, V. K., 2005. Communication and Citizenship: Mapping the Political Effects of Infotainment. *Mass Communication & Society* 8(1), pp. 111–131.

Norris, P., 2001. *A Digital Divide: Civic Engagement, Information Poverty, and the Internet in Democratic Societies.* New York, NY: Cambridge University Press.

Papacharissi, Z., 2010. *A Private Sphere: Democracy in a Digital Age.* Cambridge: Polity Press.

Pelinka, A., 2004. *Grundzüge der Politikwissenschaft.* Vienna: Böhlau.

Pfetsch, B., 2005. Politische Kommunikation. In: S. Weischenberg, H. J. Kleinsteuber and B. Pörksen, eds. *Handbuch Journalismus und Medien.* Konstanz: UVK Verlag, pp. 349–353.

Polat, R. K., 2005. The Internet and Political Participation: Exploring the Explanatory Links. *European Journal of Communication* 20(4), pp. 435–459.

Sarcinelli, U., 1994. Mediale Politikdarstellung und politisches Handeln: analytische Anmerkungen zu einer notwendigerweise spannungsreichen Beziehung. In: O. Jarren, ed. *Politische Kommunikation in Hörfunk und Fernsehen. Elektronische Medien in der Bundesrepublik Deutschland* (Gegenwartskunde, Sonderheft 8). Opladen: Leske & Budrich, pp. 35–50.

Sarcinelli, U. and Tenscher, J., 2008. Politikherstellung und Politikdarstellung. Eine Einführung. In: U. Sarcinelli and J. Tenscher, eds. *Politikherstellung und Politikdarstellung. Beiträge zur politischen Kommunikation.* Cologne: Herbert von Halem Verlag. pp. 7–19.

Sauer, B., 2001. *Die Asche des Souveräns. Staat und Demokratie in der Geschlechterdebatte.* Frankfurt am Main and New York: Campus.

Saxer, U., 2007. *Politik als Unterhaltung: zum Wandel politischer Öffentlichkeit in der Mediengesellschaft.* Konstanz: UVK Verlag.

Schulz, W., 2011. *Politische Kommunikation*. Wiesbaden: VS-Verlag für Sozialwissenschaften.

Schweiger, W. and Weihermüller, M., 2008. Öffentliche Meinung als Online-Diskurs – ein neuer empirischer Zugang. *Publizistik* 53(4), pp. 535–559.

Thomas, T., 2010. Perspektiven kritischer Medienkulturtheorie und -analyse: Aktuelle Herausforderungen und theoretische Potentiale. In: A. Hepp, M. Höhn and J. Wimmer, eds. *Medienkultur im Wandel*. Wiesbaden: VS Verlag für Sozialwissenschaften, pp. 73–89.

Vowe, G. and Dohle, M., 2007. Politische Kommunikation im Umbruch: neue Forschung zu Akteuren, Medieninhalten und Wirkungen. *Politische Vierteljahresschrift* 48(2), pp. 338–359.

Westle, B., 2001. Politische Partizipation und Geschlecht. In: A. Koch, M. Wasmer and P. Schmidt, eds. *Politische Partizipation in der Bundesrepublik Deutschland: Empirische Befunde und theoretische Erklärungen*. Opladen: Leske + Budrich, pp. 131–168.

Wimmer, J., 2007. *(Gegen-)Öffentlichkeit in der Mediengesellschaft. Analyse eines medialen Spannungsverhältnisses*. Wiesbaden: VS Verlag für Sozialwissenschaften.

Winter, C., 2010. *Widerstand im Netz*. Bielefeld: transcript.

Wright, S., 2012. Politics as Usual? Revolution, Normalization and a New Agenda for Online Deliberation. *new media & society* 14(2), pp. 244–261.

Zoonen, L. van, 2005. Entertaining the Citizen: When Politics and Popular Culture Converge. Lanham: Rowman & Littlefield.

Digital Storytelling to Empower Sex Workers: Warning, Relieving and Liberating

Sigrid Kannengießer

Introduction: Digital Storytelling for Women Empowerment

Women have used information and communication technologies (ICTs) to empower themselves or other women for a long time. The development of new ICTs leads to new challenges regarding the access and representation of women, but it also provides new possibilities of empowerment. In this article, a new strategy of empowerment using new ICTs is analysed: digital storytelling. Digital stories in this context are short films, which are produced with and distributed through digital media. In workshops for digital storytelling those production processes are conducted as processes of empowerment. Such a workshop, which was organized in South Africa by the feminist non-governmental organisation (NGO) Women'sNet[1] for sex workers in 2010, will serve as a case study for analysing digital storytelling as a tool for women's empowerment.

Within this workshop, every participant produced a digital story, a short film, about her own life. The point in time for this particular seminar was very sensitive, as the FIFA World Cup in 2010 provoked a new debate about legalising sex work in South Africa. Therefore, one aim of the workshop was to produce digital stories for the purpose of lobbying for legalising sex work. In this article, I will analyse the meanings constructed by the workshop participants regarding the digital storytelling and the workshop itself: What does it mean for the women to produce the digital stories and to be part of the seminar? I follow this question by focussing on digital storytelling as a means of empowerment. The article is structured as follows: First, I will consider the relevant research regarding digital storytelling in general and digital storytelling as an empowerment tool in particular. After that, the structure of the subsequently examined workshop for digital storytelling will be described. Before analysing the seminar, it is necessary to give some background information on sex work in South Africa. Finally, the workshop is analysed regarding the empowerment of the participants.

---

1   "Women'sNet is a feminist organisation that works to advance gender equality and justice in South Africa, through the use of Information and Communication Technologies (ICTs)" (Women'sNet, n. d.). For further information, see http://www.womensnet.org.za/.

The analysis is based on an empirical study: I conducted a participatory observation in the workshop, qualitative interviews with seven participants, and a film analysis of the digital stories. This empirical material was analysed using the Grounded Theory approach (cf. Strauss and Corbin 1996). It is important to stress that I am not making an evaluation of the seminar; instead I am interested in the meanings that the participants constructed regarding digital storytelling and the workshop in reference to empowerment.

What Is Digital Storytelling?

Digital stories are produced and distributed by digital media. The forms and format of digital stories differ, but in this context a digital story can be defined as a "short, first-person video-narrative created by combining recorded voice, still and moving images, and music or other sounds" (Center for Digital Storytelling n. d.). Digital stories are also referred to as mediatised stories (Lundby 2008b). Digital stories are *mediatised* as media are used for the process of telling as well as for the process of listening or watching. Through the use of digital media, the storytelling becomes *digital*. The format of the digital media influences the way the stories are told (Lundby 2008a: 6 and Bratteteig 2008). Nick Couldry lists four features of digital media which influence the narrative of digital stories: "first, a pressure to mix texts with other materials . . .; second, a pressure to limit the length of narrative . . .; third, a pressure towards standardization . . .; fourth, a pressure to take account of the possibility that any narrative when posted online may have unintended and undesired audiences" (Couldry 2008: 49).

As digital stories are produced with non-professional equipment (Lundby 2008a: 2), non-professional media practitioners and marginalised groups can raise their voices through these stories. They get the possibility of self-representation: Digital stories "are representations in the first person. The 'self' is social, shaped in relationships, and through the stories we tell about who we are" (ibid.: 5). The storyteller tells her or his story with her or his own voice, with her or his own words, and also chooses the pictures that visualise the story. Being self-representations, the digital stories are autobiographies and suggest authenticity (Hertzberg and Lundby 2008: 108–9).

The term digital story*telling* expresses that not only is the product of importance, but also the process of storytelling and the production of the story itself. "'Digital storytelling' is a workshop-based practice in which people are taught to use digital media to create short audio-video stories, usually about their own lives" (Hartley and McWilliam 2009: 3).

Having its origin in the U. S.-American Center for Digital Storytelling,[2] the practice of these workshops has spread all over the world. The seminar

---

2 For more information about the Center for Digital Storytelling, see http://www.storycenter.org/.

discussed later follows the workshop format, which was developed by the Center for Digital Storytelling. In a quantitative study, Kelly McWilliam lists where workshops for digital storytelling are conducted, and which institutions offer those seminars (McWilliam 2009). The main aim of the workshops is to empower the workshop participants, who are mainly socially marginalised people whose situation should be improved (ibid.: 60). The seminar provides a space where the participants get the possibility to share their experiences: "People open up and share their stories when they are provided an environment where they feel that their ideas will be valued, their stories have resonance, and they feel safe" (Lambert 2009: 86). The concrete aims depend on the group of participants and the context in which the workshop takes place. Relevant for the analysis in this article is a study analysing a project of the South African non-governmental organisations Sonke Gender Justice Network and the Center for Digital Storytelling Speaks Initiative for youths in the South African province Eastern Cape (Reed 2010). Although the author, Amber Reed, has made predominantly an evaluation of the project, some of her findings are very interesting: The workshop for digital storytelling, which was conducted as a part of the project, functions as a computer training course as well as an encouragement for the youths to tell their stories and talk about their concerns (ibid.: 277). Some of these findings are similar to the ones in the following analysis.

Workshops for Digital Storytelling

The five-day workshop "Digital Storytelling and Sex Work" analysed here took place in Johannesburg, South Africa. The participants were all female sex workers and members of the Sex Workers Education and Advocacy Task Force (SWEAT), a South African NGO which partnered with Women'sNet to organise this workshop.[3] SWEAT supports and lobbies on behalf of sex workers. The seminar was financed by OSISA, the Open Society Institute of Southern Africa. In this seminar every participant produced her film, telling her own story.

At the beginning of the workshop, every woman spoke about her experiences as a sex worker within a story circle. After this, the participants wrote their stories down using Microsoft Word on the laptops that they were provided with. Most of the participants had never used a computer before. After having typed the stories, the participants read their texts out loud, which were then recorded by the trainers using the open-source software Audacity.

Then the women searched for pictures (under the creative commons license) on the World Wide Web, or took their own photos using a small digital camera during the workshop. They used these pictures to visualise their stories. The participants were then supported by the two trainers in

---

3 For detailed information about SWEAT, visit http://www.sweat.org.za.

producing their stories with Windows Movie Maker. At the end of the seminar, every film was shown to the plenum and discussed.

Before I analyse the meanings constructed by the participants regarding the workshop and the digital storytelling, I will first frame the situation of sex workers in South Africa, which is necessary to understand the statements from my interview partners.

Sex Work in South Africa

In the following, background information about the situation of sex workers in South Africa is given, as this is essential for the workshop analysis. The following explanations focus on female sex workers, as the sex workers participating in the seminar were only females.

The situation of sex workers in South Africa is regulated by South African law, which criminalises sex work under the Sexual Offences Act of 1957 (SWEAT 2006b). Their legal status puts sex workers in a position where they easily become victims of violence:

> Sex workers . . . are considered immoral and deserving of punishment. Criminalization of sex work contributes to an environment in which violence against sex workers is tolerated, leaving them less likely to be protected from it (Rekart, cited in WHO 2005: 1).

Therefore, it is unlikely that the sex workers report experiences of violence, rape, or other crimes to the police as the role of a sex worker puts them in a criminalised position. Moreover, sex workers become the victims of discrimination or violence at the hands of the police. "Sex workers have reported to SWEAT, and studies have documented the mistreatment and abuse of sex workers when they are arrested" (Massawe 2010).

Their criminalized status also leads to social stigmatisation:

> The continued criminalization of sex workers has contributed to the stigma, isolation and violation of human rights of sex workers. Sex workers are often forced to work in isolated and remote areas. These working conditions not only make them vulnerable to violence and abuse, but also make it very difficult for intervention projects to locate them to do prevention work (Lalu 2007: 1).

A vicious circle is formed: Their criminalised status leads to social stigmatisation, which leads to further acts of violence against sex workers, which they cannot report to the police because of their criminalised status. Their status forces sex workers into a criminalised environment:

> The criminalisation of the industry increases the vulnerability of sex workers to violence and exploitation, by forcing sex workers further underground, hindering access to health and legal services and increasing the stigma attached to the work (Massawe 2010).

Sex workers are one of the most vulnerable groups for HIV infections; at the same time they are accused of spreading the virus (WHO 2005: 1–2). It is estimated that half of all female sex workers in South Africa are HIV positive (Agbiboa 2010). Many of them do not access anti-retroviral treatment as they fear discrimination and violence (WHO 2005: 2).

The legal status of sex workers in South Africa deteriorates the situation of the women but does not erase sex work at all: "Criminalising the sex work industry does not eradicate it, but simply makes it impossible to control or regulate" (SWEAT 2006b).

Many sex workers are not in full control over their lives; but not every female sex worker sees herself as a victim:

> There is also a need to recognize that not all sex workers see themselves as victims, oppressed, or exploited. . . . Some of the most successful sex work interventions have been led and run by sex workers and have allowed them to organize themselves for their own safety (WHO 2005: 3).

One example of organisation of sex workers in South Africa is the NGO Sex Workers Education and Advocacy Task Force (SWEAT), which co-organised the workshop for digital storytelling. SWEAT tries to improve the working and living conditions of its members and lobbies for the decriminalisation of sex work in South Africa. The difference between legalising and decriminalising has to be emphasised: While legalising sex work would lead to the regulation and control of sex work by the government, decriminalising would improve the situation of sex workers without regulating interferences (Sutherland 2010). The former South African police commissioner Jackie Selebi "proposed legalising or at least tolerating sex work" temporarily, "for the duration of the World Cup, arguing that the police force lacked the manpower to enforce the law in these areas. He added that legalising sex work would free his officers to deal with more pressing security issues" (Agbiboa 2010). Selbi's argumentation did not aim at improving the situation of sex workers, nor did he have enduring legalisation in mind; he only considered the capacities of the police during the World Cup and was hoping for relief for the police during this event (ibid.). This temporary legalisation of sex work during the World Cup was not realised. But, as SWEAT argues,

> [d]ecriminalising the sex work industry would preclude the need for protection outside of the police services. It would also enable sex workers to access services which are taken for granted by persons able to prove an income, such as opening a bank account, securing accommodation and access to loans, all of which are currently not available to them, and therefore makes them more vulnerable to the criminal element (SWEAT 2010).

The World Health Organisation recommends mobilising sex workers and supporting them against violence and discrimination (WHO 2005: 4–5). One example for this support is the "Digital Storytelling and Sex Work" workshop analysed in this article.

Digital Storytelling to Empower Female Sex Workers in South Africa

The participants of the "Digital Storytelling and Sex Work" workshop are in the situation described above. They are confronted with violence and crime, HIV/AIDS, drugs and the necessity to fulfil the role of the breadwinner in their families, as most of them are single mothers and many also take care of their siblings. The digital storytelling workshop aimed at empowering the women in their difficult situations. Again, the following analysis is not an evaluation of the seminar but an analysis of the meanings produced by the participants and the attitudes they formed regarding the workshop and digital storytelling in general.

Self-representation and Warning

All of the workshop participants told their personal stories in their films and described their reasons for becoming sex workers. As participant Mbali Silongo explains in an interview, "My story is about my life, . . . my background and how I get to this job of sex work." The entry into sex work is also one of the topics in Mudiwa Kalenis's story: "I told . . . about myself. Me, . . . how I went into prostitution, getting infected with HIV." 30-year-old participant Joy Bhebhe told her story in her film in Zulu, a South African language, but the pictures of women, men and children, of the police, prison and graves, allow the viewer to imagine what her experiences are like. The women tell their stories with their own voices in a voiceover; the sound dominates the image, which visualises the text. As the participants speak about their lives, the digital stories become self-representations. Their voices suggest authenticity, and as the women talk about their lives, the films become autobiographies.

Most of the participants became sex workers because they had to support themselves or their children financially. 28-year-old Scarlett Mabuza tells in her film: "I make a lot of money. I use my money to buy clothes, food, cosmetic and I pay my rent." She visualises this text with images of U. S.-American Dollar notes, clothes and vegetables. 32-year-old Mbali Silongo wants to support her siblings with the money she earns with her job; she explains in her film: "I started this job when my mother passed away. 'Cause I didn't have any choice. I decided to do it for my five siblings 'cause I was the oldest sister." Silongo shows pictures of a grave, children's shoes and a photo of herself. The picture of herself shows her from the back to avoid identification. Like Silongo, Mudiwa Kaleni explains her choice of becoming a sex worker with the early death of her mother in her film: "I believe if my mother didn't pass on, I wouldn't have gone into prostitution and getting infected with HIV/AIDS."

The participants tell about their experiences of HIV/AIDS infection and violence in their digital stories. One example is the very personal experience told by Mbali Silongo in her digital story: "There was a day that I won't forget in my life. The day when my client took me in his house and after finish[ing] his work, he kicked me out with nothing." She chooses a picture of herself walking down some stairs (taken from the back to avoid identification) to visualise how she left her client's house.

Experiences of discrimination are also represented in the films. Scarlett Mabuza states in her film: "I'm feeling bad when people are pointing fingers at me, saying I am a bitch, a criminal, an HIV-infected." She takes a picture of her back to visualise this text and puts the writing "Bitch!" on the photo in red letters. In doing so, she confronts herself in the picture with the discrimination she is confronted with in her life. She represents herself and the way she sees herself perceived by society. Therefore, the digital stories are not only self-representations of the participants but also representations of South African society through the eyes of the sex workers. In addition to their experiences with discrimination, the women also talk about their experiences with the police in their films. Amahle Mushwana shows pictures of police cars and a clenched fist while saying: "Even the police are harassing us. They beat us, also shock us or demand sex without paying."

So far my argument is that digital stories are formats of self-representation, which allow the workshop participants to represent their personal experiences. Knut Lundby stresses that digital storytelling is not only *producing* a story but also *sharing* one's own story with others (Lundby 2008a: 3). Regarding the sex workers, there is a risky moment in sharing their stories. Showing themselves in their stories and publishing them might mean provoking more discrimination against them. In showing only parts of their bodies or their backs, the sex workers find ways of self-representation which do not bear the risk of identification. Most of the women want their digital stories to be published for various reasons: They want to show people in other countries what the situation of sex workers in South Africa is like, they want other people to understand, and they want to warn others as Amahle Mushwana does in her film: "So what I want to say to other women is, that sex work is not a job that you can rely on because it's a dangerous job and you put your life on risk." Mbali Silongo also sees herself as a deterrent: "Others they will learn that to be a prostitute is not a good job. They'll learn that 'cause they will hear my advantages and . . . my disadvantages there."

Most participants agree with publishing their digital stories in an anonymous surrounding but do not want their families to see their films, because most of their relatives do not know about their jobs as sex workers.

Hope and Demands

The workshop participants address unspecific Others to inform them of their situation and warn them, but they also hope for help: "You never know . . . who's going to help you because when you say your stories . . . most of the people . . . get interested in . . . your story. And they . . . can change your life", says 36-year-old Genesis Nkosi. Joy Bhebhe hopes for advice: "Maybe if I can tell the people, maybe I'll get people they can give me advice what I must do instead to do what I'm doing. Maybe they'll help me with something."

Besides this hope for help, the sex workers also demand action from the South African government to change their situation. As Delisiwe Shabangu says:

> My story is . . . like, we just ask our government to take care of us. We just tell government: Don't take us as we're animals, we're human being[s]. We don't like to do this job but because of poverty in this country we can't feed us . . . [or] give us whatever we need.

Shabangu constructs a collective of sex workers confronting the South African government. She regards poverty as one of the reasons why women become sex workers. A similar argument is brought up by Scarlett Mabuza:

> I want sex work to be decriminalised because in South Africa there's no jobs. . . . Being a sex worker is not like you . . . [are] stealing someone's money, you grab a bag . . ., no it's just an agreement between you and your client.

If one perceives coherence between criminalisation, discrimination and violence (as it was stated above), one can understand why Amahle Mushwana regards the decriminalisation of sex work as freedom: "I am talking to government that . . . the government must . . . decriminalise, legalise sex workers so that they can be free." In her film, she addresses the South African government and demands decriminalisation of sex workers, saying: "What I want government to do is to create more jobs like building some firms. . . . Government must build some hotel so that everyone will be safe and secure. And government must hear our voices." She chooses a picture of Jacob Zuma, president of South Africa, to symbolise the South African government.

Scarlett Mabuze addresses not only Zuma but also the United Nations, which she wants to take action: "If our president can do something together with the UN, maybe they treat us with respect and get access to the law."

Relieving and Liberating

In addition to provoking other actors to take action, the women describe the telling of their stories in the workshop context as relieving. Scarlett Mabuza explains:

> [Telling the story is] a big relief for me, it's a big relief because what I'm doing now is a big secret, . . . because my family, I don't want to tell them what I'm doing; even my friends at home they don't know. . . . It's like you're in a shade or you're hiding yourself.

In the story circle the women tell their stories to like-minded people who have similar experiences. The moment Genesis Nkosi tells her story, she feels happy: "I feel happy because . . . when you've got something inside your heart you want even to tell it out, . . . you always feel guilty inside your heart but at times if you tell something out, you be happy." Mudiwa Kaleni, who was raped during her job, perceives the storytelling as pain relieving: "I feel good when I say something that's happened to me to somebody, it always changes a lot. . . . At least it's, it's out of me. . . . I don't feel much pain." In the context of the workshop, the women had the possibility to speak about their experiences without any risk of discrimination. The participants shared their experiences and formed a community of solidarity.

Delisiwe Shabangu states that she wants to learn more about the other participants: "I want to learn more about our lives. . . . I learn more about us, about how good you feel when you're doing this; outside this job we're doing now." She feels part of the group and declares during the workshop: "I am here to take care of myself." The seminar provides a secure space for the participants who repeatedly speak about the dangerous situation outside. Amahle Mushwana even feels as if she was somewhere else while participating in the seminar: "I feel that . . . I'm . . . someway outside South Africa." In the workshop setting, the participants can speak about their experiences without fear.

Telling their stories with their own voices, many participants experience an empowerment process. They explain that they gain new self-esteem through the (digital) storytelling. Mudiwa Kaleni says she is not afraid anymore after having told her story; she learned to speak her mind: "I can say anything, anytime." Mbali Silongo stresses the importance of the storytelling: "I can say it, it makes me proud of myself. . . . To be proud of what I am." Scarlett Mabuza states that she learns to stand up for herself outside of the workshop context. Amahle Mushwana has a sense of freedom while participating in the seminar. "I feel as if maybe South Africa[n] sex workers, they are free. The way I talk and the way I do the movie." South Africa for her symbolises bondage, discrimination and criminalisation. On the contrary, the workshop gives her freedom: "They give us time to think." This "time to think" also enables the participants to learn; Mudiwa Kaleni's motivation for participating is her thirst of knowledge: "I like to learn everything that comes on my way. I want to know everything so that's why I'm starting this [workshop]. I want to get more information and knowledge that I can get from this workshop." Gaining more knowledge is empowering for her.

Media Training and Change

The production of knowledge becomes concrete in the media training. For all of my interview partners it is their first time to use a computer and the World Wide Web, so getting to know how to use these ICTs is one of their biggest motivations for taking part in the workshop. Some of the women express their hopes to receive a qualification which enables them to apply for other jobs and get out of sex work, which they describe as "not a good job" or "dangerous". The sex workers hope for change in their lives, as

Scarlett Mabuza puts it: "Now, I want a better future, I wish to get a job. . . . I want a better life." This is also a motivation for Joy Bhebhe to participate in the seminar: "[I participate] because I want to change my life, what I am doing, because I' m not happy."

As media training, the workshop symbolises a way out of sex work for the participants. They describe an inhibition to ICTs, which they are able to overcome through the digital storytelling. Mbali Silongo explains that she wants to learn "the digital" in the seminar because she does not have any possibilities to do so outside the seminar. Joy Bhebhe states that the workshop was the beginning of a learning process: "I think because I know a little bit; I think now I'll carry on to learn lots of things for the computer until I understand [the] computer." And Amahle Mushwana cannot put in-to words what she learned regarding the technical devices but she stresses that she was sensitised regarding technology, saying: "My eyes are open now." Seeing the workshop as a qualification through which the partic-ipants might get a different job and quit sex work, the seminar for them becomes the hope to get out of prostitution.

But the ambition of the sex workers to become qualified for other jobs must be seen critically: Their use of the computer and the World Wide Web remains very basic and most of the participants still need a lot of support from the trainers regarding the technical devices through the end of the five-day seminar. Therefore, the workshop cannot be seen as a qualification seminar providing the women with skills for different jobs. The empower-ment the participants experience is more of a psychological one – the work-shop does not change their living condition or situation.

Conclusion: Digital Storytelling – Dimensions of Empowerment

The sex workers participating in the seminar experience different momen-tums of empowerment. They describe the workshop setting as a safe place which allows them to talk about their experiences among like-minded peo-ple. The storytelling itself is relieving and liberating for them. It is relieving as they may openly talk about their experiences as sex workers – a situation which is uncommon for them as they usually hide their jobs in fear of dis-crimination and stigmatization; this openness provokes a feeling of liber-ation. One woman actually feels that, within the workshop context, she is outside South Africa.

But at the same time, the participants are very much aware of their sit-uation in South Africa. Therefore, they also use their digital stories to, on the one hand, warn others not to go into sex work, while on the other hand they use their films to address the South African government and presi-dent and demand an improvement of their situation. For the sex workers, improvement would mainly be decriminalization. Moreover, the women hope that by publishing their stories, they will receive help.

Many women participate because they want to learn how to use computers and the Internet, and they hope that with this knowledge, they would become qualified for jobs outside prostitution. Even though the realisation of this hope is unrealistic, as the five-day workshop does not provide comprehensive computer training but is more of a "first contact" experience, the aforementioned dimensions of empowerment remain.

The empowerment perceived by the participants does not change their job situation and their role as sex workers. But it changes their identities as sex workers, as they gain in self-esteem through the experience of solidarity and being taken seriously. Even though the study I conducted does not allow a long-term analysis, as I did not follow my interview partners as they went back to their jobs, it can be stated that the women are empowered at least for the duration of the workshop.

References

Bratteteig, T., 2008. Does It Matter that It's Digital? In: K. Lundby, ed.: *Digital Storytelling, Mediatized Stories*. New York: Peter Lang, pp. 271–284.

Center for Digital Storytelling, n. d. Digital Story [online]. Available at: <http://www.storycenter.org/index1.html> [Accessed on 13 October 2011].

Couldry, N., 2008. Digital Storytelling, Media Research and Democracy: Conceptual Choices and Alternative Futures. In: K. Lundby, ed. *Mediatized Stories. Self-representation in New Media*. New York: Peter Lang, pp. 41–60.

Hartley, J. and McWilliam, K., 2009. Computational Power Meets Human Contact. In: J. Hartley and K. McWilliam, eds. *Story Circle. Digital Storytelling Around the World*. Malden: Wiley-Blackwell, pp. 3–15.

Hertzberg, B. and Lundby, K., 2008. Autobiography and assumed Authenticity in Digital Storytelling. In: K. Lundby, ed. *Mediatized Stories. Self-representation in New Media*. New York: Peter Lang, pp. 105–222.

Lalu, V., 2007. *Considering decriminalization of sex work as a health issue. The Experience of SWEAT* [online]. Available at: <http://www.kit.nl/net/KIT_Publicaties_output/ShowFile2.aspx?e=1280> [Accessed on 4 May 2010].

Lambert, J., 2009. *Where it all Started: The Center for Digital Storytelling in California*. In: J. Hartley and K. McWilliam, eds. *Story Circle. Digital Storytelling Around the World*. Malden: Wiley-Blackwell, pp. 79–90.

Lundy, K., 2008a. Digital Storytelling, Mediatized Stories. In: K. Lundby, ed. *Mediatized Stories. Self-representation in New Media*. New York: Peter Lang, pp. 1–20.

Lundby K. (2008b): *Mediatized Stories. Self-representation in New Media*. New York: Peter Lang.

Massawe, D., 2010. Advocating for Sex Workers' Rights [online]. Available at: <http://www.ngopulse.org/article/advocating-sex-workers%E2%80%99-rights> [Accessed on 04 May 2010].

McWilliam, K., 2009. The Global Diffusion of a Community Media Practice: Digital Storytelling Online. In: J. Hartley and K. McWilliam, eds. *Story Circle. Digital Storytelling Around the World*. Malden: Wiley-Blackwell, pp. 37–76.

Reed, A. 2010. "Don't keep it to yourself!": Digital Storytelling with South African Youth. In: *International Journal of Media, Technology and Lifelong Learning* 6, February 2010. Available at: <http://seminar.net/index.php/home/75-current-issue/146-dont-keep-it-toyourself-digital-storytelling-with-south-african-youth> [Accessed on 29 July 2010].

Strauss, A. L. and Corbin, J. M. 1996. *Grounded Theory: Grundlagen qualitativer Sozialforschung*. Weinheim: Beltz.

Sutherland, C., 2010. Sex work in South Africa – An argument for Decriminalisation [online]. Available at: <http://www.ngopulse.org/article/sex-work-south-africa-%E2%80%93-argument-decriminalisation> [Accessed on 16 June 2010].

SWEAT, 2010. World Cup and HIV: 2010 World Cup and Decriminalising the Sex Trade South Africa Projects [online]. Available at: <http://www.sweat.org.za/index.php?option=com_content&view=article&id=169:world-cup-and-hiv-2010-world-cup-and-decriminalising-the-sex-trade-south-africa-projects&catid=17:sweat-in-the-news> [Accessed on 04 May 2010].

SWEAT, 2006a. Different Legal Models for the Sex Work Industry [online]. Available at: <http://www.sweat.org.za/index.php?option=com_content&view=article&id=14:different-legal-models-for-the-sex-work-industry&catid=4:fact-sheets> [Accessed on 04 May 2010].

SWEAT, 2006b. The Current Context of Sex Work in South Africa [online]. Available at: http://www.sweat.org.za/index.php?option=com_content&view=article&id=13:the-current-context-of-sex-work-in-south-africa&catid=4:fact-sheets, [Accessed on 04 May 2010].

WHO, 2005. Violence against sex workers and HIV prevention [online]. Available at: <www.who.int/gender/documents/sexworkers.pdf> [Accessed on 4 May 2010].

Women'sNet, n. d. Introduction to Women'sNet [online]. Available at: <http://www.womensnet.org.za/> [Accessed on 29 February 2012].

Author interviews with:
Scarlett Mabuza, 24 February 2010
Amahle Mushwana, 26 February 2010
Joy Bhebhe, 25 February 2010
Mbali Silongo, 26 February 2010
Delisiwe Shabangu, 25 February 2010
Genesis Nkosi, 24 February 2010
Mudiwa Kaleni, 24 February 2010

All interviews were conducted in Johannesburg, South Africa. The names of the participants have been changed for their protection.

Pedagogy of Hope: Feminist Zines

Alison Piepmeier

> But you can do everything.
> That's what I think.
> Our lives are long and full and if we love and work and
> want, we can do it all.
>
> everything
> everything.
>
> even more than we are able to imagine.
> Cindy Crabb, *Doris #24* (2007)

Introduction: Feminist zines

In an essay called "Ohio" in *Doris #24*, feminist zine creator Cindy Crabb (USA) muses on a number of things – determining a turtle's age from the rings on its shell, change in her life over the years, how she has come to reconsider her own fears and assumptions, and the tools for social justice work that she's assembled from groups she's been involved with and from her own reading. It's not an essay with a linear trajectory; instead, it's a kind of rhizomatic collage of thoughts, with links that work in multiple directions. The essay consists of typewritten and handwritten text surrounded by and interspersed with small illustrations, comic strips, and hand-drawn graphics like hearts, stars, arrows, and text boxes. Grrrl zines are informal publications, often made by hand individually or in small groups, and "Ohio" is a representative grrrl zine piece – seemingly chaotic but ultimately thoughtful, rich, and multivalent. At the end of the essay, Crabb cites a friend of a friend who warns, "you can't do everything you dream of. At some point you need to narrow it down, prioritize." Crabb responds by breaking from prose into a poetic structure and offering a hopeful assertion, cited in the epigraph to this essay, about her own and the readers' ability to, in fact, do everything, "even more than we are able to imagine" (2007: 17). This typewritten statement, framed with two small, hand-drawn hearts, may not immediately seem to be making a political intervention. However, this emphatic declaration of possibility represents one kind of political work grrrl zines can do. When she suggests that "we can do it all," Crabb offers a pedagogy of hope.

In this essay, I consider the cultural and political work that zines like *Doris* do, the kinds of interventions they make into the world around them. These interventions are hopeful; indeed, they function as pedagogies of hope, showing the zines' readers ways to resist the culture of domination. This essay's case study is *Doris*, a zine that exhibits a new kind of activism emphasizing self-reflection and becoming fully human – changing the subject-position of the reader and thereby offering a model of intervention uniquely suited for this cultural moment. *Doris* models a hopeful, resistant subjectivity – what I term a "pedagogy of imagination" – and invites its readers to try it on. This pedagogy is doing political work.

Theoretical context

The political work that grrrl zines do may not be immediately obvious because this work doesn't fit with models of traditional political engagement. It doesn't fit for several reasons: because grrrl zines are generally acting at the level of the symbolic order rather than at the level of institutional change, because they operate out of personal modes of expression, and because they mobilize small-scale embodied communities rather than large-scale voting blocs. Zine creators have developed these modes of engagement in part because they see that zines are intervening in a deeply cynical culture.

The last twenty years have been a difficult time for activists and those concerned with social change. Girls' studies scholar Anita Harris describes the late twentieth century – a period starting with the Reagan era, and stretching through 9/11 and beyond – in terms of "the forces of fragmentation and decollectivization that characterize social and political life in late modernity" (2007: 1). Feminist scholar bell hooks describes this moment using the term "dominator culture," meaning a culture in which the politics of hierarchy and power over others are prevalent. She argues, "A profound cynicism is at the core of dominator culture wherever it prevails in the world" (2003: 11). Indeed, this widespread cynicism – which scholars have called "the single most pressing challenge facing American democracy today" – has emerged at this particular historical juncture because of the convergence of a backlash against the social justice movements of the 1960s and 70s and a late-capitalist, neoliberal, consumption-oriented cultural climate (Goldfarb 1999: 1). This climate, explains hooks, assures us that things can't ever be substantially better than they are right now, that private sector industries will solve all our problems, and that if we buy the right product, we'll feel much better. She calls this phenomenon "the pedagogy of domination" (hooks 2003: 11). This pedagogy teaches that since the world of consumer capitalism will solve our problems, we have no action to take. We can either view ourselves as being in the best possible position or, as zine creator Sarah McCarry puts it in a 2004 issue of her zine *Glossolalia*, we can see ourselves as being "completely, totally fucked and things are not going to get better" (2004: 30). Either viewpoint engenders apathy and resignation, leading to withdrawal from efforts at change.

Failure of imagination seems integral to this phenomenon: hope and a vision of a better future can come to seem almost pathetically naïve. In this way, cynicism forecloses social justice activism; it functions to make all forms of challenge to the status quo seem hopeless in the sense that many of us are unable to imagine something better, or to imagine that better thing actually coming into being. This translates into a cultural moment in which resistance seems limited or impossible. Feminist theory and efforts at social change, then, can appear completely outdated, irrelevant, or inadequate at the very time when they are most necessary. This is the world in which grrrl zines and third wave feminism emerged, and it's the world in which they're intervening. Because of this, grrrl zines like *Doris* are uniquely situated to awaken outrage and – perhaps more crucially – imagination, and in so doing enact what hooks and others have called for: public pedagogies of hope. hooks uses the term "pedagogy of hope" to describe the creation of hope and possibility within the realm of the classroom, but this is a concept with viability far beyond literal pedagogical spaces; indeed, I am adopting her term and broadening it to encompass the political work of grrrl zines. Pedagogies of hope – manifested in a variety of ways in grrrl zines – function as small-scale acts of resistance. By modeling process, active criticism, and imagination, grrrl zines make political interventions targeted to this late-capitalist cynical culture.

I've found a useful theoretical framework for assessing this new paradigm of activism in the work of communication scholar Clemencia Rodriguez. Rodriguez offers a formulation of the work done by what she calls "citizens' media" that identifies this work as explicitly political. Although she focuses on electronic media, particularly television and radio, zines do fit under the rubric of citizens' media, a term she uses because it "implies first that a collectivity is *enacting* its citizenship by actively intervening and transforming the established mediascape; second, that these media are contesting social codes, legitimized identities, and institutionalized social relations; and third, that these communication practices are empowering the community involved, to the point where these transformations and changes are possible" (2001: 20). As this description implies, she sees citizens' media as doing significant political work because "democratic struggles have to be understood as processes of change that also include practices of dissent in the realm of the symbolic" (2001: 20). She notes that some of the unique features of citizens' media are "blurred boundaries between sender and receiver, closeness to the audience's cultural codes, political idiosyncrasies, and noncommercial goals" (2001: 47) – all characteristics of zines.

While a cynical culture – and one attuned to old-paradigm politics – would suggest that zines are not creating social change, Rodriguez presents an alternative model for assessment, one that emphasizes political intentions rather than political effects: "While traditional scholarship weighed alternative media by their capacity to alter the empire of media megaliths, I suggest redirecting our focus to understanding how citizens' media activate subtle processes of fracture in the social, cultural, and power spheres of everyday life" (2001: xiv). Indeed, she argues for a new way of understanding the work of these media – not expecting them to eradicate corporate culture, for instance, but, instead, recognizing the local, small-scale, ephemeral ways that they foster and propagate democracy. Rodriguez suggests viewing democracy not as an endpoint but as a process, something organic and in motion. She doesn't figure transience and limited reach as automatic weaknesses but, instead, as components of a new activist paradigm (2001: 22). Citizens' media does political work because it alters power structures by strengthening individual subjectivities.

This is the work that grrrl zines are doing. They break away from linear models, they offer tools for awakening outrage and engaging in protest, and they invite readers to step into their own citizenship through pedagogies of imagination. Because of the sorts of linear expectations scholars have had of alternative media and activist work more broadly, the resistance and political interventions of grrrl zines (and third wave feminists) have been hard for many scholars to recognize, but by recognizing the dominator culture and reframing what it means to be political, these interventions become visible.

The transformative potential of imagination: A case study of *Doris*

Doris is a long-running publication, in existence since 1991, and it's all zine, in terms of philosophy, aesthetic, and distribution. *Doris* is filled with cut-and-pasted typewritten and handwritten narratives, along with small, friendly stick-figure cartoons of Crabb and her dog, Anna. The zine isn't content-driven; as with many grrrl zines, her content varies depending on what she's thinking about. The zine addresses topics such as violence

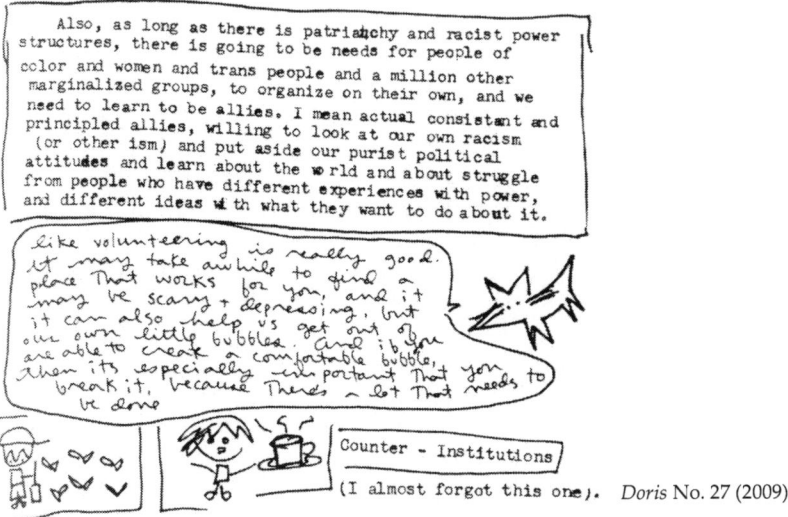

Doris No. 27 (2009)

What about your thoughts and your actions and who you love and why you love them, and your dreams and your goals, and what you've already given up, what about your desires and the things you talk about, the ways you feel about yourself, what fills your days, what permeates your nights: How much of it all is really your own?

Are you realizing your full potential? Your full humanity? Do you buy into the propaganda that you are to blame for your unhappiness? You just have to pull up your bootstraps, think positive? Do you feel meaningful? Do you feel fulfilled?

♥ i want you to feel happy+full

This is what that one book says:

For social change to happen, people need to come out of subjegations and see the oppression, and for that shift in thinking to occur, you need three things.

1. To have access to the tools that will allow you to envision a world that lies beyond subordination and imagine what you could become in that alternative space.

2. Analyze ways you have been caught up and thwarted by the relation of subordination

3. Grasp the possibility of collective struggle to overthrow the whole subordinating structure

I think a lot of us have a lot of privledge and a responsibility to use that privledge well, whether it's waking people up and changing the sturctures of our worlds, or confronting our own twisted up insides.

or both. we have to be engaged in both.

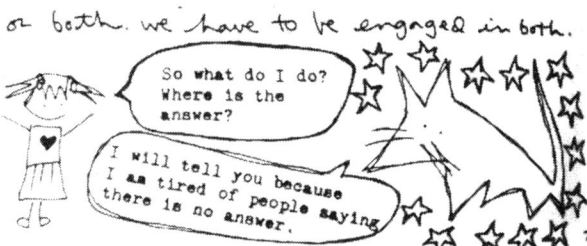

Doris No. 27 (2009), p. 2

against women, environmentalism, anarchism, bike riding, and reproductive rights, almost all of them presented in terms of personal stories and musings. But all of the zine is infused with Crabb's own theorizing about activism and resistance and what they might look like in the current cultural moment.

Although the zine started small, with only a few hundred printed in 1991, in the last several years Crabb estimates her circulation to be around 3,000 zines per issue, sold through online distros as well as through the traditional zine channels of independent book and music stores and direct mail order from Crabb herself. The emphasis in *Doris* is on the transformative potential of imagination. In some ways it reads like a twenty-one-year meditation on the possibility of individuals creating social change.

Even in the very early days of the zine, Crabb was grappling with what it meant to attempt social change in a deeply cynical culture. She identified

When I was 18, my ancient philosopher friend said that the problem with today's youth-movement was we were too transient. We were obsessed with creating community, but we wouldn't stay put. He said that real, fundamental social change had to be based in real geographical community, and that we weren't going to be very effective if we didn't stop moving around.

But it was a small town

and I was restless, and stuck inside

my self and my fears, and my lack of experience and lack of the physical knowledge of the possibilities - both for myself and for the world.

I needed to find people like me. I needed to find people who would help me feel seen and real. I needed to be around people who were so effected by the insanity of capitalism that they couldn't function in this world, and I needed to experience a world created in the cracks and fissures and forgotten places.

I needed to figure out how to be present in my body and how to say no, how to be able to dance for the fun of it and not because I thought someone might be watching. I needed to learn to feel safe among friends and like I could say what I thought without being judged. I needed to learn my anger and stop turning it inward. I needed to learn to feel good in the woods and fields and among growing things, instead of feeling kind of scared and alienated and like there was something I didn't understand, some missing part of me that was inhuman, or some human part that was cut out and thrown away.

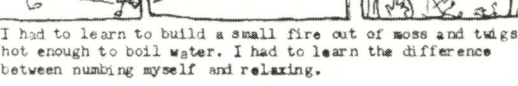

I had to learn to build a small fire out of moss and twigs, hot enough to boil water. I had to learn the difference between numbing myself and relaxing.

Doris No. 27 (2009)
p. 3

her zine as a space that would resist the cynical lure of the easy answer and would strive for complexity:

> And what I love best is the writers who embrace complexity & try to make sence [sic] of it. It makes me feel like there's so many more possibilities for fundamental social change when I'm looking at how complex everything is, and trying to fit it all together. Because simplifying seems like a huge boring trap to me & I feel surrounded by it; by people trying to make struggle understandable by making it simple, like people suck and should all die, like men suck and they should all die, like rich people suck and they should all die. It is not that easy (2005: 19).

This seems to me to be a foundational assumption on which *Doris* operates, that making things simple isn't the answer to social change. Indeed, this effort at simplicity is cynical, in part because it is so firmly rooted in a conception of politics beginning and ending with the individual: if I can't

we met weekly, hashed out ideas together, planned protests
and   conferences, and were committed to becoming part of
our city - forming coalitions with other groups and trying
to work on becoming actual allies to groups that were run
by people of color.

Different people in our group were involved in different
things, and in our weekly meetings we kept eachother updated
on what was going on. we wrote flyers and gave workshops,
and were involved in different campaigns - like working to
stop a nuclear waste dump, and working to keep and anti-
abortion conference from coming to our town.

of course there are a million different
kinds of political collectives, but I
would like to see more collectives
like that one was.

Direct Action, Protest and Community Education.

Direct Action is an essential part of social movements, but
it's often a demonized or glorified part. Property destruction,
billboard alteration, sit-ins, walk outs, puke ins, occupations
of schools and work-places, strikes and street theater.
It is good to think about what the strategic role your direct
action is going to play in the larger picture. whether your
action is going to be symbolic or more than that. It is
important not to get caught up in the ego-trip of doing
illegal things, but it's also important that we have a militant
resistance movement.

protest.)   I've seen protests come and go. times of lots of
protesting and then people giving up because their protest
didn't stop the war.
     protest is important, even in the shitty give up times.
They don't have to always be huge protests, small ones are
important to. We need visibility. We need to show that there
is resistance. We need to celebrate our resistance.

AND WHEN WE PROTEST, WE NEED TO HAVE REALLY INFOMATIVE
FLYERS AND PASS THEM OUT TO PEOPLE ON THE STREET SO
THAT THEY KNOW WHAT IS GOING ON!!!

especially if there are ways they can become involved, let
them know.

Doris No. 27 (2009),
p. 12

change it, or imagine the change easily, then change is impossible. And of
course, this sense that change is impossible is at the heart of a cynical, dominator culture. Crabb strives to capture the complexities of human life,
and rather than finding these complexities daunting, she finds them hopeful, productive.

Although Crabb certainly suggests actions to her readers, as in *Doris #15*
where she offers an extensive guide on how to deal with depression, *Doris*
is not a zine that is propelled by specific how-to tips for cultural change.
Instead, Crabb creates the zine to be a space that invites her readers to think
and feel deeply and carefully – and in complex ways – about the world
and their place in it. She explained to me, "I think there is something about
modeling a deep self-reflection, a strong desire for real emotion and real
honest closeness, that helps people to do this in their lives – counterbal-
ances the messages that tell them to stay shallow and safe" (2007, personal

correspondence). She is particularly critical of the consumer culture that encourages people to go for the quick fix, the easy answer, or to think only in terms of their individual needs.

In her zine, she consistently showcases her own emotional terrain, lets her readers see inside her own efforts at processing and making sense of the world. Reading the zine over a number of years lets you see Crabb's long-term emotional journey. The zine has both documented and been part of Crabb's own healing process. More than this, though, what Crabb is doing in *Doris* is inviting her readers to have their own emotional experience. She told me that she tries to make each issue of *Doris* contain a full range of human emotions so that the zine can provide a kind of emotional journey for the reader.

I'm intrigued with her idea of "modeling a deep self-reflection," because I do see this as both resistant and interventionist, and yet not in ways that we might recognize if we're looking for old-paradigm activism. Indeed, this might not fit many people's definition of "political" work at all. For Crabb, however, this is explicitly political, a point of view she has developed more fully in recent years. In her "Ohio" essay (2007), she writes, "I don't think our lifestyle choices are in and of themselves political. The political part is whether our lifestyle choices help us to become more human. If they help us feel a sense of personal integrity, and if that integrity gives us the power to fight further, to imagine deeper, to want more" (2007: 5).

For Crabb, then, the political is what encourages us to become more fully human. She is interested in calling her readers back to their own human integrity, a quality she believes is not nurtured in the culture at large, but which is necessary for the work of changing the world. And it's important to see that she figures this work of world change not only in terms of "fight[ing] further" but in terms of imagination and desire. Indeed, social justice activists like Paulo Freire have argued that imagination and the belief in change are crucial components of any social justice efforts. Freire argues, "In order for the oppressed to be able to wage the struggle for their liberation, they must perceive the reality of oppression not as a closed world from which there is no exit, but as a limiting situation which they can transform" (1970: 31). It's as if Crabb is taking the zine concept of emulation to a different level: not only does she invite her readers to emulate the production of the zine itself by creating a material object with "all its seams showing," but she also invites them to emulate her process of self-reflection, because she shows all the seams there, as well.

You could pick up almost any *Doris* zine and find this emphasis on becoming more fully human – an emphasis that Crabb conveys with words and imagery. For instance, in *Doris* #20 (2002), Crabb discusses the death of her mother and the friend who came to ease her through her numbness. Through these personal reminiscences, she outlines her process of healing. She describes the full human connection she feels with her friend, a connection that's manifested by them sharing stories with each other, beginning when the friend says, "tell me what you haven't told." At the bottom of this page, Crabb draws a box with a simplified, abstracted picture of a heart in a ribcage with the caption, "It is a shock to my system that I have not felt this in so long, and I can't believe all I have compromised and settled for" (2002: n. p.)

Further on in this story she explains, "This is what I think is the crazy thing. I can dream with her, and I can believe these dreams are real and not just delusion, and together we could probably make them happen" (2002: n. p.). Again, even in the context of discussing her own healing process, her emphasis is on dreaming, imagining. *Doris* invites readers to imagine more, to allow their sense of self to be transformed. The zine models an imaginative process and therefore offers what I am calling a pedagogy of imagination.

Pedagogy of imagination: political activism in *Doris*

It's a fascinating form of activism, one that might be described in terms of micropolitics, a political approach that emphasizes individual actions and choices made within a feminist interpretive framework (Budgeon, 2001: 20). Certainly this is part of what's going on in *Doris*: Crabb has developed an explicitly feminist framework, one which is broad-based and historically informed. She has studied the history of feminism along with the history of other social justice movements, and she's been involved in a number of political organizations. She incorporates these ideas into her zine through her own personal narrative. Over the years that she's produced *Doris*, Crabb has become increasingly conscious of the emotionally sensitive interventions she's making through her zine. Her pedagogy of imagination is not an unconscious or accidental process.

Unlike some grrrl zinesters, Crabb is confident that her zine has made a difference in the world. Correspondence that Crabb receives from readers confirms for her that her zine has an effect. For instance, in one letter which Crabb characterizes as typical, a woman explains, "I think it's so important for women to see that there is an empowered network of other amazing women out there. We just have to find and support each other. Please know you have my support" (2007, personal correspondence). *Doris* helped to facilitate a real human connection between Crabb and this reader, a connection that helped the reader to feel supported and inspired her to want to convey that same sense of support to Crabb in a letter. Crabb explained that this sort of response is common: "I get a lot of mail from people who I know personally it has affected . . . . I feel like it's helped some people not kill themselves. It's helped me not to kill myself, and I think it does help. I' m sure other zines are like that, too. I know *Snarla* helped me. I think it helps people to not just go where they're told to go. Zines help a lot of people to explore more options in their life, both emotionally and physically" (2007, personal interview).

In other words, Crabb sees *Doris* as a zine with a pedagogical effect, the effect of helping people "to explore more options in their life." This is clearly an important issue for Crabb, one that serves as a kind of framework for her zine. She states this idea as well in an early issue of *Doris*:

> I have this strong empathy for the way people struggle and the ways they get by in this fucked up world. I wonder all the time about what people would be doing if they were presented with options that they didn't normally see. How they would be living and relating to eachother [sic] and looking at the world and what they wanted, if there were alternatives that were real and strong (2005: 105).

She's fascinated with the options people "[don't] normally see," with real alternatives, and she sees her zine as space that can make those options visible and thereby teach people to hope. Zines like *Doris* can change power structures by giving individuals a sense of their own power, helping people "not just go where they're told to go." This is what it means to offer a pedagogy of imagination.

Zines often operate in the tiny spaces in mainstream culture, a notion which Crabb herself voices in *Doris #24*: "I needed to experience a world created in the cracks and fissures and forgotten places" (2007: 8). This level of political operation can have very tangible individual effects, such as encouraging someone not to commit suicide. And it can also have broader reaching effects that are harder to track but no less real and significant, effects such as promoting full humanity and citizenship and encouraging readers to feel that they belong in the world, that they have the right to be there and that they can make a difference. These effects are a necessary component of propagating democracy, which is why I argue that the pedagogy of imagination is, in fact, a new form of political engagement.

What does it mean to have cultural interventions that are made up of such things – of empathy, imagination, possibility, human connection? This is not what we're used to. This doesn't look like activism to many of us. And yet it's a kind of activism sensitively attuned to this cultural moment. In Stephen Duncombe's most recent book, *Dream: Re-Imagining Progressive Politics in an Age of Fantasy* (2007), he calls for just this sort of thing, a set of activist interventions that not only rely on the rational and well-argued but that also tap into our human need for something more, which he encompasses in the umbrella term "spectacle." According to Duncombe, spectacle is "a way of making an argument. Not through appeals to reason, rationality, and self-evident truth, but instead through story and myth, fears and desire, imagination and fantasy. It realizes what reality cannot represent. It is the animation of an abstraction, a transformation from ideal to expression. *Spectacle is a dream on display*" (2007: 30).

This, then, is what I argue that Crabb achieves in each issue of *Doris*. *Doris* is, in some senses, a dream on display. She imagines a world in which people are allowed to achieve their full humanity, and she offers glimpses of that world. She invites her reader to imagine with her, to feel what she is feeling. And because she has the zine medium to work with, with her own handwriting and the little pictures of Anna the dog, because she enters the reader's home and hands, she taps into the potential of the embodied community. The zine medium invites the reader to let her guard down, and Crabb steps into that small space, that fissure, where she can offer a pedagogy of hope.

I don't mean to suggest that *Doris* is a zine that offers mindless uplift. Over the years Crabb has discussed horrible pain that she's suffered – and she makes that pain viscerally real. She discusses rape, abortion, sexual harassment, the death of people she couldn't bear to lose. And she discusses the larger cultural traumas of the first and second Gulf Wars, the state-sanctioned murders of indigenous people in South America, and the halted history of union organizing in the U. S. But rather than framing these issues by resorting to easy, familiar, cynical narratives, she frames them in terms of hope:

> Do you believe in happy endings? Because sometimes they do happen. Something inside shifts, something outside comes together, and your fight becomes more purposeful, your rest becomes actually restful, your hurt becomes something you can bear, and your happiness becomes something that shines out with ease, not in lightning manic bursts that fill and then drain you, but something else, something steady, something you can almost trust to stay there (2005: 308).

In fact, Crabb's zine seems to operate within the kind of activist location bell hooks describes in *Yearning: Race, Gender, and Cultural Politics* (1990), a location of resistant marginality that allows for a new sort of subjectivity. hooks explains: "We come to this space through suffering and pain, through struggle. We know struggle to be that which pleasures, delights, and fulfills desire. We are transformed, individually, collectively, as we make radical creative space which affirms and sustains our subjectivity, which gives us a new location from which to articulate our sense of the world" (1990: 153). Crabb herself is a woman who's lived much of her adult life – the time that she's been producing *Doris* – on the margins of mainstream society. She has lived in small radical collectives in such places as Portland, Oregon, and Asheville, North Carolina. She's lived in transit and has spent time in jail. She's made money at various times through subsistence farming, public assistance, and working retail jobs. When I visited with her in July 2007 in Asheville, she was sewing funky skirts and contributing to an organic bread baking cooperative. These lifestyle choices of intentional marginality have perhaps helped her to sustain the kind of "radical creative space" hooks describes, a space that allows her – in the pages of *Doris* – to theorize social change and invite her readers to do the same.

In my book *Girl Zines* (2009) I discussed people's motivation for creating a zine. People often say they do their zine because it's fun – "tactiley" fun, fun to express themselves, and to become part of a community. Beyond this I suggest that grrrl zines are often tapping into the pleasures of social change efforts. Changing culture is hard; as hooks says, it's struggle. I've written elsewhere about the work involved: "In this era of instant gratification, we don't hear much about committing ourselves to a difficult struggle, and yet this must be the guiding philosophy of feminist consciousness in the twenty-first century" (2003: 19). Bernice Johnson Reagon (1983) articulates the visceral challenges of social justice work particularly clearly when she writes, "I feel as if I' m gonna keel over any minute and die. That is often what it feels like if you're really doing coalition work. Most of the time you feel threatened to the core and if you don't, you're not really doing no coalescing" (n. p.) Committing ourselves to a difficult challenge, one that's potentially painful and almost certainly going to experience more setbacks than successes, is not the prevailing ethos of this cultural moment. Johnson Reagon's words seem daunting.

And yet these zinesters are expressing the joy of the struggle, what hooks describes as "that which pleasures, delights, and fulfills desire." Crabb says again and again, throughout the fifteen years of *Doris*, that not trying to change the world would be boring. Other zines describe the pleasures of struggle, as well. Issues of *Bitch* repeatedly couch the publication's efforts at social change in terms of enjoyment, as in a 2008 editors' letter that explained, "As always, we've got far more questions than answers in this issue, but putting it together was more about fun than frustration" (2008: 5). In *Greenzine* Cristy Road describes her heart as "a muscle that blossomed by way of movement rather than contentment" and voices the importance of community: "The realization that kindled my impulse is the one that said I wasn't alone in this lifelong quest. That quest about hope and an agenda that went beyond a radical cliché" (2004: n. p.). Similarly, zine creator Lauren Jade Martin writes, "There is a rush, a certain kind of euphoria (way better than drugs, I' m sure) that comes with political work and organizing . . . every time I hear a domestic violence survivor assert in a workshop or a support group or on the hotline that she has a right to be safe and free from violence, I get a shiver of hope down my back" (2002: 13).

This is yet another way that grrrl zines can enact a pedagogy of hope, by demonstrating the satisfaction of involvement. Crabb told me, "When I look at my friends' lives, who don't have any hope and who are cynical, they seem to have not very happy lives. Maybe they do fun stuff a lot, but they don't seem very fulfilled, and I feel like working for social change is really fulfilling. It can be not very fulfilling, but you can find ways to make it super fulfilling, and then that gives hope, even in a hopeless situation" (2007). Zine making is one of the fulfilling ways that some girls and women have found to "give hope, even in a hopeless situation." Grrrl zines provide hope not only to the maker but also to the reader. This is one component of zines' embodied community, their ability to transmit the corporeal experience of hopefulness and the pleasures of resisting the resignation of a cynical culture.

To turn to Cherríe Moraga's ideas from *This Bridge Called My Back*, a foundation for all social justice work must be the belief "that we have the power to actually transform our experience, change our lives, save our lives" (1981: xviii). This "faith of activists" underlies, to greater or lesser extents, all grrrl zines. No matter how pessimistic or cynical the subject matter of the zine is, the fact that the zine exists – that the creator felt motivated to take action, to produce this artifact and share it with others in what can become an embodied community – gives evidence of hope. Many grrrl zines, like *Doris*, have made it their business to propagate that hope and teach others to be hopeful, as well.

Conclusion: Change is possible

In my initial assessments of grrrl zines, I found myself wanting to make them fit existing political models, in order to prove their validity. I wanted to show that they affected zinesters' and readers' engagement in political protest, that they encouraged voting, or that they helped decrease the prevalence of eating disorders or helped spread awareness of emergency contraception. And while I still think it would be interesting to know to what extent these things are true, I've come to feel that the political work of grrrl zines is more subtle and differently resistant than my earlier line of questioning allowed me to see.

What I'm interested in now are these new modes of doing politics, these micropolitical pedagogies that operate in the fissures and forgotten places, that offer dreams on display, that provoke outrage, that invite all kinds of emulation. Viewing grrrl zines in this way not only makes their interventions more visible and valuable, but it also gives a framework for evaluating the larger world of third wave feminism (see *Not My Mother's Sister*, *Third Wave Agenda, Listen Up,* and *Catching a Wave* for further information about third wave feminism), as well. These zines become case studies that materialize the arguments that third wave scholars and girls' studies scholars have been making, arguments about girls' and women's agency, and about what it means to resist in the current cultural moment.

Grrrl zines demonstrate the interpenetration of complicity and resistance; they are spaces to try out mechanisms for doing things differently – while still making use of the ephemera of the mainstream culture. They demonstrate the process, the missed attempts as well as the successes. They aren't the magic solution to social change efforts; instead, they are small, incomplete attempts, micropolitical. They function in a different way than mainstream media and than previous social justice efforts. Indeed, my work with these zines has helped me to understand one of the central paradoxes of third wave feminism: the contradiction between the emphasis on the personal and intimate on the one hand, and the need for broader collective action on the other hand. In some ways grrrl zines merge the two: they are clearly intimate, personal artifacts, and they create embodied communities. But these aren't communities that become large protest groups or voting blocs. They are communities that operate in the cracks and fissures. They show that change is still possible – "even more than we are able to imagine."

References

Budgeon, S., 2001. Emergent Feminist(?) Identities: Young Women and the Practice of Micropolitics. *The European Journal of Women's Studies* 8.1.

Crabb, C., 2002. *Doris #20.* Asheville, NC: self-published.

Crabb, C., 2007. *Doris #24.* Asheville, NC: self-published.

Crabb, C., 2005. *Doris: An Anthology, 1991–2001.* Portland, Ore: Microcosm Publishing.

Dicker, R., and Piepmeier, A., eds., 2003. *Catching a Wave: Reclaiming Feminism for the 21st Century.* Boston: Northeastern University Press.

Findlen, B., ed., 1995. *Listen Up: Voices from the Next Feminist Generation.* Seattle, WA: Seal Press.

Freire, P., 1970. *Pedagogy of the Oppressed.* New York: Continuum.

Goldfarb, J., 1999. *The Cynical Society: The Culture of Politics and the Politics of Culture in American Life.* Chicago: University of Chicago Press.

Harris, A., ed., 2007. *Next Wave Cultures: Feminism, Subcultures, Activism.* New York: Routlede.

Henry, A., 2004. *Not My Mother's Sister: Generational Conflict and Third-Wave Feminism.* Bloomington: Indiana University Press.

Heywood, L. and Drake, J., eds., 1997. *Third Wave Feminism: Being Feminist, Doing Feminism.* Minneapolis: University of Minnesota Press.

hooks, b., 2003. *Teaching Community: A Pedagogy of Hope.* New York: Routledge.

hooks, b., 1990. *Yearning: Race, Gender, and Cultural Politics.* Boston: South End Press.

Martin, L. J., 2002. *Quantify* 4. New York: self-published.

McCarry, S. 2004. Glossolalia. *The Zine Yearbook* volume 8. Toledo, OH: Clamor Magazine.

Moraga, C., 1981. Preface. In: *This Bridge Called My Back: Writings by Radical Women of Color.* New York: Kitchen Table – Women of Color Press.

Piepmeier, A., 2009. *Girl Zines: Making Media, Doing Feminism.* New York: New York University Press.

Road, C., 2004. *Greenzine* 14. Portland, OR: Microcosm Publishing.

Rodriguez, C., 2001. *Fissures in the Mediascape: An International Study of Citizens' Media.* Cresskill, NJ: Hampton.

Zeisler, A. and Jervis, L., 2008. *Bitch* 39.

Acknowledgement:
This essay is an excerpt from Alison Piepmeier's book *Girl Zines: Making Media, Doing Feminism*, NYU Press, 2009. Reprinted with kind permission from the publisher.

Images from Doris No. 27 (2009). Reprinted with kind permission from Cindy Crabb (Athens, Ohio/USA, see http://www.dorisdorisdoris.com and http://doriszineblog.blogspot.com).

From DIY to Collaborative Fields of Experimentation: Feminist Media and Cultural Production Towards Social Change – A Visual Contribution[1]

Elke Zobl

"Zines, as a DIY practice, are the very visible expression of "everyone can do it". It is a possibility of sharing and spreading information, ideas and knowledge and a means of self-teaching. It is also a way of connecting people and ideas."
Love Kills Collective
(Romania)

"I think the whole process of zine making is very empowering, both to the maker and later on the reader. Most of all, I seek satisfaction of the making, the process: dealing with what I used to write to myself as something public-politicizing the personal, and personalizing the political."
Editor of *Patrol*
zine (Israel)

"What I love about zines is that I get a lot of new perspective on things. It gives me strength."
(her) riot distro (Schweden)

1 Acknowledgement: The research on this project was funded by the Austrian Science Fund (FWF): P21187. Note: This contribution is a collage of images and quotes from interviews conducted within the project (the quotes are not necessarily from the creators of the images). The interviews can be accessed at: www.grassrootsfeminism.net. All images reprinted with permission. A warm thank you to everyone!

"It's up to you now":
Calling for participation

"DIY is a practice that can be very encouraging and empowering. Skill sharing is simply fun! This is also a kind of community building, where a lot also takes place through exchanges. DIY is a kind of alternative, that is to say: It doesn't all need to be marketable."
The Artist of *Trouble X Comics*

Flyer by *Trouble X* (Germany, www.troublex.blogsport.de). Images by Trouble X.

drag. Image by *Trouble X.* (Germany, www.troublex. blogsport.de), 2007

Taking zine-making to the community

"This DIY ethic is the cornerstone of the political aspect of Grrrl Zines A-Go-Go. We believe zine-making embodies the phrase ,the personal is political' by encouraging active participation in the creation of one's own culture, and independence from mainstream media."
Grrrl Zines A-Go-Go (USA)

"Zine-making is especially important for teen girls who discover a new avenue for expression that is uncensored; something that they can produce alone, without the need for experts or expensive tools – their tools are their mind and a pen – anyone can do it."
Grrrl Zines A-Go-Go (USA)

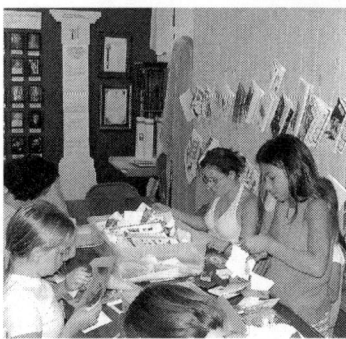

"Grrrl Zines A-Go-Go doesn't just want to encourage zine making, we also hope to inspire other groups of like-minded folks to start running workshops in their areas too."
Grrrl Zines A-Go-Go (USA)

„Making Zines, Making History" a workshop by Grrrl Zines A-Go-Go with Girl Scouts of America troop at the Women's History Museum and Education Center of San Diego (CA, USA) in October 2006. Photos by: Margarat Nee and Kim Schwenk of *Grrrl Zines A-Go-Go*.

The upper right photo is from a different event: September 8, 2007, Samuel H. Wentworth Public Library, Center Sandwich, NH, http://gzagg.org/sandwich_photos.html.

Doing-It-Together:
Towards open fields of experimentation

"DIY is an approach which understands itself clearly as action-oriented and emancipatory in the sense of detaching oneself from rigid principles. For me, DIY is only then interesting, when it becomes a Do-it-Together and is not confined to the own microcosm."
Stephanie Müller (*rag*treasure*, Germany)

rag*treasure (Munich) with their music-text-dance-textile performance "Trash-Recycled-F[e]Mtronics" at the first international women artist festival in Vienna "Her Position in Transition" (March 2006). One of the collective members, Stephanie Müller (in front with the sewing machine), has done a number of critical crafting performances and exhibitions as well as workshops with migrant youth and refugees (see http://www.flachware.de/stephanie-mueller/). Photo by scissabob.de.

"It is about making projects without the precondition of a professional education into an open field of experimentation for myself and the audience and to use my voice to indicate dedicated commitment for oneself and the needs of others."
Stephanie Müller (*rag*treasure*, Germany)

DIY feminism towards social change

"DIY feminism is about everyone doing feminism ourselves and making changes, however small they may seem at first sight. It means not waiting for others, for "professionals" or politicians, to make the world more women-friendly and to solve problems related to sexism."
Nina Nijsten (Belgium)

"DIY feminism disrupts complacent beliefs that feminism and social change are no longer on the agenda of young people."
Red Chidgey (UK)

Drawings, posters and zine fest flyer by Nina Nijsten
(Belgium, http://drawingsbynina.wordpress.com)

Appendix

Feminist Media Production in Europe: A Selected List of Projects

Compiled by Stefanie Grünangerl

This list only presents a selection of the wide range of feminist and queer European media production. For more projects and information please refer to the archive sections on grassrootsfeminism.net and grrrlzines.net. Arrows (e. g. → E-Zine) indicate further references to a change of media type, a re-launch/reconception or another medium produced within the scope of the same project. [All links checked April 2012]

Print

AEP Informationen – Feministische Zeitschrift für Politik und Gesellschaft (magazine, Austria, since 1974) <http://www.aep.at/heft/home.php>

Anattitude Magazine (magazine, Belgium, since 2005) <http://www.anattitude.net>

Andaina – Revista Galega de Pensamento Feminista (magazine, Spain, since 1983) <http://www.andainamulleres.org>

an.schläge (magazine, Austria, since 1983) <http://www.anschlaege.at> → TV

Ariadne Löng (journal, Estonia, since 2000) <http://www.enut.ee/enut.php?id=259>

ASPEKT (magazine, Slovakia, 1993–2004) <http://www.aspekt.sk> → E-Zine

AUF – Eine Frauenzeitschrift (magazine, Austria, 1974–2011) <http://www.auf-einefrauenzeitschrift.at>

Bang – Feministisk Kulturtidskrift (magazine, Sweden, since 1991) <http://www.bang.se>

a bichana (zine, Portugal, since 2008) <http://abichana.blogspot.com>

Bleck (zine, Sweden, 1998–2003?) <http://www.bleck.org/index.html>

Bloody Mary (zine, Czech Republic, since 2000) <http://bloodymary.blog.cz>

Causette (magazine, France, since 2009) <http://www.causette.fr>

Chaos Grrlz (zine, Poland, 2006–2008?) <http://www.myspace.com/chaosxgrrlz>

La Choriza (zine, France, since 2006)
<http://lachoriza.wordpress.com>
old blog: <http://sapitoverde.canalblog.com>

Chroma – A Queer Literary Journal (journal, United Kingdom, 2004–2010)
<http://www.chromajournal.co.uk>

CLARA (magazine, France, since 1987) <http://clara-magazine.fr>

Clio – Histoire, Femmes et Sociétés (journal, France, since 1995)
<http://clio.revues.org/index.html>

Clio – Die Zeitschrift für Frauengesundheit (magazine, Germany, since 1976)
<http://www.ffgz.de/07.clios_und_broschueren/CLIO_und_BROSCHUEREN-Frame.htm>

Clitocore zine (zine, Spain, 2005–2008?) <http://clitocore.blogspot.com>

Clit Rocket (zine, Italy, 1999–2009?)
<http://clitrocket.altervista.org/blog/about.htm>

Colouring Outside the Lines (zine, United Kingdom, 2005–2009)
<http://cotlzine.blogspot.com>

Coma to Action (zine, Belgium, 2009)
<http://echoproject.110mb.com/catalog.html>

Cowgirls (comic-zine, Sweden, since 2008?)
<http://karolinabang.blogspot.com>

Cuntstunt (zine, Austria, 2003–2006?)
<http://manoafreeuniversity.org/host_for/cuntstunt>

(Different Worlds) Same Heartbeats (zine, Belgium, since 2007)
<http://echoproject.110mb.com/catalog.html>

Else (zine, Germany, 2008) <http://www.myspace.com/else_zine>

Emakunde (magazine, Spain, 1989–2009)
<http://www.emakunde.euskadi.net/u72-publicac/es/contenidos/informacion/sen_revista/es_emakunde/revista_es.html>

l'émiliE (magazine, Switzerland, 2001–2009), former: Mouvement Féministe (1912–1960), Femmes suisses (1960–1999), Femmes en Suisse (1999–2001)
<http://www.lemilie.org> → E-Zine

Emma (magazine, Germany, since 1977) <http://www.emma.de>

Erreakzioa-Reacción (zine, Spain, 1994–2000)
<http://es.wikipedia.org/wiki/Erreakzioa-reacción>
<http://www.arteleku.net/argitalpenak/bildumak/feminismoak/argitalpenak/erreakzioa-aldizkaria>

Eva & Co – Eine Feministische Kulturzeitschrift (magazine, Austria, 1982–1992) <http://ursprung.mur.at/eva_co.html>

ex aequo (journal, Portugal, since 1999)
<http://www.apem-estudos.org/?page_id=26>

Faces de Eva (journal, Portugal, since 1999)
<http://www2.fcsh.unl.pt/facesdeeva>

Fair Play (magazine, Bulgaria, 1997–2002/2005)
<http://www.women-bg.org/index.php?option=com_content&view=article&id=36&Itemid=29&lang=en>

FAMA – Die feministisch-theologische Zeitschrift der Schweiz (magazine, Switzerland, since 1985) <http://www.fama.ch>

FEMA – FEministický MAgazín (magazine, Czech Republic, since 2010) <http://www.feministickymagazin.tk>

Female Sequences (magazine, Austria, 1998–2002) <http://www.female-consequences.org/femseq.html>

Feministische Studien (journal, Germany, since 1982) <http://www.feministische-studien.de>

Feminist Review (journal, United Kingdom, since 1979) <http://www.feminist-review.com>

Femka (magazine, Poland, since 2011) <http://femka.net/kwartalnik-femka>

Fett (magazine, Norway, since 2005) <http://www.fett.no>

fiber. werkstoff für feminismus und popkultur (magazine, Austria, since 2002) former: nylon. KunstStoff zu Feminismus und Popkultur (2000–2002) <http://www.fibrig.net>

FKW//Zeitschrift für Geschlechterforschung und visuelle Kultur (journal, Germany, since 2007) former: Frauen Kunst Wissenschaft (1987–2007) <http://www.frauenkunstwissenschaft.de>

Flapper Gathering (zine, Belgium, since 2002) <http://echoproject.110mb.com/catalog.html>

FrauenSicht (newspaper, Switzerland, since 2002) <http://www.frauensicht.ch/index.html>

Frauensolidarität (magazine, Austria, since 1982) <http://www.frauensolidaritaet.org> → Globale Dialoge/Radio

FRAZ Frauenzeitung (newspaper, Switzerland,1975–2009) <http://www.frauenzeitung.ch> archive: <http://www.frauenpodiumgossau-zh.ch/Archiv/FRAZArchiv/tabid/102/language/de-CH/Default.aspx>

Ful (magazine, Sweden, since 2004) <http://www.tidskriftenful.se> → Radio

Furia! (magazine, Poland, since 2010), former: Furii Pierwszej (1997–2001) <http://furia.org.pl>

Gaia (magazine, Albania, 2006–2009) <http://www.gadc.org.al/index.php?option=com_filecabinet&view=files&id=6&Itemid=54&lang=en>

Les Galopines (zine, Switzerland, since 2012) <http://feminista.ch/?p=524> first issue: <http://feminista.ch/wp-content/uploads/2012/03/2012_03 Feminizine.pdf> → Feminista!/Blog

Gender. Zeitschrift für Geschlecht, Kultur und Gesellschaft (journal, Germany, since 2009) <http://gender-zeitschrift.de>

Género y Comunicación (magazine, Spain, 1999–2007)
<http://www.nodo50.org/ameco>
<http://www.amecopress.net/spip.php?article20>

Genus (journal, Sweden, since 1999)
<http://genus.se/Publikationer/tidningen-genus>

George (magazine, Switzerland, since 2010) <http://georgemag.ch>

GirlFrenzy (zine, United Kingdom, 1991–1998)
<http://www.ampnet.co.uk/girlfrenzy.html>

GLU – Girls Like Us (magazine, The Netherlands, since 2005)
<http://www.glumagazine.com>

Görls – Die neue Mädchenzeitung (zine, Germany, since 1995)
<http://www.goerls.de>

Hugs and Kisses (magazine, Germany, since 2007)
<http://www.hugsandkissesonline.de>

IHRSINN – eine radikalfeministische Lesbenzeitschrift (magazine, Germany,
1990–2004) <http://ihrsinn.net/ende.html>

Il pleut de gouines/It's raining dykes (zine, France/Canada, 2004–2008)
<http://ilpleutdesgouines.blogspot.com>

Killed by beauty (zine, Sweden, since 2001)
<http://www.angelfire.com/on3/KBB/kbb7.htm>

KnockBack (magazine, United Kingdom, since 2006)
<http://www.knockback.co.uk>

Die Krake (zine, Germany, since 2006) <http://www.diepolytanten.de.tc>

Kvinden&Samfundet (magazine, Denmark, since 1885)
<http://danskkvindesamfund.dk/kvindensamfundet.html>

Labris novine (newspaper, Serbia, since 1995)
<http://www.labris.org.rs/labris-novine/index.html>

Lash Back (zine, Ireland, since 2009)
<http://www.myspace.com/lashbackdublin>

Lesbo (magazine, Slovenia, 1997–2005) former: fanzine Lesbozine (1987–1988)
and bulletin Pandora (1993–1996) <http://www.ljudmila.org/lesbo/lesbo.htm>

ln – lambda nordica (journal, Sweden, since 1989)
<http://www.lambdanordica.se>

LoveKills/Dragostia Ucide (zine, Romania, since 2003)
<http://aro.ecobytes.net/lovekills>

LOVER (magazine, The Netherlands, since 1974)
<http://www.tijdschriftlover.nl>

Marea (magazine, Italy, since 1994) <http://www.mareaonline.it>

Masculine Femininities (zine, United Kingdom, since 2008?)
<http://masculinefemininities.wordpress.com>

Medusa – antilookism zine (zine, Germany, since 2006)
<http://www.lookism.info/zines>

Missy Magazine (magazine, Germany, since 2008)
<http://missy-magazine.de>

MOM – Make Out Magazine (zine, Germany, since 2011)
<http://makeoutmagazine.net>

Morgenmuffel (zine, United Kingdom, since 1998?)
<http://www.morgenmuffel.co.uk>

Muze (magazine, France, since 2004) <http://blog.muze.fr>

Narobe (magazine, Slovenia, since 2007) <http://www.narobe.si>

НЕТ – ЗНАЧИТ НЕТ ("No means No") (magazine, Russia, since 2010)
<http://socialistworld.ru/kampanii/protiv-ekspluataczii-i-diskriminaczii-
zhenshhin>

Nevi Sara Kali – Roma Women's Journal (journal, Romania, since 2009)
<http://femrom.ro/nevikali.html>

NIKK magasin (magazine, Norway, since 2000)
<http://www.nikk.no/English/Publications/NIKK_magasin>

Noidonne (magazine, Italy, since 1944) <http://www.noidonne.org> → E-Zine

NORA – Nordic Journal of Feminist and Gender Research (journal, Sweden,
since 1993) <http://www.tandf.co.uk/journals/swom>

Not Ladylike (zine, Belgium, 2005)
<http://echoproject.110mb.com/catalog.html>

n.paradoxa – international feminist art journal (journal, United Kingdom,
since 1998) <http://www.ktpress.co.uk> → E-Zine

Olympe – Feministische Arbeitshefte zur Politik (magazine, Switzerland, since
1994) <http://www.olympeheft.ch>

Opzij (magazine, The Netherlands, since 1972) <http://www.opzij.nl>

Osez le féminisme! (newspaper, France, since 2009)
<http://osezlefeminisme.fr>

Остров (Ostrov) (zine, Russia, since 1999)
<http://community.livejournal.com/journal_ostrov/>
<http://www.gay.ru/lesbi/ostrov/index.htm>

outside the box – Zeitschrift für feministische Gesellschaftskritik (magazine,
Germany, since 2009) <http://outside.blogsport.de>

OvaryAction (zine, Norway, 2002–2007)
<http://www.myspace.com/ovaryaction_startariot> → Radio

Palabras/Palabres (magazine, Belgium, since 1996)
<http://www.mondefemmes.org/publications/palabras.htm>

Park It Up Your Arse (zine, France, 2008–2009?)
<http://www.myspace.com/parkitupyourarse/blog>

Pecs & Ongles – Transgouinepédémestriel (zine, France, 2008–2009)
<http://www.pantheresroses.org/Pecs-et-ongles-tous-les-numeros.html>

Pełnym Głosem (magazine, Poland, 1993–1997)
<http://efka.org.pl/?action=gl&ID=19>

Plotki femzine (zine, Germany/international, since 2006)
<http://plotkifemzine.wordpress.com>
<http://www.plotki.net/cms/index.php?option=com_content&task=blogcatego
ry&id=44&Itemid=55>
<http://www.plotki.net/cms/index.php?option=com_content&task=blogcatego
ry&id=89&Itemid=99>

Poder y Libertad (magazine, Spain, 1979–2004)
<http://www.vindicacionfeminista.com/frameset2.html>

Les Poupées en pantalon (magazine, France, since 2010)
<http://lespoupeesenpantalon.blogspot.com>

Přímá cesta (zine, Czech Republic, 2001–2006)
<http://anarchofeminismus.ecn.cz/files/casopisy.html>

punk feminist (zine, Belgium, 2001)
<http://echoproject.110mb.com/catalog.html>

Race Revolt (zine, United Kingdom, since 2007)
<http://www.racerevolt.org.uk>

Radix (zine, Belgium, 2007) <http://echoproject.110mb.com/catalog.html>

the RAG (zine, Ireland, since 2006) <http://www.ragdublin.blogspot.com>

A Rata (zine, Portugal, 1999–2004)
<http://caldeira213.net/ver.php#num=0&id=A%20Rata>
<http://membres.multimania.fr/carlacruz/zoina.htm>
<http://carlacruz.net/2011/collective/collective-two#/0>

Reassess Your Weapons (zine, United Kingdom, 2002–2009)
<http://www.myspace.com/manifestaleeds/blog/372216324>

regina (magazine, Germany, since 1994) <http://regina-magazine.de>

Riot Grrrl London zine (zine, United Kingdom, 2001–2003)
<http://riotgrrrlonline.wordpress.com/2008/04/01/riot-girl-londons-manifesto>

ROSA – Zeitschrift für Geschlechterforschung (magazine, Switzerland, since
1990) <http://www.rosa.uzh.ch>

Scumgrrrls (magazine, Belgium, since 2002) <http://scumgrrrls.org>

Shape & Situate: Posters of Inspirational European Women (zine, United
Kingdom, since 2010)
<http://remember-who-u-are.blogspot.com/2010/11/shape-and-situate-zine.
html>
<http://remember-who-u-are.blogspot.com/2011/06/shape-situate-posters-of-
inspirational.html>

Siréna (zine, Czech Republic, 2001–2002)
<http://anarchofeminismus.ecn.cz/files/casopisy.html#pci>

Slut (magazine, Sweden, 2006–2008) <http://tidskriftenslut.com>

Stichwort Newsletter (magazine, Austria, since 1996)
<http://www.stichwort.or.at/frames/newslefr.htm>

Subtext Magazine (magazine, United Kingdom, 2006–2010)
<http://www.subtextmagazine.co.uk>

Svobodna – свободна (zine, Ukraine, since 2010)
<http://svobodna.org.ua/femart/diy/spec-vypusk-svobodna> → Blog

Toilet Paper (zine, Germany, since 2002)
<http://www.myspace.com/aliensheconcerts>

Towanda! Rivista lesbica (magazine, Italy, 1994–2005/06?)
<http://www.towanda.it>

Treća (magazine, Croatia, since 1998)
<http://www.zenstud.hr/index.php?option=com_content&view=category&lay out=blog&id=49&Itemid=227>

Trouble & Strife (magazine, United Kingdom, 1983–2002)
<http://www.troubleandstrife.org>

TROUBLE X (comic-zine, Germany, since 2007)
<http://troublex.blogsport.de>

tulva – Feministinen aikakauslehti (magazine, Finland, since 2002)
<http://www.tulva.fi>

Uplift (magazine, United Kingdom, 2006)
<http://www.upliftmagazine.com>

Verge (magazine, United Kingdom, 2006)
<http://vaginamagazine.blogspot.com>

Virginia – Zeitschrift für Frauenbuchkritik (magazine, Germany, since 1986)
<http://www.virginia-frauenbuchkritik.de>

Wir Frauen – Das feministische Blatt (magazine, Germany, since 1982)
<http://www.wirfrauen.de>

Wolverette zine (zine, Germany, since 2007)
<http://wolverette.wordpress.com>

Женщина Плюс.../Woman Plus . . . (magazine, Russia, 1994–2004)
<http://www.owl.ru/win/womplus/index.htm>

xStrength & Couragex (zine, Spain, 2006)
<http://xstrengthandcouragex.webs.com>

Я – Ya (magazine, Ukraine, since 2003)
<http://www.krona.org.ua/index.php?option=com_phocadownload&view=cat egory&id=1&Itemid=222&lang=uk>

Zadra (magazine, Poland, since 1999)
<http://www.efka.org.pl/?action=gl&ID=5>

Žene protiv rata ("Women against War") (magazine, Serbia, 1994–1995)
<http://www.zeneucrnom.org>

Жарава – Zharava (magazine, Bulgaria, 1997–2000)
<http://www.women-bg.org/index.php?option=com_content&view=article&id =37&Itemid=18&lang=bg>

Zina lf_ro (zine, Romania, 2005–2007)
<http://ladyfest-ro.pimienta.org/weblog/?page_id=141> → F.I.A./Blog

Blogs

À dire d'elles (France, since 2008) <http://sandrine70.wordpress.com>

All My Independent Women (Portugal, since 2005)
<http://allmyindependentwomen.blogspot.com>

Ansats – till en feministisk frivolt (Sweden, 2008–2010)
<http://ansats.blogspot.com>

AnyBody (United Kingdom, since 2006) <http://www.any-body.org>

La Barbe (France, since 2008) <http://www.labarbelabarbe.org>

Bezimena (Serbia, 2009–2011?) <http://www.bezimena.org>

Bird of Paradox (United Kingdom, since 2008)
<http://www.birdofparadox.net/blog>
old blog: <http://birdofparadox.wordpress.com>

Blogul Medusei – lumea prin lentila feminist (Romania, since 2008)
<http://blogul-medusei.blogspot.com>

Bolletino di guerra (Italy, since 2010)
<http://bollettino-di-guerra.noblogs.org>
former Burqa Blog (2009–2010) <http://burqa.wordpress.com>

La broma – comunicación con causa, ladies, voluntariado y activism (Spain,
since 2003) <http://www.labroma.org/blog>
old blog: <http://orugachan.blogspot.com>

La Bruja Violeta – Feminotopia (Spain, since 2006)
<http://labrujavioleta.wordpress.com>

C@ucAsia – К@вкАзия (Georgia, since 2009)
<http://caucasia.at.ua> → E-Zine

Charlie Little (United Kingdom, 2008–2009)
<http://charlielittle.wordpress.com> former Blog of Feminist activism
(2006–2008) <http://charliegrrl.wordpress.com>

Collectif Debout! (France, since 2010) <http://collectif-debout.org>

Comix Grrrlz (Poland, since 2005) <http://comixgrrrlz.pl>

Crazy like us? Feminists write about mental health (United Kingdom,
2008–2011?) <http://feministmentalhealthuk.wordpress.com>

Cruella-Blog (United Kingdom, since 2004)
<http://cruellablog.blogspot.com>

Diversitat en Igualtat (Spain, since 2008)
<http://diversitatenigualtat.blogspot.com>

Dones i noves technologies (Spain, since 2006) <http://donestech.net>

Donne della réalta (Italy, since 2009) <http://donnedellarealta.wordpress.com>

Down the Rabbit Hole (Romania, 2009–2011?)
<http://alicedowntherabbithole.wordpress.com>

Dumbles (Italy, since 2001) <http://dumbles.noblogs.org>
old website: <http://www.ecologiasociale.org/pg/ecofemminismo.html>

Du Rose dans le Gris (France, 2005–2010) <http://drdlg.blogs.com>

Fel feminism (Belgium, since 2010) <http://felfeminisme.wordpress.com>

Femeko – Feministyczna Ekonomia (Poland, 2010–2011?)
<http://femeko.blox.pl/html>

Femen (Ukraine, since 2008) <http://femen.livejournal.com>

Femgerila (Macedonia, 2007–2011?) <http://femgerila.crnaovca.mk>
old blog: <http://femgerila.blog.com.mk>

Feminárium (Hungary, 2006–2008) <http://feminarium.blogter.hu>
former Egy feminista blog (2005–2006) <http://feministak.freeblog.hu>

Le féminin l'emporte (France, since 2006)
<http://femininlemporte.blogspot.com>
old blog: <http://femininlemporte.canalblog.com>

Feminism_ua (Ukraine, since 2004)
<http://feminism-ua.livejournal.com>

O Feminismo está a passar por aqui . . . (Portugal, since 2006)
<http://colectivofeminista.blogspot.com>

Feminisn'ts – Я не феминистка, но . . . (Russia, since 2008)
<http://feminisnts.ru>

Feminista! (Switzerland, since 2010)
<http://feminista.ch> → Les Galopines/Print

Feminist Carnival (United Kingdom, 2005–2010)
<http://carnivalfeminist.blogspot.com>
old blog: <http://feministcarnival.blogspot.com>

Feministinn (Iceland, since 2003) <http://www.feministinn.is>

Feministki (Russia, since 2005) <http://feministki.livejournal.com>

Feminist Memory (United Kingdom, since 2010)
<http://feministmemory.wordpress.com>

Femminismo a Sud (Italy, since 2006)
<http://femminismo-a-sud.noblogs.org>

F.I.A. blog (Romania, since 2005)
<http://ladyfest-ro.pimienta.org/weblog> → Zina lf_ro/Print

Genderblog (Germany, 2005–2011?) <http://www.genderblog.de>

gender_by (Belarus, since 2009) <http://gender-by.livejournal.com>

Girls Can Blog (Germany, since 2010) <http://girlsblogtoo.blogspot.com>

i heart digital life (Germany, since 2005) <http://www.iheartdigitallife.de>

InterAlia (Hungary, since 2008) <http://interalia.org.hu>

Knúz (Iceland, since 2011) <http://www.knuz.is>

Kvinnekongen (Norway, 2008–2011?) <http://www.kvinnekonger.no>
old blog: <http://kvinnekonge.wordpress.com>

Lezbično-feministična univerza (Slovenia, since 2010)
<http://lezbicnofeministicnauniverza.wordpress.com>

liberetutte (Perugia/Italy, since 2008) <http://liberetutte.noblogs.org>

Libere Tutte (Florence/Italy, since 2008)
<http://liberetuttefirenze.blogspot.com>

Mädchenblog (Germany, since 2006)
<http://www.maedchenblog.blogsport.de>

Mädchenmannschaft (Germany, since 2007)
<http://www.maedchenmannschaft.net>

Maman Poulet (Ireland, since 2003) <http://www.mamanpoulet.com>
old blog: <http://www.mamanpoulet.blogspot.com>

Maribolheras (Spain, since 2006) <http://maribolheras.com>

Mi feminismo y otras alteridades (Spain, 2006–2010)
<http://gaelia.wordpress.com>

Mujeres Libres Bologna (Italy, since 2009)
<http://mujeres-libres-bologna.noblogs.org>

Ni Putes Ni Soumises (France, since 2005) <http://www.npns.fr>

No Pretence (United Kingdom, 2009) <http://nopretence.wordpress.com>

Olympe et le plafond de verre (France, since 2008)
<http://blog.plafonddeverre.fr>

Panteras Rosas (Portugal, since 2005)
<http://www.panterasrosa.blogspot.com>

Penny Red (United Kingdom, since 2007)
<http://pennyred.blogspot.com>

A pinám kivan! (Hungary, since 2007) <http://pinamkivan.blog.hu>
old blog: <http://pinamkivan.freeblog.hu>

Prepih (Slovenia, since 2006) <http://prepih.blogspot.com>

Ptqk_blogzine (Spain, since 2004) <http://ptqkblogzine.blogspot.com>
old blog: <http://ptqkblogzine.blogia.com>

Ravnopravka – Moscow Feminist Group (Russia, since 2010)
<http://ravnopravka.wordpress.com>

Rdeče zore (Slovenia, since 2007) <http://rdecezore.blogspot.com>

La rete non è neutra (Italy, 2007–2009)
<http://la-rete-non-neutra.noblogs.org>

Le Ribellule (Italy, since 2007) <http://leribellule.noblogs.org>

Rmott62 (United Kingdom, since 2009) <http://rmott62.wordpress.com>

Rudax (Spain, since 2005) <http://rudaxforever.blogspot.com>

side-glance (Germany, since 2009)
<http://www.sideglance.melan-chol-ie.de>
<http://www.side-glance.de>

Sin Género de Dudas (Spain, since 2002) <http://singenerodedudas.com>

SROM – Separatystyczne Rewolucyjne Oddziały Maciczne ("Separatist Revolutionary Uterine Troops") (Poland, 2010) <http://lesmisja.blogspot.com>

Stadtpiratin (Germany, since 2009) <http://www.stadtpiratin.blogspot.com>

Strasznasztuka2 (Poland, since 2006) <http://strasznasztuka.blox.pl/html>

Svobodna – свободна (Ukraine, 2007–2011?)
<http://svobodna.org.ua> → Print

Ta det röda pillret – se världsproblemen i vitögat (Sweden, since 2008)
<http://alexanderchamberland.blogspot.com>

Têtes hautes et Regards droits! (France, since 2008)
<http://teteshautesregardsdroits.wordpress.com>

Transnational Queer Underground (Germany/international, since 2009)
<http://www.transnational-queer-underground.net>

De Tweede Sekse (Belgium, since 2008) <http://tweedesekse.wordpress.com>

UmweltWeiber (Germany, 2007–2010) <http://umweltweiber.blogsport.de>

Un altro genere di comunicazione (Italy, since 2009)
<http://comunicazionedigenere.wordpress.com>

Un Beso (Romania, 2009–2010) <http://unbeso.wordpress.com>

Vi som aldrig sa sexist (Sweden, since 2008)
<http://www.visomaldrigsasexist.net>

Women in London (United Kingdom, since 2009)
<http://www.womeninlondon.org.uk>

x0y1 – Plataforma para la investigación y la producçión artistica sobre construcçión identitaria y cultura digital blog (Spain, 2009–2010)
<http://x0y1.net/blog>

xcute'n'pastex (Poland, since 2006) <http://www.xcnpx.blogspot.com>

ЗА ФЕМИНИЗМ – Za Feminizm (Russia, since 2010)
<http://www.zafeminizm.ru/index.php>
old blog: <http://www.zafeminizm.ucoz.ru>

Ženska soba blog (Croatia, since 2009) <http://blog.vecernji.hr/zenska-soba>

E-Zines

AmecoPress – Información para la Igualdad (Spain, since 2007)
<http://www.amecopress.net>

Amphi magazine (Belarus, since 2008) <http://www.opensocium.com>

ArtMix (Poland, since 2001) <http://www.obieg.pl/artmix>
old website: <http://free.art.pl/artmix>

ASPEKTin (Slovakia, since 2004) <http://www.aspekt.sk/aspektin/title>
archive 2004–2007: <http://archiv.aspekt.sk/in_archiv.php> → Print

Aviva – Online Magazin für Frauen (Germany, since 2000)
<http://www.aviva-berlin.de>

BitchBuzz (United Kingdom, since 2008) <http://www.bitchbuzz.com>

C@ucAsia – international information-analytical electronic magazine (Georgia, 2005–2009) <http://www.gmc.ge/images/04KAVKAZIAJ-01.html> → Blog

het Continuüm – digitaal tijdschrift over genderdiversiteit en transgender (The Netherlands, since 1996) <http://www.continuum.nl>

Cunterview.net – women art media space (Croatia, 2006–2010)
<http://www.cunterview.net>
archive 2006–2009: <http://www.cunterview.net/index.php>
→ Vox Femina/E-Zine

Delt@ il tuo genere d'informazione (Italy, since 2009)
<http://www.deltanews.net>

dieStandard (Austria, since 2000) <http://diestandard.at>

emancipatie.nl (The Netherlands, since 2000) <http://www.emancipatie.nl>

Emakunde (Spain, since 2010)
<http://www.emakunde.euskadi.net/u72-revist83/es>

L'émiliE (Switzerland, since 2010) <http://www.lemilie.org> → Print

Feminisite (Turkey, since 2006) <http://www.feminisite.net>

féminisme.ch (Switzerland, since 2006) <http://www.féminisme.ch>

feminismus.cz (Czech Republic, since 1999) <http://www.feminismus.cz>

Feminist Yaklaşımlar (Turkey, since 2006)
<http://www.feministyaklasimlar.org>

Feminoteka (Poland, since 2005) <http://www.feminoteka.pl/news.php>

femka.net (Poland, since 2008) <http://femka.net>

The F-Word (United Kingdom, since 2001) <http://www.thefword.org.uk>

gaelick (Ireland, since 2008) <http://www.gaelick.com>

Gender Forum – An Internet Journal for Gender Studies (Germany, since 2002)
<http://www.genderforum.org>

gitA (Czech Republic, 2006–2009) <http://www.ta-gita.cz>

InterAlia (Poland, since 2006) <http://www.interalia.org.pl>

KILDEN – web magazine (Norway, since 1999)
<http://www.kilden.forskningsradet.no>

Konsola.org (Poland, since 2010) <http://konsola.org.pl>

Kultur & Geschlecht – Onlinejournal (Germany, since 2007)
<http://www.ruhr-uni-bochum.de/genderstudies/kulturundgeschlecht/index.
html>

KVINFOs Webmagasin (Denmark, since 1997, former: FORUM Webmagasi-
net) <http://webmagasin.kvinfo.dk>

Labris (Serbia, since 2001) <http://www.labris.org.rs>

LES Online (Portugal, since 2009)
<http://www.lespt.org/lesonline/index.php?journal=lo&page=index>

Libela – informacijski portal o rodu, spolu i demokraciji (Croatia, since 2008)
<http://www.libela.org>

LRM – El Femimagazine con Perspectiva de Género y Feminista (Spain, since
2006) <http://lady-read.blogspot.com>

Lysistrata's Path – Путь Лисистраты (Russia, since 2009)
<http://leonatus.ucoz.ru>

Melodiva – female music networking (Germany, since 2000)
<http://www.melodiva.de>

Migrazine (Austria, since 2006) <http://www.migrazine.at>

MíraLES (Spain, since 2009) <http://mirales.es> → RadiografíaLES/Radio

Miss Tilly – das Frauenmagazin im Internet (Germany, since 2006)
<http://www.misstilly.de>

Mujeres en Red – El periódico feminista (Spain, since 1997)
<http://www.mujeresenred.net>

Mujer Palabra (Spain, since 2001)
<http://www.mujerpalabra.net/index.htm>

NEWW – Polska – The Network of East-West Women (Poland/international,
since 2004) <http://www.neww.eu>

Noidonne (Italy, since 2004) <http://www.noidonne.org> → Print

Les Nouvelles News (France, since 2009)
<http://www.lesnouvellesnews.fr>

n.paradoxa – international feminist art journal (United Kingdom, 1996–2010)
<http://www.ktpress.co.uk/nparadoxa-issue-details.asp> → Print

OWL – Open Women Line (Russia, 1996–2009) <http://www.owl.ru>
archive 1997–2002: <http://owl.ru/index.htm>
archive 1996–1997: <http://www.owl.ru/win/zhif/index.htm>

Il Paese delle Donne (Italy, since 1995)
<http://www.womenews.net/spip3>

querelles-net – Rezensionszeitschrift für Frauen- und Geschlechterforschung
(Germany, since 2000) <http://www.querelles-net.de/index.php/qn>

Qunst.mag (Germany, since 2008) <http://qunst.net>

Les Quotidiennes (Switzerland, since 2007)
<http://www.lesquotidiennes.com>

RED FEMINISTA – Violencia de Género (Spain, since 2002)
<http://www.redfeminista.org>

Seksualność Kobiet (Poland, since 2009)
<http://seksualnosc-kobiet.pl>

Server Donne (Italy, since 1996) <http://www.women.it>

Trikster – Nordic Queer Journal (Denmark/international, 2008–2010?)
<http://trikster.net>

Trzy Kolory – sabatnik boginiczno-feministyczny (Poland, since 2010)
<http://sabatnik.pl/news.php>

Tüsarok (Hungary, since 2004) <http://www.tusarok.org>

Vox Feminae (Croatia, since 2010)
<http://www.voxfeminae.net> → Cunterview.net/E-Zine

Wolfsmutter (Austria, since 2002) <http://www.wolfsmutter.com>

ЖЕНСКАЯ СЕТЬ – Women's Network Infoportal (Ukraine, since 2007)
<http://www.feminist.org.ua/index.php>

Women's Views on News (United Kingdom/international, since 2009)
<http://www.womensviewsonnews.org>

Radio & TV

Bang Bang (Belgium, since 2005)
<http://www.rtbf.be/purefm/emission_bang-bang?id=626>

DégenréE – l'émission pour déranger! (France, since 2004)
<http://infokiosques.net/degenree>

Elles causent (France, 2009–2011) <http://ellescausent.blogspot.com>

Expatriarch (Germany, since 2010)
<http://www.expatriarch.com/category/radio>

Female:pressure (Austria, since 2008)
<http://o94.at/?category_name=sendereihe&id=653759>
<http://www.femalepressure.net> → Database

Fem.fm (Belarus/international, since 2012) <http://www.fem.fm>

Frauenzimmer (Austria, since 1999)
<http://radiofabrik.at/programm0/sendungenvona-z/frauenzimmer.html>

Fulradio (Sweden, since 2008)
<http://www.tidskriftenful.se/radio.php?r=ful&o=fulradio> → Print

Gender frequenz (Austria, since 2010)
<http://helsinki.at/programm/shows/gender-frequenz-sozialpolitisch-feminis-tisch-unbeugsam>
archive: <http://cba.fro.at/series/966>

Globale Dialoge – Women on Air (Austria, since 2004)
<http://o94.at/?category_name=sendereihe&id=62849>
<http://noso.at>
<http://www.frauensolidaritaet.org> → Frauensolidarität/Print

Hovory na bělidle (Czech Republic, since 2004)
<http://www.rozhlas.cz/cro6/porady/_porad/1967>
archive: <http://hledani.rozhlas.cz/iradio/?p_gt=1&p_pattern=&p_po=1967>

Jenseits der Geschlechtergrenzen (Germany, since 2005)
<http://agqueerstudies.de/radio>

Lady Radio (Italy, since 2007)
<http://www.inventati.org/radiolina/?page_id=1821>
blog: <http://ladyradio.noblogs.org>

Lezbomanija (Slovenia, since 2003)
<http://www.radiostudent.si/categories.php?catid=47&number=0>

Lilith, Martine et les Autres (France, since 2008)
<http://audioblog.arteradio.com//radiolilith/frontUser.do?method=get HomePage>

MFLA – Martedì autogestito da femministe e lesbiche (Italy, since 1995)
<http://mfla.noblogs.org>
<http://www.ondarossa.info/trx/mfla>

Mrs. Pepsteins Welt (Germany, since 1999)
<http://www.mrspepstein.blogspot.com>
old website: <http://www.mrspepstein.de>

The Other Woman (United Kingdom, since 2006)
<http://www.theotherwomanmusic.co.uk>
<http://www.myspace.com/theotherwomanmusic>

OvaryAction (Norway, 2002–2009)
<http://www.myspace.com/ovaryaction_startariot> → Print
→ RadiOrAgaZZa/Radio

Radio delle Donne (Italy, since 2009)
<http://www.radiodelledonne.org>

RadiografíaLES (Spain, since 2009)
<http://mirales.es/mirales_radio_general.php> → MíraLES/E-Zine

Radio LoRa Frauenredaktion (Switzerland, since 1983)
<http://www.lora.ch/frauen/geschichte>

RadiOrAgaZZa (France, 2010)
<http://www.myspace.com/ovaryaction_startariot>
<http://www.ekodesgarrigues.com/article.php3?id_article=1042>
→ OvaryAction/Radio

Radiorageuses (France, since 2004) <http://radiorageuses.net>

radiOrakel (Norway, since 1982) <http://radiorakel.no>

Radio Paca (Spain, since 2005) <http://69.89.22.143/~radiopac/blog>

Radio Pirate Woman (Ireland, since 1987)
<http://www.margarettadarcy.com/radio.htm>

Sektor Ž (Slovenia, since late 1990s) <http://www.radiostudent.si/družba/
sektor-ž>
archive: <http://old.radiostudent.si/categories.php?catid=44>

Sisters of Mirthy (United Kingdom, since 2011)
<http://www.londonfieldsradio.com/shows/sistersofmirthy>
<http://sistersofmirthy.tumblr.com>

SPACEfemFM Frauenradio (Austria, since 2000)
<http://www.spacefemfm.at>

Willkommen in Salzburg (Austria, since 2009)
<http://radiofabrik.at/programm0/sendungenvona-z/willkommen0.html>
<http://blog.radiofabrik.at/willkommen>

an.schläge tv (Austria, since 2005)
<http://anschlaege.at/feminismus/anschlage-tv>
<http://www.okto.tv/anschlaege> → Print

ArtFem.TV (Austria, since 2008) <http://artfem.tv>

DonnaTV (Italy, 2007–2011?) <http://www.donnatv.it>

HallonTV (Sweden, since 2008)
<http://www.hallongrottan.com/about/hallontv>

Télédebout (France, since 2010) <http://teledebout.org>

Database, (Online)Archives, Networks, Visual material, etc.

Adhesively Unchallenged (sticker, United Kingdom, 2006)
<http://adhesivelyunchallenged.wordpress.com>

Bildwechsel (archive/network, Germany/international, since 1979)
<http://www.bildwechsel.org>
Berlin: <http://bildwechselberlin.wordpress.com>
Glasgow: <http://bildwechselglasgow.wordpress.com>
Warsaw: <http://bildwechselwarszawa.wordpress.com>
Basel: <http://bildwechselbasel.wordpress.com>

Le Degenerate Magazine (blog-network, Italy, since 2010)
<http://degeneremagazine.blogspot.com>

Dig me out (archive, Austria/Spain/international, since 2009)
<http://www.digmeout.org>

Emancypunx (distro, network, record label, Poland/international, since 1996)
<http://www.emancypunx.scenaonline.org>
old website: <http://www.emancypunx.com/index2.html>

female:pressure (database, Austria, since 1998)
<http://www.femalepressure.net> → Radio

FemBio (database, Germany, since 2001) <http://www.fembio.org>

Feminist Poster Project (poster/sticker, Belgium, since 2010)
<http://feministposterproject.wordpress.com>

Femminismi (blog-network, Italy, since 2008)
<http://femminismi.noblogs.org>

GenderArtNet (database/network, Belgium, since 2009)
<http://genderartnet.constantvzw.be/emerge>

Grassrootsfeminism.net (archive/network, Austria/international, since 2008)
<http://www.grassrootsfeminism.net>

Grrrl Zine Network (archive/network, Austria/international, 2001–2008)
<http://www.grrrlzines.net>

Ka Schmitz (comics, illustration, Germany) <http://www.ka-comix.de>

Lady List (database, Ireland, since 2008) <http://www.theladylist.ie>

Lesbengeschichte (archive, Germany, since 2005)
<http://www.lesbengeschichte.de>

Migrantas (pictograms, Germany, since 2004) <http://www.migrantas.org>

Lo Personal es Político (blog-network, Spain, since 2007)
<http://lopersonalespolitico.com>

Princess Hijab (adbusting, France, since 2006) <http://www.princesshijab.org>

Queeristics (comics, Germany, since 2006) <http://www.queeristics.de>

Somewhat strident but who cares (sticker, United Kingdom, since 2007)
<http://somewhatstrident.com>
<http://www.facebook.com/group.php?gid=2467246125>

Author Biographies

Tanja Carstensen (Germany), sociologist, is a research assistant in the "Work – Gender – Technology" working group at the Hamburg University of Technology, Germany. She is currently head of the "Webbased Work" project in the cooperation project "Subject Constructions and Digital Culture". Her working fields include internet and technology studies, gender studies, and the sociology of work. Contact: carstensen@tu-harburg.de

Sandra Chatterjee (Austria/Germany/India) is a postdoctoral research assistant in the Department of Art, Music and Dance Studies at the University of Salzburg. She works at the intersections of research and choreography and is a founding member of the Post Natyam Collective. www.sandra-chatterjee.net

Red Chidgey (UK) is a PhD candidate at the Centre for Media and Culture Research, London South Bank University, researching issues of feminist cultural memory and media assemblages. Her work has appeared in *Signs: Journal of Women in Culture and Society, Feminist Media Studies, Feminist Review,* and *n.paradoxa,* and she has been involved in digital archiving projects such as *Fragen: Sharing Core European Feminist Texts Online* (www.fragen. nu) and *Grassroots Feminism: Transnational Archives, Resources and Communities* (www.grassrootsfeminism.net). She blogs about her research interests at http://feministmemory.wordpress.com.

Ricarda Drüeke (Austria) is a postdoctoral researcher in the Department of Communication at the University of Salzburg. She holds a Ph.D. from the Department of Communication at the University of Salzburg and a MA in Political Sciences and Sociology from the University of Hamburg, Germany. Her research interests are Web 2.0, theories of the public sphere and feminist media. She is also involved in a study researching the interconnections between culture, ethnicity, gender, and class in the representations of migrants in the mass media (with Elisabeth Klaus). Contact: ricarda.drueeke@ sbg.ac.at

Brigitte Geiger (Austria) is an independent communication scientist and university lecturer at the Universities of Vienna and Salzburg. Her main academic focal points are gender studies/feminist communication science; feminist public sphere and media; non-profit PR; gender and violence; feminist information. Her publications include *Feministische Kommunikations- und Medienwissenschaft* (2002, co-editor) and *Medien – Politik – Ge-*

schlecht (2008, co-editor). Further professional activities include editing and layout/graphics. She is a co-founder and chairwoman of STICHWORT: Archives of Women's and Lesbians' Movements in Vienna. Contact: brigitte.geiger@univie.ac.at

Stefanie Grünangerl (Austria) is an art historian and art mediator. She works at the Galerie 5020, Salzburg and from 2010 to 2012 was a member of the research team of the "Feminist Media Production in Europe" project based at the University of Salzburg. She is also administrator of the online archive www.grassrootsfeminism.net.

Jenny Gunnarsson Payne (Sweden) is Senior Lecturer in European Ethnology at the School of Gender, Culture and History at Södertörn University in Sweden. She has previously published on the theory and practice of feminist media outlets such as *European Journal of Women's Studies, International Journal of Cultural Studies* and *Blackwell-Wiley's International Encyclopedia of Media Studies*.

Anita Harris (Australia) is an Australian Research Council Future Fellow at Monash University, Australia. Her areas of research interest include girls' studies, youth citizenship and everyday multiculturalism. She is the author of several books, including *Future Girl* and *Young People and Everyday Multiculturalism*.

Margit Hauser (Austria), managing Director of the feminist library and archive STICHWORT in Vienna. She is active in the network connections and collaborative projects of feminist archives and libraries, and is a member of the boards of i.d.a., the umbrella organization of German language lesbian/women's archives, libraries and documentation centers, and a member of frida: the Austrian Network of Information and Documentation Centres for Women's Studies. She publishes on feminist information and documentation and on feminist philosophy. Contact: margit.hauser@tele2.at

Tea Hvala (Slovenia) is a feminist writer and organiser from Ljubljana. She completed her BA in Comparative Literature and Sociology of Culture in 2005. In 2010, she received her MA in Gender Studies. She has been co-organising the International Feminist and Queer Festival *Rdeče zore (Red Dawns)* since 2002 and running workshops in collaborative writing of feminist-queer science fiction, entitled *In Other Wor(l)ds,* since 2008. Blog: http://prepih.blogspot.com; contact: tea.hvala@gmail.com

Sigrid Kannengießer (Germany) is a researcher and project coordinator at the Center for Transnational Studies (University of Bremen and University of Oldenburg) and a member of the Center for Media, Communication and Information Research at the University of Bremen. She wrote her PhD dissertation about a translocal network of women's organisations. Her research interests are in gender media studies and transcultural/transnational communication studies.

Jessalynn Keller (USA/Canada) is a PhD candidate in the Department of Radio-Television-Film at the University of Texas at Austin. Her dissertation, funded by the Social Science and Humanities Research Council of Canada, is an ethnographic project examining how girls are producing, negotiating and articulating feminisms through the practice of blogging. Her past research has been published in *Information, Communication & Society, Women's Studies International Forum,* and *Feminist Media Studies* (forthcoming).

Elisabeth Klaus (Austria) is professor at the Department of Communication at the University of Salzburg. She received her PhD in Sociology from the University of Notre Dame (USA), and received her Habilitation in Communication and Media Studies from the University of Dormund. Her research and teaching areas include communication research and journalism studies, feminist media studies, popular culture and cultural production, and theories of the public sphere. Her numerous publications include: *Kommunikationswissenschaftliche Geschlechterforschung. Zur Bedeutung der Frauen in den Massenmedien und im Journalismus* (2005), *Media Industry, Journalism Culture and Communication Policies in Europe* (2007, co-editor), and *Identität und Inklusion im europäischen Sozialraum* (2010, co-editor). Contact: Elisabeth.Klaus@sbg.ac.at.

Verena Kuni (Germany) is a scholar in the field of history and theory of art and media cultures and a Professor of Visual Culture at Goethe University Frankfurt/Main. Her research focuses on, among other things, transfers between material and media cultures; media of imagination and technologies of transformation; alternate realities; urban biotopes; DIY and prosumer cultures; games, play and toys as tools. She has published widely (print and online) on contemporary arts and media, their histories and futures. Websites: www.kuniver.se; www.under-construction.cc; www.visuelle-kultur.info.

Cynthia Ling Lee (USA) (MFA, UCLA) instigates thoughtful, friction-filled dialogues between American postmodern dance and North Indian classical kathak. Her intercultural, interdisciplinary choreography and writing has been presented at venues such as Dance Theater Workshop (New York), REDCAT (Los Angeles), Taman Ismail Marzuki (Jakarta), Kuandu Arts Festival (Taipei), and Chandra-Mandapa: Spaces (Chennai). A member of the Post Natyam Collective, Cynthia received a 2002–3 Thomas J. Watson Fellowship, a 2006 APPEX Fellowship, and a 2010 Taipei Artist Village residency. Influential teachers include Simone Forti, Eiko & Koma, Judy Mitoma, Bandana Sen, Kumudini Lakhia, Anjani Ambegaokar, and the contact improvisation community. www.cynthialinglee.com

Margreth Lünenborg (Germany) is Professor of Communication and Journalism Studies at the Institute for Media and Communication Studies and Director of International Institute for Journalism, Free University Berlin. Her research focuses on the fields of journalism research, cultural studies, gender media studies, migration and media. Her most recent books are: *Ungleich mächtig. Das Gendering von Führungspersonen aus Politik, Wirtschaft* *und Wissenschaft in der Medienkommunikation* (2012, ed. with Jutta Röser); *Migrantinnen in den Medien. Darstellung in der Presse und deren Rezeption* (2011, with Katharina Fritsche and Annika Bach); and *Skandalisierung im Fernsehen. Strategien, Erscheinungsformen und Rezeption von Reality TV-Formaten* (2011, with Dirk Martens, Tobias Köhler, and Claudia Töpper).

Alison Piepmeier (USA) directs the Women's and Gender Studies Program at the College of Charleston in Charleston, South Carolina. She's the author of the book *Girl Zines: Making Media, Doing Feminism* (2009) and co-editor of *Catching a Wave: Reclaiming Feminism for the 21st Century* (2003). She is currently researching prenatal testing in the context of feminist disability studies and reproductive justice.

Marcus Recht (Germany) is a Visiting Professor of Didactics of Art at the Institute for Art Education of the Justus-Liebig-University Giessen and is an academic at the Goethe University Frankfurt. His research interests include image science, gender studies, television studies, aesthetics of new media, visual literacy, visual culture, philosophy and applied psychoanalysis.

Rosa Reitsamer (Austria) is an assistant professor at the Institute for Music Sociology at the University of Music and Performing Arts Vienna, Austria. She has co-edited the book *"They Say I am Different . . ." Popularmusik, Szenen und ihre Akteure* (2011), and her monograph *When Will I Be Famous? The Do-It-Yourself Careers of DJs* will be published in 2012. Her research addresses the questions of how agency is achieved in youth cultures and music scenes and how gender and ethnicity are negotiated by cultural producers.

Birgit Richard (Germany) is Professor of New Media at the Institute for Art Education of the Goethe University Frankfurt. Her research interests include new media, visual cultures, aesthetics of contemporary youth culture (youth culture archive) and pop culture (clips, games).

Linda Steiner (USA) is professor and director of graduate studies and research at the Philip Merrill College of Journalism at the University of Maryland. Since earning her PhD at the University of Illinois, she has published has coauthored or co-edited three books, and sixty journal articles and book chapters. She is president of the Association for Education in Journalism and Mass Communication, and the Council of Communication Associations.

Elke Zobl (Austria) is an assistant professor in the Department of Communication and director of the program area "Cultural Production & Contemporary Arts" at the University of Salzburg, Austria. She is currently conducting two research projects, namely "Feminist Media Production in Europe" and "P/ART/ICIPATE: Contemporary arts initiating cultural and social change." She is the founder of the two online archives, www.grassrootsfeminism.net and www.grrrlzines.net, and facilitates zine exhibits and workshops. elke.zobl@sbg.ac.at